PRAISE

WHEN BROADWAY WAS BLACh

=== ORIGINALLY PUBLISHED AS *FOOTNOTES* ===

"Exuberant and thoroughly captivating...Gaines is in full command of the material he has fastidiously researched and assembled."

—*New York Times*

"*Footnotes* is a remarkable, wonderful book. Caseen Gaines, a top-notch researcher and first-rate storyteller, vividly brings a colorful era to life, telling an important story that deserves to be better known. It's a major contribution to culture and history, all told with Gaines's usual empathy and wit."

—Brian Jay Jones, *New York Times* bestselling author of *Jim Henson: The Biography*

"With meticulous research and smooth storytelling, Caseen Gaines significantly deepens our understanding of one of the key cultural events that launched the Harlem Renaissance. *Footnotes* reminds us of the many talented, but forgotten, Black actors and musicians whose innovative productions helped shape our shared culture and history."

—A'Lelia Bundles, *New York Times* bestselling author of *On Her Own Ground: The Life and Times of Madam C. J. Walker*

"*Shuffle Along* was the first of its kind when the piece arrived on Broadway. This musical introduced Black excellence to the Great White Way. Broadway was forever changed, and we, who stand on the shoulders of our brilliant ancestors, are charged with the very often elusive task of carrying that torch into our present. I am humbled to have been part of the short-lived 2016 historical telling of how far we've come, starring as Aubrey Lyles in *Shuffle Along, or, the Making of the Musical Sensation of 1921 and All That Followed*—and happy that *Footnotes* further secures his place in history."

—Billy Porter, Tony, Grammy, and
Emmy Award–winning actor

"Think of history as a jigsaw puzzle. Caseen Gaines has unearthed one of those coveted, seemingly unremarkable pieces that suddenly turns a jumble of colors into a picture. In taking us through the story of *Shuffle Along*, Gaines brings the years surrounding the First World War to life, making a convincing case that the Roaring Twenties would have roared less loudly if it hadn't been for this once-celebrated, now-forgotten show. A story of humans at once talented, flawed, courageous, blinkered, and visionary, *Footnotes* casts a valuable light on the role African Americans have played—and continue to play—in stage history."

—Glen Berger, Emmy Award winner and author of
*Song of Spider-Man: The Inside Story of the Most
Controversial Musical in Broadway History*

"Florence Mills, Gertrude Saunders, Lottie Gee, Josephine Baker—these are just a few of the women's shoulders on which I stand. Before joining George C. Wolfe's Black Broadway 'Justice League' in *Shuffle Along, or, the Making of the Musical Sensation of 1921 and All That Followed*, I knew nothing of *Shuffle Along*, its creators, nor the scope of the immaculate talent that ascended from its company. *Shuffle Along* will always be another example of rich history within the Black community, more specifically the Black artistic community, that is so often lost, erased, and forgotten. Learning about this show and performing in the 2016 Broadway production was life-changing in more ways than one. More importantly, it affirmed the responsibility to not only discover the treasures, work, and history of our ancestors, but to also shed light on such treasures and remind the world of the excellence and greatness of our people. For there is no 'we' without 'them.'"

—Adrienne Warren, Tony Award winner

"What a gift! *Footnotes* is beautifully written, with Caseen Gaines telling a story that is absolutely vital to both the past and future of the theater."

—Rachel Chavkin, Tony Award–winning director of *Hadestown*

"Absorbing…"

—*Wall Street Journal*

In this well-researched compilation of behind-the-scenes stories and background, pop culture historian Gaines (*Inside Pee-wee's Playhouse*) celebrates the 100th anniversary of the original staging of the all-Black musical comedy *Shuffle Along*... Gaines persuasively argues that these four men shouldn't be relegated to the footnotes of history, as their work resulted in monumental gains for many Black performers. Theater buffs and students of Black history will be pleased by this cogent defense of *Shuffle Along.*"

—*Library Journal*

"In Gaines's hands, the artists come to life as groundbreakers—and later civil rights advocates (Sissle was president of the Negro Actors Guild in 1935)—who paved the way for artists to come. This vibrant history is well worth checking out."

—*Publishers Weekly*

"Through a well-paced and compelling narrative style, Gaines pays homage to the show that augured a new era for artists of color on Broadway...evocative and illuminating, *Footnotes* is an excellent addition to the canon of musical theater history."

—*Booklist*

"[A] deeply researched and thoughtful framing of this pioneering musical, its time and its influence...Gaines places the show within the broader American political and racial culture, making the book not only resonant but relevant."

—*Washington Post*

WHEN BROADWAY WAS BLACK

THE TRIUMPHANT STORY OF THE
ALL-BLACK MUSICAL THAT CHANGED THE WORLD

CASEEN GAINES

Copyright © 2021, 2023 by Caseen Gaines
Cover and internal design © 2021, 2023 by Sourcebooks
Cover design by theBookDesigners
Cover image © Anthony Barboza/Contributor/Getty Images
Internal design by Danielle McNaughton/Sourcebooks

Sourcebooks and the colophon are registered trademarks of Sourcebooks.

All rights reserved. No part of this book may be reproduced in any form or by any electronic or mechanical means including information storage and retrieval systems—except in the case of brief quotations embodied in critical articles or reviews—without permission in writing from its publisher, Sourcebooks.

This publication is designed to provide accurate and authoritative information in regard to the subject matter covered. It is sold with the understanding that the publisher is not engaged in rendering legal, accounting, or other professional service. If legal advice or other expert assistance is required, the services of a competent professional person should be sought. —*From a Declaration of Principles Jointly Adopted by a Committee of the American Bar Association and a Committee of Publishers and Associations*

All brand names and product names used in this book are trademarks, registered trademarks, or trade names of their respective holders. Sourcebooks is not associated with any product or vendor in this book.

Published by Sourcebooks
P.O. Box 4410, Naperville, Illinois 60567-4410
(630) 961-3900
sourcebooks.com

Originally published as *Footnotes* in 2021 in the United States of America by Sourcebooks.

Library of Congress Cataloging-in-Publication Data is on file with the publisher.

Printed and bound in the United States of America.
VP 10 9 8 7 6 5 4 3 2 1

For the ancestors upon whose shoulders we stand,
and for the unborn who will stand upon ours.

Black lives matter always.

History is the transformation of tumultuous conquerors into silent footnotes.

—Paul Eldridge, 1965

CONTENTS

INTRODUCTION

A s of the summer of 2016, I had never heard of *Shuffle Along*. Even though I am a Black theater educator and enthusiast, who was also a student of history, the groundbreaking all-Black Broadway musical that redefined the look and sound of American entertainment had eluded me. But once I was formally introduced to the trailblazing artists behind the production, I had to do all I could to help preserve the legacy of their crowning achievement, which disappointingly and unsurprisingly, had largely been excised from the cultural consciousness.

My orientation came by happenstance. I had unknowingly procured tickets for a matinee performance of *Shuffle Along, or the Making of the Musical Sensation of 1921 and All That Followed*, a star-studded, multiple-Tony Award nominated extravaganza written and directed by George C. Wolfe and choreographed by Savion Glover, which told a dramatized behind-the-scenes story of the forgotten Prohibition era musical.

It was July 23. The show would be ending its Broadway run the next day.

Even before the house was open, I could hear the dancers warming up inside; the unmistakable sound of the metal plates of their tap shoes piercing through the ambient noise of taxis and tourists. I snapped an obligatory selfie before stepping out of the unforgiving Manhattan heat and into the Music Box Theatre, still knowing next to nothing of the musical at the center of the show-within-a-show that Wolfe and his team had put together.

It was easy to fall in love with the lavish production, but I sat in my seat differently in the run up to intermission. The cast broke into a rousing rendition of the popular standard "I'm Just Wild About Harry," complete with dancers in vibrant costumes that iridescently caught the light as they stepped, strode, and shimmied across the stage.

When the number started—"I'm just wild about Harry / and Harry's wild about me"—I was stunned. I didn't know about *Shuffle Along* prior to that day, but I knew this song and knew it well. I could describe the exact *Looney Tunes* short where Daffy Duck croons it for Porky Pig. I remembered the scene in the 1991 film *My Girl* where Dan Aykroyd blared the song through a tuba. And although it wasn't a track I played at parties, I had downloaded Al Jolson's rendition onto my now-obsolete iPod after I saw *The Jazz Singer* in college.

I had probably heard "Harry" over a hundred times but had no idea that the song had been written by Black composers and was a standout number from the first all-Black Broadway musical to become a bona fide success. I felt excited, but mostly, I felt cheated—like my history had been stolen from me and I had been an unknowing coconspirator in its theft.

My interest in *Shuffle Along*'s mysterious disappearance from the annals of history had been piqued, and that curiosity only increased once the final curtain fell. As patrons made their way back onto West Forty-Fifth Street, inside it felt more like a funeral home. Only the most unwanted merchandise remained at the kiosks, and at a post-show talkback, several cast members expressed disappointment and frustration that the musical was coming to a premature end.

There was a palpable sense that despite Wolfe and his collaborators' attempt to justly inter the original show's creators in the pantheon of American creative geniuses of the twentieth century, the show's closing meant that their accomplishments might once again become lost to time.

When I got home, I scoured the internet for more information on the original *Shuffle Along*, with each fact further blowing my mind. The show was unique for the way it blended jazz and ragtime, music usually relegated to the speakeasies and nightspots in Harlem, with European opera to create a score unlike anything ever heard on a Manhattan stage before.

Shuffle Along ran for over five hundred performances and integrated the orchestra section of Broadway theaters. It was such an attraction that New York City changed traffic patterns to accommodate the unexpected influx of cars and pedestrians outside the theater. The show was credited with starting not only the Harlem Renaissance, but also kickstarting an unprecedented run of all-Black Broadway productions lasting nearly a decade, predating 1935's *Porgy and Bess*.

It was beloved by white critics and Black thought leaders like W.E.B. Du Bois and Claude McKay, who agreed that the show was significant in changing whites' perceptions of their colored counterparts.

And what a core creative team it had: Lyricist, vocalist, and celebrated World War I veteran Noble Sissle; musical prodigy, composer, and dexterous piano player Eubie Blake; Flournoy Miller, the quick-witted and visionary playwright who was the backbone of the operation; and Aubrey Lyles, his loyal and impulsive sidekick with a sharp tongue and larger-than-life personality.

My appreciation grew with every internet rabbit hole I found myself in, but once I learned that the show was the world-famous Josephine Baker's big break, and that Langston Hughes chose to attend Columbia University because he wanted to see it, my days-old obsession briefly turned to anger—*why didn't I know any of this?*—and then eventually, into a mission.

I didn't know exactly why *Shuffle Along* had been largely forgotten, but I was determined to do my part to reposition Sissle, Blake, Miller, Lyles, and the once-in-a-lifetime show they created nearly a century ago, into the spotlight.

Then the ground shifted underneath all of us.

While I had been researching this story for years, most of my work on this book was done while the world was on standstill due to COVID-19. The nation watched in horror as George Floyd took his last breaths, and people around the world took to the streets to ensure that Breonna Taylor's story was not only remembered, but that her name was said. And while the movement wasn't new, Black Lives Matter became an affirmation shared by people of all races and ethnicities around the world, and industries, including the professional theater community, reflected on the importance of racial inclusivity.

And while we were collectively grappling with these dual pandemics, I was at my laptop, realizing that many of the same issues and conversations were taking place a century ago. *Shuffle Along* was produced in the aftermath of a global pandemic that decimated the economy and shuttered many theaters. Broadway struggled to recover. It was staged shortly after the greatest period of racialized violence in this country since the Civil War, and in fact, the Tulsa Race Massacre was just one week after its Broadway debut.

The deck was already stacked against Blacks in so many ways, even in seemingly liberal New York, and yet even in that landscape, these artists triumphantly succeeded in a country designed to trap them in failure.

What materialized is a slightly, yet significantly, different book than what I had planned to write. Yes, it's a story of bright stage lights, backstage romances, bitter disputes, big successes, and inevitable breakups, but at its core, it's about the importance of representation, and diverse creators living in their authentic truth and sharing the stories they want to tell. It's a stark reminder of the delicate dance Black folks have to do to achieve and hold on to success in a country built on our backs, but not built for us to flourish in; a truly American tale of how, in 1921, the combined talent and determination of four men resulted in the most unlikely phenomenon of the twentieth century, and how, despite their accomplishments, they were pushed to the sidelines, unable to overcome the systemic factors that relegated them to becoming little more than historical footnotes.

Ultimately, I realized I wasn't writing a story about a show, or even about a moment in time—I was writing a story about people, phenomenal Black artists just one generation removed from slavery who were defining what Black success could look like, both personally and collectively, perhaps for the first time in this country's history. Along the way there was struggle, poverty, sacrifice, self-doubt, and racism, but there was also brilliance, bravery, laughter, allyship, heroism, and applause.

Despite their struggles, or perhaps because of them, the story of Sissle, Blake, Miller, and Lyles is ultimately one of triumph. Not only did the show bring them fame and fortune, but it reminded the greater American public that Blacks, indeed, had a soul. "The proudest day of my life was when *Shuffle Along* opened," Eubie Blake said late in his life. "At the intermission, all these white people kept saying, 'I would like to touch him, the man who wrote the music.' At last, I'm a human being."

Shuffle Along was an undeniable phenomenon that forever changed the cultural landscape, and while that's exhilarating, it raises some troubling questions: if *Shuffle Along* could be repressed in our collective memory, how many other ground-breaking works of art have become similarly overlooked over time? How many other brilliant Black Americans who left a lasting impact on this country, their country, have had their praises left unsung?

Once uncovered, let's reestablish their place in history, say their names, sing their songs, and tell their stories. Their stories are the stories of America.

NOBLE SISSLE AND EUBIE
BLAKE AT PIANO, WITH
FLOURNOY MILLER
AND AUBREY LYLES ON
TOP, REHEARSING IN A
PUBLICITY STILL FOR
SHUFFLE ALONG, 1921

*Courtesy of the archives
of Robert Kimball*

PROLOGUE

THE CROWD-PLEASER

1921

O pening night was going better than any of them could have expected, but the performers knew the rapturous applause was obscuring the truth; there was a good chance someone was going to get killed at any moment, and it was likely to be one of them. From backstage, they could hear that the controversial scene was upon them, and they hadn't forgotten the warning they had received about how the well-dressed white people in the audience might react when they saw it. While the men bore responsibility for what was about to go down, they weren't going to bear witness nor fall victim to it. Noble Sissle, who had been dubbed the greatest vocalist of his race, gathered Flournoy Miller and Aubrey Lyles, whose comically emotive brown faces were hidden beneath a layer of burnt cork. It was time for the three of them to quietly put their plan into motion. From the wings, they could see their leading players, Lottie Gee and Roger Matthews, taking center stage, which was the cue for Sissle, Miller, and Lyles to proceed to the side exit. They pushed the double doors open wide, and each placed a foot on the New York pavement, pointed toward the safe haven of Harlem. The white rioters wouldn't be able to find them here. If things suddenly turned violent, at least they had secured an escape route. Everybody else was on their own.

"Harry, you can't lose," Jessie Williams said as she crossed over to her should-be betrothed. "Jenkins or Peck beating you, why the idea is absurd."

"I know, Jessie," Harry Walton responded, his voice sullen. "But suppose—"

Before Harry could finish his thought, Eubie Blake, the conductor, dressed as if he were on his way to the opera, started the orchestra. Gee sang longingly to her partner, he recipro-cated in kind, and as the ballad hit its climax, the two locked eyes and harmonized: "Love will find a way, / though skies now are gray. / Love like ours can never be ruled. / Cupid's not schooled that way."

The men at the door kept quiet, hoping the noise from the automobiles and passersby on the Manhattan street wouldn't obscure the sound of the audience turning. They needed any head start they could get.

In the orchestra pit, Blake was unaware of what his business partners were up to. The sweeping number was one of his favorites—he was best known for ragtime and jazz, but he had longed to compose a song in the style of Leslie Stuart ever since he was a little boy—and as he directed his musicians, who were shoehorned into where the first three rows of audience seating should have been, a clear reminder that the venue was never intended to hold a musical comedy of this size, he couldn't help but sway along with the melody. Lottie Gee's lithe soprano voice was blending perfectly with Roger Matthews's affectionate tenor, but their synergy did little to assuage the feeling Sissle, Miller, and Lyles had that things were just moments away from hitting the fan.

It wasn't that white folks had a problem with seeing Black women onstage. They were comfortable with mammies—good-natured, asexual homemakers who freely doled out folksy wisdom and kept the children in line. They could laugh at sapphires—domineering women who emasculated their men and drove them away from the home. They were familiar with jezebels—sexually hungry vixens who couldn't help but satisfy their primal desires with every man they came into contact with; white men, in particular, were defenseless against their feminine wiles. And their hearts bled for tragic mulattas—light-skinned beauties who might have a chance if the Lord had blessed them with the ability to hide, or the good sense to reject, their Blackness.

Any of these were more than welcome, but a Jessie Williams, a

Black woman who expressed love for a Black man, was something different altogether. And not just love but a sincere and unfunny love, emotionally articulated in song, just like they did in Ziegfeld's *Follies* in Midtown. Even in liberal New York, the cloud of Jim Crow still hung overhead, and there were legitimate fears among many in the production that the exuberance felt in the audience during the previous song, the freewheeling and jubilant dance number with caramel-colored chorines eccentrically shimmying about, would dissipate as soon as they caught wind of where the musical was headed. There was a legitimate chance that the musical comedy could give way to an all-out race war that would almost certainly spill out onto Sixty-Third Street.

And as expected, once the number ended, the theater exploded. Hundreds jumped to their feet and began chanting at the top of their lungs, drowning out the next few lines of dialogue. As Sissle, Miller, and Lyles got ready to make their mad dash uptown, the words came into focus—*Encore! Encore! Encore! Encore!*

It was unrelenting, and Blake, ever the crowd-pleaser, nodded his bald head, swung his baton, and struck the band up for a reprise. "Love Will Find a Way" was the centerpiece of an otherwise innocent love plot that had been taboo because of the color of the characters' skin, but now, it didn't just go over well— it *killed*. The response from the mostly white audience not only validated the artistic vision of the show's creators but also their humanity, as the public accepted that the Black characters onstage were just as capable of possessing genuine emotions as the specta- tors watching them. In 1921, this was a revelation. Sissle, Miller, and Lyles let out shaky laughs and made their way back inside the theater. The color line hadn't been completely erased, but the men were content with it having become blurred. Maybe, just maybe, they'd make it through the rest of this night alive after all.

The show continued without incident, and when the act was over, Eubie Blake sprang out of the makeshift pit and ran backstage to share in the excitement he was sure his partners were feeling. It turned out they weren't only ecstatic—they were relieved. Sissle, Miller, and Lyles had a good laugh when they shared how nervous they'd been, how they'd waited at the side exit, and how they imagined the audience growing hostile, hurling tomatoes and rotten eggs at the easy target of Blake's welcoming head. It was almost time for the conductor to return to the house, but before he left, he made it clear: if any one of them tried to leave him high and dry again, they wouldn't have to worry about the audience—he'd kill them himself.

It was easy to say this was the best "all-colored" show since the days of Williams and Walker, but in actuality, New York had never seen a musical comedy like this before: a fast-moving syncopated jazz score with snappy lyrics, beautiful brown dancers, political satire, and a book that challenged the notion of what was socially taboo while also harkening back to America's familiar, albeit increasingly antiquated, tradition of minstrelsy. When the curtain closed for the final time that evening, Sissle, Blake, Miller, and Lyles had accomplished what they had been working toward for five months as a collective but for their entire lives as individuals.

They were $21,000 shy of being flat broke, in a venue that

was still under construction and seemingly violated every city ordinance in the book, but they'd made it. Now all they had to do was figure out how to stay there. But even if they closed next week, they had done the improbable: returned the Negro to Broadway. And for that, they were sure, they had secured their place in history—and *Shuffle Along* would never be forgotten.

PART ONE

THE WAY THERE

FLOURNOY MILLER
AND AUBREY LYLES
IN AN UNDATED
PUBLICITY STILL

Courtesy of Photographs
and Prints Division,
Schomburg Center
for Research in Black
Culture, New York Public
Library

1

THE BLACKER THE BAIT

1885–1915

Flournoy Eakin Miller only knew success. He was born and raised in Columbia, Tennessee, the seat of Maury, the state's most affluent county. In 1885, the city was divided into neighborhoods for the rich Blacks, poor Blacks, rich whites, and poor whites, with the Millers living in College Hill with the rest of the better-off African American folks. Their community boasted two doctors, the Black school principal, a Black-owned drug store and two grocery stores, and a newspaper, where Lee Miller,

Flournoy's father, was editor. His mother, Mary, was a social worker and elocution teacher. Columbia was a tranquil Southern hamlet to grow up in; the fragrance of honeysuckles scented the air throughout the spring and summer months, and every street was lined with respectable homes, each with a well-manicured front lawn. It was an enclave for the college-educated—Lee had attended Roger Williams University in Nashville—and folks aspired to and were expected to achieve excellence.

Yet even in this idyllic African American community, racial animus was a frequent visitor. Both of the city's segregated schools were in the aptly named College Hill section, which often led to trouble. The poor white kids walked through the affluent Black neighborhood from the industrial Cotton Factory area, where Flournoy Miller surmised that "the KKK must have hidden their sheets," on a war path every morning. When they came across the well-dressed Black kids on their way to school, they'd throw insults and punches. The daily brawls became incessant, prompting the district to stagger the start times—8:00 a.m. for the white students, an hour later for the Black ones—in an attempt to keep the peace. However, even at a young age, Flournoy was keenly aware that the rage the young white kids felt was due to their upbringing, emanating from their parents' economic anxieties and generally poor lot in life. Classism and racism were equally prevalent within city limits, and the poor whites lashed out at what they perceived to be an injustice. As they saw it, even the poor Blacks had a better chance of achieving the American dream than they did. "The Cotton Factory folks were seldom if ever seen in the better class white neighborhood for all servants there were negroes," Miller recalled. "The poor whites were not considered good enough for servants. A poor man, Black or white, when he is not needed, is not wanted."

For the first nine years of his life, Miller grew up without a want in the world, but that changed when Sissieretta Jones, who was otherwise known as the Black Patti, came to town. Jones was a classically trained, internationally renowned soprano who, with annual earnings of nearly $8,000, equivalent to more than $235,000 125 years later, also happened to be one of the highest-paid Black entertainers of the day. In 1892, she performed at the White House for President Benjamin Harrison and sang at Madison Square Garden in front of seventy-five thousand music lovers. The following year, she returned to the White House for President Grover Cleveland and became the first Black woman to headline at Carnegie Hall. By 1894, she was traveling up and down the East Coast, playing one- and two-night stands, primarily for white audiences, who saw her as a novelty. The Millers snagged tickets for her concert at the opera house in downtown Columbia, and as he watched the opening-act comedian easily draw laughs from the crowd, Miller was captivated. He was equally impressed when Jones took the stage. She was beautiful in a long gown, and as she sang, every member of the audience sat in the palm of her hand. Miller had never seen anyone as talented as her, and he realized before the night was over that when he grew up, he wanted to be onstage.

His fascination with performing grew when the Millers moved to South Pittsburg, an industrial town where people primarily made their living working in coal mines and foundries.

Lee Miller held several jobs—he served as the Black school's principal and wrote editorials for the *South Pittsburg Weekly*, a white newspaper, under the pen name "Rellim," Miller spelled backward—but the one that changed the outcome of his sons' lives was his bill-posting service, where Flournoy and his older brother, Irvin, worked. The siblings relished chatting with promoters from traveling shows about the places they had been and the unique experiences they'd had. Each conversation made the brothers more eager to pursue a life in show business. F. E., as Flournoy's friends called him, wanted to be a star, while Irvin wanted to be on the "right side of the desk."

But they knew the business had a dark side. Traveling minstrel shows usually announced their arrival in a new town with an animated parade, which, on occasion, would run them into trouble with white folks who didn't take kindly to what they saw as a brigade of "uppity niggers" disrupting their peace and quiet. Miller had heard of several incidents throughout the country, primarily in the South, that made his skin crawl. In one case, some white guys let a team of horses loose to run through a parade, nearly killing a few young Black boys in the process. Most of the instances he'd heard about were verbal assaults and efforts to disrupt the cavalcade. The disgruntled locals would attempt to shout down the Black musicians, inciting the bandleader to conduct his performers to play louder. In nearly all these incidents, the troublemakers were part of the city's lowest white class who, like the residents of Cotton Hill, took particular umbrage at the sight of African American people strutting down the street in suits with walking canes, playing music, and dancing through the street, and it incensed them even more to see the wealthier members of their race cheering them on. "As I look back, I have a feeling that the white man's hatred was motivated by jealousy more than anything else," Miller later explained. "There were cases where a white man's colored mistress would become interested in one of the flashy dressed men and if the white man would find out about it, he would ofttimes cook up some charge against him and incite the white ruffians against the entire troupe."

The incident that left the most lasting impact on Miller involved Louis Wright, a nineteen-year-old performing with the Richard and Pringle Georgia Minstrels, who was lynched by a mob of masked men. Miller had seen the group on one of their excursions through Tennessee and took special notice whenever he saw them mentioned in the paper. When he heard about what had transpired on the evening of February 12, 1902, when the performers were playing New Madrid, Missouri, he was shaken to his core. As the minstrels paraded into town past the courthouse, two white men—Richard Mott and Thomas Waters—began throwing snowballs in their direction. It was reported that Wright cursed at them, but crisis was averted when the town marshal arrived and deescalated the situation, sending everyone on their way. At that evening's performance, a group of white guys sat in front of the stage, looking for trouble. They heckled the acts, eventually provoking the colored performers to the point where they responded with witty comebacks from the stage. But the interjectors refused to let up. During ballads, they laughed; during comedy routines, they groaned; and when the other white patrons tried to quiet them down, they ignored them.

When the show was over and the house started emptying out, the men took to the stage, demanding an apology from the Black boy who shouted at them during the parade earlier. As they started toward a corridor leading backstage, one of the minstrels drew a revolver and opened fire. Shots broke out in all directions, from both the performers and the white men, and in the pandemonium, several audience members were struck or nearly missed. Five of the minstrels were arrested—while the white men were all free to leave—and later that evening, a group of masked individuals showed up at the local jail, demanding the keys to the cell that housed the entertainers. The prisoners pleaded to be left alone, but Louis Wright was taken into the mob's custody and brought to a large elm tree near the railroad tracks. The sheriff cut his dead body loose the next day.

Flournoy Miller was mortified by what had happened to Wright, but when he met Aubrey Lyles the following year, any doubts he had about his chosen career fell to the wayside. Lyles was also from Tennessee, over two hundred miles away from South Pittsburg in Jackson, a city that had already established a legacy of being outwardly hostile toward Negroes. His father was a musician who hoped to lead an orchestra one day, but he died with his goal unmet when Aubrey was just a boy. Lyles's mother remarried and maintained a modest home, and he and his siblings grew up determined to make something of themselves. He enrolled in Fisk University in Nashville before it was designated as a historically Black university, where he was working toward becoming a doctor, but once he met F. E. Miller, a charismatic upperclassman studying to be an Episcopal minister who had aspirations of a career in entertainment, he caught the acting bug.

The two hit it off right away and developed a comedy routine, which they performed on campus and at the local YMCA, capitalizing on their physical and vocal dissimilarity. Miller was five foot ten, average height, but when put next to Lyles's barely five-foot frame, he looked like a giant. And even better yet, they each sounded like their voice belonged in their partner's body, with FE's measured and gentle while his partner squawked. The centerpiece of their act was an onstage boxing match. Miller would stretch his arm and put his gloved hand on his partner's head while Lyles swung mightily, flailing about in a futile attempt to strike a body blow. They had a clear gift for comic timing and delivery, and their classmates encouraged them to write more bits and keep up the act. Their first taste of monetary success came when they generated $300 from their performances—equivalent to over $6,300 a hundred years later—which they donated toward the construction of a new science building on campus. The school repaid their generosity by placing their names on a plaque outside the hall, but they were hungry for more notoriety. They withdrew from Fisk shortly thereafter.

Immediately after leaving the university, the two realized that fame and fortune wouldn't come easily. Their first job was with John Robinson's famous touring circus, where they both performed a soft-shoe dance, and thanks to his diminutive size, Lyles also rode a bucking mule. The amateur jockey didn't mind the additional performing responsibilities, but when he and

Miller were told they'd have to help break down the tents before the circus departed for the next town, Lyles said manual labor wasn't in his job description. He and Miller quit, instead setting their sights on Chicago's South Side, which had a prosperous Black neighborhood—it would affectionately become known as "Bronzeville"—and an emerging African American theater scene.

The two arrived in the Windy City in 1905 and became acquainted with Robert T. Motts, a former saloon owner and gambler who, once he decided to "make a contribution to his race by providing entertainment along more cultural and uplifting lines," built a cabaret. Unfortunately, it had recently been demolished in a fire, but out of the ashes, Motts was planning to erect the world's first Black-owned theater. The comedians wanted in on this new venture and quickly wrote the book for *The Man from Bam*, which they envisioned as a musical comedy. The entrepreneur loved what he'd read, hired Joe Jordan, his resident pianist at the saloon, to write the score, and *The Man from Bam* became the premiere production at the Pekin Theatre on March 31, 1906. The production did well, but while Motts wanted Miller and Lyles to write another show, reality soon set in. Lyles met and married Ellamay Wallace while in Chicago, and when work was slow at the Pekin, he left the theater for a job working on the city's railroads.

While his partner was otherwise engaged, Miller began writing a new show, *The Mayor of Dixie*, which Motts fast-tracked into production. When Irvin Miller came to visit Chicago, he suggested that Flournoy and Lyles play the characters of Steve Jenkins and Sam Peck themselves, two deceitful business partners cheating to beat the other person in a mayoral race. The show's director, J. Ed Green, agreed, and Lyles took a leave from his new job to reunite with his stage partner. The show ran for three weeks to unwavering adoration, helping to put the Pekin on the map. "This little playhouse is increasing in popularity and besides enjoying the support of the Southside colored population, many white people go there for good entertainment distinctly different from any other offered in the city," *Variety* noted during *The Mayor of Dixie*'s run.

"We felt that we had arrived," Miller recalled. "But when the curtain descended on the final performance, we had the same reaction all showmen have when they see their scenery being taken out so that the following show could be set up. We stood in front of the theater. We saw our names being covered up by the coming attraction. We thought to ourselves, 'Where do we go from here?'" For Lyles, it was back to the railroad while Miller took a job in the Pekin box office, but unbeknownst to them, requests kept coming in for *The Mayor of Dixie*, prompting Motts to revive it for another brief engagement. One performance was bought out by a number of socialites from Chicago's mansion-filled Gold Coast section, and when Miller and Lyles looked out from the stage at all the cultured white folks in evening gowns and expensive jewelry laughing at their material, they knew they didn't just want to perform—they wanted to do so on Broadway.

Throughout the next two years, they continued writing and sometimes appearing in musical revues and comedies that played major cities. One of their most successful productions was 1907's *The Oyster Man*, which starred vaudevillian Ernest Hogan, who called himself the "Unbleached American," and had a brief, successful run in New York. The show didn't play on Broadway, but Miller and Lyles had made a significant contribution to Manhattan's growing interest in Black theater, which began in 1896 with *A Trip to Coontown*, the first all-Black full-length musical comedy. It was essentially a three-act minstrel show, complete with Black actors in both black- and whiteface, watermelon eating, shucking and jiving, and racially stereotypical songs by Bob Cole and Billy Johnson. After brief engagements throughout the East Coast, *Coontown* became the first African American musical to play in New York City when the show had a short-lived run at the modest Third Avenue Theater in April 1898, far away from the impressive Broadway houses.

Bert Williams and George Walker, the top Black vaudevillian duo who marketed themselves as "the Real Coons," had the most success in elevating the status of Black performers in theater. The two popularized the cakewalk, a high-leg prance created to mimic and parody the pretention of Southern gents and debutants. It became a hit throughout the United States and Europe—the joke was seemingly lost on the white social elite—and in 1898, they inspired *Clorindy: The Origin of the Cakewalk*, an hour-long one-act musical written by Will Marion Cook, a musician eager to bring the first Negro show to Broadway, and poet Paul Laurence Dunbar. *Clorindy* opened on Broadway on July 5 at the top—the rooftop, to be precise—of the Casino Roof Garden theater. It wasn't a Broadway house in the conventional sense, and there was only seating for about

875 people, but the team declared victory nonetheless. "Negroes were at last on Broadway," Cook said, "and there to stay."

Williams, Walker, Cook, and Dunbar made it to Broadway proper when they collaborated a few years later on 1903's *In Dahomey*. Jesse A. Shipp Jr., a dynamic writer for Williams and Walker's vaudeville act, directed the show and wrote its book—Dunbar remained Cook's lyricist—which satirized American colonization of African nations. As the show was the first all-Black production to play on Broadway, there were concerns that white audiences would turn hostile, and anxieties were high on opening night. "A thundercloud has been gathering of late in the faces of the established Broadway managers," a journalist wrote in the *New York Times* following its Manhattan debut. "Since it was announced that Williams and Walker, with their all-negro musical comedy, *In Dahomey*, were booked to appear at the New York Theatre, there have been times when the trouble-breeders have foreboded a race war. But all went merrily last night."

In Dahomey ran for a respectable fifty-three performances before touring the United States and United Kingdom, paving the way for two more Williams and Walker musicals on Broadway: 1906's *Abyssinia*, which entertained for forty-eight performances and introduced the self-deprecating "Nobody," which became Williams's signature number, and 1908's *Bandanna Land*, which played eighty-nine performances. Throughout their decade-long tenure on Broadway, the team demonstrated that Black artists were just as worthy of playing legitimate houses as their white counterparts.

However, just as quickly as all-Black musicals caught fire,

they began to disappear from major New York theaters due to a number of factors. George Walker became ill in 1909 during a post-Broadway tour of *Bandanna Land*, which forced him into early retirement. He would ultimately die from syphilis two years later. While Williams continued without him, starring in the musical *Mr. Lode of Koal* later that year, he failed to replicate their previous successes. Its run ended during its pre-Broadway tryout, and that same year, the Black theater community also suffered the loss of *The Oyster Man*'s Ernest Hogan. The *New York Age* evaluated the ever-whitening state of Broadway in a 1910 editorial: "In speaking of the colored theatrical situation as it exists to-day one can, with apologies to the weather forecaster, without hesitation use the familiar term 'cloudy and unsettled,'" they said. "It has been a long, long time since conditions have such been a deep indigo hue."

Coincidentally, as Blacks were becoming but a faint memory on Broadway, Manhattan's theater district garnered a new nickname. Each night, Midtown was bathed in bright lights, thanks to the ubiquitous trend of electric bulbs being used to shine the names of the shows and stars currently playing. By 1910, Broadway was regularly being referred to by its new moniker, the Great White Way.

While opportunities on Broadway had become nonexistent for African Americans, Miller and Lyles were undeterred in their mission to play there. They believed their best approach was to develop their own vaudeville act, as all the Black Broadway stars had done before them, except they would have the added benefit of having written their own material. By the end of the decade, enterprising entrepreneurs were capitalizing on the public's desire for live entertainment by converting storefront shops into nickelodeons, crude performing spaces with little more than a small platform to serve as a stage and a few hundred seats crammed in. There were no fancy amenities for the talent,

FLOURNOY MILLER AND AUBREY
LYLES, CIRCA 1910

Photo by Apeda Studio / Courtesy of Photographs
and Prints Division, Schomburg Center for
Research and Black Culture, The New York
Public Library

like dressing rooms or even a backstage; the acts on the bill had to sit in the front row and wait their turn to step onto the makeshift podium and do their few minutes.

Even with the homely accommodations, Miller and Lyles were determined to set themselves up for success. They'd noticed that the African American acts that did the best had singing and dancing, and while the men had a little rhythm, vocalizing was not in their wheelhouse. For added insurance, they hired three women as chorus girls and branded the act the "Ebony Five." Booking agent Frank O'Doyle quickly found them work playing fifteen shows a day at a small house on State Street, near the Loop in Chicago. The comedians barely had money left over for themselves after paying the chorus girls their salary, which became even more irritating when the women began showing up late to performances. As their first week approached its end, Miller and Lyles called a group meeting to address their lack of professionalism. The women laughed in their faces. "Can you imagine the nerve of them?

They can't sing or dance, and without us, they wouldn't have an act! We are carrying them."

The comedians were furious. They had decided to grab a bite so they could blow off some steam and weigh their options when they ran into Frank Frabito, manager of the ramshackle theater. He complimented their comedic ability, and if they'd agree to play another week, he was willing to increase their salary. Miller and Lyles confided that they were planning on taking some time away from the stage so they could replace their chorus, but they'd misunderstood. The manager liked the comedians; he thought the chorus girls were superfluous. Miller and Lyles ran back to the theater and laid it on thick, telling the women they didn't want to be a burden anymore and thanking them for carrying the show this past week. The chorus girls grabbed their things and, on their way out, they saw the sign being changed out front—MILLER AND LYLES. HELD OVER FOR ANOTHER WEEK. They turned on their heels, bursting with excitement over the news. "Say," one of the women said. "We're being held over for another week!"

"Not you," Lyles said, dropping the facade. "*Miller and Lyles* are being held over." But the women thought they'd have the last laugh. The next day, they returned to the theater, this time as spectators, certain they'd see the comedians fall on their faces. Miller and Lyles stepped onto the makeshift stage in burnt cork makeup, just as Hogan and Bert Williams had done before them. For the comedians, darkening their skin was a necessary means to an end. "Blackface was the bait to draw them in," Miller explained. "Once on the inside, they would enjoy our fine art."

The two performed what they called a "syncopated argument," a rhythmic exchange of one-upmanship and unfinished sentence bits, where they seemingly used telepathy to finish each other's statements. They ended with their old boxing routine from their days at Fisk, which once again brought the house down. Their former colleagues left without saying goodbye.

While the practice of European performers darkening their skin to play people of color onstage traces back to the 1400s, by the 1830s, it became commonplace for white minstrels to imitate Blacks by darkening their skin with burnt cork. They would cover their faces until they were the color of tar, leaving just enough space to paint on a wide mouth with bright red or white exaggerated lips. The look would become complete with a natty wig, tattered clothing, white gloves on occasion, and a heavy Southern drawl with English so broken, it was hardly intelligible. These imitations were purely for the enjoyment of white audiences, and through humor, music, and dance—theatricality—they often played up to the idea that Blacks were uneducated, inarticulate, shiftless, lazy, superstitious, and longed for life on the master's plantation. Its use became popularized in 1828, when white song-and-dance man Thomas D. Rice wrote and performed the song "Jump Jim Crow," which inadvertently coined the term that would later refer to a set of racially discriminatory laws.

While blackface was created by whites for their own gratification, by 1840, African American performers were getting into the act too, darkening their already colored skin for comedic effect. While history would look on these artists with derision, by entering the minstrelsy arena, they were asserting a power and privilege that leveled the playing field. Why should their white competitors have free rein to make a buck, and at Black folks' expense no less? The African Americans beneath the cork often claimed to be recently freed slaves, a marketing tactic more than anything else, which made them more desirable to white audiences eager to see an "authentic" Negro performance. But Black minstrels' material was just as rife with stereotypes as that of their white counterparts, complicating and polarizing their relationship with the Black community. On one hand, they were validating white people's worst perceptions and fears, but on the other, they were showcasing and monetizing their genuine artistic abilities and giving white minstrels a run for their money in the process. This was a vital step in Blacks gaining representation in all-white spaces. Frederick Douglass, who despised the practice of blackface, explained this dichotomy in 1849 when he conceded that "it is something to be gained when the colored man in any form can appear before a white audience."

After an eight-week tour playing dodgy venues throughout Chicago for $40 a week, Miller and Lyles met Harry Weber, a better-connected agent who booked them at the city's Majestic Theatre, the best vaudeville house in the Midwest. After seven years together, the duo had finally become overnight sensations. "We were the first 'talking act' on the big time," Miller claimed. "Up until then, the public had been trained to expect nothing but singing and dancing from Negroes on the stage. Officials of the Keith circuit were afraid that the white public would not listen to such an act. So although we performed as blackfaced comedians, we had to create the illusion that we were white.

"We wore wigs so that the audience might think we were white men," he continued. "I was careful to let my skin show between my gloved hands and shirt cuff to further help the illusion. Finally, however, the wigs became a nuisance in our boxing act and once, after they had fallen off, we decided not to wear them again. In the meantime, so many inquiries had been made as to whether we were white or colored, and our reputation had been so established, that we were not molested after we had stopped trying to pass for white in blackface."

They played consistently on the highly coveted Keith circuit of vaudeville theaters, and because theater remained their first love and ultimate goal, they took a brief hiatus from vaudeville in 1912 to appear in *The Charity Girl*, an integrated musical comedy by Edward Henry Peple, a white playwright who didn't shy away from dialectical humor at the expense of Black folks. Miller joined the show thinking about Broadway, but once production was underway, his attention turned to Bessie Oliver, one of the chorines in the cast. They married in New York the following year, where she picked up work as a domestic while he continued on the circuit with Lyles. A daughter, Olivette, soon followed.

After over a decade pursuing Broadway together, Miller and Lyles finally hit the jackpot when they were tapped to star in 1915's *Darkydom*, a highly anticipated musical that Lester Walton, the show's main producer, declared would usher in "a new era for the colored musical show, which has not enjoyed the widespread popularity of former years since the passing away of the Williams and Walker, Cole and Johnson, and Ernest Hogan Companies." As the most celebrated vaudeville comedians of the day, Miller and

Lyles were clearly the heirs apparent to help bring Black folks back to the heart of Manhattan's theater district. Not only were they asked to lead the expansive company, but they were able to play Steve Jenkins and Sam Peck, the characters they debuted in *The Mayor of Dixie*. There was only one thing left to work out: *Where do we sign?*

Noble Sissle and
Eubie Blake in a 1921
publicity still

Courtesy of the Maryland
Center for History
and Culture, Item ID
#PP301.170

2

KNOW YOUR AUDIENCE

1915

J oe Porter's Famous Dixie Serenaders were stuck on the front
steps of an East Baltimore row house, out of small talk and
time, and it was all Frank Fowler Brown's fault. Maybe they
should have seen this coming. He'd been playing with the group
throughout the spring, and the shows were going well—in fact,
just a little bit too well as far as his wife was concerned. Brown
was a good-looking guy with a silky voice, and from the moment
he stepped onstage, women would holler and make him the

object of their attention. They only got louder when he opened his mouth to sing. It was great for business but cancerous for his marriage. Mrs. Brown had finally had enough and forced him into early retirement, leaving Joe Porter, the band's arranger, in a lurch. Porter found a replacement whom he believed could match Brown's stage presence and vocal prowess and offered him a job throughout the summer. The catch? The singer had to travel over five hundred miles from Indiana to take it.

Despite coming highly recommended, the new guy was late. It was past time for the Serenaders to leave for Riverview Park, where they were scheduled to entertain on the bandstand stage, and the quintet was growing increasingly impatient. There were real consequences to tardiness, and none of them could afford to mess with their money. They'd held out as long as they could, and after gathering their packed instruments, they rushed to the amusement park. Shortly after they arrived, they were approached by a man—sharply dressed, mustachioed, with bright and inquisitive eyes behind round-frame glasses—carrying a patent leather valise. He apologized for his unpunctuality and the late departure of his train but said he was ready to perform with them. There wasn't any time to litigate the situation, and Arthur Porter, Joe's brother, hastily introduced the newcomer to each of his new band members before they took the stage.

"You didn't give me an introduction to Mr. Sissle." The Serenaders' pianist, Eubie Blake, had inadvertently been skipped over. As Arthur Porter quickly acquainted the two men, something rang a bell in Blake's mind. "Sissle, Sissle... Didn't I see your name on a song once?" Two years before, Noble Sissle had written the lyrics for Russell Johnson's "My Heart for You

Pines Away," an obscure number from an even more obscure Black musical, Salem Tutt Whitney and J. Homer Tutt's *The Wrong Mr. President*, about two vagabonds who pose as the leaders of the free world. Sissle said as much, but Blake hadn't heard of the song. The pianist fired back, "Did it hit?" It hadn't. "If you write one with *me*," Blake said with his characteristic charm, "it'll hit."

The piano player was only kidding—he knew better than to make predictions about success in show business—but it provided the perfect opening for the two to begin a fast friendship. Over the coming weeks, they learned they had more in common than a shared love for music. Noble's father, George, was born into slavery on the Cecil plantation in Lexington, Kentucky, in 1852. After Emancipation, he and the other newly freed Black folks, who all shared the same name as their former master, established a church. George was installed as pastor, and to distinguish himself from his flock and separate himself from their painful shared past, he tinkered around with his last name, rebranding himself as Reverend Sissle.

By the time Noble was born in 1889, George and his wife, Martha, also from Kentucky, had moved to a small rural community on the outskirts of Indianapolis. Martha was born after slavery had ended, but she still lived in the shadow it cast. Her mother spent most of her life enslaved, and when she was freed, she left the plantation without a cent to her name. Child-rearing proved too financially burdensome, and the more prudent decision was to allow the institution to separate one final generation of the family. Martha was given to her mother's close friend, whom she lived with until she married George at nineteen years old, a year before Noble was born. She ultimately became a school teacher, probation officer, and matriarch of Simpson Methodist Episcopal Chapel, where George preached and she taught Sunday school. The Sissles were strong advocates for social justice who were both vocal in church about the lasting impact of slavery and the current state of the "race problem" in America.

Noble Sissle also grew into himself at church. He had a great singing voice, even as a child, and was arguably an even more dynamic showman than he was vocalist. Each spiritual sung was an opportunity to perform and each congregant a potential acolyte. "I used to get a great thrill when my father or some member of the congregation would lead us in hymn, reading off the lyrics ahead of us," Sissle recalled. "Then everyone would join in and every foot would keep time, and soon the whole church would be swaying in rhythm or patting their hands and feet." Music became a passion, and while he and his family believed he would grow up to be a minister like his old man, he was going to seize every opportunity to perform that presented itself.

In 1906, the family relocated to Cleveland, Ohio. Sissle's parents enrolled him in Central High School, which John D. Rockefeller attended and Langston Hughes would later attend. Of the fifteen hundred students, he was one of only six Black children. Nevertheless, Sissle was warmly welcomed at Central. He joined the school's baseball and football teams and quickly rose through the ranks in the glee club from featured tenor soloist to their elected leader in his senior year.

Instead of choosing his preordained path of following in his father's footsteps, Sissle took musical odd jobs during his time at Central. His first professional engagement was a stint with the Edward Thomas Male Quartet, and once he graduated high school at twenty-one years old—music repeatedly obstructed the road to commencement—he continued to tour with various bands across the state. The tension between wanting to further his education and advance his career continued. While enrolled at DePauw University in Indiana in the fall of 1913, Sissle wrote his song for *The Wrong Mr. President*. He transferred to Butler University the following semester, where he wrote the school's fight song, "Butler Will Shine Tonight." He dropped out soon thereafter, picking up work at the grandiose Severin Hotel, the newly opened crown jewel of downtown Indianapolis.

Although Sissle was a server, his life gravitated back toward music when, in early 1915, his boss took him aside to put him on a special assignment. While spending the Christmas holiday in New York, the manager had visited hotels where Negro musicians entertained the guests. He felt the Severin would benefit from that same draw and asked Sissle to assemble a twelve-piece orchestra for the hotel's entertainment. Within ten days, a band was performing in the lobby, and Sissle was its lead singer. But as much as he enjoyed playing for the upper echelon, he was eager to get in front of new audiences. When he received an offer to join Joe Porter's band for the summer, he couldn't wait to purchase a train ticket.

Sissle arrived in Baltimore on May 16, and with a handshake, he began a musical partnership with Eubie Blake that would last a lifetime. The two had barely gotten to know each other, but something felt promising from the jump. Beyond being a charismatic vocalist, Sissle had a way with words. Blake quickly picked up on the singer's pedigree and ascribed to him the nickname "college man," but perhaps some of that polish would go a long way. Blake's own schooling ended in eighth grade after a teacher falsely accused him of erasing math equations on the chalkboard during recess. He was talkative in class, and the principal called him the worst kid in the building, so given this golden opportunity, the administrator sent Blake packing. "Now, I wasn't no angel," Blake recalled. "But I wasn't the worst boy in the school."

Even without formal education, he was regarded among the locals as a musical genius, an honorific first bestowed upon him when he was just a toddler. It was a Saturday night, and Little Hubie—he was born James Hubert Blake in 1887 and had many childhood nicknames—was dragged along by his mother as she shopped at the local market. Instead of discarding their unsold produce at the day's end, the store owners were savvy enough to offer reduced-price produce before a fresh shipment arrived the next day. As Emily Blake, his mother, searched for bargains, her spirited child slipped away. By the time she found him, it was too late. Music had gotten him.

"This child is a *genius*!" The precocious youngster had discovered an organ in a nearby music store, and as his fingers struck the keys, the shop's manager laid it on thick like the salesman he was. "It would be criminal to deprive him of the chance to make use of such a sublime, God-given talent!" He'd inadvertently hit on the magic word. Emily Blake was a deeply religious woman—Eubie used to say she carried Jesus around with her in her pocket—and would do nearly anything if it would please the Lord. She wasn't exactly fanatical, Eubie'd say, but she was just short of it. While her love for Christ was deep, her pockets were not. She managed to bypass the double onslaught of an eager store manager and a headstrong toddler and make it out the door with her son in hand and every cent in her pocketbook in place. But in the melee, she had thoughtlessly mentioned where she lived, and on Monday morning, a brand-new organ arrived at the Blake home. For Eubie, it was a miracle, but for his parents, it was an unwanted—and unaffordable—intruder. When they refused the delivery, the manager offered financing on the $75 instrument at a quarter a week. It'd take nearly six years to pay off, but with a low monetary commitment and an enthusiastic son, the Blakes signed on the dotted line and accepted the instrument.

If God gave their son talent, who were they to get in the way of it?

It wasn't long before the young Blake started to develop into a bona fide musician, even without a lick of training. After a year of toying around, he was able to plunk out the Civil War–era tune "Marching Through Georgia," which his father, John Sumner Blake, would sing around the house. A year later, he could pretty much play any song he heard. Indeed, it seemed the Lord had truly blessed the Blakes at long last. Eubie was their eleventh child and, because of a lack of prenatal care, the only one to survive beyond infancy. His parents were protective of him, but as he developed as a young musician, their support was seemingly endless. They asked their next-door neighbor, Margaret Marshall, the pump organist at Waters Chapel Methodist Church, to give him proper lessons. It'd run them another quarter a week, but even though they barely had two spare nickels to rub together on their best day, they considered it a worthwhile investment.

While his no-nonsense mother hadn't given him explicit directions at the start, Blake knew his piano playing would only be tolerated if he stuck to godly music. Otherwise, she would, quite literally, attempt to beat the devil out of him. While he thought he was obliging his mother's wishes, keeping his piano playing strictly to classics and church hymns, Emily soon took objection not to what her son was playing but *how* it was being played. As his fingers danced over the ivories, suspending beats, ragging the rhythm, and wobbling the bass with his left hand, his observant mother heard the unmistakable sound of the devil's music filling her home.

"Mister Blake," she scolded. When he was in trouble, he was always "Mister Blake" to his mother. "Take that ragtime out of my house!"

Ragtime. He had never heard the word before and couldn't understand how what he was doing was unholy. In church, the organist would often lean on the keys and wobble the bass with their left hand. When funeral processions would make their way through the Baltimore streets, full bands would give the dearly departed a raucous musical send-off into the afterlife. He wasn't trying to rebel against the music he'd heard growing up; he was emulating it. But Mrs. Blake would have no part of it and ordered him to straighten up.

At fifteen years old, the young pianist took "that ragtime" out of his mother's home and, without her knowledge, parlayed his skills into a nightly engagement when a local piano player, Basil Chase, received an inheritance and quit his job playing in a sporting house. By then, Blake had made a bit of a name for himself, and Chase gave the teenager an address in Baltimore's red-light district, an area the young pianist had never visited before, and told him to apply. Blake was led to a bordello run by Aggie Shelton, "a great big woman—German woman," he recalled. "She must have weighed three hundred pounds. Not fat, just a big woman." His playing was good enough for her. If he wanted the job, all he had to do was come back at 9:00 p.m. in a pair of long pants, ready to play.

He returned that evening in ill-fitting rented slacks, with the waist sitting at his chest and the length extended nearly to the soles of his shoes. The smoke-filled atmosphere, with liquor flowing freely, was a far cry from the churches his mother dreamed of him playing in. But it could have been worse. Aggie's was a classy establishment, a $5 spot, the kind of place where the illicit activity was kept off the main floor. While he was focused on playing and trying to not eye the merchandise too hard, Blake couldn't help but notice the effect his music had on the patrons. "All the girls'd come into the piano room, see, and the men would sit there and drink," he recalled. "And they'd dance just like in a cabaret. Then they'd go upstairs." He played there for weeks, sneaking out of his second-story bedroom, climbing down the roof, running from his neighborhood to the tawdry part of the city, slipping into his performance pants, and playing into the twilight hours. Even though Aggie never made good on the $3 a night she'd promised him, Blake could still bring in $18 on a good day from tips alone.

All was well until some of the church parishioners heard a familiar sound while walking home from a late choir practice. The next morning, Sister Reed made a beeline to the Blakes'. "We heard somebody playing the piano at Aggie Shelton's," she said. "Sounded just like Little Hubie." This meant nothing to Mrs. Blake until she was told that Aggie ran a bawdy house— she misheard it as "body house," but it still fit. Then she was willing to entertain the conversation further.

"What time was it?"

"About one o'clock in the morning."

Now Mrs. Blake knew Sister Reed was mistaken. Her son went to bed dutifully at nine every night and slept soundly until the next morning. And besides, unless the respectable Sister Reed had been inside the establishment, how did she know who it was?

"Nobody wobbles the bass like him," the whistleblower said. "Ain't anybody plays like him."

Blake's mother could hardly wait for him to wake up, and once he did, he received a full interrogation. He confessed to having worked there for three or four days, although it really had been three or four weeks, and he received three whippings for his deception. Once his father got home, Emily instructed he give their son a fourth. The father and son went to Eubie's room, but when the teenager showed him the rolls of bills he'd saved, nearly $100, his father's tone changed. Mr. Blake worked as a stevedore, unloading cargo from ships for $9 a week. As long as Eubie promised to keep it quiet and didn't partake in any of the salacious transactions taking place under Aggie's roof, he could keep playing.

"We kept it from Mama for a long time," Blake recalled. "You gotta know how it was back then, to understand it. That was back when eatin' was the main consideration."

Like Noble Sissle's father, both of Blake's parents were born enslaved. While other families were broken up and sold to different owners, John Sumner Blake and his brothers, Eubie's uncles, were kept together. They were all large, strong, strapping men, and as a result, the whites who owned the plantation would gather them up and feed them fresh meat and "the best of everything, just the same as the white people had" a few days before they were used to stud. Usually for about three days, the slave master would lock six of his male slaves in a barn with twelve of his female ones, with the expectation that there would be a dozen pregnancies by the time the wooden doors were opened again. Ultimately, John sired twenty-seven children that he knew about, and likely even more. He was routinely whipped by the overseer, and when Eubie was a boy, John would sit with his shirt off, with the raised marks of his lashings clearly visible across his back, and tell his son about the countless hours he spent picking cotton and the cruel and unjust treatment he experienced.

The patriarch spoke about his life in bondage openly, much to the chagrin of his wife, who tried her best to forget her past. "I want him to know about it, Em," John said. "Everybody, especially every colored child, needs to know." But she begged to differ. She thought that period of American history—and her life—was better left in the past. In fact, in stark contrast to her husband, Emily Blake never admitted to being enslaved, even though she and John married before they'd been given their freedom. He'd tease her about her denial, asking her if she ever picked cotton and, when she said yes, asking her how much she got paid for it. Of course, she hadn't been, and her husband could call that "slavery" if he wanted to, but she was never going to use the word in regard to herself.

However, despite having endured unjust treatment at the hands of the slave owners and overseers, John Blake never harbored resentment against the entire white race. When Eubie would get beaten up by white kids on his way to and from school, he'd run back home to his father. One time, he walked through the door with a bloody nose and two black eyes, and he told his father, "Papa, I hate white people. I don't care what you say, I don't like 'em." But just as his son predicted, John would have none of it. He had taught his son that all white people aren't alike, even though Eubie had trouble believing that. After all, white people had allowed the "peculiar institution" of slavery to exist in the first place and last for almost 250 years. Besides his belief that one shouldn't be judged solely by the color of their skin, John had a more practical reason why his son shouldn't harbor ill will toward whites. "A smart man never bites the hand that feeds him," he said. "And don't ever forget it. A white man paid for this house we're living in, and he lets us rent it. It was a white man—a foreigner, Lord Baltimore— that gave us this land. Don't you ever let me hear you say you hate white people. When you hate anybody, you suffer more than the people you hate."

Eubie Blake took his father's words under advisement and understood where he was coming from. After all, Aggie Shelton, a white woman, had given him a path to a generous income. The father and son successfully kept the young piano player's nightly activities secret, and soon, Blake moved on to play at Annie Gilly's $1 establishment of ill repute, a shoddier joint where the women sat in the window, inviting the passersby. The proprietor paid Blake on time—$1.50 nightly—and he was officially a working musician. He played ragtime for hours on end, taking requests and practicing his craft. The pianist continued to play seedy shops throughout Baltimore until he grew tired and left the city limits.

Blake found his way into a stint with Dr. Frazier's traveling medicine show, where he played the melodeon, a small pump organ, and buck danced with four other boys on the back of a horse-drawn wagon to prime the crowd before the presentation. When they arrived in Fairfield, Pennsylvania, the local children ran up to the dancers in amazement. They had never seen Black people before. Their white parents would follow along behind them, and as if they were looking at animals in a zoo, they'd point and explain to their children, "Here's what we call a 'nigger.'" Blake and his partners wouldn't say anything in response, even when the children ran up to them and tried to rub the color off their skin.

Their time dancing for the medicine show began on the Fourth of July in 1901, and while things were going well enough, when Frazier started to withhold the meals and the $3 a week he'd promised them, Blake and two of the other young men jumped ship, walking more than sixty miles back to Baltimore from Fairfield. He then ventured to New York the next year to perform as a buck dancer in *In Old Kentucky*, a plantation-themed revue, but once again, that was short-lived. The following year, Blake found himself back in Baltimore as the resident pianist at Alfred Greenfeld's Saloon, where he earned $1.25 a night for the pleasure of wading through sawdust caked onto the floor higher than the soles of his shoes. The place made Annie Gilly's look like heaven. There were no chairs, and the patrons would sit on whatever they could find—beer barrels, wooden crates—and pull up to the iron tables that were spread around. Fights broke out regularly, and to mask the ruckus, Blake was instructed to just play louder.

He wasn't happy working in these places, but it was an opportunity to be heard. He developed lots of trick ways to play the piano and even learned to write his own music. In 1899, when he was just twelve years old, he wrote his first song, which he later titled "The Charleston Rag." Three years later, around the time he started playing at Aggie Shelton's, his mother paid for him to study with Llewellyn Wilson, a local Baltimorean who taught him an invaluable lesson in composing. One day, Wilson gave Blake an hour to write a song. The teenager sat at the piano, working tirelessly on a tune, and when his teacher returned, he ripped the paper in half and threw it in the waste-basket. "He taught me one of the greatest lessons of my life," Blake recalled. "He said, 'When you compose music, you only use the piano to test it. Write it down out of your head. That way, no matter where you are, even on a desert island, you can write music.' I never forgot it."

In 1906, Eubie Blake began spending his summers on the New Jersey shore in Atlantic City, where he found a reprieve from the Baltimore heat and ample opportunities for work. He continued this for several years, and in 1910, he was reintroduced to Avis Lee, one of his former elementary school classmates. She was also a pianist, having been taught by Fanny Hurst, a classically trained Black woman who attended Baltimore's segregated Peabody Conservatory by passing for white. The two dated for several months, and Blake finally felt they were ready to take their relationship to the next level. He borrowed a car and hired a chauffeur to take them on a date, as he didn't know how to drive yet, and on the ride back to Avis's house, Blake finally asked the big question. Not only did she *not* want to have sex with him that night, she was well aware of his reputation as a local Casanova. "I know all about you, Eubie Blake," she said, "and I know all about all your women. You better understand right now that that's not what I want out of life." But Blake wasn't just interested in a one-night fling, and on the spot, he decided to ask Avis to marry him instead. She said she'd take it under consideration, and by that summer, the two were married in Atlantic City.

Blake was making enough money to support his household, but he still longed to see his name on a piece of sheet music, something that he had written down out of his head and that a publisher deemed worthy of release. It wasn't until 1914, during one of his summers at the Jersey Shore, that he scored a shot. Charles "Luckey" Roberts, a talented Black pianist, happened to be in Atlantic City and saw Blake playing some of his original songs. A year earlier, Joseph Stern, a music publisher, had released Roberts's "Junk Man Rag," which was a big hit. Stern added lyrics to the song, branded the rag a one-step, capitalizing on the musical trend of the day, and added a photograph of Maurice and Florence Walton, a white married couple who were well-known for their social dances, to the cover. The appeal to the sensibilities of well-off white people paid off, and before long, it was easy to find people playing the rag in homes and bars and at exclusive parties.

Roberts convinced Stern to acquire the rights to two of Blake's songs: "Fizz Water" and "Chevy Chase." Once again, the publisher made an effort to increase their commercial appeal. As Blake's instrumentation was considered too complex for the average pianist to play, Stern had a white employee rearrange and simplify the music; he labeled the songs as both a foxtrot and a one-step—the terms were becoming interchangeable—and featured illustrations of white people on the sheet music. "Chevy Chase" also included an inexplicable photo inset of Betty Bond, a white performer.

However, in the end, neither song was financially fruitful. "Fizz Water," the tune that sounded more in line with the standard social dance rags of the day, sold a disappointing 388 copies, while "Chevy Chase," the more dynamic and unique song, did mildly better, moving 1617 units. But Eubie Blake had little to show for it. The pianist was paid a $1 advance against a one-cent royalty for each copy sold, and after his two compositions had run their course, the young composer had made about as much money as he had in a night at Aggie Shelton's. It wasn't lost on him that Luckey Roberts had lyrics to his song while Blake did not, and the pianist knew what he needed was a collaborator who could write lyrics to the tunes that filled his head.

Throughout Noble Sissle's first few months in Baltimore, he and Blake continued discussing their shared goal of publishing a song together, and a chance came when Sophie Tucker, the Ukrainian-born star of the Keith-Albee vaudeville circuit, announced she would be playing the Maryland Theatre downtown that August. They knew that if they could convince her to perform one of their songs, she could make it a hit. They hadn't figured out the logistics of their plan, but opportunities were few and far between in show business. They were going to seize this one.

By 1915, Tucker had already cemented her reputation as a dynamic, albeit iconoclastic performer. She rose to prominence as "America's Greatest Coon Shouter," performing blackface minstrelsy on the circuit, but quickly jettisoned the burnt-cork routine after her first visit to the southern part of the country. "I began to walk about the streets and study the Negro character of the South intimately," she recalled. "I realized how far away I and other performers were from the real thing." She vowed to be "through with blackface forever," and her career never suffered for it. In fact, her popularity grew. Bucking conventionality became a defining aspect of her persona, as she contradicted everything that should make a woman desirable:

she wasn't conventionally beautiful, her dresses were too snug, and she wasn't petite. However, she was confident and clearly comfortable in her own skin, as one of her stage hits, "I Don't Want to Get Thin," suggests.

And of the utmost importance to Sissle and Blake, her biggest hit, "Some of These Days," was written in 1909 by Shelton Brooks, a young and untested Black composer. Initially, she refused to meet with him, overburdened with the constant barrage of songwriters pitching her their next big hit, but on the advice of her trusted African American maid, Mollie Elkins, she changed her tune. "See here, young lady," Elkins told her boss, "since when are you so important that you can't hear a song by a colored writer?" Tucker agreed to meet with Brooks and, upon hearing the song, nearly kicked herself for having passed up the opportunity. She worked the number into her act the following evening, and it never left.

Tucker gave Brooks a chance, and in exchange, he gave her what would become her signature song. If only Sissle and Blake would be so lucky. Over their time playing various spots, they learned how to give the audience what they wanted, and in this case, their job was made easier. They had an audience of one, and they knew what kind of material resonated with her and, more importantly, her fans. The two quickly wrote an up-tempo breakup song, "It's All Your Fault," with a little help from Eddie Nelson, a white musician who also performed at Riverview Park.

Sissle and Blake went to the Maryland Theatre downtown on her opening night but weren't sure how to get their sheet music to her. As Blake tried to come up with a plan, Sissle was already working on how to get backstage. The pianist chalked up his partner's brazenness to the fact that he was "all brass" and, because of his upbringing, was generally fearless when it came to dealing with white people. "Sissle was more aggressive than I was," Blake said. "He was a fighter, he's a go-getter. I was never that way. If you don't like my music, I just took it and walked away, but he'd argue with you and sell it to you." The two managed to talk their way backstage and steal a few minutes of Tucker's time. Blake took to the piano, and Sissle didn't just sing the song—he *performed*. It was the first time the duo had an audience for an original song of theirs, and they clearly knocked it out of the park. The song was worked into Tucker's act a few days later. "It was an instant hit, at least in Baltimore," Blake recalled. "Everybody whistled it in the street."

Although the number was only known to those in attendance at Tucker's shows, "It's All Your Fault" was released by a Maryland-based music publisher the following month. It ultimately moved about thirty thousand copies, fifteen times what Blake's first two songs had sold combined. The sheet music was published with two different covers in 1915: one with a photo of Sophie Tucker with a hand on her hip and the other with a small photo of Eddie Nelson. Anyone purchasing the song would be forgiven for thinking that only white artists were behind the number. But for Sissle and Blake, it made no difference. They quickly followed up "It's All Your Fault" by collaborating with Nelson on "See America First," an ode to the United States that was also promptly published.

Their faces weren't on the music, but their names were, side by side, and even though they had only done it locally, Blake was right. Together, they hit.

The Serenaders disbanded at the end of the summer, and it immediately became clear how difficult it would be to keep the Sissle and Blake partnership together. Bob Young, the Serenaders' drummer, asked Sissle to be part of his sextet, which scored work playing the Hotel Kernan, while Blake started another band on the other side of the city. But while they had become separated by circumstances, the two continued to write together. Sophie Tucker accepted another one of their songs, "Have a Good Time, Everybody," and while it wasn't met with the same enthusiasm as its predecessor, it served as enough of a springboard for the duo to perform a short set at the Howard Theatre in Washington, DC, in early October. But as fall prepared to turn to winter, Bob Young was asked to bring his band to play in Palm Beach, Florida, for several months. Blake stayed in his hometown while Sissle moved on with the sextet. There were no certainties in show business, but they each had a suspicion they'd see the other again soon.

James Reese Europe's String Octett, with Noble Sissle second from right

Courtesy Photographs and Prints Division, Schomburg Center for Research in Black Culture, New York Public Library

3

HIGH SOCIETY

1915–1917

Less than a week after Sissle and Blake vacated the star dressing room at the Howard Theatre in Washington, DC, Miller and Lyles were moving in. *Darkydom* had just had a brief tryout in Trenton, New Jersey, and was poised for a more proper engagement in the nation's capital, beginning October 18, 1915. Miller and Lyles appeared in the show once again as Steve Jenkins and Sam Peck, vagabonds running away from someone who is trying to give them a $500 reward, all because they mistakenly think he's a detective looking to arrest them. In his effort to reinvigorate life in the African American theater scene, producer Lester Walton had reassembled some of the giants responsible for putting Black shows on the map the first time: *In Dahomey*'s Jesse A. Shipp Jr., who codirected with comedian Will A. Cook, and *Clorindy*'s Will Marion Cook, who wrote the music and conducted the orchestra.

The show lived up to its high expectations, and the beautiful sets and costume pieces, coupled with the top-notch acting and Cook's enthusiastic leading of the orchestra, all but guaranteed that it would kick-start a Negro renaissance on the legitimate stage. But there were warning signs early on that success may not come. R. W. Thompson, a reviewer for the *Indianapolis Freeman*, the first Negro paper in the nation, who flew out to review the opening-night show, gave *Darkydom* his blessing but felt it was a relic of an era best left forgotten. Many in the Black community had grown tired of seeing themselves caricatured as dim-witted fools and were growing increasingly fed up with burnt-cork comedians being considered high-end entertainment for wealthy white people. Thompson acknowledged that for a show to succeed, it would have to win over the social elites, but he stated that even the show's title confirmed that *Darkydom* was not meant to be enjoyed by the race that created it. "If the management consults the wishes of the masses of the colored patrons of the show, they will select a title that will convey the idea that it is a genuine Negro entertainment without using a term that is banned by polite society," he warned. However, the show proceeded, title unchanged, throughout the rest of the week, with the noted and well-respected Black bandleader James Reese Europe substituting for Cook as the orchestra's conductor.

The show opened at the Lafayette Theatre in Harlem the following week, to enthusiasm and stellar reviews, with the highest praise bestowed on the show's leading players. "Miller and Lyles, as per their work in this production, take first rank among all actual colored teams on the stage, in current or past time," *Variety*'s founder, Sime Silverman, wrote in the trade, "for it would not belittle Bert Williams as the great single comedian he is, to say that Miller and Lyles are a funnier team than Williams and Walker were... It looks like a show that can be rounded into a standard colored attraction, good for touring purposes for a long time to come, while those two crackerjack funny men, Miller and Lyles (who are both young), remain the standard bearers." It was also reported that John Cort, a comedian-turned-theatrical mogul, and his son, Harry, were arranging for the show to play $2 houses throughout the country, then bringing it to Broadway before an engagement in London. The elder Cort started one of the first vaudeville circuits before seamlessly evolving into one of New York's most powerful producers. News of his interest in the show was a boon to ticket sales, particularly as the show continued to its previously scheduled stops in New Jersey and Philadelphia, but public enthusiasm soon waned. *Darkydom* had everything Black producers thought white audiences wanted in terms of talent and spectacle, but it lacked what had made its predecessors so successful—originality.

Perhaps more importantly, while Black folks were hungry for representation on Broadway, the community was becoming increasingly vocal about negative portrayals of their race on the stage and screen. D. W. Griffith's epic film *The Birth of a Nation* was released that year and included a "historical" portrayal of South Carolinians during their first legislative session under Reconstruction. In an unbridled sequence, the Black elected officials eat fried chicken, sneak sips of liquor, sit with their bare feet on top of their desks, and vote to legalize interracial marriage and require that "all whites must salute negro officers on the streets," to the dismay of the "helpless white minority." The movie used white actors in blackface to paint African Americans as rapists and murderers, while glorifying and ultimately leading to a real-life reinvigoration of the Ku Klux Klan. *The Birth of a Nation* was a nationwide smash, earning praise from sitting President Woodrow Wilson himself, prompting the National Association for the Advancement of Colored People (NAACP) and Black activists like William Monroe Trotter, who was a Harvard classmate of W. E. B. Du Bois, to organize peaceful protests in an attempt to get the film banned for its racial depictions. While white patronage was important to any successful African American musical comedy, Black support was too, and against this backdrop, *Darkydom* wasn't going to garner many fans within the race.

However, despite the mixed response, Miller and Lyles were undeterred. The show folded prematurely, but the press they had received significantly raised their profile. In March 1916, they traveled to England for a string of dates; Bessie and

Olivette Miller accompanied Flournoy overseas, but Aubrey and Ellamay Lyles would divorce the next year. Miller and Lyles made their European debut at the Alhambra in Glasgow, with their tour including a high-profile engagement at the Victoria Palace in London.

Meanwhile, as the comedians were setting sail across the ocean, Noble Sissle was enjoying a scenic view of a Palm Beach lagoon. Boasting five-star accommodations, over a thousand rooms, tennis courts, a swimming pool, its own postal service, ice cream shop, and six stories set against a picturesque background, the Royal Poinciana Hotel wasn't just the largest resort in the world—it was a wonderland. Newspapers touted the arrival of notable visitors on a near-daily basis, as the newly reopened establishment's guestbook read like a who's who of the world's most-respected power brokers in business, politics, entertainment, and other aspects of high society. It was a perfect place for Sissle to spend his winter months, a welcome departure from the Midwestern cold, but part of him missed Indiana. When the Poinciana's owners invited C. I. Taylor, founder of the first Negro baseball league, to host his winter series on site, Sissle wrote a recap of their February 6, 1916, game for the *Indianapolis Freeman*. Most of the players were from the Indianapolis ABCs team, and since he was a local boy himself, he wanted to share this moment with everyone back home.

Sissle was used to playing classy spots, but the Poinciana required the highest standard of excellence and professionalism. Every day, he and the rest of the sextet dressed to the nines— Palm Beach suits by day, dinner jackets by night—and did their part to ensure the guests enjoyed their stay. While he couldn't do much more than pluck at the strings, he held a bandolin and sang while the rest of the musicians provided the actual instrumental accompaniment to the guests' dinner and dancing. The sun-kissed clientele on holiday couldn't have been more different from the Baltimoreans who watched him perform with the Serenaders just a few months earlier. His charm won over many of the New Yorkers seeking southern comfort during the winter months, and one socialite, Mary Brown Warburton, was so taken with his professionalism and talent that she took it upon herself to write him a letter of recommendation and give him a piece of advice. If he ever made it to New York, she said, he had to look up James Reese Europe. She was certain the two would hit it off.

Sissle didn't know it at the time, but a trip to Manhattan was more imminent than he expected. Vaudeville star Nora Bayes played a highly publicized benefit in the hotel's ballroom on February 28, and E. F. Albee, one of the heads of the Keith-Albee circuit, was among those in attendance. Throughout the performance, Noble Sissle and the rest of the sextet supported Bayes's act, and when the show concluded, Albee asked them to play for "Palm Beach Week" at New York's prestigious Palace Theatre. Bayes was on board, and once Bob Young agreed to let his group accompany her, Sissle was on the move again, leaving paradise for the show business capital of the world.

New York was where he—and every entertainer who wanted to make it to the big time—wanted to be, and Sissle was eager to make James Reese Europe's acquaintance. The bandleader was a true giant in the music world, not only to those of his race. He was born in Mobile, Alabama, and was raised in Washington, DC, where he studied the violin alongside Frederick Douglass's grandson, Joseph. Upon moving to New York in 1904, Europe discovered that he could find more work playing piano. He quickly ingratiated himself in the budding Black theater scene, writing songs for and conducting several musicals. By the end of his first half decade in show business, he had already established himself as one of the most significant Negro musicians in the country.

While his individual accomplishments would have been impressive enough, Europe revolutionized Negro musicianship when, in 1910, he cofounded the Clef Club, a consortium of colored instrumentalists and vocalists. The organization was dedicated to the promotion of the professional endeavors and social welfare of Black musicians, and it was groundbreaking for serving as both a union to ensure fair wages for artists of color and a centralized booking agency for New York's high society. The crème de la crème needed the best colored musicians playing their soirees, and as long as they were willing to pay for the honor, James Reese Europe was happy to assist. Under his leadership as their first elected president, membership grew into the hundreds.

But Europe's goals extended beyond economic equity. He believed that Black musicians were *at least* as talented as their white counterparts, and they would have the greatest professional success if they avoided imitating the European musical conventions. "Our symphony orchestra never tries to play white folks' music," he said. "We should be foolish to attempt such a thing. We are no more fitted for that than a white orchestra is to play our music." He wasn't advocating for musical segregation as much as he was rejecting the idea of assimilation. African American folks were best equipped to play music born out of their culture, he said, and if they had skill, their talent would be clear to members of all races, just as artists of European descent achieved success in America by holding on to their roots.

By the time Sissle arrived in New York, James Reese Europe was a household name, in large part because of his working relationship with Irene and Vernon Castle, white married ballroom dancers who were world-famous from the stage and screen. Once they settled in Manhattan, the couple capitalized on their notoriety by teaching social dances, like the foxtrot—which was created by W. C. Handy, the Black composer behind 1909's "The Memphis Blues"—to the city's debutants and throwing lavish parties that were covered in the press. The Castles knew a party was only as good as its music, and they needed the best. Europe's Society Orchestra became their house band in the most literal sense, often with several different ensembles spread out across various rooms. With their swinging ragtime, Europe provided just what the couple needed to preserve their reputation as having their finger on the pulse of popular entertainment.

Sissle was impressed by Europe and wanted everything he had to offer: steady work, kinship with the best colored musicians in the business, and the prestige and fair pay that should come alongside. He secured an audition with the bandleader and nearly immediately became a staple of the Society Orchestra that crisscrossed the city. Just as quickly, their business relationship gave way to a genuine friendship. Europe valued talent, competency, and ambition equally, and Sissle had all three in spades. In addition to being a frequently hired-out vocalist, Sissle was soon tasked with helping with Europe's business fairs and managing the bands with logistics at bookings.

Musicians often came and went, and by the spring, Europe was in need of another pianist. Sissle had been eager for Eubie Blake to join him where the action was. He lobbied Jim Europe, as his friends called him, to hire his old partner sight unseen, and as a testament to the trust the bandleader had in Sissle, he agreed. Eubie and Avis Blake packed their things and relocated to New York.

Almost immediately upon the Blakes' arrival, the three men seemed as if they had known one another all their lives. Europe arranged for Blake to play piano on Long Island during the day, and in the evenings, the pianist joined back up with the Society Orchestra. It was an adjustment wearing a tuxedo and long tails each day, and while Blake enjoyed having steady work and playing comfortable places, he was less impressed by the likes of the Astors and Schwabs than Sissle clearly was. The singer was quick to rub elbows with the socialites, but Blake always retained what he felt was a healthy skepticism.

He remembered one night in particular when he was reminded exactly where he was on the social ladder—and what Negroes had to do to reach the next rung. The Society Orchestra was playing a party for John Wanamaker, and while the musicians were supposed to have been fed, the Black waitstaff were too busy waiting on the guests. Contract or not, the white folks were going to be taken care of first. When the musicians' hunger—or perhaps just their complaining—became intolerable, Europe took their concerns to the Black staff manager. "Now, this butler, see—he's workin' for the great John Wanamaker, see—he thinks he ain't like *other* Negroes," Blake recounted. "He don't like it when Jim complains." After a few minutes, the musicians were all invited to a big room in the house, and they were each served soup out of a large china dish. The men all grabbed a spoon, but just as soon as the warm liquid touched Blake's lips, he spit it back out. It was dishwater. The other musicians also pushed their bowls aside, but when Blake looked over, Europe was still taking his dinner in by the spoonful. "My God, I thought, that Europe will eat anything," Blake recalled. "I realize[d] Jim Europe didn't get where he is with the white folks by complainin'."

While working with Europe, Blake picked up an important trick of the trade. Most of the Society Orchestra were "legitimate" musicians, as in they'd had some level of formal training or at least could read music, but even the most well-meaning white folks wanted to hold on to the idea that Blacks weren't educated enough to have been taught how to play; their talent was innate. Once Blake became assistant conductor for one of Europe's bands, he'd purchase the latest Broadway music and rehearse the musicians until they could play it flawlessly without sheet music. It'd take hours before everything was perfect, but Blake wouldn't accept anything less because Europe wouldn't, because their clients wouldn't. It was thankless and demeaning work that betrayed their true skill at mastering ragtime's intricacies and perpetuated the idea that Blacks were incapable of learning. It would strike Blake's attuned ear like nails on a chalkboard when they'd go to play parties and "all the high-tone, big-time folks would say, 'Isn't it wonderful how these untrained, primitive musicians can pick up all the latest songs?'"

Europe was adept at navigating white spaces, but he wasn't blind to racial discrimination. By the time Sissle and Blake hit New York, the bandleader had essentially monopolized the market for those seeking ragtime musicians for their social events. White players had also jumped on the current music and dance craze, but even the best of them lacked the same sense of rhythm and were too technical in their approach. "The colored bands jazz a tune," Irene Castle explained. "That is to say, they slur the notes, they syncopate, and each instrument puts in a world of little fancy bits of its own." It wasn't that white musicians didn't try to recreate that style, but just as Europe felt that Black folks couldn't ever surpass white folks at playing music they'd developed, ragtime's roots traced back to the Negro spirituals and church hymns from the Deep South. There were generations of history embedded in every note, passed down into the soul of every player. Playing ragtime required a lived experience white musicians would never have.

But jealousy eventually set in. Europe's musicians were doing well—in 1915, they had revenues of over $100,000, equivalent to over $2.3 million a century later—and there was a growing sense among some that the Society Orchestras were taking opportunities from white musicians. When a journalist asked Europe how he had achieved such success, the bandleader responded frankly. "In this occupation, as in all other desirable ones here in America, the Negro's color is a handicap," he said. "And wherever he achieves success he does so in the face of doubly severe competition." Additionally, while Europe may have been among the most profitable Negro musicians, when it came to sales of his music, publishing houses were still paying him a fraction of what he deserved. "I myself have written probably more of these new dances than any other composer, and one of my compositions, 'The Castle Lame Duck Waltz,' is, perhaps, the most widely known of any dance now before the public," he said in a 1914 interview. "Yet we negroes are under a great handicap. For 'The Castle Lame Duck' I receive only one cent a copy royalty and the phonograph royalties in the like proportion. A white man would receive from six to twelve times the royalty I receive, and compositions far less popular than mine, but written by white men, gain for their composers vastly greater rewards.

"I have done my best to put a stop to this discrimination, but I have found that it was no use," he continued. "The music world is controlled by a trust, and the negro must submit to its demands or fail to have his compositions produced. I am not bitter about it. It is, after all, but a slight portion of the price my race must pay in its at times almost hopeless fight for a place in the sun. Someday it will be different and justice will prevail."

While New York was coming together around ragtime, the rest of the world was falling apart. The United States had so far remained neutral in the conflict that Europe was entangled in, but after Germany sank a British ocean liner with over a hundred Americans on board, President Woodrow Wilson signaled that his troops may need to enter the fray. At the time, there were approximately ten thousand Black soldiers spread out across four segregated regular units of the U.S. Army, but Negroes in New York were eager for a National Guard unit of their own. Adhering to public pressure, the state's governor, Charles S. Whitman, created the 15th Infantry Regiment of the New York National Guard, with virtually no support from the federal government. Whitman began recruiting on June 29, 1916, and while there was interest in the creation of the unit, he struggled to get African American folks to volunteer. Most Black New Yorkers were new arrivals to the city and were more focused on making ends meet than signing up for the army.

Although he seemingly had little reason to jump in, on September 18, James Reese Europe enlisted as a private in the 15th New York National Guard Regiment—and he wanted Noble Sissle to sign up as well. The singer was reluctant. The Society Orchestras were keeping them both very busy, and Sissle felt that joining the army would be too demanding on their time. However, he agreed to hear his friend out. Europe said that he had initially shared Sissle's concerns but had just recently changed his mind. The army, he felt, was the best way for Black men in the city to organize. "Our race will never amount to anything, politically or economically, in New York or anywhere else, unless there are strong organizations of men who stand for something in our community," Europe said, adding that he envisioned an armory in Harlem where young Black men could not only have their bodies strengthened—with a swimming pool and gym equipment—but also their minds. This was an opportunity for a genuine investment in what was fast becoming their part of the city, but he told Sissle it would not happen if "the best and most sincere...men like you and I...sit back and say we have not got time. No, New York cannot afford to lose this great chance for such a strong, powerful institution, for the development of the negro manhood of Harlem."

This conversation came at a difficult time for Sissle. A month earlier, his mother, Martha Angeline Sissle, had died of cancer in Indianapolis on her forty-seventh birthday after undergoing two unsuccessful operations. However, while he wasn't sure how ready he was for another major life change, he trusted Europe completely and supported his vision. A week after they spoke, Noble Sissle was sworn in as a private and James Reese Europe was appointed first sergeant. But despite Europe's recruitment of Sissle, overall enrollment in the 15th remained low throughout the fall. William Hayward, the white colonel in charge of the colored regiment, had an idea to increase their presence and, in turn, their numbers. He wanted Europe to organize an army band, and while he expected the bandleader-turned-sergeant to enthusiastically agree, Europe was reluctant. He met up with Sissle upon leaving Hayward's office on Broadway, and the two discussed the opportunity over a late-night lunch at the Libya Restaurant on 131st.

There were many concerns. For one, Europe knew he couldn't just put together any band. Because of his reputation, it would have to be the best one in the U.S. Army. He also had a personal dislike for military bands, believing they were too loud and too brassy and lacked the beautiful musicality of strings. Crashing cymbals were not his style. Perhaps most importantly, Europe hadn't signed up for the army to play music; he had signed up to prove his worth to his country by fighting on the front lines for it.

While he understood Europe's concerns, Sissle thought Hayward's request was sensible. Europe was a musician above all else, and if the army thought he could best serve his country by leading a five-star band, he should consider it. He thought about it for a few days and returned to Hayward with an offer: if the colonel would provide any resource Europe requested to ensure the band met the musician's highest standards, he would do it. That would not only mean an unprecedented budget of about $15,000 but also bending the army's rules that a regimental band consist of exactly twenty-eight pieces. Europe said this was an "entirely impractical combination of instruments to play well-balanced music." He wouldn't do it unless he had at least forty-four men, but "sixty-odd would be better." He was certain the colonel wouldn't be able to meet his demands, but after a few days of figuring out how he was going to pull it off, Hayward agreed.

Just as funding was secured and the green light was given for a band to be assembled, Europe was preparing to depart to the Royal Poinciana Hotel in Palm Beach where he was providing two dance orchestras throughout January and February 1917. Sissle was supposed to join him, but instead, Europe asked him to stay behind and begin recruitment. Sissle took out advertisements in all the colored newspapers across the nation, and while it was easy to find interested drummers and brass players—many were untrained musicians struggling to make ends meet or former members of army bands in the Philippine-American war—Europe knew there was a shortage of qualified colored reed players. To find clarinet, flute, and saxophone players, he would have to recruit in Puerto Rico. In anticipation of the impending involvement in the war, President Wilson had recently signed the Jones-Shafroth Act, granting U.S. citizenship to Puerto Ricans and allowing them to enlist. The success of the regimental band relied on their involvement. With only three days to recruit, Europe left for San Juan on May 2, 1917. He returned with fifteen of the best players the island had to offer, just days before the 15th Regiment was scheduled to leave for its two-week training in field duties and rifle practice in Peekskill, New York.

While Europe and Sissle were preparing to fight and play for America, Eubie Blake wanted no part of the war effort. He claimed his age was the main reason why he didn't want to go—he was thirty years old at the time—but in actuality, he was comfortable in New York. He had well-paid, steady work, Avis was in the city with him, and he wasn't too interested in putting his life on the line for Uncle Sam. Europe never pushed the issue, but he and Sissle, who had recently joined his mentor in obtaining the rank of sergeant, enjoyed giving Blake the business. When they'd run into a group of women at a party or out on the town, they'd make a point of introducing themselves as army men and their third-wheel as "Eubie Blake, the slacker." The pianist didn't pay them much mind. It was all in good fun, and after all, he'd been called worse. Instead of going overseas, Blake agreed to help manage Europe's business affairs stateside, a win for all involved.

The 15th New York Infantry Regiment was ordered to Camp Wadsworth in Spartanburg, South Carolina for basic training in August 1917, but many feared they might also be embroiling themselves in the race war that seemed to be percolating within the armed forces itself. That same month, Black soldiers from the 24th Infantry got into a gun battle with white citizens in Houston, Texas, where they were stationed. The army men had been provoked with taunts and insults, and after they were pushed to the brink, nearly twenty whites were dead. Thirteen of the soldiers involved were tried and hanged for their involvement, while another forty-one were sentenced to life in prison. Tensions were high when news broke that troops from Harlem were headed down South, with Spartanburg Mayor J. F. Floyd making it clear to the *New York Times* that he felt the soldiers would be best served if they didn't come to his municipality. "With their northern ideas about race equality, they probably expect to be treated like white men," he said. "I can say right here that they will not be treated as anything except negroes. We shall treat them exactly as we treat our resident negroes. This thing is like waving a red flag in the face of a bull."

The *Times* story was concerning and seemed representative of a systemic problem. A week before the men left their safe harbor of Manhattan, there was another case of racial violence involving Black soldiers that made headlines, with this one exposing dissension in the army's own ranks. A group of Southern troops stationed at Camp Dix in Wrightstown, New Jersey, put up a sign stating NO NIGGERS ALLOWED on one of the buildings. The sign was taken down by a guard, but the troops quickly replaced it with one that said FOR WHITE SOLDIERS ONLY. A fight nearly erupted between two hundred armed men, which was only stopped by intervention from the battalion's officers.

The increase in tension between Black soldiers and whites, those also serving and civilians alike, shone a light on a debate taking place in the colored community. Emancipation was just a little over a half century earlier, the Reconstruction Era was murky and short-lived, and Jim Crow laws were still being implemented in states across the nation. African American folks were no longer enslaved, but even if they lived separately and unequally, they were still guaranteed second-class citizenship in the land of the free. It would be another several months before W. E. B. Du Bois advocated that his fellow Black men should "forget our special grievances and close ranks shoulder to shoulder with our own white fellow citizens" by joining the war effort, but African Americans were already engaged in a public conversation about whether they should fight for a country that systematically fought against them.

But James Reese Europe believed that fighting and playing was how Negroes could show their worth and contributions to America. While much of the discourse around whether African American folks should fight was about the war, Europe was more interested in the possibilities that might await them once they returned. On October 10, 1917, the 15th Regiment arrived by train in Spartanburg. While the mayor had made it clear they weren't welcome, some locals were quick to distance themselves from his sentiments although, they conceded, it still may have been ill-advised for the men to have been stationed there. The infantry was cautious, adhering to the best of their ability to the Jim Crow laws, but tensions continued to rise. At one point, soldiers from the 7th Regiment, a white brigade also stationed in Spartanburg, saw a Black soldier attacked by a group of towns-people while walking down the street. When they first arrived in town, the men from the 15th promised never to retaliate with violence while they were there, no matter the circumstances, but having made no such promise, the soldiers from the 7th beat the civilians for their mistreatment of their comrades in service. The following week, a misunderstanding led to a swiftly spread rumor that two Negro soldiers had been hanged. The infantry was already threatening to abandon their promise of pacifism. As many of them were New Yorkers, they were not used to this level of blatant racial injustice and were even less inclined to tolerate it while wearing the uniform of the United States.

Confrontations could occur on any street corner, and no Black soldier was immune from the threat, including Noble Sissle. On the evening of October 20, he was headed back to camp with Europe and about seventy-five other soldiers from the regiment after having performed at a local church. As they waited for their transportation, Europe asked Sissle to purchase a copy of every New York paper from a nearby hotel lobby. "Go on over, Siss," he said. "I never knew how sweet New York was until I landed here." The hotel was for whites only, but a local assured Europe that African American folks purchased papers from there all the time and they weren't met with any trouble.

Sissle put on a brave face but was secretly hesitant as he walked over. He saw several white officers through the hotel's large lobby window and a newspaper stand right next to the entryway. In his best effort to be unobtrusive, he quietly opened the door, grabbed the papers, and passed a white soldier, who was reading. Sissle smiled and approached the newsstand, where the cashier was in conversation with some policemen. The officer stepped back as he approached, and the clerk waited on the army man with all the honor and dignity a soldier in uniform, regardless of his race, deserved. Sissle had received his change and was headed for the door, reflecting on the anxiety he felt during the transaction, when he was hit from behind, his cap knocked from his head.

"Say, nigger, don't you know enough to take your hat off?"

Sissle genuinely believed he had violated a norm of the hotel but quickly realized the issue wasn't the headwear but the skin color of the person beneath it. He looked around and saw everyone in the lobby was wearing a hat. "Do you realize you are abusing a United States soldier," Sissle asked as he regained his footing, "and that is a government hat you knocked on the floor?"

As Sissle reached down for his hat and made his way out the door, the man, who happened to be the hotel owner, cursed and kicked at him until he was back on the street. "Damn you and the government too," the owner said. "No nigger can come into my place without taking off his hat."

The infantrymen had seen the whole encounter through the lobby's large windows, and the white soldier—"a Jewish boy from New York"—was also furious at what had transpired. He confirmed that Sissle was a victim of the "southern hospitality" the mayor had promised and, as best he could tell, was guilty of no further offense. All bets were off, and the colored men's pledge of civility was a distant memory. They quickly joined forces with about forty or fifty white soldiers on an impromptu mission to storm the hotel, assault its owner, and raze it to the ground. The newly founded mixed-race battalion entered the hotel, and before they could execute their plan, they heard a booming voice calling them to order. "Get your hats and coats and leave this place, quietly." The voice belonged to Europe. "And walk out, separately in twos, to Main Street." They followed his directions, leaving him and Sissle alone with the hotel owner and the white police officers who were still on duty inside.

Europe asked what had happened, and the proprietor, who was even more worked up than he was earlier in the day, maintained his innocence. As he saw it, the issue was that "that nigger did not take his hat off." The owner evaluated Europe. He was tall and built but even-keeled in nature, looking every bit as heroic as he felt in his army uniform and its accompanying hat. "No nigger can come into my place without taking off his hat—and you take off your hat."

Sissle's anxiety returned. He looked outside and saw the

troops still seething, and he looked at all six feet of his friend Jim
Europe, who didn't take kindly to being insulted, especially on the
basis of his race. *Well,* Sissle thought, *I know this place is going
to get wrecked now.*

Europe kept his attention on the hotel's owner and, slowly
and deliberately, removed the hat from his head. "I'll take my
hat off, just to find out one thing," he said. "What did Sgt. Sissle
do? Did he commit any offense?"

"I told you, he did not take his hat off, and I knocked it off.
Now you get out of here!"

Europe stood silently and locked eyes with the proprietor. He stayed there for several moments and then, with what
Sissle saw as "quiet dignity," the sergeant turned his back on
the owner and walked toward the large doors leading into the
country he had sworn to defend.

At that moment, the military police arrived on the scene,
and after saluting Europe, they asked what the trouble was. The
commanding officer of the military police assured him that the
proprietor would be punished accordingly. As they took the
hotel owner aside, the white local police officers commended the
army men on their professionalism and restraint. They made it
clear that they hadn't seen Sissle do anything wrong and that the
actions of the hotel owner were "un-American." Once outside,
Europe realized the troops weren't satisfied with the outcome.
Before heading back to camp, he reminded them of what Colonel
Hayward had said. They had a mission greater than fighting the
Germans; they were also fighting for their race. One hotel owner
shouldn't get in the way of that.

While they had planned to spend the remainder of their time training in Spartanburg, on October 24, 1917, just two weeks after they arrived, the 15th Regiment was prematurely being sent to France. Word of the various incidents had made their way back to Washington, DC, and because none had manifested into any serious violence, the higher-ups thought the Negro troops had earned the right to represent the country on foreign land. "In France, there is no color line. In France, your regiment can complete its training for modern warfare," Colonel Hayward was told. "To France, every fighting regiment of our army must go sooner or later," and for the Black boys from New York, it was going to be sooner.

With their bags packed and instruments in tow, the men prepared for the next leg on their journey. While it was said that their early departure was a "reward" for their resolve and dignity, James Reese Europe, perhaps only jokingly, said the army had no choice but to ship them off to another country that would treat them better.

"I'm sure sorry I sent you in after those papers," Europe told Sissle, somewhat in jest. "The man kicked us right to France."

James Reese Europe (left, with glasses), returning from France with the 369th Infantry

Courtesy of National Archives/165-WW-127(22)

4

NO MAN'S LAND

1917–1919

The dozen stone steps leading up to the grandiose opera house were completely obscured by the nearly thousand music lovers who were anticipating a show unlike anything they'd ever seen. It would be at least another hour before the curtain, but the crowd outside sizzled with excitement. The great American president Abraham Lincoln had been born 109 years ago on this day, and because that event was important to their allies, it was important to the French. Just slightly more than eight hundred people held tickets to the 9:00 p.m. concert, but there were another several hundred gathered around the towering Corinthian columns in front of the doors to the vestibule.

Then the band arrived. Before making their way inside, the soldiers took out their instruments and served as their own opening act, playing several songs on the plaza as the audience cheered them on. The enthusiasm with which James Reese Europe punctuated each baton movement belied the fact that morale had been waning among the men of the 15th New York Infantry. They had come to France on the promise of playing music and seeing war, and now, at least half of that promise was being meaningfully fulfilled.

The trip overseas had been an unmitigated disaster, taking nearly seventy days and four attempts for the troops to make it across the Atlantic. When the regiment departed from Spartanburg, they were excited to be leaving a place fraught with racial tension and moving one step closer to combat. But their trip was disastrous from the start. They'd arrived back in New York just in time to miss their convoy and were stuck waiting at Camp Mills on Long Island for two weeks while other arrangements were worked out. On November 11, 1917, they traveled across the Hudson River to Hoboken, New Jersey, and boarded the USS *Pocahontas*. It had barely made it offshore before they were returning to port due to engine trouble. Three weeks later, in early December, they attempted to sail out again with a new convoy, but a fire broke out in a coal bunker on shore, and the infantry was unable to leave with their scheduled caravan. The fourth attempt on December 13 began with a similarly disastrous start, when the soldiers on board were woken up in the middle of the night by an explosion. A British oil tanker had inadvertently torn a hole in the starboard side of the ship. It seemed as if the *Pocahontas* was destined to return to the port yet again, but a small fleet of metal workers made the necessary repairs for the nearly two-week journey to France to begin the next morning. "I believe that no less than ninety percent of the soldier men on that ship would have burst into tears if we had failed for the fourth time," Major Arthur W. Little of the infantry recalled.

The 15th New York Infantry made history on New Year's Day, 1918, when they became the first Black combat troops on French soil. Once they stepped off the *Pocahontas* at the harbor at Brest on the Brittany coast, the soldiers took out their instruments and enthusiastically played "La Marseillaise," the national anthem of their new temporary home. The French soldiers who received them looked perplexed, causing the American soldiers to wonder if they had committed some faux pas, but after playing close to a dozen bars, the locals snapped to attention. Astonishment rippled across each of their faces as, finally, they recognized the tune. They'd heard it hundreds of times before, but never with syncopation and a jazz rhythm. The dance craze that was taking over the United States had yet to reach their country, and as a result, its corresponding music hadn't made its way yet either.

But just as the Black soldiers were getting started, their planned contributions to the war effort were derailed once again. The regiment was ordered farther down the coast to Saint-Nazaire, where accommodations were being made to receive several million U.S. troops. Instead of proceeding to the battlefield, the pioneering Black army men were ordered to work duty, helping to lay a railroad, build a dock, and perform other essential tasks necessary to receive their forthcoming brethren in arms. It was long and arduous labor, a different kind of sacrifice and service than they'd signed up for, but on February 10, the newly promoted Lieutenant James Reese Europe and Sergeant Noble Sissle were ordered to Aix-les-Bains along with fifty-six other men. And even better yet, along their way, they'd have a chance to play a special performance on Lincoln's birthday at the Théâtre Graslin in Nantes.

It was standing room only in the Graslin, with each of its five levels of seating bustling with eager concertgoers. After some opening addresses, Europe signaled with his baton, and the band struck up a French march, followed by selections from the male vocal quartet. The audience's applause laid a strong foundation for the next number, John Philip Sousa's "The Stars and Stripes Forever," and before the last note was struck, the halls of the venue were filled with a rapturous applause that caught the musicians by surprise. The next set was a number of "plantation melodies," and once it was over, the musicians readied themselves for the big finale. Europe twitched his shoulders to ensure there was enough give in the underarm seam in his military coat for what was to come. The brass players blew the saliva from their instruments, and the percussionists tightened their drumheads. The musicians all settled back in their seats and closed their eyes just slightly, as if preparing for a transcendental experience.

Europe raised his baton high in the air and, with what Sissle described as "a swoop that came down with a soul-rousing crash," led his men in a high-octane rendition of W. C. Handy's "The Memphis Blues." The band was in rare form, with each instrument freeing notes that had been pent-up inside their players for months, eagerly waiting for appreciative ears. The Puerto Rican members of the infantry proved to be particularly dexterous, playing their cornets and clarinets in a rhythm that had yet to be recorded on paper by anyone, and by the time the song was done, the drummers were shaking in time to the beat they had created. Then Sissle saw a transformation in front of his very eyes. "Lieut. Europe was no longer the Lieut. Europe of a moment ago," he said, "but Jim Europe, who a few months ago rocked New York with his syncopated baton." The bandleader's body swayed along with the rhythm, his head bobbed, and like a bolt of lightning had run through him, he turned to the trombone players and commanded them to play a "jazz spasm," blurting a note with their slides fully extended, only for it to be sharply drawn back in. The audience couldn't stand it, working themselves into an "eagle rocking fit," where their bodies relaxed and their extremities swayed along with the rhythm. Prior to the concert, Sissle was hesitant about playing such a jubilant concert for the French, who were deep in the throes of war, but as "The Memphis Blues" danced to a close, he realized the fallacy of his thinking. "When the band had finished and the people were roaring with laughter, their faces wreathed in smiles," he recalled, "I was forced to say that this is just what France needed at this critical moment."

The remainder of their pilgrimage to the front lines was filled with impromptu performances for fellow American troops and French civilians alike. On one memorable occasion, the regiment played a concert at an orphanage in Chambéry, and as Europe was conducting, he noticed a small child moving his arms, imitating the bandleader with the utmost adoration. Once the song was finished, Europe whispered to his musicians, quietly advising them of the tempo for the next number, before he placed his baton in the hand of his young admirer. The child lit up brightly, and as he started waving his arms like the sorcerer's apprentice with the musicians seemingly following along, the crowd went wild. Europe stayed off to the side, proud not only of the band for being so charitable but also of the work that was being done to ensure the infantry was a positive reflection of their race. While on the way to Aix-les-Bains, the small coastal community where the 15th was to be stationed, Major General Kernan, the commanding officer of the region, reminded the colored soldiers that they were literally marching on new ground. As the men from New York were likely the first African American folks many of the French would have seen, they were advised to be extra cautious to make a good first impression. "The eyes of France would be upon them," Kernan said to Colonel Hayward, "and through the eyes of France, the eyes of the world."

As the 15th New York Infantry was expected to help prevent the establishment of a color line, their skin color was keeping them stuck behind a wall. The U.S. Army would not assign them to fight alongside white American soldiers, leaving the regiment only two choices: they could either return to the States in the hopes that they could join a future Black combat division, should one be established, or they could be transferred to fight with the French Army. The decision was an easy one. The wanted to serve their country in battle, and even if that meant being loaned out to an ally, they were game. But the irony wasn't lost on them. "Our great American general simply put the black orphan in a basket, set it on the doorstep of the French, pulled the bell, and went away," Colonel Hayward recalled.

The troops in search of a country arrived at Connantre in the northeastern part of France on March 20, 1918, and upon their arrival, they were rebranded the Trois Cent Soixante-Neuvieme RIUS, the 369th Infantry Regiment, U.S. Army, and temporarily assigned to the 16th Division of the French Army before embarking to their training site near Givry-en-Argonne. They had been anticipating going to the front lines since they enlisted, but just as they began their combat training, they received word that Vernon Castle, James Reese Europe's friend who helped popularize ragtime dance music among the white upper class and subsequently joined Britain's Royal Flying Corps, had died in a war-related incident. The news was devastating for Europe, who saw Castle as not only a friend but a true ally, the "one white absolutely without prejudice."

Europe was still in mourning when he received a letter from Eubie Blake, who was embroiled in his own battles back in New York. The bustling nightlife had nearly slowed to a complete standstill, with many of the city's elite donating their time and money to the Red Cross and other war relief efforts, thus limiting the demand for colored musicians. Blake was tending to James Reese Europe's business affairs, but with the country in less of a mood for revelry, there weren't many affairs to tend to. He voiced his displeasure with his current status in a letter to Europe, but the bandleader would have no part of the pianist's complaining. "If you think of the comfort you are having over there and think of the hardships we are having over here, you'd be happy, I am sure, to go on 'suffering,'" he said. Europe urged Blake to stay the course. Once the war was over and the musicians returned from France, things were certain to pick up. "I have some wonderful opportunities for you to make all the money you need," he continued. "Eubie, the thing to do is to build for the future, and build securely, and that is what I am doing. When I go up, I will take you with me, you can be sure of that."

Blake was despondent but finding ways to make ends meet. He recorded several songs onto piano rolls for Ampico, the American Piano Company; formed a new band, the Eubie Blake Trio; and released three dance tracks—"Hungarian Rag," "American Jubilee," and "Sarah from Sahara"—through Pathé Records.

Meanwhile in France, the men of the 369th had finally reached the front lines. They'd retained their uniforms from New York's 15th Infantry, but they also wore the French steel Adrian helmet, a visual reminder of their displacement from their native country. Europe was soon out dodging enemy fire— he was also a machine gun company officer, the first Black officer to lead troops into combat—and his band played on without him, with Sergeant Eugene Mikell, one of his coronet and saxophone players, serving as interim bandleader. Noble Sissle often organized makeshift vaudeville-style shows to give the band opportunities to perform in addition to the concerts they played to entertain the troops. They were safe and removed from combat, but playing at the funerals of fallen soldiers was a constant reminder of the true expense of war. The stakes were high every time they played, but no performance caused more anxiety than when Irvin S. Cobb, a noted writer from New York by way of Kentucky, showed up at the 369th Infantry headquarters in Maffrécourt in the second week of May with two other reporters. The journalists had made the trip to France to see the oddity of colored American soldiers fighting alongside the French for themselves, and upon their arrival, they were to be treated to a concert by the band.

Cobb was a divisive figure among the infantrymen. Over the course of his decades-long career, he rose to prominence in part because of his mockery of Blacks. When he arrived, the men of the regiment gave him an icy reception, doing their best to busy themselves around the station to avoid making eye contact with him. The last thing they wanted was for their dedication and competency to be misrepresented by a Southerner with a chip on his shoulder. As drum major, Noble Sissle worked alongside Eugene Mikell on a special set list in the hopes that they could play on Cobb's nostalgia for antebellum tunes. "We were both of the same opinion," Sissle recalled, "that if Irvin Cobb had any heart in him at all after going through the trenches and seeing our boys isolated from their own American army and cheerfully going about their allotted duties, and then hear...some typical Southern American melodies, his attitude would certainly be softened in some degree towards us as a race, and that 'poisoned pen'...would be at least modified, if not stilled forever."

With their shared goal in mind, the band struck up "The Stars and Stripes Forever" before transitioning into a medley of plantation songs. Accompanied by only the trombonist and a few other select instruments, Sissle crooned Stephen Foster's "Old Folks at Home" as the full moon in the sky provided enough light to silhouette the half-deserted town's church steeples in the background. Once they completed their set, they played an encore of "Dixie," beginning softly but slowly building into their characteristic finale of crashing cymbals, punched brass notes, and punctuated drums.

It wasn't confirmed until his report was published in the *Saturday Evening Post* that August, but Cobb was moved by the performance. "If I live to be 101, I shall never forget the... night," he wrote. "When the band got to 'Way Down Upon the Swanee River' I wanted to cry, and when Noble Sissle, the drum major, who likewise had a splendid baritone voice, sang as an interpolated number, 'Joan of Arc,' first in English and then in excellent French, the villagers openly cried; and an elderly peasant, heavily whiskered, with tears of a joyous and thankful enthusiasm running down his bearded cheeks, was with difficulty restrained from throwing his arms about the soloist and kissing him."

While the soldiers were pleased with their write-up, their

performance was only the second most impressive thing that occurred on the day Cobb arrived. Early that morning, two Black soldiers from the 369th—Henry Johnson of Albany, New York, and Needham Roberts of Trenton, New Jersey—found themselves outnumbered ten to one by German combat troops on patrol. They were both badly injured by grenades, with the impact from the explosion leaving Roberts nearly unconscious. Johnson ran out of ammunition quickly but fought like hell, annihilating the Germans with the butt of his rifle, fists, and ultimately the deadliest weapon he had available—an eight-inch French bolo knife. Johnson's unbridled grit outmatched the German's numbers and artillery, and they were soon set off on their heels, dragging their four dead soldiers as well as the wounded ones back to safety. Roberts suffered twenty-one injuries from the brawl, but from that point on, he was known as "Black Death," and the 369th Infantry Regiment had earned the nickname of "Hellfighters." Lincoln Eyre of the *New York World* and Martin Green of the *Evening World*, the two journalists accompanying Cobb, cabled their stories back to the States, and within a few days, the world knew of not only the musical prowess but also the courageousness of the Black American soldiers.

But while Roberts was receiving accolades both in America and France for his heroism, it wouldn't be until Cobb's piece ran in the *Saturday Evening Post* that the battle took on legendary status. The journalist was unequivocal in his praise, writing that "if ever proof were needed, which it is not, that the colour of a man's skin has nothing to do with his soul, the war was it." But what stood out most about his account of spending time with the Hellfighters was his belief that, upon their return, they would—and should—be finally welcomed as full citizens in their home country. "I make the assertion with all the better grace, I think, seeing that I am a Southerner with all of the Southerner's inherited prejudices touching on the race question," he wrote, "that as a result of what our black soldiers are going to do in this war, a word that has been uttered billions of times in our country, sometimes in derision, sometimes in hate, sometimes in all kindliness—but which I am sure never fell on black ears but it left behind a sting for the heart—is going to have a new meaning for all of us, South and North too, and that hereafter n-i-g-g-e-r will merely be another way of spelling the word American." Despite the evocation of the racial epithet, for Irvin Cobb, this was high praise.

The sounds of New York were resonating throughout France, and not exclusively by the infantry band. Louis A. Mitchell, a drummer and vocalist from the States, had recently come to the country with a group he dubbed the Jazz Kings. He was in need of more qualified musicians from the United States to join his efforts and wrote to his old pal Eubie Blake, whom he knew from Baltimore, asking him to relocate to France at $75 a week to play with his group, the Seven Spades. "This is the finest country in the world, and if you once get over here, you will never want to come back to New York again," he said in his offer. "You are treated white wherever you go as they like spades here and these Yanks can't teach these French people any different. I intend to stay here forever, and I am sure that you will feel the same way if you come over." However, despite the promise of a racial utopia, Mitchell's offer went unrequited; Eubie Blake remained in America, where he felt more comfortable, even though there were more opportunities abroad.

Throughout the summer of 1918, things remained relatively unchanged for Noble Sissle as well, until he received word that Europe was recovering from an attack of heavy German fire and a thick cloud of poisonous gas. Sissle rushed to the small hospital at Gézaincourt where the lieutenant was being treated, and they found the recovering soldier sitting upright with a notebook propped on his knees. A broad smile washed over Europe's face, and his eyes twinkled through his shell-rimmed glasses. "Gee, I am glad to see you boys," he said, seemingly unconcerned with his physical condition. "Sissle, here's a wonderful idea for a song that just came to me. In fact, it was [from the] experience that I had last night during the bombardment that nearly knocked me out." Europe showed his friend the chorus of "On Patrol in No Man's Land," an ode to life on the front lines.

By September, Europe, Sissle, and the majority of the 369th were transferred to Paris. The lieutenant resumed his position as bandleader—a role he hadn't played since February—and the regimental band kick-started their tour through the French capital with a concert at the Théâtre des Champs-Élysées. Nearly two thousand people attended, and just as they had done upon their arrival in Nantes, the band exceeded even their own expectations. Instead of returning to combat, the band was assigned out of harm's way. The war was escalating, and the army felt the best service the men could provide was to help boost the morale of the rest of the enlisted men and entertain the locals, most of whom had still never heard the rollicking music the band had become famous for. Throughout their eight weeks in Paris, riots broke out everywhere the musicians played as jazz, a term that was increasingly becoming en vogue overseas and back home in America to describe the syncopated sounds, filled every segment of the city. "When our country was dance mad a few years ago, we quite agreed with the popular Broadway song composer who wrote: 'Syncopation rules the nation, you can't get away from it,'" Noble Sissle said, referring to a tune made popular by Bert Williams in 1913. "But if you could see the effect our good, old 'jazz' melodies have on the people of every race and creed, you would change the world 'nation'...to 'world.'"

The most memorable performance in Paris took place in the Tuileries Garden, where the infantrymen were invited to give a concert alongside the British Band of the Grenadier Guards, the French Republican Guard Band, and the Royal Italian Band. These were the best military musicians in the world, and sincerely, Europe knew his performers could not compare. More than fifty thousand people were in attendance, and while the four different bands were playing at once, the crowd gravitated to where Europe was conducting. The French had decided on that day, the 369th

POSTCARD FROM NOBLE SISSLE INSCRIBED TO EUBIE BLAKE ON MAY 28, 1918, FROM PARIS

Courtesy of the Maryland Center for History and Culture, Item ID #PP301.1355

Infantry Regimental Band was the best in the world. They impressed not only the audience but the other musicians, with the bandleader of the Republican Guard asking to inspect the Black players' instruments, as he was sure they had been augmented in some way to create the unique sounds they produced. For Europe, the time spent in Paris was confirmation of his long-held theory that Black artists would have the greatest chance of success if they stuck with what they did best. "We have our own racial feeling and if we try to copy whites, we will make bad copies," he said. "We won France by playing music which was ours and not a pale imitation of others, and if we are to develop in America, we must develop along our own lines. Our musicians do their best work when doing negro material."

While things were going well in France, Sissle, who ultimately achieved the rank of lieutenant, was looking ahead to his return to the States and, more specifically, reuniting with Eubie Blake. On October 14, 1918, he wrote his old friend in New York a letter letting him know how well things were going overseas—"Jim and I have Paris by the balls in a bigger way than anyone you know"—and reminding him that the best of their careers was yet to come. Sissle had received word from Louis A. Mitchell that Blake was still having a rough time in New York. "Well old boy, hang on," Sissle wrote his friend. "We will be able to knock them cold after the war. It will be over soon."

"Soon" came on November 11, 1918, when Germany signed an armistice agreement to end all combat. The Great War was over, and after nearly two more months of primarily playing celebrations throughout France, the men of the 369th received word that they were headed back home. They were prepared to leave from Brest for New York on January 11, but when they arrived at the French port, they were greeted with hostility. The Black soldiers had been celebrated in France as both musicians and heroes of war, and the army command was worried they might have gotten too big for their American britches. They warned that the colored soldiers may have become infected with "foreign radicalism" and would return with the preposterous belief that the United States should be just as absent of color discrimination as France. To that end, they instructed the officers at Brest to treat them harshly to remind them of the colored man's place in the country they were returning to. "Our niggers were feeling their oats," they were told. "Take it out of them quickly…as to not have any trouble later on."

The treatment the soldiers received at Brest was unlike anything they had experienced throughout their time overseas. The officers in charge sanctioned them for insignificant infractions, threatening to delay their departure unless the colored infantry straightened up their acts. The disparity in treatment wasn't lost on the men, who had done all they could to fight tyranny from foreign enemies, and as one of their regiment wrote in a diary entry, "it seem[ed] as if [they] at last had struck something worse than the Germans." On January 31, the men of the 369th ended their thirteen months in France, and as Europe, Sissle, and the rest of the band departed on the SS *Stockholm*, they played happily and bid bon voyage to the country that opened its arms so widely to them.

After an uneventful trip back across the ocean, the last of the three ships carrying the 369th Infantry arrived in New York on Lincoln's Birthday, 1919, to a sea of thousands welcoming their arrival. Streamers flew through the air, seemingly given wings by the sounds of horns that filled the Manhattan streets, as tugboats also occupying the harbor shot streams of water into the sky. Five days later, on February 17, the city gave a formal heroes' welcome to the three thousand men who'd served in the trailblazing Negro regiment. Once again, thousands took to the streets along the parade route, which began at East Twenty-Third Street, up Fifth Avenue, and then ultimately to Harlem, where the men anticipated being most warmly received. "They did not give us their welcome because ours was a regiment of colored soldiers—they did not give us their welcome in spite of ours being a regiment of colored soldiers," Major Arthur Little said. "They greeted us that day from hearts filled with gratitude and with pride and with love, because ours was a regiment of men, who had done the work of men."

Throughout the entire voyage back to the States, James Reese Europe, Noble Sissle, and the rest of the musicians discussed and dreamed about how they could best capitalize on their return. They would certainly be greeted as full Americans, and despite their country's long-standing refusal to see the Negro as deserving of true acceptance, the war effort, they believed, had likely moved the needle. Irvin Cobb's recounting of his time with the infantry had captivated the nation, and while it was imperfect—the stereotypical Negro dialect and "darky humor" he was known for still permeated the piece—it had done wonders for solidifying their place in history. Throughout his time overseas, Europe frequently encouraged his musicians to stay by his side—including those who were in New York, like Eubie Blake—and he was more determined than ever to repay them for the dedication they had shown him and their country.

NEW YORKERS
CELEBRATE THE RETURN
OF THE 369TH INFANTRY

*Courtesy of National
Archives/165-
WW-127(63)*

5

THE RED SUMMER

1919

Peace had broken out in Europe, but the American soldiers returning home found a country very different from the one they had left, and for many, the opportunities they anticipated were mere optimistic fantasies. The United States had fallen into an economic recession brought on by the Treasury printing more money to finance the war effort instead of increasing taxes, which was a political nonstarter. This resulted in inflation, an increase in unemployment, and ballooning interest rates.

Southern Blacks continued to migrate to the North in droves, partially to escape discriminatory Jim Crow laws but also to capitalize on labor jobs that needed to be filled while hundreds of thousands of men were overseas at war. Once white army men returned home and discovered that their neighborhoods had changed and their vacated jobs had been filled by men they viewed as interlopers, dissension occasionally led to conflict and violence.

The economic uncertainty was further exacerbated by the ongoing health crisis—the global pandemic, caused by an unforgiving strain of the H1N1 virus—that began a year earlier. The powerful influenza would ultimately kill over two hundred thousand New Yorkers, nearly a third of the total lives lost in the nation. By early 1919, most citizens had stopped taking the preventative measure of covering the lower half of their faces with white gauze masks, but the virus remained a silent killer, rapidly circulating throughout tenements and overcrowded neighborhoods. Poverty and discriminatory housing practices placed people of color in harm's way at a disproportionate rate, making them most susceptible to what should have been a color-blind pandemic. While classrooms were closed around the nation, New York's health commissioner, Dr. Royal S. Copeland, made the unpopular decision to keep their schools open, as they were well-ventilated, clean, and spacious and had routine inspections for symptoms. With over 75 percent of enrolled students living in overcrowded tenements, it was healthier for kids to remain in school. Besides subpar living conditions and a higher likelihood of getting sick, Blacks had the added detriment of inadequate access to health care and treatment, as hospitals were segregated nationwide, and the ones for African American folks were unanimously inferior. In some cases, the disparity in care extended even into death. In October 1918, white sanitation workers in Baltimore refused to dig new graves in Mount Auburn Cemetery, the city's only site where Black bodies were accepted, fearing they may open themselves up to infection on the job. The city's mayor called on the army for assistance, and a group of Negro soldiers prepared 175 final resting places in just a day.

The end of the war also brought about a significant uptick in racial violence, particularly directed at Black soldiers returning from war. On December 16, 1918, Charles Lewis, a uniformed African American in Hickman, Kentucky, was approached by an officer who said he fit the description of a suspected robber. When the veteran explained that he had recently been honorably discharged and hadn't robbed anyone, the officer accused him of assault and brought him to the local jail. The next day, a white mob broke in, kidnapped the soldier, and hanged him. The NAACP demanded the state's governor hold the vigilantes to account. "In the opinion of the Association, this lynching has a tremendous significance in that the victim, Charles Lewis, had at the request of the government entered the service of the United States Army where he was prepared, if necessary, to lay down his life to see that the ideals of democracy were perpetuated," they said. The Boston branch of the National Equal Rights League issued a similar request to President Woodrow Wilson, but in the end, both cries fell on deaf ears. No one was ever charged for Lewis's murder.

In March 1919, a Black man in Nashville, Tennessee, submitted a letter to the *Chattanooga Daily Times*'s editor voicing the frustrations many in the race felt. "There are about 13,000,000 of us in this country who are only asking to be treated as American citizens," he wrote. "And we are asking that the door of hope and the gate of opportunity be not closed in our faces. We want to be encouraged when we do right. We do not condone crime nor do we harbor criminals. We are trying to live life as an American people—supporting the Constitution, fighting for the flag, and helping to build up business enterprises in every community where we live." Colored men and women rushed to join organizations to fight for the rights the country owed them, and between 1918 and 1919, a hundred new branches of the NAACP were established nationwide, increasing overall membership from nine thousand to forty-eight thousand in just a year. The association scheduled an antilynching conference in New York City later that spring, open to "all white people who love justice and all colored people who love liberty," and in their announcement, they drew attention to the incongruity of the treatment Lewis received in Kentucky—what they saw as the reality of race relations, particularly in the South—with the celebrated heroism of the 369th regiment. Even if only for their service to this country, the American Negro, they argued, was deserving of a "square deal."

The United States had become a place of increased tension and despair. While many African American folks attempted to seize this moment to create positive change for their race, many in the nation's upper class were keen on picking up where they had left off before the conflict. With the Great War over and their men back home, the social elite, most of whom were unaffected by the recent economic downturn, were ready to dance again—and James Reese Europe was eager to provide the soundtrack. The Hellfighters recorded a number of songs for Pathé that would be released over the next several months, and alongside booking agent Pat Casey, Europe quickly arranged a ten-week tour, primarily made up of two-night stands, where folks as far west as Chicago could experience the wartime heroes up close and personal. They had retained their uniforms, which they proudly wore to each performance and public appearance. As the publicity effort for the tour was about to begin, Casey raced to get his client's approval on the promotional materials. "Lieutenant Europe, we're about to go to press on the advertising posters. How do you want your name to appear on the lithographs? Shall we print it out in full, like this, JAMES REESE EUROPE?"

"No, Mr. Casey," the bandleader replied. "Just plain 'Jim' Europe. That is how I was known before I went to France, and I am the same Jim Europe now."

The tour kicked off on March 16, 1919, at the Manhattan Opera House on West Thirty-Fourth Street, the grandiose venue owned and operated by Oscar Hammerstein. Over three thousand people filled the seats, with the wealthiest among the audience occupying the boxes. At 8:30 p.m., a stagehand raised the asbestos curtain into the fly space, unveiling the eighty-five-member 369th Infantry Regimental Band seated in concert formation, ready for their American debut. Jim Europe stood in front of them in his khaki officer's uniform and, with his back to the audience, pierced the air with his baton to signal the concert's commencement. The response to the opening number was reminiscent of the Théâtre Graslin, and as the musicians listened to the vociferous ovation, they knew this was a night they would never forget. The rest of the concert was received just as well, and after the audience had heard the multiple encores they begged for, a public reception followed on the stage. It was a promising start to what would be a world tour, which the bandleader hoped would be a transformative experience in each city they visited.

The remaining weeks went by in a whirl. The Regimental Band took off to Boston, followed by a tour of major cities in upstate New York, then several dates in Ohio, a short stay in Noble Sissle's hometown of Indianapolis, over to St. Louis, then up to Michigan. All the concerts went well, save for a snag in Chicago on April 21. Once a local paper announced that seating at the show would be segregated, colored and white folks of the city banded together in protest. One journalist noted that "never before has such unity of oneness of purpose been displayed in this city," as the NAACP and local clergy distributed flyers— "The Shame of Segregation"—advocating for a boycott of the concert. On the evening of the event, an organized group of Black women formed a mile-long barricade around the hall, determined to inflict economic pain on the venue and stop every person with brown skin who tried to cross the racial picket line. In the end, only two Black people made it through, and with two hundred white ticket holders added in, over fifteen hundred seats went unfilled inside. The manager of the theater stormed toward the protesters during the demonstration, vowing to never let another colored person inside the theater again, prompting a woman to shout back at him from the crowd, "That is a matter for the courts to decide and not you!"

The demonstration in Chicago came on the heels of an event that rocked the Black community. Just a week earlier, a white mob had wreaked havoc on a Black neighborhood in Jenkins County, Georgia. Louis Ruffin, an Army veteran, shot and killed a police officer who was beating Ruffin's father with a pistol. Another officer drew his gun on Ruffin and was shot and killed as well. When word spread, the white residents of the rural community took the law into their own hands, killing two of Ruffin's sons—one was only thirteen years old—and throwing their dead bodies in flames they had created that were demolishing the local Negro church. Their rampage continued throughout the night, with the rioters setting cars and several other colored lodges and churches on fire. In the end, both Ruffin and his father were charged with the murder of the white officers and threatened with lynching, but no one in the white mob was held to account for his sons' deaths or the destruction of property. This marked the beginning of what would become known as the Red Summer, a prolonged period of racialized antagonism and violence, primarily in the South. While Black leaders had advocated for African American men to enlist in the army, believing it would lead to Jim Crow's end, they were now impressing upon them the urgency for the fight for democracy to continue on domestic soil. In the aftermath of the hate crimes in Georgia, W. E. B. Du Bois stated, "By the God of Heaven, we are cowards and jackasses if now that war is over, we do not marshal every ounce of our brain and brawn to fight a sterner, longer, more unbending battle against the forces of hell in our own land."

But despite the nation's growing racial discord, the tour moved on without further incident. They proceeded back through Ohio to Pennsylvania, then ultimately to Boston on May 9, where they had a return engagement. Instead of playing at the Boston Opera Club, as they had previously, they were booked at Mechanics Hall, a sizable venue on Huntington Avenue. The morning they returned to Massachusetts began in similar fashion to the days before it, in a major city hotel room. The weather was rainy and irksome, and a cloud hung over the band members. War had brought them together, and their homecoming tour had kept them there, but the former had ended and the latter was ending. After a two-week break, a few of the players would continue on with Europe and Sissle, playing the Shelburne Hotel at New York's Brighton Beach throughout the summer, but the rest would essentially be furloughed until the fall. Although they were scheduled to reunite, the reality remained that the next "gig"—a term Europe coined to describe a one-night performance, which quickly caught on in the jazz community—is never guaranteed in show business.

But despite the weather and an incorrigible head cold that caused him to quietly seek medical attention that morning, Jim Europe remained in relatively high spirits, even after seeing the modest amenities of the day's performance venue, which had a cavernous and cold auditorium. Vaudeville and Broadway star Al Jolson happened to be in the city, performing at a benefit without the blackface makeup that had made him a household name, and surprised his old friend Jim by coming to the matinee, which had a smaller crowd than expected. However, what they lacked in numbers, they made up for in enthusiasm. Europe slipped away to the doctor again after the afternoon show, as he was still feeling weak and ill. The weather had been unforgiving, the winds antagonistic, and he was advised that morning that he was on the verge of developing pneumonia. If he didn't play it safe, Dr. Bennie Robinson told him, he might end the day in the hospital.

Just prior to the 8:30 p.m. curtain being raised, the band's manager, John Fisher, came backstage bearing news. Massachusetts governor Calvin Coolidge had invited the band to play a special concert on the State House steps the next afternoon. He would then present Europe with a wreath to place at the monument of Robert Gould Shaw, colonel of the 54th Massachusetts Volunteer Infantry Regiment of Negro Soldiers during the Civil War, which was adjacent to the capitol building, an acknowledgment of the ongoing contributions Black servicemen made to the country.

The show began as usual, with rapturous applause, the swift swoop of Europe's baton, and an explosion of energy. Noble Sissle remained backstage in a sizable dressing room he shared with Europe, which served as a meeting room when the venue was otherwise dark. He wasn't scheduled to perform until later in the show and was able to read the newspaper while the band played in the background. Two numbers before the end of the first half, one of the musicians ran into the dressing room, pushing the ajar door open. "Lieutenant Sissle," he said. "Lieutenant Europe said to find Herbert Wright and send him back on the stage!" Apparently, Wright, who was half of a drumming duo, had stormed off during the second number and hadn't returned. Sissle could hear that the finale was next, and as it was to feature a drum duet between Herbert and his "stage brother" Steve Wright, finding the missing musician was imperative. Sissle ran into the hallway, opening doors until he found Herbert Wright behind one, nonchalantly lying on a bench with his performance attire—his army uniform coat—off.

Sissle could tell Wright was in a foul mood. As part of his drum major responsibilities overseas, the vocalist had been responsible for handling band member discipline, and Wright was often in need of addressing. He wore being argumentative as a badge of honor, but when given an opportunity to vent his frustration, he usually calmed down. "You know, Lieutenant Sissle, I work hard and Steve never does anything right," Herbert Wright said while shifting his body to sit up. "He makes mistakes, and then Lieutenant Europe looks back in the drummer section and commences to frowning at me." Sissle heard his colleague out, then reassured him that he'd misinterpreted the bandleader's actions. More was expected of Herbert because Europe knew he was the better drummer. "Well, for you, Lieutenant Sissle, I will go back onstage," the drummer said. "But you know I work hard and Jim has no right to frown at me."

Wright returned to the stage, and Sissle returned to his

dressing room. From what the vocalist could hear, the first act finale went off without a hitch, but as the audience was still applauding at the beginning of intermission, Europe came into the dressing room with Herbert—who still had his drum fastened around his neck—and Steve right behind. Europe sat at the table beside Sissle, who barely looked up from his newspaper, and let the Wrights know he wasn't in an arguing mood. He wasn't feeling well and, according to his doctor, should be at the hospital this evening instead of onstage. He was just trying to finish these last few dates so he could take a much-needed break, from which they all could benefit. The band members had been away from their homes for years, and some of them— the Wrights in particular—obviously needed to clear their heads. "You two boys above anybody else in the band should cause me the least worry," Europe told the drummers. "I have at all times tried to be a father to you both and there is nothing I wouldn't do to help both of you, and I don't want either one of you to worry me anymore."

"All right, Lieutenant," Steve, usually the more combative of the Wrights, said after the lecture. "I promise I will not cause you any more worry."

"What about you, Herbert?"

"Lieutenant Europe, you don't treat me right," the other drummer answered. "Look at my hands, they're all swollen where I have been drumming, trying to hold the time and yet, Steve, he makes all kinds of mistakes and you never say anything to him."

Just as Europe was set to respond, Roland Hayes, a gifted

Black tenor vocalist who happened to be at the show, entered the room with three of the Harmony Kings—a vocal quartet Europe and Sissle had discovered while in Chicago made up of Horace Berry, Harold Browning, Exodus Drayton, and William Hann. In the commotion of their arrival, Sissle whispered to Wright to drop it, but it seemed to him that the drummer was being plagued by more than just casual glances in his direction during performances. As the Harmony Kings took Europe's attention, Sissle asked Wright to leave, as to avoid making a scene. The drummer reluctantly left the room.

Wright had only been gone for a few moments when he burst back in, seemingly having a change of heart. He cast his drum off and threw it in the corner of the room, surprising and confounding the newest arrivals to the dressing room, who instinctively took a step backward. The drummer pulled his arms out of his uniform coat, throwing it down, and with Europe still behind the table, Wright raced toward him, yelling, "I'll kill anybody who takes advantage of me!" The drummer flashed a knife he'd been concealing in his closed fist and screamed, "Jim Europe, I'll kill you!"

Sissle and the rest of the men in the room stood paralyzed as Europe backed up between the table and the wall. The bandleader quickly grabbed a chair and raised it in an attempt to create a blockade between himself and Wright, who was now crouched down like an animal preparing to pounce. The stand-off had broken the spell on the other men in the room, and they began hollering and screaming for Europe to knock the knife out of the crazed drummer's hand. Perhaps the bandleader sensed that Wright felt just as cornered as he was, leading Europe to attempt to deescalate the situation, or he was simply blinded by optimism and unable to comprehend the reality of what was happening, but at the height of the frenzy, Europe relaxed his body and lowered himself to set the chair down. Wright moved too, lunging toward Europe, who turned away to shield himself from the attack. Wright swung his knife wildly at Europe's face, and with a scream, the bandleader sank to the floor. Sissle ran over and put his hands on his friend's shoulders in an attempt to calm him down. It seemed to work. With Europe safe and tranquil, Sissle turned his attention to Herbert Wright.

Europe's second-in-command reassumed his role as disciplinarian. "What's the matter with you? Are you crazy to cause this embarrassment here before strangers?" He demanded Wright follow him to another dressing room, which the drummer did willingly, and just as Sissle began to tell him off for his unacceptable behavior, one of the Harmony Kings barged in. "Sissle, come in the room at once," he said. "Herbert stabbed Lieutenant Europe."

Sissle didn't realize that Wright's knife had made contact, but when he ran back to their shared dressing room, it was a crime scene. The Harmony King stayed with Wright, and when Sissle reunited with Europe, he found his old friend tugging at the collar of his uniform. When he had finally gotten it unfastened and loosened his white tie from around his neck, blood spurted from a wound that was barely visible. One of the other Harmony Kings raced to apply pressure to the site with a towel.

Everything was going to be all right. The drummer was

promptly taken into police custody, and it was decided that, as to not alarm the audience, the show would go on. As the intermission drew to an end, the band resumed their positions, and an announcement was made that Europe had fallen ill and that the rest of the evening would be led by assistant conductor Felix Weir. Meanwhile, unbeknownst to the applauding audience members ready for the second act, an ambulance had quietly parked behind Mechanics Hall, and a stretcher was brought through the back entrance. Sissle stayed by Europe's side throughout the ordeal, and just before the bandleader was wheeled out, he looked back at his friend.

"Sissle, don't forget to have the band down before the State House at 9:00 in the morning," he said. "I am going to the hospital, and I will have my wound dressed, and I will be at the Commons in the morning in time to conduct the band. See that the rest of the program is gone through with. I leave everything for you to carry on."

Europe was rushed to Boston City Hospital, just a mile away, where the diagnosis was bleaker than everyone had thought backstage at the venue. "Lieutenant Europe, we have very little hopes for your recovering," the doctor said. "Our only possible means of saving your life is by an operation." The door to the operating room opened cautiously, and an officer in plain clothes walked in, with Herbert Wright tethered with handcuffs.

"Lieutenant Europe, is this the boy who stabbed you?"

"Yes, that is Herbert," he replied. "But don't lock him up. He's a good boy—just got a little excited tonight."

The medical situation was growing more dire by the minute, and if there was any chance of saving Europe's life, the chief surgeon would have to start now. "Lieutenant Europe, you are in serious condition," he said. "If you have anything to say, you must say it now. We have hardly any hopes of your recovery."

"I'll get along all right," Europe replied. "Herbert didn't mean to do it—just hotheaded. Go ahead and operate. I'll get well." The doctors quickly administered the anesthetic, rendering Jim Europe unconscious so they could proceed. He never woke up.

Noble Sissle and two of the Harmony Kings were at the police station giving their statements when they received word that Europe's health had taken a turn for the worse. They linked up with the third member of the quartet who was present during the incident and took a taxi to the hospital. They were told that the bandleader would need a blood transfusion, but just a few minutes later, an orderly returned with the final update—James Reese Europe was dead. The next morning, Sissle did as his friend had directed. He ensured the band met at the capitol steps on time, and after playing, Governor Coolidge gave them the wreath he had intended to be laid at the monument of Robert Gould Shaw as a token of his appreciation and respect for the recently deceased Lieutenant Europe.

News spread quickly around the world, but New York, Jim Europe's home for a decade and a half, felt the loss most significantly. The tour was intended to end on May 12 with a triumphant one-night stand at the Manhattan Casino in Harlem, where the Clef Club Orchestra had its first performance in 1910. Eubie

Blake was the manager of the event, in charge of ticket sales, but instead, on May 13, Europe had a different kind of homecoming, as the city held a public funeral the likes of which had never been seen for a member of the Negro race. When the cortege left the parlor on West 131st, it was greeted by thousands of Harlemites, who filled the sidewalks and stuck their heads out of the building windows to catch a glimpse of the caravan escorting Lieutenant Europe. The procession passed the headquarters of the Clef Club on Fifty-Third before proceeding to St. Mark's Methodist Episcopal Church, which was filled hours before the services were to start. The march was led by the Hellfighters Band, under the direction of Ford Dabney, a close friend and frequent collaborator of Europe, and included members of the old 15th Infantry Regiment and many prominent civilians. The memorial was notable not only for the quantity of people but also the number of white people in attendance, including Colonel William Hayward, Captain John Wanamaker Jr., Lieutenant J. P. Gillespie of the French 59th Artillery, and Pat Casey, who helped book the ill-fated tour. Following the services, Europe's body was sent from Pennsylvania Station to Washington, DC, where he was to be buried the next day in Arlington Cemetery with military honors.

The country's Black newspapers, like the *New York Age*, were eager to secure Europe's legacy. It was important to establish that he had not succeeded despite of his race but, in many ways, because of his embrace of it as well as his unbridled ambition. "He was not ashamed of being a Negro or being called a Negro," they wrote, "believing that instead of worrying and arguing about what he should be called, the proper thing was to dignify the term 'Negro,' just as he helped dignify Negro music… He was the Roosevelt of the Negro musicians—a dynamic force that did things—big things. His death comes as a big loss to the musical world, but a still greater loss to the race of which he was proud to be a member."

Noble Sissle took Europe's death particularly hard. The two had known each other for only three years, but it seemed like a lifetime. He didn't simply mourn the loss of Europe but also his unrealized dream, which Sissle felt the bandleader was on the cusp of making come true. "You see, Siss," Europe said to him in 1916, shortly after the two met. "I have always wanted to see one thing materialize before I die. And I don't care whether I am at the head of it or not, but I want to someday see an American Negro Symphony Orchestra organized. It's my life's dream, and I would like to see an organization of trained Negro musicians specialize in the rendition of Negro music, written by Negro composers." But Europe had no delusions about how challenging this would be. The biggest issue, as he saw it, would be securing financing during a rehearsal period until the musicians were of an appropriate caliber. Otherwise, they'd risk putting less than their best onstage. "I would never come before the public with a musical organization that I was not positive would be a revelation and a credit to the race," he said, "because it would hurt our race and set it back in the minds of the world more than anything else inasmuch as any race's progress is rated by its artistic attainments."

For the bandleader, performing for and maintaining relationships with the wealthy was simply a means to that end.

When he was ready to organize an effort to rival all the great symphonies in the world, having white folks with money on his side would go a long way. Sissle listened to Europe intently as he spelled out his plan, and by the end of the conversation, he had made a decision. "I vowed that if I ever did anything else in life other than to aid him in the realization of this beneficent ideal, I would not have lived my life in vain," Sissle recounted. "Unlike many of his fame, he did not seek to ape other races, but his whole life's desire was to bring out the original talents and artists' attainments of his own race."

I leave everything for you to carry on. Europe's final words to Sissle kept replaying in his head. The bandleader was referring specifically to the evening's performance, but given what followed, they took on a new, prophetic meaning. The issue was, the vocalist didn't know how to best continue Europe's legacy. "There was only one Jim Europe," Sissle said. "There were years of experience behind that sweep of his arms, and anyone who tried to follow would just be out of their mind." As he brainstormed how to best "carry on," Pat Casey, Europe's booking manager, and B. S. Moss, a booking agent on the Keith vaudeville circuit, approached Sissle with an idea. The tour had been a success, in large part because of the notoriety the Hellfighters had received overseas. Irvin Cobb had specifically named Sissle in his write-up, earning him the moniker of "the Greatest Singer of his race," and Casey said he would be wise to capitalize on his newfound notoriety while opportunities existed. They suggested he go on tour with a fifteen-piece band, but the singer countered. He didn't want a horde of musicians alongside him;

he only needed one. During the ten-week tour, Sissle and Europe concluded each concert with a duet, with Europe at the piano and Sissle singing, and the segment always went over well. Sissle was sure that with Eubie Blake at the piano bench, they'd have a shot at replicating the magic that had driven audiences wild. The two had already proven to make a successful team, and if anyone was deserving of coming along for this ride, it was his old partner.

Blake loved the idea, as he was no stranger to vaudeville. In fact, while Europe and Sissle were in France and work slowed with the Society Orchestra, Blake joined forces with Broadway Jones, a big, flashy guy with a strong baritone voice—Blake said he never saw Jones wear the same suit twice—for a series of dates at the Gossler Brothers' Campus Restaurant at 104th Street and Columbus Avenue, and a string of other engagements on the Keith vaudeville circuit. Working with Jones gave the pianist experience collaborating consistently with a partner and some practical lessons in professionalism. "He come on stage, and you know, they got chalk marks on the floor, so you got to stand by the chalk marks," Blake said. "Now Broadway comes out smilin', see. Now he looks perfect. He's right on the chalk where he's supposed to be, see. Well, if you move the piano ten feet away, he still stays on his mark—like either he's afraid to leave it or he doesn't see that the piano is moved."

Sissle and Blake quickly put together an act and set off on the road. Ensuring that no opportunity for publicity went untaken, advertisements and newspaper write-ups in advance of their appearances often noted that both men had worked alongside James Reese Europe and that Sissle was formerly part of the Harlem Hellfighters. They were branded as the heirs apparent to Europe's legacy, a responsibility they welcomed and took seriously. Just as they had done when performing with the Society Orchestra, they donned black tuxedos, and before stepping out onstage, they used a handheld whisk broom to pick off any errant flecks of dust or dandruff that threatened to ruin the perception of perfection. The vaudeville audience was different from the big spenders they were used to, but Sissle was confident that he and Blake would win them over in the nine minutes they were given to perform just the same. The only thing left to do was let the audiences weigh in for themselves.

Noble Sissle and Eubie Blake

Courtesy of Glasshouse Images/Shutterstock

6

PARTNERED

1919–1921

Hey you! You follow that act?"

As they had been over a dozen times before, Noble Sissle and Eubie Blake were in the wings on opposite ends of the stage, sharp as tacks, waiting for their cue to run on. Their tuxedos were crisp and clean, and each of Sissle's low-cut wavy hairs lay perfectly atop his head. If his partner had had any left, they would have been in place too. This had become business as usual, but as their time to step in front of the audience neared, a white guy stood alongside Blake, clearly with something on his mind.

"Did you hear what I said?"

"Sure, I heard what you said." Blake wasn't in the mood. He was in his hometown of Baltimore, enjoying one hell of a homecoming, the Dixie Duo taking the Keith vaudeville circuit by storm after only a few weeks. The pianist knew what the man was getting at and quickly grew annoyed with the unsolicited and unwanted song-and-dance routine. "You said I follow that act," Blake continued. "I know. I'm here, aren't I?"

"Ah," his sparring partner said before leaning closer. "When you gonna make up?"

Blake knew he wasn't talking about a little powder to hide the sweat that would soon be running off his head from the stage lights. But instead, the pianist played dumb. "Make up?" His feigned confusion took the man by surprise. "What do you mean 'make up'?"

"When you gonna put cork on!"

"I was *born* with cork," Blake said, his voice competing with the growing applause for the act that had just ended. "I'm gonna spend money to pay for what I've already got?"

Before the man could respond, the emcee introduced the Dixie Duo, the band struck up, and Sissle and Blake made their grand entrance. There was no shiftless buffoonery, just the clean, upscale entertainment the two were known for. As expected, the audience ate it up. Blake had completely forgotten about the altercation before the performance, but when the two left the stage, the man was in the exact same spot, armed with a retort: "Wise guy."

It had been just a few weeks since Sissle and Blake had begun touring together, but in that short time, they had made a name for themselves. The strong sales of Pathé's recordings of the 369th Infantry Band helped Noble Sissle become an even better-known figure nationally. The act he and Blake had developed was perfectly calibrated to resonate with white audiences. Their new name, the Dixie Duo, evoked the Confederate States of America, even while they were paradoxically dressed in the most debonair formal wear from head to toe. Their set was entirely comprised of original songs, and while many of them were contemporary tunes suitable for dancing, others were stereotypical numbers reminiscent of the standard minstrel fare that Sissle and Blake personally resented. The musicians felt it was all about balance and ultimately giving the audience what they wanted to see. But while Blake was amenable to telling a few light jokes at the expense of the colored race during their onstage banter, Sissle never went down that route. Nostalgic ballads were one thing, but inviting white folks to make fun of Black people, he felt, was another.

In fact, despite the slight antebellum aspects of their act, the number that always garnered the most attention and applause was their finale, "On Patrol in No Man's Land," which Sissle wrote with Jim Europe overseas. Even though the song wasn't a genuine Dixie Duo original, it served as a tribute to the heroism of the 369th and contributions of Europe, both as a musician and patriot, and the two felt it was the perfect way to leave the crowd wanting more. "I didn't have nothin' to do with those tunes," Blake recalled, referring to both "On

Patrol in No Man's Land" and "All of No Man's Land Is Ours," another Europe and Sissle war-era hit. "But they put my name on them right alongside theirs, because that's the kind of partners they were. I've been lucky to have such friends in my life."

Through the power of music, the stage transformed into a war zone. When the number was played by the Hellfighters, the entire band would simulate the sounds of machine guns rapidly expelling bullets, grenades being tossed, explosions, and whirring sirens to create an immersive experience. However, with Sissle and Blake operating as a twosome, it was up to Blake to fill in for the entire regimental ensemble. The pianist loudly struck his keys at various points in the song, and with every interjection, Sissle jumped, slid, and ducked as if he were dodging oncoming fire:

> Don't start to bombing with those hand
> grenades,
> There's a machine gun, holy spades!
> Alert, gas, put on your mask,
> Adjust it correctly and hurry up fast.
> Drop! There's a rocket for the Boche barrage,
> Down, hug the ground, close as you can, don't
> stand.
> Creep and crawl, follow me, that's all.
> What do you hear? Nothing near. All is clear,
> don't fear.

That's the life of a stroll when you take a
    patrol
Out in no man's land. Ain't it grand?
Out in no man's land.

The Dixie Duo made their debut in Bridgeport, Connecticut, and based on the strong response, Pat Casey quickly arranged for them to play the Harlem Opera House. The following week, Sissle and Blake presented their set for bookers of the highly coveted Palace Theatre, "the pride of the Keith circuit." The venue's manager loved the original songs and their presence but thought their set would go over better if they were more in line with the typical Negro theatrical norms of the day—blackface, white gloves, Southern dialect, and comedy that communicated a clear lack of intellect. He envisioned Sissle and Blake entering the stage from two separate sides, in oversize patched overalls, dressed as if they'd just stepped off the plantation. Sissle would gesture to a big box on the stage. "Say," he'd ask his partner, "what's dat thing over there?" Then Blake would look at the box as if it had landed from Mars and say, "I don't know what 'tis!" Then he'd approach the object tentatively and, with his crooked pointer finger, strike one of the ivory keys concealed by the box's facade. A surprised look would appear on his face to punctuate the sound of the note he'd just played, and with all the feigned astonishment he could muster, the first-rate pianist would cry out—"That's a pie-anna!"—before taking his place at the instrument to begin their set.

Pat Casey was a barrel-chested, no-nonsense veteran of the

business with a reputation for impertinence and a love of four-letter words. When he was pitched this idea at the Palace, he made it clear that his performers weren't going to play coons onstage. "They're not going to wear any grotesque clothes," he said. "They're going to wear tuxes. Did you see them at the Harlem Opera House? That's what they're going to wear. Tuxedos. And they're not going to have no piano in the box that the piano came in on the stage. And they're not going to say they don't know what it is. They're going to walk right out to the piano and play it. These men played with James Reese Europe in the million-aires' homes of the whole United States. Now, you're going to take them and put cork on their faces? They're not that kind."

The great Black vaudeville comedian Bert Williams had headlined the Palace just a few months earlier. His engagement was supported by a robust promotional campaign, with lobby cards featuring a prominent illustration of the comedian just slightly hunched over, outfitted in a top hat, jacket, checkered pants, white gloves, and slick black shoes. Williams's skin was painted completely black, making the borders of his jacket and hat indistinguishable from his head. The only contrasting colors on his body were the whites of his eyes and his soft pink lips. His run at the Palace was unprecedented—it was rare for a colored artist to headline any vaudeville house, let alone the crown jewel of the circuit, right in the heart of the entertainment capital of the world. However, while Williams performed regularly in black-face, Sissle and Blake did not. Casey offered an ultimatum: the theater's manager could either book the Dixie Duo as they had been performing, or Casey would offer the act to the Shuberts, who had an ever-expanding theatrical empire throughout major cities on the East Coast. The manager promptly dropped his idea and gave Sissle and Blake a spot on the bill.

Even though some aspects of their set played to the base interests of the white vaudevillian audience, the Dixie Duo was as far away from minstrelsy as Black vaudevillians were permitted to be. Nearly eighty years after blackface became an American pastime, most vaudevillians, Black and white, were still wearing burnt cork, but when Sissle and Blake debuted at the Palace on June 30, 1919, they remained part of a small contingent of Black performers who appeared on the stage in their natural skin tone. They were advertised as Jim Europe's protégés and given the second performance spot—a slight, to be sure, as reviewers saw performers who played early in the night as openers and rarely came to a vaudeville show until the third act. Sissle and Blake's first performance at the venue got off to a lukewarm start, but by the time they hit their novelty finale, they'd generated some of the loudest applause of the night. "You play the Palace and then you die and [go] to Heaven, for there's nowhere else to play," Blake said.

Of course, there *were* more places to play—and lots of them. The Dixie Duo did a week at the Maryland Theatre in Baltimore before proceeding to Keith's Amusement Center in Boston. They had become a hard act to follow, and by the time they hit the stage in Massachusetts, they were given higher billing than some of the white critics in the audience thought they deserved. But despite the skepticism they faced from some in the chattering class, Sissle and Blake were becoming overnight sensations. Thanks to their newfound success in vaudeville, the two signed a nonexclusive deal in July 1919 as songwriters with M. Witmark & Sons, their first major publishing agreement. They were paid a salary of $25 a week to provide the company with songs on a regular basis, and they would receive two cents commission on every copy of sheet music sold. As the act grew in popularity and with recording and publishing contracts in hand, the two continued to write at breakneck speed, often testing out new material onstage before handing it over to the Witmarks for consideration.

The two continued cranking out new music and playing major cities, consistently impressing audiences. "Sissle and Blake stop the show every time they appear," *Billboard* magazine reported of their September engagement in Brooklyn at the RKO 81st Street Theater. "The songs they offer, which are all written by themselves, are absolutely unique and possess a snap and originality quite uncommon. That the duo know how to put them over goes without saying. They are marvels of efficiency and smartness... The two...scored such a hit and the applause attending each of their numbers grew so rapidly that by the time their act was ended it seemed as though the Brooklynites might not allow the performance to proceed."

Their warm reception was replicated throughout the fall at the Royal Theatre in the Bronx, Keith's on Chestnut Street in Philadelphia, the Empress in Grand Rapids, Michigan, and the E. F. Albee Theatre in Providence, Rhode Island. Throughout the barn-burning tour, the Dixie Duo continued to climb further up the bill, ultimately moving to the penultimate spot, a testament to their ability to win over a crowd and serve as a box office draw for theater managers. But while they were able to ascend on the circuit, there were plenty of factors behind the scenes that prevented them from forgetting where they were in the social hierarchy. The duo always received the same pay regardless of their billing, and at $300 a week, it paled in comparison to the wages their white counterparts commanded. Their dressing rooms were always the smallest, least hospitable, and farthest away from the stage, accessible only after taking several flights of stairs and weaving through unwelcoming corridors.

Outside the theater, the treatment they received was often worse. Finding adequate hotels was a challenge, even in the seemingly liberal North, and Sissle and Blake occasionally had to utilize their networks and crash at their acquaintances' homes. "If you show up at a hotel where you got a reservation, they see you're colored and find out that 'there must be some mistake, we haven't got a record of that. All our rooms are taken,'" Blake explained. "I don't blame all white people for them things. That's just the way things were... A lot of white people don't know what we went through."

While their early December dates in Hartford, Connecticut, were written up positively by the press—one of the local papers noted the oddity of them not receiving top billing, even though they had the best act—their trip through the city was sullied by a negative experience. They had just left the theater through the stage door and crossed the street to grab a bite at a small diner. Someone had stolen Sissle's overcoat, so he was sporting his officer's jacket to shield himself from the winter's cold. But Uncle Sam's uniform earned him no special privileges. As he and Blake walked inside, a white guy wearing a grimy apron approached them. "What can I do for you, boy?"

"I think I'll take a cup of tea," Sissle answered sincerely. "And a donut."

"You do, huh," the worker responded. "Well, both of you together can pack up and leave. We don't serve your kind here." This sort of treatment had become par for the course.

"They found ways to keep you out of...restaurants even in the North," Blake recalled. "You go into a restaurant that don't want any Negro trade, they put so much salt in your food you can't eat it."

Nonetheless, Blake was bothered, while Sissle simply laughed it off. He had endured worse treatment in nicer places and from more dignified people. The incident had drawn the attention of the only customer in the shop, a Jewish man who happened to work for a local paper. As they were walking away, the reporter followed, asking for their names so he could write a story on what had occurred. Blake was quick to "get that free advertising," not only stating who they were but also mentioning that they could be seen playing at the theater across the street throughout the rest of the week. Broadway star Al Jolson, who was playing the Shuberts' theater in town, saw the story in the paper the next day. As a Jewish person who had experienced his share of discrimination, he was particularly sensitive to acts of injustice. Jolson had his valet drive to the theater where Sissle and Blake were performing and send for them, much to the surprise of the up-and-coming musicians. "We were two very unimportant guys whom he'd never heard of until that morning," Sissle recalled, "[but] he was so sore about the story he wanted to make it up to us."

"They put you out of that joint across the street?"

Blake responded in the affirmative.

"Well, I'm gonna take you to the finest hotel in Hartford—"

Before Jolson could get the rest of his sentence out, Blake was already interrupting. "You ain't gonna take *me* to the finest hotel in Hartford!"

"And if they don't serve you," Jolson said, "I'll raise up hell in there."

"Oh no, stop, don't do that," Blake said. "Listen, let me tell you something. If the rabbit bites you first, that's the rabbit's fault. Now, you go back and let that same rabbit bite you again? That's your fault." Yet despite his reservations, he and Sissle agreed to be Jolson's guests at dinner the following day, which led to a long-standing friendship between the three men.

While their first five months on the road had gone well enough, Sissle and Blake were managing nomadic life differently. Blake had always enjoyed traveling and playing and had no problem laying his hat in whatever city Pat Casey put next on the itinerary. "I've never been homesick," he recalled. "When I was a kid, the house I lived in wasn't the kind of place you want to come back to. Yeah, I wanted to see my mother and my father, but that house was nothin'. You get in a good hotel room with your own bathtub and your own toilet, it's not easy to go back and stay in the kind of place I grew up in." Even though Avis was waiting for him back home, Blake was happy to see different cities, despite not always being treated justly by the locals. As long as the performances went well and they were paid on time, he was content.

Sissle, however, had grown tired of being constantly on the move. The singer had stayed close to his family's home until he left for Baltimore in 1915, and he had been essentially traveling ever since. He enjoyed the camaraderie but often found living out of suitcases unbearable. And unlike Blake, he wasn't impressed by any of their accommodations. "No matter where we played, Sissle *always* complained," his partner recalled. "The food, the water. Nothing suited him. The room was never clean enough. He was a guy [who] wiped a doorknob before he went in anyplace. And he always carried twice as much baggage as me... Now, you know, Sissle grew up in a nicer place than I did and maybe these hotels were not as nice as *his* house, but they were nicer than my house."

The tour continued through the next few weeks of December, with a stop in Rhode Island where they were heralded as "the most remarkable Negro entertainers before the public," and afterward, the two took a brief respite for the holiday season. Sissle slipped away to Montclair, New Jersey, where he married Harriett Toye, the widow of Patrick Toye, a former pianist who had died at sea in October 1918 while serving in the U.S. Navy. Sissle and Harriet had a private ceremony on Christmas Day and honeymooned at the Pinehurst Inn on Maple Avenue in town. The marriage was sudden—the details surrounding exactly when and where they met have been lost to time—but the couple was happy. Not only was Sissle a new husband but also a stepfather to Harriett's six-year-old daughter, Helen.

Sissle and Blake spent nearly every week in a different theater throughout 1920 as they continued to crisscross the East Coast and Midwest of the United States, with a brief stint in Canada thrown in for good measure. As hard as it was for Sissle to return to the road, his time away was even more difficult for Harriett. She was still mourning the loss of her first husband and indefinitely separated from her second, whom she had just married, and she soon became bored, depressed, and dependent on bootleg alcohol. Noble, in turn, found his own way to manage. "If you didn't know Sissle, you'd think he always behaved himself," Blake said. "But he never got tired of the women. You'd be standin' on a corner or in front of the theater talkin' to him and a girl comes by and his head turns just like a piano stool, and he keeps lookin' till he can't see her no more."

Of course, Blake's hands weren't exactly clean either. He enjoyed the company of women—lots of them—and while he loved Avis, the adultery clause in their marital contract was malleable. "I missed my wife when I was away from her, but if show business is your life, it's not the same as other people's lives," he explained. "You just got to know how it is. Avis learned how to work them things out for herself. To tell the truth, I wasn't no angel on the road."

Sissle and Blake had settled into a rhythm. They had been on tour for about eighteen months, and while they were enjoying their success, the musicians were beginning to find the circuit a bit monotonous and isolating. While they had seen lots of talented entertainers in their travels, none of them were African American. Booking agents and house managers never put more than one Black act on the vaudeville bill, as colored performers, regardless of quality, were considered a novelty. It wasn't until they were invited to perform at an NAACP benefit at the Dunbar Theatre in Philadelphia that they gained an opportunity to see other Black acts. Sissle and Blake performed some of their original numbers, followed by an encore of audience requests—"Margie" and "Apple Blossom Time," two recent hits. Sissle sang with his typical theatrical bravado, and Blake's fingers confidently danced over the keys, even though he was figuring out the accompaniment as he went along. They headed backstage once their set was over, where they were approached by an incongruous-looking duo—one tall, light-skinned, and mild-mannered; the other short, dark, and bustling with personality. The musicians recognized them straightaway as Flournoy Miller and Aubrey Lyles.

Although the comedians were expected to remain in Europe for at least three years, Miller and Lyles had come back to the United States in 1917, almost a year to the day they left. By that time, America had joined the Great War, and while the two toyed with the idea of enlisting, they instead returned to the Keith circuit, writing and performing new material. They doubled back through the East Coast several times but maintained a nagging feeling that they should do as many other African American men had and enlist to serve their country. They finally filled out their draft cards on September 12, 1918, which they did between sets while they were playing the Palace Theatre in New York City. They were both scheduled to depart for training on November 12, but the armistice was signed the day before, keeping the comedians on the circuit.

But even though they weren't entering the war, things *were* changing. Lyles remarried in July 1919—he met Meryl Porter while on the road—and while it had been over a decade since a Black show had been on Broadway and half a decade since they'd missed their best chance with *Darkydom*, Miller and Lyles were itching to give it another shot. They had been writing material nonstop, but they had never forgotten about some of their earliest successes at the Pekin Theatre, how the audiences clamored for more and the way it catapulted their long careers. They began to ruminate on an idea—what if they revived one of their old shows in a new and exciting way? As Miller was tinkering around with the concept, he and Lyles received an invitation to do a bit at an NAACP benefit in Philadelphia. They were happy for a chance to scope out the other entertainers—it was nearly impossible to see other colored acts while on the circuit, let alone have an opportunity to collaborate with them—and when they saw Eubie Blake and Noble Sissle's syncopated set, the comedians sensed that they had been blessed with another chance at the big time.

"You guys are so good with your *own* stuff, you ought to leave those songs to Frank Crumit and Julia Sanderson," Aubrey Lyles said. The comedian was impressed with the original songs Sissle and Blake had performed—it seemed everyone in the Dunbar was—but thought they were better than playing covers of songs by white singers. He could make a compliment sound like an insult, but Sissle and Blake didn't take any offense.

They had enjoyed the comedians' act earlier that evening, and Sissle told them as much. The four men weren't previously acquainted but were familiar with—and had a great deal of respect for—each other's work.

They engaged in some small talk before Miller shifted the conversation to the comedians' future plans. He and Lyles were working on a new full-length show culled from the best of their vaudeville material. "Broadway was the goal," he recalled. "We knew that the American public would support a Negro play once we got there... We knew that Negro personalities on the stage had made friends for our race. We wanted to keep them." The comedian was confident in the quality of their material, but they knew that to make it to the big time, they would need catchy and clever music. When it came to contemporary colored songwriters, Miller said, there were none better than Sissle and Blake. The musicians were flattered and, as they had done in polite conversation before, made a vague commitment to collaborate in the future.

As luck would have it, the two teams were both playing New York City in January 1921, where they serendipitously ran into each other on a Manhattan street. Miller and Lyles picked up the conversation where they had left off, except this time, they were better prepared for the pitch. Miller saw the potential for a new version of *The Mayor of Dixie* to be a hit. As he started describing the plot, he began to embody different characters, gesticulating and changing the tone and inflection of his voice. The city became his stage and the three men watching him his audience. As Lyles cheered his partner on, Sissle and

Blake were caught up in his energy, enthusiasm, and his clearly thought-out plan.

As they stood on the sidewalk, with the noises of the city providing the soundtrack to Miller's theatrics, the musicians couldn't help but think about Jim Europe. The three had talked about writing a musical comedy together after the war, as Europe was disappointed that the Negro had completely disappeared from Broadway houses. Blake believed in fate and couldn't help but wonder if this unexpected reunion was a sign from some higher power. And even if it wasn't, they had gotten this far by taking chances—what did they have to lose by rolling the dice with Miller and Lyles? The four men were aware of their long odds but thought if anyone could bring Black folks back to Broadway, they were the ones. The comedians had written musicals before and already had the skeleton of a story; the musicians had dozens of songs they could work into a narrative. With nothing but a handshake agreement in place, the quartet agreed to give it a shot. They had excitement, ambition, and material, but they lacked what they needed most—a benefactor.

PART TWO

MAKING IT

From top: Flournoy Miller, Noble Sissle, Eubie Blake, and Aubrey Lyles in an undated publicity still

Courtesy of the Maryland Center for History and Culture, Item ID #PP301.633

7

BLACK BOHEMIANS

1921

All the unlined sheets of white paper that F. E. Miller wrote bits of dialogue on, in blue ink and wispy cursive, were ready to be put to good use. He crafted a detailed plot description with some bits of dialogue interspersed throughout and, along with Lyles, Sissle, and Blake, sought out E. C. Brown to produce the show. The businessman was the director of Brown & Stevens Colored Bank of Philadelphia, the financier behind Harlem's Lafayette and Philadelphia's

Dunbar theaters. He also had a large financial stake in the Howard Theatre in Washington, DC, all Black owned and operated venues, making him a natural choice to get behind this venture.

The pitch: Miller, Lyles, and Sissle would write and appear in the show while Blake would compose the music and conduct the orchestra. They would each work for $75 a week—significantly less than either act made in vaudeville—and only maintain a half interest in the show. Like *Darkydom* before them, they figured they'd begin by touring Black houses, then eventually some white venues until they built up enough of a following that Broadway would come calling. "We were sure we were following the right procedure," Sissle recounted, "and were confident we had an unusual show, the style and entertainment of which both the white and colored lovers of good, clean, wholesome entertainment would enjoy. Both of our teams originated with the Keith vaudeville school of strictly censored high-class show business."

But the banker didn't bite. Unbeknownst to the four collaborators, his company, Quality Amusement Corporation, was going through a rough patch. Within a few months, Brown would first sell the Avenue, Brown and Stevens's theater in Chicago, followed shortly thereafter by the sale of his entire company.

Instead, Miller and Lyles approached their vaudeville booking manager, Al Mayer, to see if he had any ideas. Mayer had been in the business for a long time, and in recent years, he had regularly worked with colored artists. He was instrumental in maintaining the comedians' steady work on the vaudeville circuit, and over the years, he had earned their trust. The manager knew Miller and Lyles were still hell-bent on Broadway, but when he learned of his clients' partnership with Sissle and Blake, he shared their optimism for the first time. "I had always believed there was room for a good Negro show, but I had never found the right show," he recalled. "But I saw the possibilities as outlined by Miller and Lyles, and Sissle and Blake, and got busy." Mayer offered to manage the project, doing what he could to get the embryonic show to one of Manhattan's finest stages in exchange for a cut of the proceeds once it arrived. The five men agreed to get into business together, once again cementing the agreement with nothing but a handshake. "There has never been a piece of paper between us," Mayer explained. "We have nothing but the pledged word of each other, but that verbal contract is as good as gold."

Sissle, Blake, Miller, and Lyles had a manager, but they still lacked a benefactor. Mayer's first responsibility was to find someone to back the project, and he immediately thought of John Cort, an acquaintance of his who tried and failed to move the ill-fated *Darkydom* to Broadway. The producer had done respectable business in recent years with 1915's *The Princess Pat*, 1917's *Flo-Flo*, and 1918's *Listen Lester*, which were all staged at his beautiful 1,082-seat Cort Theatre on West Forty-Eighth Street, an exquisite building modeled after the Petit Trianon in Versailles. However, instead of going directly to John, Al Mayer invited his son, Harry, who was also in the business, to talk shop over lunch instead. The younger Cort was a playwright and

producer as well—he cowrote *Listen Lester*'s book and lyrics—
and Mayer thought the show idea might be more attractive to
his sensibilities.

Harry Cort agreed to a sit-down, but the manager didn't
have the requisite money to take him out. The economy had
rebounded slightly in 1919, but by January 1920, it was free-
falling back into a recession. New York City and the entertainment industry were hit especially hard, and even though Mayer
had one of the hottest acts on the Keith circuit, he was barely
able to live off his cut of their salary. When the four performers
learned that the meeting with Harry Cort was in jeopardy, they
each chipped in $1.25 toward the cause. Miller also offered the
new sharp overcoat that he had just purchased, an attractive
necessity for him to combat the city's violent winter. It was too
large and came down to Mayer's ankles, but he borrowed it
anyway, hoping it would help him make a good impression. In
the end, it seemed their investment had paid off. Harry Cort was
intrigued, but he and his father would need to hear some music
from the show before either committed to invest.

Sissle and Blake culled their best material for the hastily
arranged audition, and at the tryout, they took to the piano with
their typical theatricality and energy. They were certain they'd
knock Old Man Cort dead, but a stone-cold expression never left
their potential backer's face throughout any of their jazz tunes.
They played and sang through several numbers before turning to
"Love Will Find a Way," a new ballad written specially for the
show, cast from the standard musical theater mold. Sissle and
Blake were sure this would turn the audition around, but in the

middle of the number, Cort stood up and walked out. "Thank you, boys," he said on his way to the door. "Thank you very much." The musicians left feeling dejected, until they received word from Al Mayer that "Love" had won the producer over.

Manhattan had changed significantly since the days of *Darkydom*. The economy remained in shambles, with one of the most significant losses of revenue in the city due to the ratification of the Eighteenth Amendment to the Constitution, which prohibited the manufacture, sale, or transportation of alcohol. This social and legislative experiment went into full effect in January 1920, and its impact was felt immediately throughout New York State, which derived 75 percent of its total revenue from liquor taxes. In response to the widespread ban on alcohol, folks took their parties underground. Illicit speakeasies popped up throughout the city, bootlegging became a dissident industry—on average, a thousand people died each year during the Prohibition Era as a result of drinking homemade alcohol unfit for consumption—and an amendment meant to create a more puritanical society ultimately created one that increased poverty and encouraged illegality.

The city was being remade in other ways as well, as women were finally being acknowledged for their importance to society. They had contributed significantly to the labor force while the country's men were overseas, and in many ways, pursuing employment was seen as a patriotic contribution to the war effort. Just as Black soldiers found it difficult to assimilate back into a country that did not see them as whole citizens, many women struggled to readjust when they were pulled away from their new jobs and consigned solely to a life of homemaking and child-rearing without any real say in the matter. Many continued to work, and with these newfound responsibilities came independence. The divorce rate in America skyrocketed, spiking in 1920 to the highest it had ever been. That same year, director Alan Crosland captured "the new woman" in the silent film *The Flapper*, wherein the young flirty, fashionable, and fun-loving female protagonist, played by Olive Thomas, is whisked away to a boarding school after she is caught in the scandalous act of sharing a soda with a young man while unchaperoned. The film was the first to capitalize on the growing cultural trend, introducing the flapper to moviegoers nationwide. Art had begun to imitate the carefree life that many young women were enjoying in postwar America.

This watershed moment for women coincided with the ratification of the Nineteenth Amendment to the Constitution in August 1920, which, on paper, granted over twenty-six million women the franchise, while in reality, for Black women, at least at the time, very little changed. Women of color had always been instrumental suffragettes, but they were often exiled to the margins of the movement. Instead, they created their own advocacy organizations, such as the National Association of Colored Women (NACW), which was founded in 1896 and largely sought to establish women as a viable voting block to overturn racially discriminatory laws. But with many states still living under Jim Crow well into the twentieth century and racialized violence toward Blacks on the rise after the war, many white suffragettes felt the efforts of their African

American sisters threatened to make it harder for legislators from the South to support the amendment. "With us as colored women, this struggle becomes two-fold," Mary B. Talbert, one of the NACW leaders, wrote in the NAACP's *The Crisis* magazine in 1915. "First, because we are women and second, because we are colored women." Unfortunately (and unsurprisingly), after the amendment was ratified, just as Black men had before them, many of the Black suffragettes who fought for the franchise found it difficult or impossible to register to vote or cast a ballot due to discriminatory policies like poll taxes and literacy tests.

But even though the national landscape for African Americans remained bleak in the early 1920s, Harlem was on the rise. While uptown Manhattan was originally conceived as a high-end hamlet for wealthy whites, middle-class Black families soon relocated there from the "Black Bohemia" section of the city. At the center of the well-maintained residential neighborhood stood a restaurant, the Marshallette, its identifier a portmanteau derived from the last names of its owners, Jim Marshall and Jim Lett. It was originally located in Manhattan's crime and sex-ridden Tenderloin District but became a hot spot in 1900 when it found a new home inside a converted brownstone at Fifty-Third Street and Sixth Avenue, two doors away from the largest Baptist church in the city. The sophisticated establishment had an air of exclusivity, with several small, private dining rooms—not the salacious kind in the city's red-light district— which led to it becoming a meeting spot for colored entertainers. Show business folks like Bert Williams, George Walker, and Ernest Hogan discovered the Marshallette first, but it soon became a popular haunt for all well-known members of the race. Sissieretta Jones and Paul Lawrence Dunbar were also known to stop by while in town, but the most consistent patrons were jazz musicians. For them, the establishment was a safe haven to try out new material, and the other patrons were free to dance and cut loose without having to worry about white folks.

But shortly thereafter, the party headed uptown. Despite visions of an upper-class white enclave in Harlem, the neighborhood became overdeveloped with row houses and large apartment buildings that, by the time they were completed, landlords were unable to rent at top-tier rates. Eastern European Jews were quick to move into those housing units at a deep discount, despite being met with resistance and anti-Semitism, and Italian immigrants soon followed. However, the influx of lower-class whites was soon thwarted by the efforts of the Afro-American Realty Company, founded by Philip A. Payton Jr., which changed the face of Harlem for the next hundred years. Payton was a former Livingstone College athlete, barber, and porter in a real estate office, where he got the idea to try starting his own business. The company was founded in 1900 but struggled to find its footing. His wife, Maggie, took up sewing work to help keep the business afloat, and the couple soon moved into one of the many vacant brownstones in Harlem. One of Payton's earliest successes came when a murder occurred on West 133rd Street, and the tenants of an apartment house there moved out in droves. The budding entrepreneur approached the manager of the property and encouraged him to fill the building with

Black families instead. During that time, African American folks were still largely relegated to overpopulated tenements—white landlords refused to rent to them—and Payton sensed this was his best chance to relocate as many members of his race as possible into a nicer part of the city.

About a year into owning the business, Payton was managing an entire housing tenement in Harlem on his own. Two landlords who each owned property on West 134th Street had gotten into a dispute, and to "get even" with the other, one of them asked Payton to fill his building with Black tenants. He was easily able to rent and manage the property, and over time, he convinced more landlords to allow him to do the same. Despite the reservations some had about Harlem becoming increasingly populated with African American folks, the white landlords felt that a fully rented building, managed by a competent businessman, was better than a vacant one. It wasn't long before a cycle, one beneficial to Payton and his Black clients, was established. As more Black folks moved in, whites moved out. This continued to diminish property values, putting Payton's services in higher demand.

By 1904, he was ready to take his real estate business to the next level. He solicited investments from Manhattan's monied Blacks, promising them a 10 percent return, to purchase apartment buildings in Harlem. In his pitch, Payton stressed that his venture was less about profits and more about justice. "Now is the time to buy, if you want to be numbered among those of the race who are doing something toward trying to solve the so-called 'Race Problem,'" he wrote to potential investors. "Race prejudice is a luxury, and, like all other luxuries, can be made very expensive in New York City. The very prejudice which has heretofore worked against us can be turned and used to our profit." The well-off Blacks bought in, with many relocating themselves uptown as well, from Black Bohemia and beyond.

It wasn't long before there was a whitelash, with the beginning of what the *New York Times* referred to as a "real estate race war." In 1905, the white-owned Hudson Realty Company purchased a tract of land on West 135th Street near Lenox Avenue with the intention of developing it. The company bought the neighboring tenements from the Afro-American Realty Company and promptly evicted their Black residents. Philip Payton responded by purchasing two apartment buildings adjacent to the ones Hudson Realty had just bought and moving all the displaced residents there instead. The cat-and-mouse proved too much of a headache for the white developers, and they eventually decided to take their prospects elsewhere, selling the buildings they had purchased back to Payton at a significant loss. African American folks were winning the realty wars, and it wasn't before long before more investors—and Black residents, not only from within the city but also Southerners and Caribbean immigrants in search of the American dream—moved into the emerging mecca.

However, just as his vision was being realized, Philip Payton found himself in financial and legal trouble. He was unable to provide the return on investment he had promised, and although the company had $1 million in assets by 1906, he was sued by thirty-five of his backers that October. He was charged with fraud the following year. His business never recovered, and in 1908, the Afro-American Realty Company folded. Payton started another enterprise, the eponymous Philip A. Payton Jr. Company, and continued to buy properties throughout Harlem and Long Island to rent to Black tenants. Additionally, two of his former directors at the Afro-American Realty Company, John E. Nail and Henry G. Parker, founded their own successful real estate company in 1907. By the time Payton died of liver cancer in 1917, over three-quarters of the city's Black population lived in Harlem. The NAACP's membership and influence continued to grow, and Marcus Garvey, a Jamaican-born racial justice activist and founder of the Universal Negro Improvement Association and African Communities League, a fraternal organization dedicated to the advancement of all individuals from the African diaspora, began empowering the community as well. The neighborhood was becoming a cultural hot spot, developing quickly as other parts of Manhattan struggled to stay afloat.

Against the backdrop of this changing city and the growing cultural jazz movement, John Cort believed a Black show could once again play on Broadway. However, his involvement in his old pal Al Mayer's latest venture came with caveats. Cort had been hit hard by the economic recession as well, and Broadway was in the midst of a fiscally subpar season. He was unable to provide the creative team with his own seed money, but he was willing to draw on the other resources he had. In exchange for his help, his son, Harry, would have to be given a financial interest in the show. Mayer and the vaudevillians agreed that this was an easy stipulation, and the show officially went into preproduction.

News leaked almost immediately, and by January 29, 1921, J. A. Jackson, a Black journalist who reported colored entertainment news and gossip for *Billboard*, had caught wind of the budding project. "MILLER AND LYLES; SISSLE AND BLAKE— Doesn't that headline sound promising," he mused in print. In his tease that the vaudevillians were developing "a big colored show of the highest possible caliber," he made an early endorsement in the nationwide trade magazine as to the talents of the show's collaborators. "What a show this quartet of big-time boys could put together," Jackson added. "Among the four are a most comprehensive knowledge of the business, a thoro [*sic*] appreciation of comedy values, and some musical abilities far above the average."

But despite the eagerness of the show's writers to get to work, there were still logistics to figure out. The two vaudeville acts still had to negotiate out of their dates on the Keith circuit, and until then, the musicians and comedians would have to write their parts separately. For Sissle and Blake, the task was relatively easy. They had written enough music for M. Witmark & Sons—some had been published, some the company had rejected, and there was even some that the musicians had kept in their back pocket because they were too good to "give away"— and all they needed was a finished book by Miller and Lyles into which they could incorporate their material.

The comedians completed a draft relatively quickly, titling

their new show *The Mayor of Jimtown*, to both evoke and separate their latest project from its predecessor at the Pekin. The overall plot remained largely unchanged. The story centered on a mayoral race. Steve Jenkins and Sam Peck, two business partners who own the local grocery store, played by Miller and Lyles in blackface, decide to run. The two poke fun at each other's electoral chances—after Jenkins calls Peck a long-shot candidate, the other retorts that "I maght be de dark horse, but you ain't gwine never be no Black Mayor"—but they make a pact that if one of them wins, they'll appoint the other to serve as chief of police. ("That's the way they were expected to talk," Eubie Blake explained. "Mixing verbs and things like that. 'Is you going out?' and 'We is here?' That was very funny to white people. That's what they wanted to hear.") Of course, Jenkins and Peck are comically dishonest, but they agree to trust each other nonetheless. However, there's a third candidate in the race, Harry Walton, an upstanding gentleman who has nothing but pure intentions for entering politics. One of Walton's supporters is Jim Williams, the proprietor of the Jimtown Hotel. Jim's daughter, Jessie, and Harry Walton are in love, but while Jim has no doubts that the mayoral candidate would be a perfect husband, he will only approve of them marrying if Harry wins the election.

While Harry faithfully attempts to gain support, Steve and Sam take the unscrupulous route. They both start stealing from the grocery store cash register, without the other's knowledge, to crookedly finance their campaign, and when they begin to suspect their business partner is doing the same, they (accidentally) hire the same private detective to keep an eye on the other. Political boss Tom Sharper, Steve Jenkins's equally unprincipled campaign manager, helps him steal the election, and Steve immediately reneges on his promise to appoint Sam Peck police chief. "Oh, I said dat befo' I was 'lected," Jenkins says. "If you ain't got no better sense den to pay any 'tention to dem 'lection promises, you ain't got sense 'nough to be no Chief of Police." They settle the score with a boxing match—a reprise of Miller and Lyles's now-classic routine—which turns into a highly choreographed number complete with time steps, buck-and-wing dances, and an ample number of musically punctuated punches. "The fight lasted about twenty minutes," Flournoy Miller explained. "We wrote it out and then ad-libbed too. Lyles would fuss at me until we both began swinging—and one point I knocked him down, and he jumped over my back. Jack Benny once told us that our timing was the best he'd ever seen." Sam manages to give Steve a run for his money, and the next time Sam is seen onstage, it's in a royal-blue uniform. By the end of the show, the private detective reveals that both Steve and Sam had corrupted the election. The two lose their positions, and Harry Walton is declared the mayor of Jimtown—and Jessie Williams's future husband. Then, with the show's plot over, Eubie Blake would hop up onstage from the orchestra pit and perform "a few minutes" of his vaudeville act with Noble Sissle.

With a script in place, John Cort offered the Standard Theatre, his small, two-story house on the corner of Ninetieth and Broadway uptown, for auditions. While Black folks weren't working on the main stages in the heart of the theater district, there were still plenty in vaudeville who were eager to try out for a new musical comedy. Word spread quickly, but a few days before Sissle and Blake were set to see prospective talent, they realized an error. The audition notice said that the casting call would be held at the Cort Theatre in Times Square, not the smaller and more modest performing space he owned dozens of blocks away. Sissle begged John J. Scholl, who did Cort's bookings, to let them use their flagship house. Scholl assumed it would only be a half dozen or so people and granted them permission, and when over eighty people showed up, he hardly believed his eyes. People had come from all over for their chance to be seen. "There were a lot of good Negro vaudeville acts to pick from," Sissle recalled. "The players knew that they had little future in vaudeville because of their race and when we told them we had no money, but would not take them farther than walking distance from New York, they agreed to gamble with us."

The show's creative team had their pick of the litter, which emboldened them to be highly selective during the casting call. Twenty-six-year-old Alberta Hunter, who would eventually go on to have a seven-decades-long career as a celebrated jazz singer, was among the many who failed to make the final cut. She sang just fine, but Sissle said her skin was too dark. It was ironic, she thought, that she had recently come back from a tour of London and Paris, where she hadn't experienced any racial discrimination at all, only for an African American man to tell her she was too dark for an all-Black show in America. Ultimately, she chalked up Sissle's attitude to the fact that he was a "dicty," a pretentious man, with a color complex. Ethel

Waters, a blues singer who had recently relocated to Harlem, was also turned away. She, too, would go on to have a long and prosperous career—she was a dozen years away from popularizing the song "Stormy Weather" in Harlem's Cotton Club—but she was dismissed during the auditions as "just a cheap honky-tonk singer."

Of the eighty or so who auditioned, nearly half were cast in the show's three female singing and dancing choruses, as either Happy Honeysuckles, Jazz Jasmines, or Majestic Magnolias. The male chorus members were designated Syncopated Sunflowers. Lottie Gee, an acquaintance of Eubie Blake who had been performing since her teenage years, was cast as Jessie Williams, the romantic lead. This opportunity couldn't have come at a better time for her. She had separated from her husband, Wilson Kyer, in 1919, and while she had just concluded a tour of England with the Southern Syncopated Orchestra, she was in search of steady work that would settle her in New York. She was cast alongside Roger Matthews, a relatively unknown actor who won the role of candidate Harry Walton, her love interest. Of course, Miller and Lyles would revive their Steve Jenkins and Sam Peck roles, while Noble Sissle cast himself as the dubious Tom Sharper.

Mattie Wilkes, a prima donna vaudevillian with a rich soprano voice who also happened to be the former Mrs. Ernest Hogan, was cast as Mrs. Peck, Sam's politically ambitious wife, who is helping her husband's campaign out of a desire to be Jimtown's First Lady. For a country that had only elected one woman to Congress—Republican Jeannette

Rankin from Montana in 1917—and granted women the right to vote only a year earlier, Mrs. Peck's interest in politics was a wink and nod to the suffragettes who were still making headlines nationwide. Gertrude Saunders, who had spent years with the Billy King Stock Company in Chicago, was tapped for the show's ingenue, Ruth Little, Jessie Williams's flapper friend. Early in the show, she tells Jessie that "none of that wedding stuff" is for her before singing "I'm Just Simply Full of Jazz," a number from Sissle and Blake's vaudeville act. The snappy song was the most musically contemporary piece in the show, perfectly at home in a vaudeville theater, but with its lyrics that referenced current social dance crazes, it was unlike anything on Broadway.

"I'm Just Simply Full of Jazz" was conceived to be a frenzied number where sixteen chorines would run out onstage in dazzling costumes, hoofing with all the energy their bodies could generate. Lawrence Deas, a versatile performer who had previously appeared with Ernest Hogan in Miller and Lyles's *The Oyster Man*, was brought on by the comedians early and asked to "stage"—direct and choreograph—*Jimtown*. He had spent two decades playing vaudeville and burlesque houses—often with his wife, Ella, who was also in *The Oyster Man*—earning recognition for his comic delivery, dancing, and singing abilities. In addition to staging the show, Deas was also cast as Jack Penrose, the private detective. With money tight, he agreed to accept producer credit on the show, forgoing any compensation until the production made good financially.

As the cast took shape, Harry Cort went rummaging through

his storage, pulling out set pieces that could be repurposed—even if it was ultimately done imperfectly. "I'll show you how inconsistent it was," Eubie Blake explained. "The grocery store was on this side, and the hotel was over there... [But in] the scenery, they had it wrong. But we had to take it because that was the way they had it from this other show, where they got the drop from." Cort also found costumes from some of the previous shows he and his father had brought to the stage. They were better suited for the landfill than the theater, with irremovable sweat stains under the arms, but considering their lack of funds, they would have to do.

Upon hearing of Cort's finds, the show's writers found ways to incorporate the new pieces into the show by any means necessary. For example, when Harry discovered a collection of patched and polka-dotted antebellum frocks from *Roly-Boly Eyes*, Sissle and Blake wrote "Bandana Days" over the phone, while the lyricist was in Boston and the composer in New York. The song was a modern twist on a minstrel song, with lyrical references to "mammies" and strumming banjos in the pale moonlight. Although the song harkened back to the cotton-picking days, Blake's music was just as contemporary and syncopated as anything else in the score, and Sissle infused the song with the same melodic wordplay he excelled at: "In those dear old bandana days / Cane-and-cotton-ne'er-forgotten bandana days." Miller and Lyles shoehorned it into the show by adding an ancillary character—Uncle Ned, a reference to the popular 1848 Stephen Foster minstrel song. Tom Sharper attempts to pay Uncle Ned to vote for Steve

Jenkins, but the old-timer declines, saying—in full Southern Negro dialect—that he grew up in the "bandana days" when people valued honesty and integrity. Luckily, when Cort found some kimonos and other Asian garments, Sissle and Blake already had the perfect song ready to go, "Oriental Blues," which they wrote in 1920. The song wasn't one of their hits per se, but it fit the bill, even though Blake hated the title; he didn't think it sounded from the Orient, nor did it have a single blue note.

Although Miller and Lyles had only begun working with Sissle and Blake two months earlier, by March 1921, the show was readying for its first performance. Al Mayer booked the musical for a limited run in a few cities within hours of Manhattan, starting with the Grand Theatre in Trenton, New Jersey, as John Cort attempted to solidify a Broadway house. There wasn't a finalized script for the show—Miller and Lyles were continuing to make edits throughout the process—but the cast quickly developed a rhythm and rapport. Lawrence Deas worked alongside the chorus girls to conceptualize the show's dance numbers. Theater is a collaborative medium, and by working together as a collective, with the chorines suggesting and demonstrating moves they knew would look great on their bodies, the show's creators were certain *Jimtown* wouldn't be criticized for being too much like the colored shows of yesterday. While the environment was likely welcoming of input, some of Sissle's lyrics dictated the specific moves that should be done, like "Baltimore Buzz," an instruction song that ended the show with a full company dance number:

Now, first, you take your babe and then you
hold her,
Then, you lay your head upon her shoulder,
Next, you walk just like your legs are
breaking,
Do a bangle like a jangle then you start to tip
and a-tangle.
Then, you do a raggy-braggy motion,
Just like any ship upon the ocean,
Glide! And then you hesitate,
Slide, oh, honey, ain't it great?
You will simply go in a trance with the
Baltimore Buzzin' dance!

Rehearsals were going well until Lottie Gee took exception with one of her character's songs. After Jessie Williams learns that Steve Jenkins will be appointed mayor and her father won't give his blessing to her marrying Harry Walton, the lovestruck woman sings "I'm Just Wild About Harry." The number was repurposed from "My Loving Baby," which Sissle and Blake wrote in 1916. While some of the lyrics and melody were changed slightly for *Jimtown*, the original iteration of the song provided a solid foundation for Sissle and Blake to crib from: "I'm just wild about Baby / And Baby's wild about me / And when I look into his dreamy eyes / His very soul I can see. / He's sweet just like 'lasses candy / Sweeter than the honey from the Bee."

Blake had written "Harry" as a Viennese waltz, with a

beautifully romantic melody suitable for ballroom dancing, but when he played it for Lottie Gee, she said the song was too slow, too romantic, and most importantly, too white. *Who'd ever heard of a waltz in a colored show?* she asked him. Blake reminded her of "When the Pale Moon Shines" from 1906's *Abyssinia*, but she quickly retorted that the song wasn't a hit. She wanted him to pick up the tempo and add some syncopation, as it felt unnatural for her to sing and nearly impossible for her to dance to its current iteration. In order to communicate just how "wild" her character was about Harry Walton, she thought the song necessitated a dance with more drive—a one-step—instead of a graceful glide across the stage. Blake pushed back, but she remained adamant. "That cut me to the quick," Blake recalled. "She was going to destroy my beautiful melody. I loved that waltz." The pianist called in Sissle to back him up, but his partner agreed with their leading lady. When she rehearsed the peppier version of "Harry," she began punctuating the syllable on every fourth beat, giving the number a new sense of urgency. Once the chorus girls were added into the number to dance behind her, it was clear that Lottie Gee's instincts were right.

The musical had taken shape, and even though they still hadn't a penny to their names or a Broadway house secured, Al Mayer prepared to take the show on tour. The goal was to test the musical out of town with a different name and, based on the critical response, bring it back to New York with its proper title, *The Mayor of Jimtown*. The thought was that if they were a flop outside Manhattan, they'd shed the bad press by rebranding the musical before what they hoped would be its Broadway run. They temporarily adopted the name *Shuffle Along*. Not only was it a sly reference to the nomadic tour they were set to embark on, but it was also the title of the high-octane start of the show's second act, where fast-moving tap dancer Charlie Davis, dressed as a traffic cop, rhythmically rushed the passersby to their destinations. "I could do all variety of dances, but my own was strictly Buck and Wing and flash," he said, acknowledging the contributions of Black dancer Toots Davis, who rose to notoriety in *Darktown Follies*, to his own performance. "Toots started Over the Top and Trenches, two of my biggest assets in *Shuffle Along*." The song was an enthusiastic burst to encourage the audience to return to their seats after intermission, with lyrics that highlighted the unifying potential of music and the necessity to forge ahead despite life's challenges:

> *Everyone in town is always singing this song:*
> *"Shuffle Along"—"Shuffle Along."*
> *Doctors, bakers, undertakers, do a step*
> *That's full of pep and syncopation.*
> *"Shuffle Along,"—oh, "Shuffle Along."*
> *Why, life's but a chance, and when times*
>   *comes to choose,*
> *If you lose, don't start a-singing the blues,*
> *But just you shuffle along,*
> *And whistle a song.*
> *Why, sometimes a smile will right every wrong.*
> *Keep smiling and shuffle along.*

With their bags packed and their raggedy costumes, props, and set backdrops in tow, Al Mayer and the performers headed from their rehearsal space in Harlem to Penn Station. However, when they arrived, they realized they didn't have enough money for train fare to Trenton. Eubie Blake took this as a sign. He started to sneak away and head back to his home on West 132nd Street, but Sissle stopped him. "He said we'd get there somehow," Blake recalled. "I think Sissle still felt Jim Europe's hand guiding us."

Throughout the rehearsal process, Milton Gosdorfer, an acquaintance of Al Mayer's, often hung around, watching the show come together. He was a shabbily dressed white guy, and the cast assumed he was just there to keep an unwanted watchful eye on the young ladies. But Mayer said he was on the level, and in fact, they should invite him along for the tour. The show's writers didn't put up much of a fuss, and when they realized they were stuck at Penn Station, the manager gave the man a half share of his stake in the show in exchange for him covering transportation for this leg of the trip.

After just two months gestating, on March 24, 1921, *Shuffle Along* had its first performance at the Grand Theatre in Trenton. The show was a clear amalgamation of a lot of disparate moving pieces, and when it came to the large dance numbers, the chorines were clunky in their entrances and exits, in stark contrast to the gliding beauties who traversed across the stage in white revues like Ziegfeld's *Follies*. Al Mayer explained this away in the press by saying that with a company so large, it was difficult to find Black performers with the requisite stage experience, and instead, they had prioritized their raw vocal talent, bodies, and youth while casting. Nevertheless, despite the rough edges, the chorus numbers—and the women in them—immediately drew attention from reviewers. "Lawrence Deas, whose experience as a director dates back to the days of Ernest Rogan [sic], has introduced dance numbers that have the true spirit of Negro folk-lore with the rhythm and grace for which these people are famous," J. A. Jackson wrote in *Billboard* of the debut performance. "His numbers are interpreted by a chorus of vari-complexioned beauties who can really sing and dance, and do it with an air of actual enjoyment. The girls are typical of their race, ranging in color from seeming white, thru high yellow to tantalizing brown skins, and they were not made up either as to face or manners to imitate a white chorus."

With the exception of criticism for the costumes, which Jackson assumed were unfinished when they were actually just unsuitable, the critic was overwhelmingly positive. He reserved his highest praise for Sissle and Blake's songs, which he predicted would "set the country to humming, once they are heard in big cities." While he singled out several of the numbers—he seemed particularly impressed with Gertrude Saunders—he predicted that Lottie Gee's "I'm Just Wild About Harry" and "Love Will Find a Way" would be remembered, noting that several members of the audience left the theater singing them. Unfortunately, despite the enthusiasm of the audience and critics, there was very little in the way of audience to speak of. Perhaps as a result of the torrential downpour that persisted throughout the night, the Grand was less than half full when the curtain was raised.

After expenses, Al Mayer was $20 shy of what he needed to get the troupe to their next stop in Washington, DC, where they were scheduled to play the Howard Theatre.

Exactly how the group funded their trip to the nation's capital remains a mystery. Mayer recalled that he found an usher at the Grand who had some extra cash on him, as he had been saving for a new suit. The manager sweet-talked him into loaning the show $20, with the promise that Mayer would pay him back with 50 percent interest once they arrived at their next stop. "We had a guarantee in Washington, so we breathed easy there," the manager explained. However, Eubie Blake recalled a different series of events. In his memory, they all proceeded to the train station before they realized they were short. While the manager was pacing up and down on the platform, trying to figure out how to solve their poverty problem, a man approached him. "Say," he said. "You see that nigger show in town here last night?... That was the best thing I ever saw, that nigger show. Yes, sir!"

"That's my show," Mayer said. "I'm the manager."

"Well, you've got a gold mine there."

"Well, sir, that's nice to hear, but we don't even have enough money to get to the next town." The man excused himself to speak with the station manager, and when he came back, he had tickets for the entire company. It turned out he was one of the owners of the railroad. Regardless of which version of the story is accurate, the group played a successful week in Washington between March 28 and April 9. "Noble Sissle and Eubie Blake, the well-known writers and entertainers, scored a decided hit at the Howard Theatre, where a musical riot by the 'pair' was played before capacity audiences," a local journalist noted. While the group had a guarantee, money remained an issue. One of the theater's employees was busted stealing from the box office during the show's run, and while he was fired, the group had to once again depend on the kindness of strangers to afford fare to the next location.

The next leg of their tour was highly anticipated, as *Shuffle Along* would be playing the Dunbar Theatre in Philadelphia, where Sissle and Blake met Miller and Lyles just a few months ago. It was a site of new beginnings, and while in town, the group began to make formal preparations in advance of what they still hoped would be their Broadway run. They arranged to use the theater during the day to audition more chorus girls in the event that they had to shake up the cast before playing Manhattan.

It was pouring outside the Dunbar the day of the tryouts, but there was still a long line of women wrapped around the corner. The most fortunate found refuge under the fire escape, but most just endured the elements on their small plot of sidewalk. Torn stockings and thin dresses hugged the women's bodies, and for those who were more fortunate, a thin coat too. While there were dozens waiting to walk through the theater's large glass doors, one was being slipped in through the side entrance. As she confidently strode toward the auditioning room, she couldn't help but think about the unlikely circumstances that led her there. What if she hadn't run into her old classmate from St. Louis, Wilsie Caldwell, in a bar the night before? What if Wilsie and her brother hadn't been part of the *Shuffle Along* company—she was a chorus girl, he was a dancer—and what if they hadn't been unable to stop talking about how the show and its creators were poised to take New York by storm? "They're just full of ideas!" Wilsie exclaimed. "For example, all of the chorus girls will be mulattoes."

The young woman decided to audition the next day. While she didn't know much about the show or the four men behind it, she was familiar with "I'm Just Simply Full of Jazz," and that was good enough for her. She walked into the theater still shivering from the cold, with wet hair, looking as if she had skipped more than a few meals. Eubie Blake was hunched over at the piano, his head buried in sheet music, barely taking notice of who walked in, while the show's other three writers looked her over. She did a dance routine, but before she had a chance to sing, Miller and Sissle had a quick sidebar. Then Sissle stopped the meeting in its tracks. "Too young," he said.

She quickly turned on the charm. "But I'm seventeen," she lied.

"Sorry," he continued. "Too small, too thin, too dark."

She was embarrassed, hurt, angry—and sent on her way. Tears filled her eyes, and as she walked back toward the stage door entrance, half stumbling down the stairs that led to the street, the men inside could hear her faint sobs giving way to wails. When she met back up with her friend at the stage door, she vented her frustration at what had just happened, saying the thin man with the mustache was ashamed of his kind. "It's just the opposite," Wilsie said. "He's hoping to beat the whites at their own game. Since they prefer blackface shows to real black performers, he's decided to give them white black folks. *Shuffle Along* isn't variety or burlesque. It's a real good comedy with a plot." Wilsie tried to convince her old classmate to ask for a job with the show as a dresser, assisting with costumes backstage, but the fifteen-year-old had done that already. She had been performing since she'd dropped out of school in the fifth grade—mostly on the streets and in nightspots, both of which shamed her mother—and had been married twice. She was nearly nine hundred miles from her hometown, but a few days later, she decided to travel about a hundred miles farther. She went to the train station, and with the last few dollars she had, Josephine Baker bought a one-way ticket to New York, determined not to let her skin color stop her from reaching the big time.

While she was heading to Manhattan, John Cort was traveling to Philadelphia with Abe Erlanger, another theatrical producer, alongside him. It was announced that *Shuffle Along* would be opening at the Greenwich Village Theatre on Manhattan's West Side on May 9, a modestly sized venue with only five hundred seats, and with them finally having a New York booking, Al Mayer invited Cort to see the show. The musical had been playing to full houses—grossing $9,000 weekly, with the highest ticket prices only ninety cents—and technically, the show was getting sharper. "A splendid performance from the beginning to the final curtain," *Billboard* reported during the Dunbar run. "The roughness referred to in the initial review has been eliminated and it is a smooth-running show. There are no dull moments." Al Mayer thought that if Cort saw an audience's reaction for himself, he might be motivated to find them a proper Broadway house. The visitors watched a performance and, in Sissle's words, "laughed themselves sick" over the idea that because Black folks were enjoying it at Black theaters, it suggested anything about whether whites would as well. They would have to prove that the musical would appeal to the reliably bankable theater crowd, the types of people who would pay at least $2 a ticket, and the only way to do that was to put the show in front of white audiences and gauge their reactions. The company was already scheduled to play a week in Baltimore next, and afterward, Cort arranged for them to go on a two-week "graveyard tour" of one- and two-night stands, with dates as far west as Pittsburgh.

While Cort's idea had merit as a means for the company to prove their commercial appeal to whites, this proved to be the most grueling and least fruitful aspect of their run. "No one knew us, so they'd only book us for a short time," Eubie Blake recalled. "We'd get good reviews in one town, but before they could do us any good, we'd be on to another town." Traversing with a company that large was a drain on their nonexistent budget, and there was the foreboding sense that, purely based on economic reasons, every stop could be their last. One evening, Sissle and Blake were sitting on the steps of a municipal building writing out checks that, if they were cashed that day, would have bounced. They wouldn't be good until the production wired their latest box office haul to their bank in New York, and it would take at least another day for things to clear. As the two were taking pen to paper, Blake looked up. "Sissle," he said. "Do you know where you're sitting?" They were on the local jailhouse steps, and the two fell out laughing. If anyone found out they were writing bad checks, at least they'd have a short commute to their cell.

While Sissle and Blake were occasionally tasked with paying out the company, Blake was usually able to escape the more tedious aspects of being a theatrical producer. For the most part, the only dollars he was interested in counting were the ones in his hand. "Blake and Lyles were always playing poker and kidding around, while Sissle and I took care of business," Flournoy Miller explained. "Everything we made, we gave to the cast right away. One night everybody got only $2, and Eubie Blake—we called him Mouse then—nearly cried he was so disappointed. So I said, 'Sissle, give him your two dollars, Lyles, give him yours,' and I gave him mine. That made him happy. A few minutes later, we all borrowed the money back, and then Mouse felt like a big shot."

The financial situation was dire overall, and the company had to not only keep the show going but themselves as well. "We didn't have money for nothin'," Eubie Blake recalled. "It just seemed that we found everything just when we needed it." Before long, the company's survival instincts set in, and they were finding clever ways to adapt to impoverished life. On one occasion, a penniless Al Mayer offered a waitress a complimentary ticket to the show in exchange for two sandwiches and two bottles of milk. "At the next town we put sandwiches and milk on the property list so we would be sure to get food," Mayer said.

"You learn a lot of tricks on the road," Flournoy Miller explained. "Sissle and I would visit people who were boarding some members of the cast—always at mealtime—and I would take a bite of everything on the table and insist that Sissle taste it too, because it was so delicious. Then we'd go to another house and do the same thing. We usually had plenty to eat."

In another city, he talked a cab driver into fronting them cash for lodging on the promise that the company would pay him back once they got to New York in a few weeks. The man drove Miller and Lyles, Sissle and Blake, and actor Paul Floyd to a dodgy boardinghouse. All the men shared a room, with Miller and Lyles in one bed, Blake and Floyd in another, and somehow, Sissle had his all to himself—*mostly.* The men hardly got a good night's sleep, as they were fending off bedbugs. When they weren't stirring because of the bites, they were woken up by the sounds of their colleagues' palms slapping their own skin in an attempt to assassinate the insects. The next morning, the quintet tried to sneak out of the dive, as they were almost certain the cab driver hadn't paid their bill. Lyles led the way down the stairs to the entrance, as conspicuous as ever, with a big cigar in his mouth. The group was greeted at the bottom by a large Black man, the boardinghouse's owner, blocking the door and demanding his money. "I didn't trust you minstrel niggers! You all are no good!"

Lyles took the cigar out of his mouth. "Sir," he said calmly and with all the sincerity he could muster, "the boy will be here with the money very soon." To everyone's surprise, that happened to be true. After several tense minutes, the cab driver showed up, freeing the performers to go on their way unscathed—save for the bug bites.

However, as the tour of the "graveyard" neared its end, *Shuffle Along* was given another shot at life. While the show was hemorrhaging money on a daily basis, audiences—*white* audiences—came through in droves. The response was just as positive as John Cort had seen at the Dunbar, and while he still couldn't find a proper Broadway venue to take the show, he had an idea. He owned an old lecture hall on Sixty-Third Street—dilapidated, dark, and without a proper stage or orchestra pit—which he agreed to lease to his son, Harry. The unassuming building was wedged between several garages, could be easily missed even if you were looking for it, and was about a half mile away from the heart of the theater district. It wasn't what Miller, Lyles, Sissle, and Blake had in mind, and the building would need major renovations to even make it somewhat suitable, but if they wanted it, it was theirs. With the group's blessing, the May 9 engagement in Greenwich Village was dropped, and a May 16 opening on Sixty-Third was scheduled. With their extra week, they booked a return engagement at the Dunbar. Not only was it where they had made the most money, but the venue had become a sort of good luck charm, making it a fitting last stop before their return to Manhattan.

On May 9, 1921, *Shuffle Along* returned to Philadelphia, and the *New York Times* announced that it would be opening shortly at the Sixty-Third Street Theatre.(With its tryout having gone so well, the producers decided to keep the name.) However, despite the abundance of good news, a few concerns remained. Someone who worked at a local newspaper told John Cort that audiences wouldn't stand for Negroes displaying genuine love for each other onstage, suggesting that the romantic plot between Jessie Williams and Harry Walton be tempered or removed altogether. "It was only a thread because we didn't know whether they would accept it," Blake explained. "They'd never had a thread of love in a colored show before." There had, in fact, been romantic partnerships depicted in Black musical comedies before, but they were either never to be taken too seriously or the desires of the characters were never as clearly communicated as they were in *Shuffle Along*.

The song that caused the most concern was "Love Will Find a Way," the tune that initially won Cort over in the first place, as it was not only a genuine ballad but also a duet. "If anything approaching a love duet was introduced in a musical comedy, it had to be broadly burlesqued," explained writer and activist James Weldon Johnson, who was then the executive secretary of the NAACP. "The reason...lay in the belief that a love scene between two Negroes could not strike a white audience except as ridiculous."

While there were concerns, the team decided to leave "Love" in the show until New York audiences had a chance to weigh in for themselves. In fact, if any song were going to get the ax, it would be "I'm Just Wild About Harry." While J. A. Jackson saw the potential for the song to be a hit early on, most of the local reviewers failed to give it high marks. It wasn't that they disliked it; most just ignored it. The song appears early in the second act, wedged between the foot-stomping "Shuffle Along" and the gut-busting "Jimtown Fisticuffs" sequence, with Miller and Lyles's boxing match. A number that brought down the energy at that moment could kill the show in New York, and the show's creators weren't in a position to take many more chances.

However, fate—and the good luck of the Dunbar—conspired. One of the male chorus members fell ill during the return engagement, and Bob Lee, who was in the singing ensemble, was told to fill in. Lee was an excellent singer but a pretty lousy dancer, so Lawrence Deas had him lead the line during "Harry" so he would both be the first one offstage and not get in the way of the rest of the chorines who knew what they were doing. While Sissle, Miller, and Lyles were in their dressing room changing costumes, they heard an explosion of sustained laugher coming from the audience. Lyles said Lee had probably fallen flat on his face, and as the three quickly finished dressing and ran to the wings of the stage to see what all the fuss was about, the laughter gave way to noisy applause. Eubie Blake yelled over the audience from the orchestra pit, where he could see his partners peeking their heads out: "Keep him in! Keep him in!" The trio still had no idea what was going on until Blake struck up the pit again for the encore. Bob Lee clearly didn't know the choreography and had given up trying. Instead, he flashed a big smile and went into his own high-stepping dance routine. As the title and lyrics suggested, audiences were wild about "Harry," solidifying Lee's place in the number and the song's place in the show.

While Lottie Gee's love songs garnered a lot of discussion and debate, Gertrude Saunders's were met with unanimous adoration. She was such a standout that, even before the show hit New York, she recorded two of her songs—"I'm Craving That Kind of Love" and "Daddy, Won't You Please Come Home"— for Okeh, a white-owned record label that had recently started releasing "race records" of Black artists. Saunders's ability to hit high notes at an almost operatic range made her a novelty to white and Black audiences alike. "Miss Saunders's inimitable singing style is so well known to the colored lovers of music," J. A. Jackson wrote in *Billboard* upon the announcement of her recordings of songs from *Shuffle Along*. "She is one of the very few sopranos with a voice of such timbre as to qualify for the successful production of records. This is in itself an unusual distinction."

The return engagement at the Dunbar was a smash, but after expenses, the production arrived in New York about $21,000 in debt. Additionally, the show's opening was delayed a week to allow for renovations to be done to the music hall. Several rows of seating had to be removed to build a makeshift orchestra pit, and the platform that was serving as a stage was built out to accommodate the show's large cast. While things were less than ideal, there was a bit of good news. M. Witmark & Sons acquired the publication rights to the show's music,continuing their fruitful relationship with Sissle and Blake, which all but guaranteed that *Shuffle Along* would soon gain visibility beyond Manhattan's reach. Additionally, while there were several unofficial business agreements in place, Harry Cort, Al Mayer, and the show's writers formed the Nikko Producing Company in the days before their New York opening. Cort and Mayer were the two leading executives and would collectively lay claim to 50 percent of the earnings, while Sissle, Blake, Miller, and Lyles were all appointed to the board of directors and collectively shared the other half. Now all they had to do was bring in an audience.

But while construction was underway, it was difficult to appraise how easily that would happen. Not only was the Sixty-Third Street Theatre far from Times Square, it didn't even look like it belonged there. Rehearsals continued at the venue while construction workers and maintenance men worked around the clock to ready the building for opening night, with sawdust and the sounds of stomping feet frequently filling the air. Nevertheless, Sissle, Blake, Miller, and Lyles remained optimistic—for the most part. A few days before opening, when the four were walking to the theater, they ran into Sime Silverman, the editor of *Variety*, at Fifty-Ninth Street and Broadway in Columbus Park. He recognized them from their work in vaudeville. "What are you four fellas doing together?"

"We're getting ready to do a show!"

"Show? What are you gonna do? A minstrel show?"

"No, a musical comedy."

Silverman looked at them as if they each had three heads. "You all're crazy," he said. "Musical comedies have got to have women. White women ain't gonna come to the show and see colored women. Are there any in vaudeville?"

They were glad the question was rhetorical, because they couldn't think of any. Silverman walked away, and the men lingered, with the wind knocked out of their sails. When the coast was clear—none of them would dare talk out of turn about a white man in his presence—Aubrey Lyles made it clear that he wasn't having it. "Oh, that guy's crazy," he said before pointing upward. "They said *this guy* was crazy too!" Sissle, Blake, and Miller looked skyward, and on top of a granite column several stories high, they saw a fourteen-foot statue of Christopher Columbus staring toward the horizon. The men laughed and felt a bit better, hoping that, like in the romanticized story of the explorer standing high above them, the next leg of their journey would help create a new world—or at least a better and more inclusive America.

AUBREY LYLES
(STANDING) AND
FLOURNOY MILLER IN
CHARACTER AS SAM PECK
AND STEVE JENKINS IN
A PROMOTIONAL STILL
FOR *SHUFFLE ALONG*, 1921

*Photo by White Studio,
© New York Public
Library for the
Performing Arts*

8

NEVERTHELESS, THEY SUCCEEDED

1921–1922

B y mid-May 1921, it was clear that Broadway was experiencing one of its bleakest seasons on record, and with theaters preparing to close for the summer to escape the unforgiving and stifling Manhattan heat, things seemed unlikely to turn around. Many of the houses had prematurely gone dark, finding it financially unviable to keep their doors open, and it was several weeks before old reliable revues like Ziegfeld's *Follies* and Frank Fay's *Fables* were anticipated to arrive later that summer. But there was a glimmer of hope. *The Last Waltz*, a three-act musical produced by the Shuberts, was doing respectable business at the Century Theatre on Sixty-Second, just around the corner from the Sixty-Third Street Theatre. It was heralded a smash, raking in $33,000 in the week of its May 10 opening, with a $2.50 top ticket price. The show appeared to be on track to compete with *Sally*, a musical comedy produced by Florenz Ziegfeld Jr., about a dishwasher who becomes famous by posing as a ballerina and joining his *Follies* revue. The show had been running since December 1920 and managed to survive an otherwise desolate season.

No one anticipated that four Black vaudevillians would have much to add to the Manhattan theater scene. *Shuffle Along* arrived in the city with a few advance notices in the papers, respectable press from its brief tryout, and a potentially lethal dose of indifference and skepticism. The Sixty-Third Street Theatre was designed to be a lecture hall, and aesthetically, it still left much to be desired. The apron of the stage was extended into the first three rows of the audience, which made it difficult for folks to enter and exit from the house. A gridiron was built for scenery to be hung from, and while dressing rooms were planned, they were nonexistent as the show began its run in New York. "You could hear hammering during the performances," Flournoy Miller recalled. "We had to run out to the men's room to wash up." The best thing the theater had going for it was its capacity for over a thousand people, as well as a balcony and a gallery, giving just the slightest semblance that it was a suitable house for a major production after all.

The show's preview performance on May 22—they formally opened the next day—couldn't have gone better. The theater was packed with an integrated audience—African American folks sat as close as the fifth row of the orchestra section—and the white patrons didn't reject "Love Will Find a Way." In fact, they couldn't get enough of the groundbreaking show. Lottie Gee, Roger Matthews, and Gertrude Saunders were begged for encores—"I'm Just Simply Full of Jazz" was requested and performed thrice—and Miller and Lyles's boxing match elicited the most uninhibited laughter of the night. Before the show concluded, Sissle and Blake took to the stage in their regular tuxedos, cozied up to the Aeolian piano, and gave everyone a taste of vaudeville. Before the duo concluded their set, Sissle stepped forward and announced the following song was coming from "our benefactor, the late Jim Europe," before going into a high-stepping rendition of "On Patrol in No Man's Land."

And just as it seemed the evening couldn't get any better, the full company returned for one last dance number, "Baltimore Buzz." As the adrenaline rushed through the cast and orchestra, the energy in the audience became electric and insurmountable. The evening's program noted that the finale would be performed by "the entire outfit, including you," and whether because the audience followed directions or were independently motivated to take to their feet, the venue became less like a theater and more like a dance hall. "People cheered," Noble Sissle recalled. "I almost fell off the stage when I looked out into the audience—there was old John Cort dancing in the aisles! His faith in us had been borne out. That night it looked like we were home."

Shuffle Along was off to a strong start, and while Sissle, Blake, Miller, and Lyles weren't actually on the Great White Way, their ticket pricing, which started off ranging between fifty cents and $2, was in line with other shows in Times Square, thus qualifying it for the distinction, with the trades covering the show just as they did the "legitimate" productions in Midtown. As a result, according to Eubie Blake, *Shuffle Along* marked the first time Black performers had truly broken that glass ceiling. "It was the first Negro show on Broadway, but it wasn't the first Negro show to *play on* Broadway," he explained. "You see, Williams and Walker, Cole and Johnson, Ernest R. Hogan—they played on Broadway, too... [But] they never got $5 for a ticket. It was a dollar, top. See, it's the price that makes Broadway... Otherwise you can put a flea circus next to a theater and call it a Broadway show. I don't mean Williams and Walker and the rest of those people weren't high-class shows... When it comes to quality, there was nobody could touch Bert Williams and George Walker. Bob Cole and J. Rosamund [*sic*] Johnson were musical *geniuses*. Great! But they could never bring even their greatest shows to Broadway."

While reviews were generally positive at the outset, several critics noted the shoddiness of the venue, the unpolished look of the costumes and sets, and the somewhat disappointing and inconsistent quality of Miller and Lyles's book, with perhaps the most stringent criticism of the comedians' script coming from James Whittaker of the *New York Daily News*: "Between songs at the Sixty-Third Street Theatre is a good time to read the rest of last Sunday's paper." However, the negative comments were largely ignored by the public, and the show quickly gained traction with the white theatergoers John Cort knew were essential for the musical to become a hit. Sissle and Blake credited positive reviews from Jack Pulaski in *Variety* and Alan Dale's write-up in the *American* with piquing the interest of potential patrons who may not have ordinarily sought the show out.

One of the most routinely acknowledged aspects of *Shuffle Along* was its music, and while Sissle and Blake were often credited for its quality, William Vodery, who orchestrated the show, was also deserving of praise. The composer was born in Pennsylvania to a mother who was a pianist and a father who taught at Lincoln University. His parents rented rooms, and show folks would often stay at the house, giving the youngster another access point to see working artists up close. He ultimately attended the University of Pittsburgh on a music scholarship, and by 1910, he was the musical director for performances at the Howard Theatre in Washington, DC.

Vodery composed the arrangements for each of the show's fifteen pit musicians, including not only African Americans but also Puerto Ricans. While it is difficult to know exactly how many due to recent arrivals to America often anglicizing their names in order to assimilate and find work, several musicians who played in the *Shuffle Along* orchestra had also been in James Reese Europe's 369th Infantry Regimental Band. They were each trained zarzuela musicians who weren't just talented players but could read sheet music, which not all the Negro instrumentalists could do despite their proficiency. Having Boricuas—Puerto Ricans living in mainland America—in the pit was a win for everyone; Eubie Blake had incredibly gifted musicians who would help elevate the sound of songs and William Vodery's orchestrations to work with, and the Puerto Ricans were provided an opportunity to make a living doing something they enjoyed and excelled at. While there were about 150,000 African Americans living in New York, there were only 35,000 Puerto Ricans. They had yet to develop an enclave or organize their community, as Black Americans had in Harlem, making it difficult to find work. Their brown skin prohibited them from playing in white orchestras, but they fit in comfortably alongside Negro musicians.

While the opening on Sixty-Third was a blessing to the show's writers, for Lawrence Deas, who staged the show, it was bittersweet. Just before the musical opened in Manhattan and even though his staging was left largely intact, Al Mayer and John Cort replaced him. "They brought in a white director named Walter Brooks to give the show 'that Broadway touch,'" Eubie Blake explained. "He got two percent of the production, and Lawrence Deas, who had done all the work, was paid off with a small amount of cash and dropped." Brooks had previously staged Flo-Flo, which Cort produced, and the old man thought that it would lend the show a bit of gravitas if his former colleague was attached. Deas remained in the cast as Jack Penrose, and while he would later argue deservedly that he was chiefly responsible for the unbridled, peppy dancing that made the show famous, Brooks unilaterally received credit on paper and in payment.

By the end of *Shuffle Along*'s first week, the musical comedy had brought in receipts of $6,800, an impressive number for a relatively unknown show that wore its poverty on its tattered sleeves. *Variety* noted the strength of its opening, citing that "despite handicaps with an improvised stage and poor production, the colored show stands a chance" within the anemic theatrical landscape, and by the end of its second week, when the show made $8,000, it seemed their odds of sticking around were getting better. While the Nikko Producing Company had barely begun to climb out of debt, their second week box office returns provided a lot to be optimistic about. Their weekly break-even point was $7,500, meaning that, for the first time, the show had managed to earn a small profit.

The unlikeliness of this uptick was somewhat surprising, especially considering the social ills that were commanding the country's attention. New York's economy remained in dire straits, and anti-Black racism was still exploding into incidents of violence and terrorism. Just days after *Shuffle Along*'s New York opening, on May 30, Dick Rowland, a Black teenager, stepped into an elevator in an office building in Tulsa, Oklahoma. A few minutes later, Sarah Page, the young, white elevator operator, was heard screaming. When the doors opened, Rowland fled. He was arrested the next morning, but in the interim, rumors spread like wildfire throughout the city. The afternoon he was arrested, a front-page story in the *Tulsa Tribune* claimed that Rowland had sexually assaulted Page.

Later that evening, in a scene that had played out in too many small towns and cities throughout the United States, an angry white mob showed up at the courthouse and demanded the sheriff turn the teenager over to them. Law enforcement refused, and twenty-five armed Black men, many of them veterans, offered their assistance to help protect Rowland inside. The sheriff turned them away, but the Black men returned an hour later with fifty more, all bearing weapons, and when they did, they were met with fifteen hundred whites who also had arms. Shots rang out, chaos ensued, and Greenwood—a prosperous section of the city devoid of whites that would later become known as "Black Wall Street"—burned for over eighteen hours straight: 1,256 houses were set ablaze, rendering residents homeless, as well as thirty-five blocks' worth of Black-owned businesses, a school, a library, a hospital, churches, and hotels. The next day, whites ransacked the community, with the looters pillaging all they could abscond with in their bare hands. By the time the National Guard arrived on the scene shortly before noon on May 31, the riot had essentially ended, and the community had been permanently lost.

Shortly thereafter, all charges were dropped against Dick Rowland. The police determined that he had stumbled in the elevator, and Sarah Page's scream was the result of him accidentally stepping on her foot. He slipped out of town the next day and never returned.

According to local residents, for a long time, whites and Blacks had coexisted happily in their "progressive"—yet segregated—city, until the war exposed the racial animus that had been concealed by many of the well-meaning whites in the community. "The United States placed them on the same footing in the army as the white soldiers, and many of them when they returned walked through the streets with an arrogance that they never would have dreamed of assuming before the war," a white pastor, Reverend Harold G. Cooke of the Centenary Southern Methodist Church, one of the largest religious institutions in Tulsa, told the press in the aftermath of the riots.

"White people have been forced either to step aside on the sidewalk or be brushed aside by negroes," he continued. "Negroes have ignored the Jim Crow laws on the street cars, which have been divided into two sections, one for whites and one for negroes. They have overflowed into the white section of the cars and have remained seated there while white women have been forced to stand in the aisle. This has resulted in a number of individual altercations between white men and negroes, although there has been no general conflict between the races until Tuesday night. It helped widen the breach though."

However, even with the news out of Tulsa hitting the New York papers, the colored performers on Sixty-Third continued to do well, and perhaps counterintuitively, Noble Sissle chalked up *Shuffle Along*'s initial success to folks' desire for escapism. "Very few people of the Broadway theatrical managerial staff believed us and there were few among our own group who felt we had a chance," he said. "However, we felt we had a message—we felt that the gloom and depression as an aftermath of the war had left the country hungry for laughter. That was so expressed in our music and rhythm."

Besides word of mouth, positive press, and the need for lighthearted entertainment, the increase in ticket sales can be credited, at least in part, to the show's producers canceling the Wednesday afternoon performance and replacing it with a "midnight matinee"—which actually started at 11:30 p.m.—instead. The novelty of being able to see a show—an all-Black, contemporary, jazz-infused show—late at night helped further distinguish *Shuffle Along* from the rest of the pack. The Sixty-Third Street Theatre was the only game in town for those looking for clean entertainment at that hour, and the late curtain time meant performers from other shows throughout the city were also free to drop by and see what all the buzz was about. "White show people spread the word," Noble Sissle said, with Flournoy Miller adding, "Then Negroes came to see the celebrities."

"Irving Berlin used to sit behind me at *Shuffle Along*," Eubie Blake recalled. "He'd say, 'Tell Mr. Sissle I take my hat off to those lyrics.'" Fiorello La Guardia, president of New York City's Board of Aldermen, was also a frequent visitor. The politician was particularly fond of Miller and Lyles's satirical take on municipal leadership, with their boxing match being his favorite scene. "La Guardia came three nights in one week," Blake said.

While Broadway continued to be in a slump—nearly 50 percent of theaters in the vicinity of Times Square were dark by the first week of June—word of *Shuffle Along* continued to spread, confounding at least one white producer. As his competing production was flailing financially while the African American musical on Sixty-Third thrived, the Broadway backer told a reporter, "That *Shuffle Along* show is just one of those things that happen. It's a 'wow' and you can't stop it." On June 5, 1921, Burns Mantle, a special correspondent writing for the *Louisville Courier Journal* newspaper, encouraged Kentuckians who planned on vacationing in New York to see the new Black musical comedy. "The negro is a natural and frequently a gifted comedian; he can always dance and usually he can sing better than most of his white brothers, and his dark-skinned sisters are a melodious and peppery group of choristers," he wrote. "Since Walker died and Williams went over to *Follies*, there have been few colored companies organized and we have missed them."

The producers of *Shuffle Along* quickly capitalized on their newfound popularity—particularly among white people with expendable income—by briefly flirting with a $3 top ticket price in early June, as their weekly intake continued to increase. In fact, the show caused such a stir before and after performances that, early in the summer of 1921, the city designated Sixty-Third Street as a one-way to alleviate the congestion.

However, white audiences' perceptions and their fiscal intake were not the primary concerns for the show's writers. Sissle, Blake, Miller, and Lyles felt the greatest sense of pride in the belief that they were making a positive contribution to their race. Just a month after they opened on Sixty-Third, the *Baltimore Afro-American* ran an editorial, "*Shuffle Along—What it Means to the Colored Artist*," which may not have moved as many tickets as Jack Pulaski or Alan Dale to the clientele John Cort was attracting, but for the show's writers, it was just as important. "*Shuffle Along* is an established artistic success; without regard to the commercial possibilities, which are great. To the Negro performer, this means much," they wrote. "It means that notwithstanding the suppression; the prejudice; the handicaps and the struggle directly due to race; that the pinnacle of every American performer's ambition may be reached. This show is a 'rainbow' of hope and encouragement to every artist of the race."

However, the newspaper made clear that *Shuffle Along*'s success wasn't simply due to its existence and the inevitability of colored shows to play well but because, at its core, it was a quality musical mélange that, despite its rough edges, was created by clearly gifted artists who appealed to a wide cross-section of theatergoers. "Achievement is possible only to those who may possess exceptional talent, originality, and the willingness to work, to illustrate," they concluded. "The show succeeded... without smut, profanity, vulgarity, suggestiveness, or double entendre jokes... That means that a clean show is acceptable. All in all, it means brace up—be clean—have talented initiative— and you may work with reasonable hope of just reward. This page did not err when it said, 'The time is now ripe for a big colored show.'"

The editors of the *Baltimore Afro-American* weren't unique in thinking the moment was right for "a big colored show." In August 1921, *Put and Take*, an all-Black revue written and coproduced by Irvin C. Miller, Flournoy's brother, debuted at the town hall on West Forty-Third Street between Sixth Avenue and Broadway, in the heart of the theater district. Like the Sixty-Third Street Theatre, the venue's stage had to be extended to accommodate all the performers, as the 1,495-seat house was also conceived for lectures and speeches, not theatrical ventures. The show reportedly received the support of several wealthy backers from both uptown and downtown—whites and Blacks—a clear signal that colored musicals were now considered a worthwhile investment.

Just before the show's opening, it was announced that the production would star former heavyweight champion Jack Johnson, who was to receive a $2,000 weekly salary and a cut of the proceeds. However, when the show opened on August 23, after having sold all their tickets to an enthusiastic audience by twenty minutes before curtain, Miller appeared in his place. The *Baltimore Afro-American* expressed optimism after its debut, predicting that "the show is destined to last a long time, thus more firmly establishing the race on the top row of theatricals." *Variety*'s Jack Lait disagreed, describing *Put and Take* as a vanity project from a writer, producer, and actor eager to capitalize on his brother's success. But beyond Miller's so-called self-indulgence, Lait took exception with the show's attempt to pass itself off as just another mainstream—white—revue. "There is, throughout, too much effort to be 'dressed up' and dignified," he wrote. "Only at the very end does it become the novelty that it should be if it wants to survive at all and have any excuse for invading Times Square. Colored performers cannot vie with white ones, and colored producers cannot play within an apple's throw of Ziegfeld and try and compete with him... The mere novelty of a colored revue near Broadway may put *Put and Take* over. If it does, any colored show can do it."

Ultimately, Lait proved to be prophetic. While there was

favorable press surrounding the show—particularly for the music by Spencer Williams, Tim Brymn, and Perry Bradford, as well as the large chorus of dancing girls who seemed "bent on outgyrating each other"—*Put and Take* survived for only thirty-two performances, closing abruptly with reports that the cast and crew had been left unpaid. The show began by bringing in $8,000 weekly, but by its third week, it was already being deemed an "awful flop" financially. It was mused in the trades that its failure was an indication that the novelty of Black folks on Broadway was wearing off; however, these journalistic prognostications couldn't have been further from the truth. By the end of August 1921, *Shuffle Along* had not only survived the summer's dog days but had thrived in them, increasing its weekly box office returns to over $9,000. "The way this colored revue is going, it is liable to run well into the fall," *Variety* reported. The musical was in such demand that Charles B. Cochran, a top English producer, opened negotiations with John Cort to bring *Shuffle Along* to London once it closed in New York. Cochran offered transportation for the entire production team and to pay the Nikko Producing Company $5,000 for each week the show ran in London, but Cort balked. He countered that the show was worth at least $1,000 more, adding that if the Englishman wanted it at that price, he would have to wait until after the New Year, as the musical was expected to run in Manhattan at least that long. Conversations between the two producers continued, with updates leaked regularly to the trades, serving as a regular reminder that Sissle, Blake, Miller, and Lyles were in high demand.

The summer sustainability of *Shuffle Along* was in spite of—or perhaps due to—a high-profile casting shake-up. Gertrude Saunders, the bright-eyed darling of the critics, left the show in early August after well-known white manager Joe Hurtig offered to pay her more than she was earning in *Shuffle Along* to perform in his lavish burlesque extravaganza several blocks away. She gave her notice, and after spending a few weeks singing at Reisenweber's Café, the popular jazz club restaurant in Columbus Circle on Fifty-Eight Street and Eighth Avenue, she was onstage for Hurtig in early September. Her decision came as a surprise—and a headache—to *Shuffle Along*'s production team, especially since Sissle and Blake wrote "Daddy, Won't You Please Come Home" and "I'm Craving That Kind of Love" specifically for her. "She was the sensation of our show—stopped it cold every night. But like so many artists in show business who had become a sensation overnight, Gertrude, in spite of our efforts at persuasion, left the show, and we had just got started," Noble Sissle explained, with Eubie Blake adding, "She threw it all away for $5 more a week in a burlesque show." For her part, Saunders maintained she "never missed a thing" by leaving *Shuffle Along*, as she would go on to have a fruitful career.

Sissle, Blake, Miller, and Lyles racked their brains figuring out how to replace Saunders quickly and quietly. Gertrude had light-brown skin, soft curly hair, big brown eyes, a unique soprano voice, and, as Blake put it, a figure that "looked like someone had molded it." Now the show's creators weren't just looking for someone who could learn her part but an actress whom the audience would be quick to fall in love with. While

Harriett Sissle, Noble's wife, was typically removed from his business affairs, she proved instrumental in finding Saunders's replacement. Harriett's drinking problem had worsened significantly since she and Noble married, and while she was out one night at Barron Wilkins's popular Harlem nightspot on West 134th Street at Seventh Avenue, she ran into Ada Smith, a popular singer better known as Bricktop. Smith had heard through the grapevine that Saunders was splitting with *Shuffle Along*, and she had the perfect replacement in mind—her friend Florence Mills, whom she had known for a long time and had also gotten a job performing at the club. "Flo was a star for years on the colored circuit," Eubie Blake explained, "but it was very tough for us to be recognized in the white world." Harriett agreed to bring the idea to her husband, but he dismissed it outright. "She's a ballad singer," Sissle said. "Gertrude's part calls for dancing and singing blues." But Harriett told him not to take her word for it; Mills was already performing "I'm Craving That Kind of Love" every night at the club, and Sissle could go check her out himself. "At her insistence, I went to see her without saying anything to my partners," he explained. "The next night I told them we were saved, but Lyles, in his dry way, said, 'She *ought* to sing—she has legs like a canary.'"

Mills was offered $100 a week, to which Sissle added $25 after some back-and-forth, putting her just that amount shy of what star Lottie Gee was making. Additionally, as a condition of her joining the show, her husband and manager, U. S. "Slow Kid" Thompson, joined the cast, replacing acrobatic dancer Tommy Woods as a porter in Jimtown's mayor's office, performing an eccentric legomania dance where he swung and kicked his legs wildly, as if they were made of rubber. Thompson and Mills were inseparable, having toured for years on the Keith vaudeville circuit in an act called the Tennessee Ten, and if she were kick-starting her career in the top African American show in over a decade, she was going to bring her life and stage partner with her. The cast was excited to meet Saunders's replacement, but on her first day, when the petite performer showed up backstage, looking homely in a simple black dress that hung off her shoulders over her shapeless frame, her new colleagues were far from impressed. "She looked like one of those little girls you would see walking into a store," chorus member Bee Freeman recalled. "We thought, 'How dare they inflict this thing on us.'"

Her husband knew how important it was for Mills to make a strong impression, so on the evening of her first perfor-mance, he purchased tickets for twenty ringers, who were spread throughout the audience, to applaud wildly when she began her chorus in what was one of Gertrude Saunders's signature songs. But it turned out he didn't need the insur-ance. "She had these beautiful eyes and she stole the show," Eubie Blake recalled. "When she sang, 'I'm Craving That Kind of Love,' the audience

FLORENCE MILLS, ROGER MATTHEWS, AND LOTTIE GEE IN A PUBLICITY STILL FOR *SHUFFLE ALONG*, 1921

Courtesy of the archives of Robert Kimball

never heard the punch line because they were throwing up their hats and cheering before she could finish the song."

As it turned out, Mills's interpretation of the number was what distinguished her most. In its original conception and with Saunders's performance, the song was one of desire, just short of sexual in its interpretation: "Kiss me, kiss me, kiss me with his tempting lips / Sweet as honey drops / Press me, press me, press me to his loving breast." However, Mills's interpretation was softer, more "lovable," and she communicated a more hopeful sense of longing with the same lyrics and music. Additionally, she elevated the piece from being a simple novelty number. "She sang a song with soul," Saunders said. "I was a trickster. I just did tricks." With an unassuming presence and melodic, "birdlike" voice, Florence Mills was the perfect person to replace Saunders—primarily because the two were nothing alike. And to the delight and surprise of the show's four writers, she was someone the audience fell in love with nightly.

"She had a little figure; she had nothing in the world to help her," Eubie Blake recalled. "When the woman's on the stage, you gotta have a woman that men can say, 'Oh God, I'd like to [go] out with that girl.' I've never heard anybody in my life say they'd like to go out with her. But, brother, when she walked on the stage, she lit the stage up... One time I was going down Broadway, and there were two women, white women, behind me. And Florence was coming up Broadway. The woman behind me says, 'Look, look, look, there's Florence Mills.' And the other woman says, 'Where?' And she's looking right at her... She looked like nothing, scrawny little thing."

Despite the initial trepidation by the cast, the new star of *Shuffle Along* fit right in. While she and Lottie Gee were cast as best friends in the show, they quickly slipped into those same roles offstage as well. "If Lottie mentioned to Florence that she couldn't make that B-flat above the staff in 'Love Will Find a Way,' Florence would make the note for her," Blake recalled. Not only did the audience and cast fall head over heels for her, the press did as well. Like Saunders, Florence Mills became a star overnight. Word spread far, with one of the show's long-distance devotees—a young, emerging African American poet from Ohio—keeping the actress in the forefront of his mind as he was deciding where to attend college. His father urged the teenager to attend school in Switzerland, primarily to have a respite from American racism, but his son, Langston Hughes, had his sights set on the Sixty-Third Street Theatre. "*Shuffle Along* had just burst into being, and I wanted to hear Florence Mills sing," he recalled. "So I told my father I'd rather go to Columbia." Once he arrived in the city, Hughes "sat up in the gallery night after night at *Shuffle Along*," where he "adored Florence Mills."

Concurrent with Gertrude Saunders's departure from the cast, the Harmony Kings, three of whose members had been in the dressing room with Noble Sissle when James Reese Europe was fatally stabbed in May 1919 during their postwar tour, joined the cast at $275 a week for the collective. Just as Sissle and Blake had "a few minutes" at the end of each show, the Harmony Kings were given some time during the second act to perform some numbers. Additionally, while this was not initially part of the deal, Ivan Harold Browning also substituted in as romantic lead Harry Walton until early September, as Roger Matthews had coincidentally fallen ill around the same time.

Despite not having a proper place in the show's narrative, when the four men took to the stage in identical tuxedos and top hats, holding their wooden canes, the audience was happy to indulge them. Of the numbers they performed during their short set, "Ain't It a Shame" routinely received the biggest response of the night. After they sang the short rhythmic spiritual—"Ain't it a shame to sin on Sunday? / Ain't it a shame to sin on Sunday? / Ain't it a shame? / When you got Monday, Tuesday, Wednesday / Thursday, Friday, and Saturday, too. / Ain't it a shame?"— William Hann, who had a deep bass voice "of phenomenal sweetness," would sing, "It sho' is!" The audience would eat it up, with one journalist noting that "had he been born white, [Hann] would be singing at the Metropolitan Opera House."

Broadway arose from its summer slump in the fall, and *Shuffle Along* followed suit, achieving its best week to date in mid-October with $11,000 in ticket sales. While nearly all the shows in the heart of the theater district were doing better business than that each week, with its shoestring budget, limited overhead, and threadbare production values, the fact that *Shuffle Along* had lasted until the fall and was increasing its weekly intake was significant. Although the show was bringing in money primarily from white patrons, the cast sought opportunities to make the show accessible to the Black community, as they did on October 17, 1921, when they performed a benefit for the NAACP at Harlem's Lafayette Theatre. On the night of the event, 132nd Street was packed with hundreds of patrons who had been turned away, and the police had to manage the boisterous overflow crowd when a fight nearly broke out between folks trying to gain admittance. In the melee, a pane of glass was broken in the lobby door. But despite the chaos outside, the event, which was billed as "Miss Florence Mills and the Jazz Girls and Boys," was nothing but jubilant. The audience was not only filled by everyday Harlemites eager to see the latest Black theatrical attraction but also several notable members of Black society, such as novelist Jessie Fauset, who volunteered as an usher, and Dr. Gertrude Curtis, New York's first Black female dentist, who helped the NAACP with publicity. With ticket prices ranging from $1.50 for box seats and fifty cents for the balcony, by the end of the evening, $1,026 was made for the organization. The rogue extra $1 was donated by a cast member.

Harlem had become a literal home for Noble Sissle, Eubie Blake, Flournoy Miller, Aubrey Lyles, and nearly all the cast during the run of the show. While the average person uptown didn't necessarily have the disposable funds for the best seats at the Sixty-Third Street Theatre—by November 1921, Black folks only made up about 10 percent of the audience—the sounds of *Shuffle Along* were regularly heard throughout Harlem as club singers performed the show's hits at the microphone in late-night spots, and Eubie Blake and the Shuffle Along Orchestra made themselves available to play "all occasions. No job too small or too large." While they were regularly hired for white social events, just as he and Noble Sissle had done with James Reese Europe, Blake also became a staple of "house rent parties," which were becoming regular occurrences throughout the neighborhood. Blacks were still flocking to Harlem in droves, but it didn't take long before enterprising landlords capitalized on this mass migration and began doubling and, in some cases, even tripling their tenants' rent, knowing the African American folks they were renting to had limited options in terms of other places to go. To help make ends meet, neighbors would collaborate to bring fried chicken, baked ham, pig's feet, gumbo—and plenty of bootleg liquor—to the apartment of the person in need. Then they'd charge a few dollars for admission and host a rollicking party that wouldn't subside until well into the twilight hours. The neighbors would hire a pianist and drummer—the going rate was about $10 for the duo—and by the end of the evening, they'd typically have made enough money to last at least a few months. Eubie Blake enjoyed being part of these community revelries and was often able to hit up three or four different parties in a given night.

However, while many in Harlem were eager for more shows like *Shuffle Along*, the show still had its share of critics within the Black community. William H. Ferris, an author and intellectual who had worked with W. E. B. Du Bois and spoken critically about Booker T. Washington's more conservative path to racial justice, cautioned against the show painting a simplistic view of Black life and setting an unbreakable precedent that would limit the types of representation African American folks would have on the stage in future productions. "The average Negro feels that when a Negro artist portrays a Negro in his grotesque and ludicrous aspects, to get the applause of the gallery gods, that he is catering to a race prejudice for a few dimes and shekels," he wrote. "The Negro no more regards the darkey and the coon who plays the monkey as the typical Negro than the Jew regards the rag peddler as the typical Jew or the Italian regards the banana vendor as the typical Italian or the Irishman regards 'Pat' with his broken vogue as the typical Irishman.

"The average Negro is not narrow," he continued. "He doesn't object to the Uncle Toms, the mammies, the pickaninnies, the buck and wing dancers, etc., being depicted on the stages. But he wants the higher type of the Negro also depicted. He regards Toussaint L'Ouverture, Sir William Conrad Reeves, Henry Highland Garnet, William Highland Day, Frederick Douglass, Alexander Crumwell, Edward Wilmot Blyden, Dusé Mohamed Ali, Marcus Garvey, William Monroe Trotter, and Dr. W. E. B. Du Bois as worthy of presentation on the stage as the banjo players and *Shuffle Along* dancers."

The opportunity to see "the higher type" of Black folks on the stage seemed more imminent than some would have predicted before *Shuffle Along*'s run. A bold black headline ran across the full width of the December 9 issue of *Variety*'s front page—PLAN NEGRO GRAND OPERA—with a claim that John and Harry Cort were set to assemble the greatest Black vocalists for an indefinite engagement beginning in February of the following year. "Negro grand opera has often been spoken about in the past, but has never come to actuality," the trade wrote. "The colored race holds many noted voices, some heard in other stage performances of the past, like Abbie Mitchell's. It appears the success of *Shuffle Along* has convinced the promising backers negro opera could make money in attracting whites, as *Shuffle Along* is doing." While the Corts' plans ultimately failed to materialize, the prominent announcement highlighted just how eager many were for more African American entertainment, even beyond the musical comedy variety, and just how successful *Shuffle Along* had been in advancing the national conversation around Black artistry. By this time, ticket sales had grown to $3 for top seating—they'd be up to $4 by New Year's Eve—with the show bringing in about $15,000 weekly.

As their banner year came to an end, the cast of *Shuffle Along* gave back to the city and community that had given them so much. They organized a pair of benefit performances for the Lincoln Settlement House on 202 West Sixty-Third Street, a community and recreation center established for Black kids. At the first, on December 10, the company played to 210 children, who were each given a box of candy to enjoy while they watched the show. The following week, on December 17, a hundred children from the settlement house attended, as well as three classes from one of New York's public schools. Finally, on Christmas, the production purchased dinner for a thousand children in need throughout Harlem. Just before the New Year, NAACP executive secretary James Weldon Johnson commended the cast and crew on behalf of the organization, stating that, "The members of this company, whose performance is a vital contribution to the welfare of colored people in the United States, deserve the highest praise for their readiness to share with others the pleasure they can give. In addition to having proved that the colored musical comedy can rank with the best productions on Broadway, they have given several benefit performances, including one for the NAACP, and have demonstrated that they can not only be successful, but generous."

With *Shuffle Along* surpassing its three hundredth performance at the Sixty-Third Street Theatre by late January 1922—a significant milestone for any Broadway show, let alone an African American musical comedy—Harry Cort announced that while the main company would remain in Manhattan, a second group was being assembled to begin touring on February 12, playing one-night stands along the East Coast. While this was seemingly reminiscent of the graveyard tour the cast and crew had embarked on before arriving in New York, the success of the show guaranteed this would be a different endeavor altogether. Train fare would be guaranteed, and the show's stars wouldn't have to crash on anyone's floor. Lew Payton and Joe Simms, a vaudeville comedy duo, filled in for the roles originated by Flournoy Miller and Aubrey Lyles, and the two drew rave reviews at every stop, particularly from Black newspapers.

In less than a year, *Shuffle Along* had become one of the theater industry's most surprising sensations, achieving the praise of white and Black audiences alike, which musicals like *Darkydom* had been unable to do. "We were afraid people would think of it as a freak show and it wouldn't appeal to white people," Eubie Blake explained. "Others thought that if it was a colored show it might be dirty. One man bought a front row seat for himself every night for a week. I'd noticed him—down in the pit you notice things in the audience—and finally, after the whole week was past, he came up and told me that now he could bring his wife and children because there was no foul language and not one double-entendre."

Shuffle Along's influence was spreading throughout the entertainment industry in ways the show's creators couldn't have predicted. Every night, over a thousand people attended a musical with a syncopated score, bringing the sounds of the city's hidden night spots into a "legitimate," albeit still ramshackle, theater. In two hours, the show celebrated and highlighted Black artistry, sparking an interest that would last in New York throughout the remainder of the decade. "The 1920s were the years of Manhattan's Black Renaissance. It began with *Shuffle Along*...a honey of a show," Langston Hughes recalled. "Swift, bright, funny, rollicking, and gay, with a dozen danceable, singable tunes... Everybody was in the audience—including me. People came back to see it innumerable times. It was always packed... It gave just the proper push—a pre-Charleston kick—to that Negro vogue of the '20s, that spread to books, African sculpture, music, and dancing."

The economics of the show—low overhead, novel

CLOCKWISE FROM TOP: AUBREY LYLES, EUBIE BLAKE, FLOURNOY MILLER, AND NOBLE SISSLE IN AN UNDATED PUBLICITY PHOTOGRAPH

Photo by White Studio, © New York Public Library for the Performing Arts

content—were simple to understand and imitate. The return of a high-profile all-colored musical comedy all but guaranteed that other producers would seek to capitalize on the market that clearly existed for Negro entertainment, and Lew Leslie, a white cutthroat businessman with an otherwise friendly disposition, was one of the first to ride the wave. Leslie was a former performer who earned a comfortable living by discovering and advancing new talent, and his first major foray presenting Black talent on the Manhattan stage was in George White's *Scandals of 1921*, that year's installment of his annual revue, which was fashioned in the style of Ziegfeld's *Follies*. Leslie successfully lobbied for one of his protégés, Tess Gardella, a white vaudeville performer who often donned blackface to play Aunt Jemima, to have a spot in the show as her popular character, singing ragtime and plantation songs with a polka-dot kerchief and matching top for $1,000 a week. However, Leslie's career took a dramatic turn when he attended a performance of *Shuffle Along* with cabaret owner Sam Salvin in August 1921. "We really went to hear a girl named Gertrude Saunders, but this night…an understudy did her songs," Leslie recalled. "The understudy rolled a pair of flashing black eyes… Her name was Florence Mills." From the moment he saw her, the producer wanted to promote Black showgirls in the same way that Florenz Ziegfeld was doing for white ones in his *Follies*. According to Noble Sissle, Lew Leslie "was the pioneer of the Negro nightclub revue, the first to glamorize Negro girls and the one who set the pattern for such clubs at the Cotton Club, the Alabam, and others."

In January 1922, Leslie offered Mills a five-week contract to play seven performances a week, with only one of them starting before midnight, in exchange for $1,000 at Sam Salvin's Folies Bergère cabaret, located above the Winter Garden Theater on Broadway. As the engagement wouldn't interfere with her work in *Shuffle Along* and this side opportunity paid more than she was earning on Sixty-Third Street, she agreed. Salvin's venue was in need of renovating, and Leslie encouraged him to create a truly unique and novel aesthetic, inspired by his new star and the rest of the Black performers the producer would employ. When it reopened, the cabaret was renamed the Plantation, as it was a completely immersive, theatrically lavish, antebellum experience. Patrons would enter a large gate that led to a large room with a log cabin where, inside, a Mammy was cooking pancakes. There was a ten-piece band led by Lieutenant Tim Brynn, all in pickaninny costumes, and the dance floor, which was where the show took place, was surrounded by a wooden picket fence and a cotton field in the background. Seemingly no expense was spared in creating an extravagant, yet stereotypical, African American production.

Florence Mills was the star attraction in *Plantation Revue*, which was subtitled "Night Time Frolics in Dixieland," an evening of cabaret performances by Black artists. Its opening was celebrated with a gala and an exclusive ticket price of $10—five times what the normal admission fee would be—which drew the ire and condemnation of at least one New York columnist in attendance, who was overheard asking, "Who ever heard of evening dress to go in and see a lot of niggers?" Yet despite the clearly racist commentator's incredulity, *Plantation Revue* was immediately profitable. As Mills's five weeks came to an end, Leslie confessed to her that he had always had designs on expanding the floor show, and his initial offer was just to buy him time to prove the concept before fully committing. What he was proposing was transformative, not only for her but for Black entertainers overall—an opportunity to have a show built around her, in the heart of Times Square. Not only that but they were willing to give her a 50 percent increase in pay, more than twice what she was making in *Shuffle Along*. It was a no-brainer.

In March 1922, when the managers of *Shuffle Along* were told that Mills was leaving, they sought an injunction to keep her in the musical comedy on the basis that she had a contract. However, when her attorneys pointed out that she had a two-week cancellation clause, the Nikko Producing Company let her go without a fuss. At least not a formal fuss. Aubrey Lyles was the most skeptical about Florence Mills when she was brought into the show and the most incensed when he learned she was leaving. *Shuffle Along* was a hit, and he couldn't believe that "Slow Kid" Thompson would allow her to leave that behind. "What kind of [man] is you," he asked her husband. "You got a girl here, she's a jewel."

"Well, it's a gamble, so the man's going to give her $300."

"But goddammit, you're working in a damned restaurant, so I don't give a damn if you're making high C with a pork chop in your mouth."

Shuffle Along continued without Mills—she was replaced in late April by vaudevillian Edith Spencer—while in Midtown, *Plantation Revue* flourished. Florence Mills's name glistened in bright lights above the Winter Garden, illuminated with precisely a hundred bulbs, with attendance increasing significantly after *Make It Snappy*, a musical revue starring Eddie Cantor, opened at the theater downstairs that month. For just two more dollars, patrons could walk upstairs and be treated to a forty-five-minute revue, headlined by one of the former stars of *Shuffle Along*. The show quickly spawned several imitators, with *Variety* reporting on new "Plantations" cropping up in Paris and Chicago, just months after Leslie expanded his venture. In some ways, the profitability of the producer's endeavor was surprising, but with its lush budget, premiere location, headlining star, the increasing appetite for Black artistry, and its wink and nod to the nostalgia many cultured white folks still felt for the Southern traditions, one can easily see why the show caught on as quickly as it did.

In fact, the strength of *Plantation Revue* led *Shuffle Along* manager Al Mayer to produce his own carbon copy, *Bandanaland*, which was staged at Reisenweber's Café and cast from the same mold Lew Leslie created for his floor show downtown. The show opened on April 27, preceded by a newspaper advertisement— with two smiling illustrated Black faces that looked more like Al Jolson in burnt cork than actual Black people—highlighting that the show was by "Miller & Lyles and Sissle & Blake, originators of *Shuffle Along*." With the exception of just one song, Mayer's forty-two-minute revue was made up of entirely new music by Noble Sissle and Eubie Blake and starred Lottie Gee, the Palm Beach Four (a quartet that performed specialty numbers in *Shuffle Along*), Willie Wood (a dancer from the show's touring company), and eight chorine dancers who easily captured the interest of the audience, with *Variety* noting that they were "of the creole type, all good-looking and shapely. They loom up best in a number when they wore but brief skirtings over bare thighs and legs." The dancers performed within inches of the tables where the patrons sat, strutting, shimmying, and doing a stylized version of the cakewalk, while the Black orchestra played in front of a painting of a steamboat on the Mississippi River. Mayer was given a $1,350 weekly guarantee and a cut of the door, and with a seating capacity of four hundred and minimal $1 cover charge, the expectation was that *Bandanaland* would replicate both *Shuffle Along* and *Plantation Revue*'s success—and it did.

The opening at Reisenweber's coincided with another significant milestone. *Shuffle Along's* producers were celebrating the one-year anniversary of its opening on Broadway—albeit a few weeks early—and they marked the historic occasion on May 5, 1922 with a party at the home of their new musical revue. The touring company was in New York as well, doing a short run at Teller's Shubert Theatre in Brooklyn, and were able to partake in the festivities. In the year since they'd formally begun this venture, the lives of all involved with the production had changed dramatically. On April 14, *Variety* described the lavish lifestyles of the show's creators, who were now firmly seated in the lap of luxury: "The four featured colored artists are in on the piece, and financial prosperity has been evidenced in a number of ways. Sissle and Blake, and Miller and Lyles, are the 'boys' getting a percentage weekly. All have motor cars, plus chauffeurs. This week Lyles appeared, sporting one of the fanciest watches ever flashed on the uptown belt. It is studded with diamonds and cost the comic $1,100. Sissle appears to be the businessman of the quartet. He has opened an auto accessory shop and a music store."

J. A. Jackson, who had been a strong supporter of *Shuffle Along* since word leaked that the four were collaborating, evaluated their banner year in *Billboard*, stating that the show "did what has been regarded as impossible. This colored-attraction has stayed in the metropolitan district on the sheer merit of its producers and its cast, overcoming the handicap of bad location, inadequate capitalization, and a management that was not entirely confident of the possibilities. In fact, the business management that sponsored the company added little to the assets of the artists. Nevertheless, they have succeeded." In addition to their unlikely success and the doors they opened for theatrical ventures, Jackson noted that the show had resulted in several "indirect benefits" for the race, including noticeable changing perceptions toward African American folks more generally, which was illustrated in the way hotel managers were becoming more welcoming of Black patrons and "destroying some previous opinions not so favorable to us."

The anniversary of *Shuffle Along*'s inception was cause to celebrate, particularly in the wake of the Black theater community experiencing yet another prominent loss. Bert Williams, who had been instrumental with George Walker at breaking barriers for Black performers onstage, had died a few months earlier on March 4 after a bout of pneumonia and a blood transfusion to which he'd failed to respond. Just a few days earlier, the comedian collapsed onstage in Detroit, Michigan, during a production of the musical comedy *Under the Bamboo Tree*. The audience thought Williams's fall was part of the show until the comedian had to be assisted to his dressing room. "That's a nice way to die," he said as he walked backstage. "They was laughing when I made my last exit." The performer was brought back to New York but never made a successful recovery. While he was a blackface comedian, Williams was disappointed in the continuing state of race relations in the United States, and on his deathbed, he wrote to a friend in what would be his final correspondence, reflecting on his life and ruminating on the future he was certain he wouldn't live to see.

"I was thinking about all the honors that are showered my way at the theatre. How everyone wishes to shake my hand and get an autograph. A real hero, you'd naturally think," he wrote. "However, when I reached [*sic*] my hotel, I am refused permission to ride the passenger elevator, cannot enter the dining room for my meals, and am Jim Crowed generally. But Bill, I'm not complaining particularly since I know this is an unbelievable custom. I am just wondering. I'd like to know when ultimate changes come and those persons I meet at the theatre eliminate through education and common decency the kind that run such establishments what will happen. I wonder if the new human beings will believe such persons as I am writing you about actually lived."

Bert Williams and Eubie Blake were well acquainted—the pianist lived just a few doors down for a period of time after he moved to Harlem from Baltimore—and had a mutual respect for each other, both professionally and personally. "I think if Bert Williams had lived, I might sometime have done a show with him. It would have been a good show and a great honor. He was a great artist and a great man," Blake said. "He was a man who liked to see everybody do good. When our show was such a big hit, he [was] just as happy as if it was his show... He did a lot for our people. If it wasn't for him and Jim Europe, I don't know where Negroes in show business would be today. I wish everybody would understand that."

Bert Williams received a hero's send-off, while the state of Black theater in New York continued to change. While *Put and Take* stumbled in trying to replicate the *Shuffle Along* formula with a full all-colored musical revue a year earlier, by the summer of 1922, more white producers were taking their shot at replicating what was happening at the Sixty-Third Street Theatre. The previous Broadway season had been the worst on record, leading more producers to exploit not only the trend of Black theatrical entertainment but also the performers themselves, whom they could hire at cut rates. "Just now there is much bidding for Negro talent in New York," J. A. Jackson wrote in *Variety*. "As a consequence, there is a lot of unethical methods being used to secure talent with name value or with especially strong personality."

And while most of the Black dancers who had come to New York in search of stardom were not well-known, especially to white audiences, their value to white producers— and white shows—was frequently noted in the press. "Many of our more legitimate chorus sisters could get lessons in 'ginger' by attending a performance of *Shuffle Along* and watching the sprightliness of its Creole belles," Elmer J. Walters wrote in *Billboard*. Alan Dale also called special attention to the attributes of the *Shuffle Along* chorus in his review for the *New York American*, noting how those traits were absent in Midtown. "At times it seemed as though nothing would stop the chorus from singing and dancing except bringing down the curtain," he wrote. "They reveled in their work; they simply pulsed with it, and there was no let-up at all. And gradually any tired feeling you might have been nursing vanished in the sun of their good humor and you didn't mind how they 'shuffled along.' You even felt like shuffling a bit with them. All of which I admit isn't usual in dear old Forty-second street."

For their part, the creators of *Shuffle Along* were pleased with the amount of attention the young women of the chorus were receiving. Never before had female dancers moved so enthusiastically onstage or been praised for their talent and not just their looks, which was a testament not only to the cast but also to those who selected them. "Such girls are hard to find," Flournoy Miller said. "But it pays to search for them, because you can get more work out of them and they dance better and more gracefully than older girls. I have often heard people remark of the work these girls do in our company and wonder how they can stand it. Why, if people only knew, the Happy Honeysuckle girls in *Shuffle Along* with several entire changes of costume to make and as many different dancing specialties, complain most of the time of not being kept busy."

While finding top-tier chorus dancers was hard work, many producers gave it a try. One of the most ambitious attempts was *Strut, Miss Lizzie*, a Black revue by Henry Creamer and J. Turner Layton, Black songwriters who scored a foxtrot hit with a song of the same name, which began a three-week engagement on June 19, 1922, at the Times Square Theatre on West Forty-Second. Like *Plantation Revue* and *Bandanaland*, the two-act musical revue was once again set below the Mason-Dixon line. The cast featured four African American female leads, coined "high brown babies," and twenty-two chorines, with Jack Pulaski of *Variety* noting that they were "all of light tan" complexion, except for one, Alice Brown, who was "a blue-eyed, high brown." In the first number, "Dear Old Southland," an adolescent returns home from up north to take his mammy to New York, explaining to her that this is "a colored year on Broadway."

That sentiment was echoed a week later in *Ziegfeld Follies of 1922*, which presented what Noble Sissle described as "glorified minstrelsy with girls." Florenz Ziegfeld's annual revue regularly showcased conventionally beautiful white women; however, recognizing the changing face of Manhattan's theater scene, a different sort of number materialized in June 1922. The main attraction in the show was Gilda Gray, a performer who rose to prominence when she began performing in New York City in 1919, the year she claimed to originate the shimmy. The Austria-Hungary native took to the stage in a white lace costume that, by way of a lighting trick, could make her skin appear dark brown in an instant. She was accompanied by sixteen white female dancers, similarly dressed, who all performed an eccentric buck dance, while she sang "It's Getting Dark on Old Broadway":

> *It's getting very dark on old Broadway,*
> *You see the change in ev'ry cabaret;*
> *Just like an eclipse of the moon,*
> *Ev'ry café now has the dancing coon.*
> *Pretty chocolate babies,*
> *Shake and shimmie ev'rywhere.*
> *Real darktown entertainers hold the stage,*
> *You must black up to be the latest rage.*
> *Yes, the great white way is white no more,*
> *It's just like a street on a Swanee shore;*
> *It's getting very dark on old Broadway.*

Although this was the sixteenth installment of Florenz Ziegfeld's famous *Follies*, it was the first to bear what would become his standard slogan, "Glorifying the American Girl," making Gilda Gray's number all the more curious. By decrying the changing state of Broadway, were audiences to understand that African American shows were undeserving of accolades and Black female performers not sufficiently American? The number was an enormous hit, singled out in nearly every print review for the show, but it almost appeared very differently onstage. The original concept was for Gray to dance alongside sixteen Black chorus dancers, but they were fired during the rehearsal process. "It was figured that the idea of this ditty, which tells of the 'invasion' of the cabaret field by the colored performer, would not jibe with chorus girls of that type in the show," Gordon Whyte wrote in *Billboard*. "They were given two weeks' salary and dismissed."

It wasn't just the look of Broadway that was changing, it was also the sound. *Shuffle Along* was revolutionary in bringing syncopation to the stage, fusing jazz with operatic musical theater elements. However, a year later, a score that once was novel was quickly becoming the template for the industry standard, with one reporter noting that on Broadway, "jazz crowded out the Viennese waltz." However, while a few noted the impact of Black artists—specifically musicians Noble Sissle and Eubie Blake—most white Broadway composers failed to acknowledge where they had drawn inspiration from in the year since *Shuffle Along* opened. "The Negro has made such a thorough job of nationalizing our music," Blake said, "that he himself had been forgotten."

As Gilda Gray won raves in *Follies of 1922*, Sissle and Blake were helping to pioneer a revolutionary development in the film industry. Inventor Lee de Forest had patented an innovative process, which he called Phonofilm, that allowed for electronic waves to be optically printed photographically onto film so that when it was played using special equipment, audiences could enjoy synchronous sound and moving images. A half decade before the first "all-talking" feature would hit cinemas, de Forest had come up with the technology. Sissle and Blake consented to being filmed for his experimental venture, along with several other performers, with each act having their own time in front of cameras, making them the first Black artists to be part of a moving, talking, and singing picture.

The filming took place at a theater in Manhattan—Eubie Blake recalled it being the Metropolitan Opera House, although later in his life, he wasn't completely sure—where they performed "Affectionate Dan," which was typically the second song in their vaudeville act after "Gee! I'm Glad That I'm from Dixie." The duo decided to perform that number, as it was a high-energy ditty that captured the audience's attention. But while it was exciting to take part in this great experiment, Sissle and Blake found the experience a bit stifling. "This was the first time we worked in front of a camera, and in those days they couldn't move the camera around on wheels or turn it every way, so naturally it couldn't follow you," Blake explained. "That didn't bother me too much because I'm sittin' at the piano anyway, I ain't goin' nowhere. But Sissle, he's all over the stage, see. If he has to just stand still and sing, it's just real hard for him to do that. He's an *actor*, and that cramps his style. So when you see the film—and if you know how he is the rest of the time—you can see he's not up to his best.

"Another thing," he continued. "If you play to a theater audience, you have to learn how to stage smile. Now that means you show your teeth. The audience is too far away to see if you're laughin' or cryin' or if you *really* look sad. But if those people out there see teeth, they're satisfied. Now if you do the stage smile and the camera is eight feet away, then when the films come out your stage smile looks like a Hallowe'en mask. The audience can see you're not happy at all if you're not. You can't hide *nothin'* from that camera. So me and Sissle don't look natural in that film. We sound real good. There ain't nothin' fake about the sound. At the time I didn't think too much about the whole thing, but then as time went on I realized that we made show-business history that day. The first Negro act in talking pictures! The first film music!"

It would take until April 15, 1923, for an audience to see their short movie, but in the interim, their bread and butter, *Shuffle Along*, was losing steam. The number two touring company was still doing respectable business in Brooklyn, but the weekly box office returns at the Sixty-Third Street Theatre had slipped to just over $6,000 by June 16, 1922. The main cast was booked for a two-week engagement at Boston's beautiful Selwyn Theatre the following month, and while John and Harry Cort had thought the show might continue running in New York with a different cast, when they had to resort to selling two-for-one tickets to keep the house full on Sixty-Third, it seemed the show's days were numbered. To make matters worse, just as the cast and crew prepared to change their focus toward their forthcoming Massachusetts run, William Hann, the deep-voiced Harmony King, became ill and had to leave the show. By chance, Ivan Harold Browning, another member of the quartet, ran into his old acquaintance Paul Robeson on the streets of New York just after Hann began his temporary leave. Browning thought his old pal would make a perfect replacement, and after floating the idea up the chain and just one rehearsal, the Harmony Kings gained a new interim member.

Robeson was a native of Princeton, New Jersey, who gained national attention after he became the third Black student to enroll at the state's Rutgers University in 1915, which he attended on a football scholarship. He ultimately became an All-American athlete while at the school, and his proficiency at the game earned him a write-up as one of the "Men of the Month" in the NAACP's *The Crisis* magazine in March 1918. In addition to sports, Robeson was also a bass soloist and informal member of the university's glee club, as formal membership would have required him to attend social events that were limited to white students. By the end of his undergraduate studies in 1919, he was elected valedictorian by his class, giving a speech that urged his white classmates to do their part to end racial disharmony and help unite the nation. "We of this less favored race realize that our future lies chiefly in our own hands," he said. "We know that neither institutions nor friends can make a race stand unless it has strength in its own foundation; that races like individuals must stand or fall by their own merit; that to fully succeed they must practice their virtues of self-reliance, self-respect, industry, perseverance, and economy. But in order for us to successfully do all these things it is necessary that you of the favored race catch a new vision and exemplify in your actions this new American spirit."

The graduate enrolled in New York Law School in the fall of 1919. After one semester, he moved to Harlem and transferred to Columbia but took a leave shortly thereafter to begin a career on the stage, first in *Simon the Cyrenian*, written by Ridgely Torrence, a white playwright who regularly wrote dramas for Black actors, then 1922's *Taboo*, a play by Mary Hoyt Wiborg, one of the city's white socialites, written for a primarily colored cast—there was one white actress—and set on a plantation in Louisiana. *Taboo* had just wrapped when Robeson and Browning reconnected, freeing the student up to join *Shuffle Along.*

However, while their chance meeting seemed to be a positive sign, Robeson's first moments at the Sixty-Third Street Theatre began disastrously. As he excitedly strode onto the stage with his straw hat and cane, he bent to get through a narrow doorway and tripped, knocking over the three other Harmony Kings in the process "like ninepins" with such a force that Eubie Blake feared Robeson was going to barrel on top of him into the orchestra pit. However, nearly as soon as each member of the quartet hit the deck, they each sprang back up, smiling as if nothing had happened, and proceeded with their set, assuring Blake that they had chosen a winner in casting Robeson. "That boy will bear watching," he said. "Anybody who can fall like that and come up with a million-dollar smile has got some personality!"

By July, William Hann had recuperated, Paul Robeson was on his way to Britain to appear in an overseas engagement of *Taboo*, and after 504 performances, *Shuffle Along* ended its triumphant and unprecedented run at the Sixty-Third Street Theatre. When it staged its final performance on the July 15, after having played for sixty weeks in Manhattan, the show was the longest-running musical attraction in the city. The African American musical's ability to last was made all the more impressive in comparison with its competition. While the previous Broadway season had been the worst on record, 1922 had been even worse. Noble

Sissle, Eubie Blake, Flournoy Miller, and Aubrey Lyles had much to be proud of and little time to reflect on their New York run. They'd made their mark on Manhattan. Now all they had to do was catch lightning in a bottle once again when they arrived in Boston next month.

THE SELWYN THEATRE IN BOSTON, 1922

Courtesy of the Maryland Center for History and Culture, Item ID #PP301.94

9

VAMPED BY
A BROWN SKIN

1922–1923

Although *Shuffle Along* had far exceeded expectations in Manhattan, there was no guarantee that it would play equally as well beyond city limits. "New York is a freak town which can take a freak show," big-name producers would say outside Manhattan. "But other towns won't go for it." While industry titans like the Shuberts and Abraham Lincoln Erlanger wouldn't book the show in their theaters, producer Arch Selwyn ultimately allowed the show to play his eponymous venue in Boston "when nobody else wanted it because of the stifling heat and no business," Noble Sissle explained.

Nevertheless, Selwyn did his part to ensure the city received *Shuffle Along* just as warmly. The illuminated protruding marquee that stretched out from the theater boasted that the show was "The Hit of the Season," while its smaller accompanying board placed the show's creators—MILLER AND LYLES, SISSLE AND BLAKE—in bright lights together for the first time. The side of the venue displayed a large billboard advertisement boldly displaying the show's title in large capital letters, with silhouettes of the show's stars—comedians in costume as the mayor and chief of police, the musicians at the piano in tuxedos—and pint-sized black figures of a dancing chorus between them.

Sissle and Blake went to the theater on the day the box office opened for advance tickets, excited to read the tea leaves of how they would fare, and they were amazed to see a long line of African American folks ready with cash in hand. It was a stark difference from the primarily white audiences they had been playing to since they'd embarked on their graveyard tour and through their run in New York. "The management was scared to death that the audience would be top-heavy with colored people," Eubie Blake recalled. However, after some inquiring, it turned out those patiently queued up were mostly maids and chauffeurs who had been sent out on an errand for their employers. It seemed like things were going to be about the same for *Shuffle Along* after all.

When the show opened on July 29, 1922, the company once again played to a largely white audience of theatergoers, and just as they had done in New York, the critics raved. "The power of syncopation, interpreted by those who delight in revealing its possibilities, is seen at its height. The best colored talent romps through choruses and dances while a joy-filled audience thunders its applause," the *Boston Globe* noted in its opening night review. "*Shuffle Along* is both novel and speedy, in fact, it is bursting with jazz and tunefulness. Dancers who seem no less than human dynamos and singers with voices of excellent quality maintain a spirited performance accompanied by a most efficient colored orchestra." The opening brought in $1,763—with only a $2 top ticket price—which quickly made the company local celebrities, especially within the Black community. On one day, Mrs. Butler Wilson, president of the Women's Service Club of Boston, the most exclusive organization for Black women in the nation, hosted a reception for the women of the cast, and that evening, a similar event was sponsored for the entire production team by Tom E. Lucas, a restaurateur whose establishment was the largest to be patronized by Blacks.

Arch Selwyn had booked the Shakespearean team of Sothern and Marlowe to come in after *Shuffle Along* concluded its two-week run, but with the show doing big business, its engagement was instead extended indefinitely. The proprietor devised a clever promotional stunt to help him move tickets for the added dates. Boston's mayor, James Michael Curley, had a flair for the theatrical and agreed to meet with the show's four writers for a photo opportunity. However, Flournoy Miller got cold feet about the meeting, sensing something wasn't completely on the level about it, and let Lyles, Sissle, and Blake go without him. When the trio arrived at the mayor's offices

NOBLE SISSLE, AUBREY LYLES, AN UNIDENTIFIED PERSON, AND EUBIE BLAKE WITH BOSTON MAYOR JAMES MICHAEL CURLEY (SEATED)

Photo by Egan-James Photography / Courtesy of Photographs and Prints Division, Schomburg Center for Research and Black Culture, The New York Public Library

in sharp business suits, neckties, and pocket squares, looking as politick as possible, Curley was upset and asked, "Where's the mayor?" Somehow the plan hadn't been fully communicated to the performers, but the goal was to have Boston's mayor and Jimtown's mayor—since Miller played Steve Jenkins—be photographed meeting. The other three took turns fabricating excuses for their partner's absence, and when Miller saw the photo in the paper, he realized he had made a mistake. He went down to city hall by himself and, in a sharp brown double-breasted suit, was presented an oversize key to the city, from one mayor to another, as Curley had typically done when municipal leaders visited.

Boston's mayor wasn't the only notable white figure who wanted face time with the show's creators. Jack Dempsey, the boxing heavyweight champion of the world, happened into a controversy while he was in Boston, because his manager, Ted Rickard, refused to let him fight Harry Wills, who was Black and largely perceived to be his most worthy challenger for the title. The champ was accused of having racist motivations for not boxing Wills, which Dempsey maintained couldn't have been further from the truth. After he attended a performance of *Shuffle Along*, the boxer went backstage and asked to borrow a minute of Sissle, Blake, Miller, and Lyles's time. Dempsey shyly acknowledged that he was aware of the controversy in which he was entangled but assured the men that race had nothing to do with why he and Wills weren't going to square off. The boxer asked if he could accompany the quartet to a forthcoming benefit they were appearing at as a sign of solidarity. It wasn't clear if Dempsey was being sincere or was simply doing damage control, but the performers were happy to have him tag along either way.

The show's creators were aware of the potential they had to play a part in healing the country's racial divide. At one performance in Boston, a woman who Eubie Blake recognized as being "socially very prominent" took her front row seat, and when the orchestra entered the pit, she was aghast. "Great heavens," she said to her neighbor, clearly not realizing exactly what she had bought tickets for. "We are at a Colored show." Blake heard the woman, but instead of taking offense, he put his game face on. "I paid no attention, but considered it a challenge for me to do everything that I could that evening to conduct as spiritedly as possible," he said. "I wanted a particularly good performance." Blake did his best, and thanks to his extra efforts, the first act was flawless.

During intermission, the woman beckoned to him. "Did you hear what I said when you first came in?" she asked.

Blake shook his head.

"Honestly?"

He shook his head again to assure her that he hadn't.

"If you did, I want to apologize for it," she said. "And if you did or if you didn't, I want to tell you that I have never enjoyed myself more in a single evening in the theater. I admire what you, your partner, and everyone else in the company has done tonight and I want to say so."

"Now, strange as it may appear to you, that whole evening made me very happy," Eubie Blake explained to a journalist after the fact. "My partner and I had done something that we have been endeavoring to do and which we shall continue to endeavor to do. We had made at least one prejudiced person not of our Race think a little more kindly of the American Colored entertainer."

Although the main company had been performing together for over a year—save for the occasional casting change—they were still in need of a tune-up every now and then. Revella Hughes, a Black soprano vocalist who had just made her stage debut in the ironically named flop *Dumb Luck*, was hired during the Boston run as a vocal coach. "The production had small problems, and kinks had crept in that needed straightening out," she said. "They needed someone qualified to help with the choral work and the other preparation." Every Monday at 1:00 p.m., the full cast reported for rehearsal, with Hughes paid $150 a week to not only correct vocals but also serve as a pseudo stage manager. "I did not do anything in the show, but I was supposed to see that everybody did their part," she explained. "I had to be sure that everybody made their cues because they didn't have all the marvelous sound system[s] like they have now. The kids had to stand in the wings to back the soloists."

Flournoy Miller also ran dance rehearsals for the chorus, who knew they had to work twice as hard to maintain their reputation as the best movers on the legitimate stage. On one occasion, Miller was "drilling the company in parts of the performance in which they had been getting careless" until he finally realized he was being too hard on them. He excused them so they could return to their hotel and rest up for the evening's performance, but after about fifteen minutes, he realized there were eight of the young women on the side of the stage, working through the steps by themselves and correcting one another's errors. Miller once again told them to leave, but they were equally insistent. "O, yes sir," one of the dancers said. "We heard you, but we like to rehearse better than anything else, and if you have no objection, and we don't bother you too much, we will stay here and practice a little."

Just as in New York, the Boston press raved about the dancers, particularly "one of the unique sights of the year, a chorus girl who literally 'walks off with the show' in several instances, not by mere beauty—as has been done—but by her comedy dancing." While she wasn't mentioned by name, the journalist was referring to sixteen-year-old Josephine Baker, who had managed to become part of the cast after having been turned down a year earlier in Philadelphia. She'd boarded a train for New York shortly after her negative experience with Noble Sissle at the Dunbar, but once she arrived, she was even more destitute than before she'd left. Once *Shuffle Along* opened and the critics crowned it a winner, Baker went to visit her old classmate Wilsie Caldwell at the stage door. She had slept on park benches the previous two nights and her cheeks were sunken in, a far cry from the spry girl Wilsie had seen just a month or so earlier. She and her brother insisted that Baker move into their small rented apartment. The vagabond in search of a stage agreed, but while the Caldwells were looking to help her out, Josephine only had one thing on her mind: "Is Mr. Sissle any nicer?"

"He's thrilled to death, Josephine! The show is so successful that they're forming a touring company. Cities all over the country are asking for bookings." Then Wilsie Caldwell had an idea. "Why don't you talk to him again?"

Baker agreed to try out for *Shuffle Along* a second time, and on this occasion, she was seen by Al Mayer instead. She walked into the meeting with her face coated with the lightest shade of powdered foundation she could find, and when the show's manager took one look at her, history nearly repeated itself. "Too young, too skinny," he said, prompting Wilsie to interject quickly, "What about hiring her as a dresser?" Baker had already said she didn't want to help out backstage when she and Wilsie had this conversation in Philadelphia, but her friend was adamant that this was the best way to get a foot in the door. "At least it'll keep you going for a while," she said. "The thing to do is to learn all the songs and dance steps. Someone is sure to get sick."

Baker joined in with the touring company, unsnapping buttons, brushing the young women's hair, fastening skirts, and secretly praying that someone would get sick. *Lord, I'm not asking for anything dramatic,* she prayed at night, *but please do something!* A few days later, her prayers were answered. One of the chorines, who had been hiding a pregnancy, became sick shortly before the curtain, and Baker, realizing the dancer would be out of the show for at least four months, sweet-talked her way onto the stage. "If it's any help, I know all the songs and dances," she told the road manager. Within minutes, she was put into a costume and out onstage, where she had wanted to be for over a year. "When I saw those watching faces a giddiness swept over me," she recalled. "I let the music carry me away." The night had been everything she had dreamed of, until she returned backstage and found that none of the other dancers would speak to her. "She stole the show with her stupid faces," one of the lead actresses told the road manager. "Get rid of her. It's her or me." He acquiesced to the ultimatum and said he'd get a replacement for her in the morning.

Just as easily as opportunity came, it went. Baker had squandered her chance. She wrapped herself in an old dressing gown and stayed the night curled up in one of the theater's box seats until she was woken up the next morning by the manager. "On your feet, girl," he said, waving a newspaper under her nose. "Listen to what the critics say!" He proceeded to read the reviews of the previous night's performance—A revelation! Unique sense of rhythm! A born comic! Baker wasn't sure why she was getting credit for the notices until he got to the final one: "It's impossible to take your eyes off the little cross-eyed girl." She knew the steps well enough, but during the show, she had made funny faces at the other girls and put her own interpretation on all the moves.

In a chorus of standout dancers, she made it a point to stand out the most. Baker stayed with the show, and as they continued to tour, it became common to hear patrons at the box office ask if "the little cross-eyed girl" was performing that evening.

It wasn't exactly stardom—Baker was still just a silly face in the crowd—but it was a start. However, although she earned accolades from the audience, the rest of the dancers were furious with the show's latest headline grabber. To them, she wasn't Josephine but "Monkey," and on one occasion, one of the other girls tripped her while they were making their entrance for a number. Baker comically nose-dived onto the deck, sending the audience into a fit of laughter and applause and the backstage bully into a fit of anger that her plan had backfired. Ultimately, the mistreatment became so bad that the teenager bucked the dressing room altogether, opting to change her clothes in the bathroom alone instead. Just as things seemed like they couldn't get worse, Baker learned that Sissle, Blake, Miller, and Lyles wanted her to join the main company in Boston. "Word got back to us that a comedy chorus girl joined the company after we had rehearsed it and sent it on the road," Noble Sissle recalled. "She had slipped out on the road to join that company because she thought we didn't like her or want to hire her. How glad we were to get her back." She packed her bag and boarded a train to New York, where she was greeted by Wilsie Caldwell at the station: "Who would have thought you'd upstage us all!"

When the young performer arrived in Boston, she was at a loss for words when she ran into Noble Sissle again. He remembered her well, and sensing her discomfort, he attempted to break the ice. "Miss Baker, do you know why I didn't hire you last year in Philadelphia?"

She knew, mumbling, "Too small, too thin, too dark."

"No. Too *young*. It's against the law to employ anyone under sixteen in New York." Sissle hadn't believed her when she claimed to be seventeen years old at her first audition, but he said that since the age requirement was just a state law, she was free to join them on the road. What he hadn't realized was that it wouldn't have mattered either way, as Baker's birthday had just passed and she was now fully legal to join the company wherever their itinerary took them. "She had such a wonderful disposition," Eubie Blake recalled, "and kept us in stitches off the stage as well as on."

Baker was excited for the fresh start and quickly befriended a few of the young women, including Fredi Washington, an eighteen-year-old who was making her stage debut in *Shuffle Along*. She was born in Savannah, Georgia, to parents who were both of African American and European descent, and she had ivory-colored skin, finely textured wavy hair, green eyes, and facial features that were somewhere between ethnically ambiguous and "anything but Black." Her mother died when she was eleven, her father remarried, and by 1921, she was living with her grandmother and aunt, who had relocated to Harlem as part of the Great Migration. She was working as a bookkeeper at Black Swan Record Company, which was owned by African American musician W. C. Handy, when she heard that *Shuffle Along* was auditioning dancers for a national tour in advance of their first stop in Boston.

Fredi knew how to dance—it was something she'd learned

from her mother, who used to perform professionally—and she figured she had nothing to lose by trying out. "It wasn't that I wanted to get into show business," she explained. "But somebody told me they were paying more to chorus girls than I was making as a bookkeeper." Not only had she never thought about being onstage, she had never stepped foot in a theater before she auditioned for the musical comedy. "I had never seen a play or show until I went into *Shuffle Along*," she said. "I had never had lipstick on until that day, I knew nothing about makeup, and I bought everything they told me I needed and I proceeded to put it on. I looked like a clown." Luckily another chorine, Maude Russell, saw her bright-eyed, helpless, painted face and took Fredi under her wing: "I got to get this off you and make you look human." Although she couldn't sing and wasn't particularly funny, Fredi moved well enough to claim a spot among the *Shuffle Along* main company for its Boston run, where she and Baker hit it off immediately.

With her moxie that could be seen from a mile away, it didn't take long before Josephine Baker also caught the eye of Lottie Gee. The teenage firecracker didn't shy away from her ambition—she was determined to be a star and she didn't see any benefit in keeping that a secret—and the lead in *Shuffle Along* believed Baker's goals were more than just pipedreams. Gee became her mentor, which likely resulted in more than a few side eyes from Baker's colleagues in the chorus, and the young performer soon amended her goal: she didn't just want to be a star, she wanted to be as much like Lottie Gee as possible. The two developed a friendship that would last decades, and even though their lives would go on to take very separate paths, Baker would never forget the support Gee gave her, especially when she was at one of her lowest points emotionally.

However, for the most part, Josephine Baker's treatment by the main company was no better than what she had previously experienced on the road. In some ways, it was worse. She had deliberately chosen to pull focus on the stage, doing comical variations of the choreography, crossing her legs and her beautifully expressive eyes—all to the delight of the audience and annoyance of her chorus colleagues. Most of the other young women saw the young standout as an uneducated and uncultured showboat who was getting by on silliness, not skill, and they'd find ways to get into petty arguments with her backstage. On one occasion, some of the choral clique took it upon themselves to evict her from their shared dressing room at the Selwyn. "That's where I blew my top," Fredi Washington said. "All her stuff was in the hallway, and I knew exactly what had happened. All those girls thought they were a big deal and looked down on Josephine, who was so much darker." Fredi stormed into the changing space, mad as hell, screaming at the top of her lungs to everyone and no one in particular: "Who told you you own this dressing room? You go and get her stuff!" And to her surprise, they did.

While Josephine Baker's treatment based on the color of her skin was cruel, in a lot of ways, it was the result of a systemic culture of colorism that emanated from the top. It was an open secret that *Shuffle Along* hired only young women who would pass the brown paper bag test—as in their complexions were lighter than a brown paper bag—for the chorus, and even among those who made the cut, those who were more of a bronze skin tone were often relegated to singing from the wings offstage. "Talk about discrimination," Katherine Yarborough, a member of the company who was an operatic soprano vocalist, said. "I had that beautiful voice, but I was too black to be onstage." Black author Claude McKay, writing in the socialist *Liberator* magazine, expressed his displeasure with the chorines' nearly monochromatic palette prior to Josephine Baker joining the main company. "The ensemble is a little disappointing and lacking in harmony. Instead of making up to achieve a uniform near-white complexion, the chorus might have made up to accentuate the diversity of shades among 'Afro-Americans,' and let the white audience in on the secret of the color nomenclature of the Negro world," he wrote. "For, as whites have their blonde and brunette, so do the blacks have their chocolate, chocolate-to-the-bone, brown, low-brown, teasing-brown, high-brown, yellow, high-yellow, and so on. The difference on our side is so much more interesting and funny.

"It is whispered in some circles that the 'Blue-vein' [fair-complexioned Blacks who climbed the social ladder by passing as whites] Societies among the Afro-American elite bar the black girls from the stage," he continued. "There is a dearth of black girls in Negro theatricals whose presence would surely give more distinction and realism to the stage. I believe that the colored actors prefer the lighter-skinned girls. The latter are vivacious, pushing, and pretty, but prettiness is always plentiful, while beauty is rare and hard to find. If black

men in general favor the lighter women of their race, it is a
natural phenomenon beyond criticism... Still, despite this fact,
Negro artists ought not to ignore the variety of the material
at hand."

Skin color was clearly on the minds of the show's four
creators before the casting process was underway, not only by
their decision to have the "ignoramus" comedic characters appear
in blackface but also by including "If You've Never Been Vamped
by a Brown Skin," a sprightly number that is the centerpiece of
one of the show's ancillary plot points. In the second act, Jimtown
mayor Steve Jenkins, played by Flournoy Miller, asks Police Chief
Sam Peck, played by Aubrey Lyles—in full Southern dialect—to
"tell dem 'bout old Deacon Birch and dat brown skin vamp down
de court de other day. Dey ain't heard no scandal!" Peck recounts,
in song, that the church official's wife had caught him being
adulterous. However, while the deacon didn't deny the charges, he
explained to the judge that he couldn't be found guilty of anything
because he couldn't help himself. Then he pled his case:

> If you've never been vamped by a brown skin,
> You've never been vamped at all,
> For the vampingest vamp is a brown skin.
> Believe me now, that ain't no stall.
> A high brown gal will make you break out of jail,
> A choc'late brown will make a tadpole smack
>   a whale,
> But a pretty sealskin brown, I mean one long
>   and tall,

Would make the silent Sphinx out in the desert
brawl.
If you've never been vamped by a brown skin,
You've never been vamped at all.

The comedic, high-energy number always went over well, even though white and Black audience members may have interpreted the song differently. It is likely the former saw the number as being about a binary choice between a Black woman and white woman, while African American folks probably picked up on the song's true implications: darker-skinned women were seen as sexually hungry jezebels—the vampingest vamps—and even good church elders would be forgiven for succumbing to their powers of persuasion.

It's impossible to know whether the *Shuffle Along* chorines were primarily of a fair complexion because that was considered most acceptable—or desirable—to white audiences or if the show's creators truly did have a "color complex." Either way, the young ladies in the cast garnered a great deal of attention, including among themselves. "We girls would share a room because of the cost," Maude Russell, the member of the chorus who fixed Fredi Washington's bad makeup job, explained. "Well, many of us had been kind of abused by producers, directors, leading men—if they liked girls. In those days, men only wanted what they wanted. They didn't care about pleasing a girl, and girls needed tenderness, so we had girl friendships—the famous lady lovers. But lesbians weren't accepted in show business, they were called 'bull dykers.' I guess we were bisexual, is what you would call it today." Among the clandestine trysts offstage, Josephine Baker frequently enjoyed the company of one colleague in particular. "She was crazy about [chorus girl] Evelyn Sheppard," Russell continued. "I didn't think she was gay, she got around with too many men, but she didn't talk about those things."

Outside their own squad, the young women of the cast also received extra attention from Eubie Blake, who freely admitted to enjoying the chorines for more than their singing and dancing abilities. "I always did like pretty girls," he recalled. "Men always liked dancin' girls, even back in Bible days. You can look it up. I'm not gonna tell you I didn't do my share of playin' around—in fact, almost every time I ever got the chance—but I really wasn't no ladies' man like [band member William Grant] Still and Sissle. The girls would just hang around them. And remember, when I made it to Broadway, I was a lot older than those guys.

"No man can resist," he continued. "You meet a Josephine Baker in her prime, you know she's a *girl*. That's the first thing you notice. If that ain't the first thing you notice you need to see a doctor. Valaida Snow, Adelaide Hall, Florence Mills. They got the whole city of

NOBLE SISSLE (SEATED) AND CHORINES IN A PUBLICITY STILL FOR *SHUFFLE ALONG*, 1921

Courtesy of the Maryland Center for History and Culture, Item ID #PP301.2

New York excited, so how ain't they gonna get me excited? How can you resist 'em if you know 'em face to face?"

While the quartet who created *Shuffle Along* all had wives, it's likely that only Flournoy Miller and Aubrey Lyles remained faithful on the road. Noble Sissle may have been more covert about his extramarital affairs, but Eubie Blake wasn't particularly shy about admitting to his infidelity, chalking his wild oat–sowing to being a rudimentary aspect of what people in show business do. "Eubie would pore over pictures of *Shuffle Along*, recalling the chorus girls he slept with," a friend of his explained. "He would just point with his finger—'This one, this one, this one.'" And while the ladies on the line might have temporarily served as the object of his infatuation, the musician was genuinely enamored with the show's star, Lottie Gee. The two met in Baltimore in 1911 when she was performing at Ford's Theatre with an act called Two Indian Girls. They didn't keep in touch, but the pianist kept tabs on her career, and when she joined the company of *Shuffle Along* a decade later, things sparked during rehearsals. Blake put her up in an apartment, and the two began a semicovert relationship that would last a decade. "I guess I have to say I was smitten," he recalled. "When I was at a party and she was there, she acted like she barely knew me. Called me 'Mr. Blake' because, of course, nobody is supposed to know I'm livin' with her, see. But she never came near me in public. Alone though, she called me 'Daddy.'"

Throughout this period Eubie and Avis Blake remained happily married, frequently speaking of having children together. He divided his time between both the women in his life, and while he was "smitten" with Lottie Gee, he never professed to be in love with her. "I never bought her a thing," he says. "I put a piano in her house, but just so I can teach her the new songs." In contrast, Eubie made sure Avis knew where she stood in the pecking order. On one occasion, a friend of hers stopped by their lavish apartment to let her know what Eubie had been up to. "Avis, that niggah you married to, he got an apartment for a chippie in his show," the friend said. "An' that niggah goes up there to be wit' her every day. You might be a saint, Avis. You shouldn't have to put up with a niggah like that."

After listening to the report, a knowing smile came over Avis's face. "Honey, you see that li'l ol' box on the vanity? Just go over there and open it." Inside, there were diamonds and emeralds. "My husband, that no-good niggah, gave me those. Now, baby, will you just slide open that closet door and count the fur coats?" There were several, and Avis proudly gave the rundown of the inventory, gesturing toward each one—mink, sable, beaver, fox. "That niggah gave me all those things. Now, tonight, after the show is over, where do you think that niggah's goin'? He's coming right back here where he goes every night and"—with a point toward their boudoir—"gets into that bed next to *this* niggah.

"Kitten, what are you going to do in the morning?" Avis asked her friend—it was a weekday. Her friend was going to go to work. "Not me, kiddo," Avis said, her lighthearted attitude giving way to smugness. "I'm stayin' right here in bed until I feel like gettin' up. That no-good niggah husband of mine bought me those jewels and those furs. He takes care of me so I don't have to lift a finger. I don't have a maid, because I don't want one around, but I've got a car and a chauffeur. I can't drive, you know. And I'm gonna worry what that no-good niggah might be doin' behind my back? No, Gal, you need to get *you* a low-down cheater like my Eubie."

For Lottie's part, sharing Eubie Blake was difficult, even though she knew what she was getting into when she and the musician had taken up with one another. She had a history of mental illness and struggled with coping mechanisms, and while Blake filled certain voids in her life, in other ways, he exacerbated her issues. Lottie Gee freely admitted to being jealous and insecure—despite her strong exterior, Avis often felt the same—and she regularly self-medicated with alcohol. She often received the attention of other men while in New York and on the road, as she was talented, beautiful, and the star of a hit show, but in her heart, Eubie Blake was her man. She just wasn't able to have him all to herself.

However, even though Blake's affections were divided, when they were on the road away from Avis, who remained in Harlem, Lottie Gee found it easier to pretend he was all hers. Although it was only scheduled to stay two weeks, *Shuffle Along* lasted at the Selwyn for fifteen, earning an average of $14,500 a week while playing to capacity audiences, with hundreds turned away at the box office most days. It had been announced that the show was headed to Chicago next—"We had to jump all the way [there because] nobody else would take us," Eubie Blake said—but as its run in Boston was indefinitely extended, their engagement at the Windy City's Olympic Theatre continued to be pushed back as well. Despite the reasonable explanation, word began to spread within the Black community that the show's producers were having trouble securing bookings in legitimate theaters, due to prejudicial theater owners. Much had been written of the show's initial struggles to secure a proper venue in Manhattan—having to settle instead for the Sixty-Third Street Theatre—and their inability to find investors for proper sets and costumes. The show had already secured its legacy as being culturally significant, but while *Shuffle Along* was demonstrating its value on a nightly basis with two different touring companies, many Black folks across the nation felt Sissle, Blake, Miller, and Lyles were still working twice as hard to get half as far.

W. E. B. Du Bois addressed the controversy in a straightforward and scathing editorial in the September 1922 issue of the NAACP's *The Crisis*, where he took issue with the white gatekeepers who he felt were actively preventing the show from reaching its zenith. "For a solid year colored artists have maintained on Broadway, New York, one of the cleanest, tunefulest, and cleverest variety shows ever given," he began. "We accuse white America of prejudice, and God knows it has aplenty. But worse than the prejudice is the ignorance. White folk hate and discriminate because they do not realize or know. When they do know they become usually honest, sympathetic human souls. Thousands of them were prejudiced against 'nigger shows,' but when they had a chance to see *Shuffle Along*, they applauded generously. The real devils in America are those who deny the mass of white folk any opportunity of forming real honest judgment concerning Negroes. They stretch a veil of untruth and ignorance.

"These monopolists have determined that *Shuffle Along* shall not be permitted to play in their theaters in the United States," he continued. "One was very frank: 'No, you can't play in any of our theaters. We'll take Miller and Lyles and let them write their own comedy, but they must play in a white company. We are not going to have any colored women on the stage.' The other company was not so plain, but equally firm: 'No, the manager has not decided to book you. I do not know the reason!' And this for one of the greatest theatrical successes of the season... Two attempts to secure independent theatres in Chicago have failed because of threats against managers by the trust... Thus Monopoly aids Ignorance to manufacture Prejudice. And thus this stupid land shuffles along."

Theophilus Lewis, a Black drama critic for *The Messenger*, A. Philip Randolph and Chandler Owen's social and cultural magazine, agreed with Du Bois's sentiment. He was a staunch believer in the power of theater to bring about social change, and as he saw it, the only way Black folks would truly succeed on that front was by forming their own entertainment enterprises and cutting out the gatekeepers—a difficult but worthwhile task. "Without economic autonomy, the Negro stage can never become the flexible medium for the expression of the spirit of Negro people it ought to be," he wrote.

As Black thought leaders debated in print about the best way for performers of the race to most effectively influence the American public, Sissle, Blake, Miller, and Lyles proceeded to Chicago, where critics declared that "*Shuffle Along* is the Negro 'Lightnin'!" and "Any Caucasian producer who achieves an ensemble of such spirit and abandon would regard it as a triumph." During one performance, it was noted that the company responded to twenty-three requests for encores before intermission, causing the show to end close to midnight. After a barn-burning fifteen weeks, the main company brought the house down in Milwaukee, Des Moines, Peoria, and Indianapolis. Their next stop was St. Louis.

Long after she appeared in *Shuffle Along*, Josephine Baker recalled their trek through her hometown. After the company arrived on a snowy day in December, she hailed a taxi to her family's home on Bernard Street, on the wrong side of town for a young woman dressed in a fur coat and earning $30 a week. When she arrived home, the living conditions were worse than she could have imagined. The house was filled with boarders, and there was no electricity—kerosene lamps provided the lighting—a communal washtub, and dirty dishes hidden underneath the bed. Her family believed their little girl had become a star, and Baker did little to dissuade them. It wasn't until Christmas Eve that things went south. "I was at the theater tonight," her mother said, and before the teenager could ask how she enjoyed the show, Baker felt her mother's hand rush across her face so hard and fast, she thought her neck would break. "My own flesh and blood up there with naked women!"

"But, Mama, they're not naked! All you can see is their legs."

"And everything else!" Her mother rushed off crying while Baker was left confused and upset. However, the next day, with the encouragement of the rest of her family, in the spirit of Christmas, the teenager forgave and forgot what had transpired the night before.

However, while Baker's recounting was vivid, it was likely also fictitious. She was the consummate performer ever since she was a young girl, a characteristic that only grew once she reached adulthood, and since the *Shuffle Along* company didn't arrive in St. Louis until March 1923, it's difficult to tell exactly how much truth—if any—her anecdote contains. ("I don't lie," she once famously said. "I improve on life.") Instead, Adelaide Hall, a friend of Baker who had been in the chorus since the show's earliest days, recalled a different story altogether. Carrie McDonald, Baker's mother, never saw her daughter perform because when *Shuffle Along* arrived in St. Louis, the young dancer took an unexpected—and unexplained—temporary leave. Carrie went to the theater one day after a show, and as the performers were gathering their belongings to leave, she shyly asked to see Baker. The woman looked as if she had seen better days, and after telling her that the young dancer wasn't there, Adelaide gave Carrie a $5 bill. "I'm sure Josephine would want me to give you this," she said. "It's just a little something to help you get home safely. In fact, I know she'd want you to have it." With a half smile at the gesture, the mother embarrassingly accepted the offering.

However, whether Josephine Baker was in the show or not, the *Shuffle Along* company sustained its streak of success while in Missouri, where critics remained surprised at how contemporary the colored show felt. "*Shuffle Along* is scarcely a negro show at all; it is a musical comedy that happens to be performed by negroes," Richard L. Stokes wrote in the *St. Louis Post-Dispatch*. "Although the scene is laid in Dixie, the characters are of the Northern, rather than Southern, type. The plantation darky has virtually disappeared. Instead, we have negro merchants, whose children have attended high school, lost every trace of dialect, and learned to sing according to the Italian method." However, even despite this praise for the show depicting what W. E. B. Du Bois referred to as the "New Negro," Stokes did call attention to the continued use of blackface, not just as a means of comedy but also to draw a distinction between the different kinds of colored characters. "It was interesting to note that whenever a character was indicated as a full-blooded negro, it was necessary to use burnt cork," he wrote.

As the show continued to be introduced to new audiences across the nation, another auxiliary cast hit the road in March 1923, with the licensing rights granted to white producer George Wintz. It became the third version of the musical to play throughout the East Coast, Midwest, and even the Deep South. While Wintz was helping to expand *Shuffle Along*'s reach throughout previously uncharted territories across the United States, Shuffle Along Inc., the new name for the Nikko Producing Company, was battling in court to protect its copyright. For several months, the show's producers had been fighting to stop Lawrence Deas, who staged *Shuffle Along* and was replaced before its New York opening, from using "Gypsy Blues," "I'm Craving That Kind of Love," and "Bandana Days" in *Plantation Days*, the musical revue he created after leaving the show. After hearing that Deas had not complied with the injunction to stop performing songs from *Shuffle Along* and advertising himself as one of its producers, the company hired a private detective to investigate—a funny turn of events, since Deas had played Jack Penrose, the detective in *Shuffle Along*. The artist said that he was entitled to use the songs as he was a part owner of the show. He had been given a producer credit in 1921 in lieu of proper payment, but it was discovered that his title was purely a professional courtesy. Deas had no real stake in the show, and his performers were ultimately forced to cease and desist.

And the illegal use of *Shuffle Along* songs wasn't the only thing coming to an end. After stops in Toledo, Grand Rapids, Detroit, Buffalo, Rochester, and Philadelphia, the original company of *Shuffle Along* played its final performane on June 23, 1923, in Atlantic City. There was no comparison to what Noble Sissle, Eubie Blake, Flournoy Miller, and Aubrey Lyles had accomplished, and as the two pairs prepared to take their first vacation in nearly twenty-seven months, the sand was silently shifting beneath their feet. The four had agreed to collaborate on another show together, but after months of the musicians asking how the book was coming along and the comedians playing it close to the vest, it had become clear that something was awry. When the press announced that the main company was ending its run, the news came with two more bombshells: *Shuffle Along* would return to the road in the fall, but when it did, it would be without Flournoy Miller and Aubrey Lyles.

PART THREE

—

HOLDING ON

FLOURNOY MILLER
AND AUBREY LYLES
STAGE THEIR FAMOUS
BOXING ROUTINE IN
RUNNIN' WILD, 1923

Photo by White Studio,
© New York Public
Library
for the Performing Arts

10

PARTIAL OWNERSHIP

1923–1924

While the passersby outside the Apollo Theatre in Atlantic City, just off the Boardwalk, were enjoying the beginning of summer, inside, the mood was anything but lighthearted. For months, audiences had no idea that Noble Sissle, Eubie Blake, Flournoy Miller, and Aubrey Lyles had been regularly butting heads, but on the evening of their final performance on June 23, the fissures were clear. It was predetermined that the entire company would remain onstage after the curtain call for a triumphant rendition of "Auld Lang Syne" to mark the conclusion of their historic run, but as the number began, some of the cast stormed offstage. After having grossed an estimated $1.5 million—equivalent to nearly $25 million a hundred years later—the main company of *Shuffle Along* had finally reached the end of the road.

The backstage drama started sometime in the spring, when Miller and Lyles demanded to be paid royalties for the sale of sheet music and piano rolls of songs from the show. As they saw it, while most of the numbers were from Sissle and Blake's vaudeville repertoire and were written before they had met the comedians, their profits emanated from the success of *Shuffle Along*, a collaborative venture. Although each duo was receiving an equal weekly salary from the production and owned 25 percent of Shuffle Along Inc., the musicians were earning more than the comics, not only from music royalties but also since they could supplement their income by playing hits from the show at private events after hours. Of course, Sissle and Blake saw it differently and told the comedians the songs were theirs to perform—and profit from—as they saw fit. While the two musicians thought the matter was settled and plans were moving ahead for the four to collaborate on a new musical comedy, Miller and Lyles were quietly negotiating with George White, a highly successful and well-respected Broadway producer, to secure his backing for a new show.

George White was Florenz Ziegfeld's largest competitor and the producer of *Scandals*, an annual revue that rivaled *Follies*.

Miller secretly wrote a new show and laid the groundwork to stage it quickly. While they hadn't caught wind of the full extent of what the comedians were planning, Sissle and Blake promptly staged their own revue, *Plantation Days*—a name blatantly ripped off from Lawrence Deas—at Café La Marne on the Broadway in Atlantic City, debuting in July. The show included new musical numbers and starred some *Shuffle Along* alumni, including Lottie Gee and the Harmony Kings. Opening night was a smash, with the audience demanding five encores.

Things were going relatively well until Shuffle Along Inc. filed an injunction against Miller and Lyles in New York Superior Court, which made waves throughout the industry trades. The comedians had announced that they were planning on naming their new show *Miller and Lyles' Shuffle Along of 1923–1924*, which didn't sit well with their former business partners. Shuffle Along Inc. argued that the comedians had no right to use the name of the show, even though they had written its book. Additionally, Sissle and Blake decided that they would go back on the road with the musical comedy once the summer was done, and since Miller and Lyles were legally bound to remain with the show throughout the duration of its run, the company argued that they were prohibited from starring in their own production. They were irreplaceable, the show's lawyers argued, and would have to remain with *Shuffle Along* instead. When the complaint was filed with the court, George White formally assisted the comedians, stating on the record that he didn't have any financial interest in their upcoming venture and that his "only purpose was to help these colored people." He argued

237

that Miller and Lyles had been mistreated by the company and, more importantly, had not received their fair share of the royalties from *Shuffle Along*'s touring troupes.

On August 3, 1923, Justice William P. Barr rendered a split decision. "From the papers submitted on this motion, Miller and Lyles appear to me to be nothing more than ordinary actors performing parts well," he said. "I can see nothing special, unique, or extraordinary in their services, nor do I consider them 'irreplaceable' in their several parts, particularly in view of the fact that other *Shuffle Along* road companies have been producing the play with the consent of the plaintiff." Miller and Lyles were free to stage their own show but were unable to use the words "Shuffle Along" in conjunction with it. Nevertheless, the comedians considered this a significant win and took to the press to begin promoting their forthcoming project, which they hoped would hit Broadway after a brief out-of-town tryout. "Flournoy Miller warrants us in predicting that they will come before the public with something out of the ordinary and something which we are all looking forward to with pleasurable anticipation," a journalist wrote in the *New York Amsterdam News*, one of the city's Black-owned papers. "No stone will be left unturned in trying to make this latest show one of the best of its kind ever produced, with a real story brimful of humor running throughout."

Just days after receiving the green light, Miller and Lyles declared that their new show, which had yet to be renamed, was in rehearsals and scheduled to open in just a few weeks. The cast would be comprised of sixty people, and James P. "Jimmy"

Johnson—who had written the new songs for Lawrence Deas's *Plantation Days* revue—was composing original music, with Cecil Mack providing the lyrics. Not to be outdone, Sissle and Blake announced that they were preparing a new version of *Shuffle Along* to debut around the same time, which would once again star Lottie Gee and feature the Harmony Kings, but with a largely new cast and storyline. However, while the performing duos were publicly attempting to one-up each other, they were united in another legal effort that would likely have a far more significant impact on their finances.

Although they collectively owned 67.5 percent of Shuffle Along Inc., along with investors John J. Scholl and Louis I. Isquith, the show's four creators filed a lawsuit alleging that they had fallen victim to a scheme by the minority stakeholders, John and Harry Cort, to install Milton Gosdorfer as company president. Gosdorfer was the benefactor who was given a share of the company in exchange for purchasing the train tickets to Trenton before the musical comedy hit New York, and as the performers felt he had nothing to do with the show's inception and little to do with its success, they saw the move as a duplicitous hostile takeover. However, after hearing the case and reviewing the process, the New York Supreme Court ruled that the election by the board of directors had been conducted legally, and Gosdorfer was free to serve as the company's new head decision-maker.

However, for the time being, Miller and Lyles couldn't worry themselves over *Shuffle Along*. Although the show hadn't produced as large of a windfall for them as it had for Sissle and Blake, the comedians had made a considerable amount of money—over $52,000 between the two of them in the last year alone, on top of their weekly $625 salary—and whatever else they netted from that point on would be icing on the cake. After considering naming their new show *George White's Black Scandals*, which was thought to be too similar to the producer's popular revue, and *Miller and Lyles's Cakewalkers*, the triumvirate settled on *Runnin' Wild* just before its opening at the Howard Theatre in Washington, DC, on August 20, 1923. Unlike the deal the comedians had struck with their previous musical comedy, where they were partners in the production, George White owned the show wholly, with Miller and Lyles paid a weekly salary of $2,000, a significant increase over what they had been earning just a few months before. The two reprised their famous Steve Jenkins and Sam Peck characters in a "thin thread of a story" that saw the two shiftless grifters getting into a series of comical situations while attempting to navigate through life putting in the least amount of effort possible. The cast drew heavily from former members of *Shuffle Along*'s main company, including Mattie Wilkes, Katherine Yarborough, vocal coach Revella Hughes, and Adelaide Hall, who had graduated from the chorus to play a featured part. Will Marion Cook conducted the orchestra, with dances staged by *Shuffle Along* chorine Elida Webb.

Opening night was a resounding hit, with over $800 brought in on that day alone. For the first week, nearly two-thirds of the audience was white—business as usual for the performers but an unusual occurrence for the management of the Howard—and the reviews were promising. A theater critic for *Variety* noted that Adelaide Hall "jazzes a number as [white performer] Paul Whiteman would have done it" before calling her a "knock-out," but among the overall praise, the reviewer took issue with *Runnin' Wild*'s reliance on stereotypical racial comedy tropes. "There is but one complaint with the show," he said. "The one opportunity to show the real Negro and his generally accepted environment is allotted but a few minutes. More should have been done with this bit, and possibly will before the show is finally shaped up." Miller and Lyles's reliance on blackface comedy, Southern dialectical humor, and racist tropes was beginning to wear thin for some, regardless of how talented the artists who were playing up to these stereotypes were onstage.

Runnin' Wild sold out its first week in DC—$8,000 earned from ten performances—but the show was far from financially solvent. George White told the comedians that their $1 top ticket pricing was unsustainable, but instead of raising the cost for the audience, which was becoming increasingly blacker as performances went on, Miller and Lyles agreed to forgo their salary for the first week. Even better, they said, the entire company was willing to do the same. However, when Saturday night rolled around and Clarence Gray, the show's manager, hadn't handed out the payroll envelopes with checks inside, it was clear there had been some misunderstanding and the cast and crew hadn't agreed to work for free. As the performers grew increasingly hostile, Gray telegraphed George White in New York, telling the producer they had a big problem on their hands. White replied that if proper salaries were remitted, the show would close, and when Gray relayed that message, the company said they wouldn't work for free; if that meant the show was over, then so be it. They quickly worked out a deal: Miller and Lyles would honor their original agreement to waive their salary for the first week, with the rest of the company—which included a fifteen-piece band costing $1,200 weekly—agreeing to accept partial payment for the week.

As *Runnin' Wild* was struggling to pay the bills, *Shuffle Along* had picked back up. The show reopened on August 27 in Toronto at the Royal Alexandra Theatre, with Lew Payton and Joe Simms as Steve Jenkins and Sam Peck, respectively, where it found an incredibly inviting audience. "When Joe Simms sang 'If You've Never Been Vamped by a Brownskin'... he sang a parable," Robert P. Edwards, the Canadian representative for the Negro Associated Press, wrote. "For the sixty-odd brown-skinned, flexible-voiced singers and versatile dancers, in gorgeous costumes, set in the most lavish and original scenery that ever graced a Canadian stage, so completely vamped the exacting patrons of this famous playhouse that hundreds were turned away nightly and various movements were inaugurated to persuade the management to lengthen their stay. As it was, the usually reserved patrons were so enthusiastic that they ignored all time limits to curtain calls and held the show until 11:30 nightly... When the curtain fell for the last time, it left the exacting Toronto society folk asking for more. Said the Africanadian: 'If you've never been vamped by brownskins,'—'You needn't finish!' replied the Caucanadian. 'I have and am.'"

While Miller and Lyles were in the nation's capital and

Sissle and Blake were out of the country, Milton Gosdorfer was in New York, exerting his newfound power as president of Shuffle Along Inc. He petitioned the New York Superior Court to appoint a receiver to take control of the company, arguing that the other stockholders had been spending beyond their means and were not upholding their own established bylaws when it came to holding board elections. Gosdorfer's request was denied, but he still had more avenues to achieve his desired goal. Of the company's forty total shares, the president now owned six and a half. He quickly made moves to buy out John and Harry Cort's positions, which would give him fifteen, and *Variety* reported that Gosdorfer was negotiating to purchase Miller and Lyles's ten shares, as the duo had become increasingly disinterested in *Shuffle Along*'s business affairs and were desperate for cash on hand. The successful completion of those transactions would give Gosdorfer a majority stake in the company and the ability to steer the ship in the direction he saw fit. However, in the interim, Shuffle Along Inc. tipped off the press that they were preparing to file a motion against Miller and Lyles for contempt of court. The *Runnin' Wild* promotional materials declared that the comedians were "formerly of *Shuffle Along*," which the company argued violated the judge's ruling that they couldn't use the show title in conjunction with their latest project.

However, even with the public rivalry between Miller, Lyles, Sissle, and Blake and the increasing litigiousness of the company they had partial ownership in, the fact that there were now more Black productions being staged throughout North America—and

more representation of the race in all aspects of entertainment—
was being celebrated as a net positive by the community. "Talk
all you may of the good old days, but measured in terms of
actual facts, the present is the high spot of Negro theatricals.
Envy, emotion, and all preferences aside, the Negro artist is in
the heyday of his glory and financial favor," J. A. Jackson wrote.
"There are many more Negro music publishing houses in the
field than ever before in the history of the business. If the advertising bills that are being constantly made and as constantly paid
for when due are any harbingers, they are receiving their share
of the business in their field of endeavor. Record manufacturers
are employing more Negro artists at recording and having more
accompanists and arrangers of the race working for these artists
in presenting to a bigger public more compositions of the race
than ever before.

"Burlesque companies, a group that was one time
completely closed to the colored comedian and dancer, and
to whom the Negro woman artists was an unheard of possi-
bility, today employ more than a hundred performers of the
race," he continued. "Once we just had Williams and Walker's
show. This season we have in the musical comedy top row:
The *Shuffle Along* road show, Sissle and Blake's *Shuffle Along*
company, the new Miller and Lyles production, Eddie Hunter
and the *How Come* show, the *Plantation Days* Company,
which recently opened in Chicago, as did Izzy Weingarden's
second *Follow Me*."

Although they were still in financial trouble, Miller and
Lyles returned to Boston's Selwyn Theatre, where *Runnin' Wild*

played to full houses. By September 20, the show was in its third week at the venue—where it was grossing just shy of $11,000 weekly—and George White was teasing in the press that a New York run was imminent and likely at Daly's Sixty-Third Street Theatre, the recently renamed venue that was home to *Shuffle Along* in Manhattan. Just as it seemed things couldn't get any better, New York Supreme Court Justice Barr ruled that Miller and Lyles hadn't violated their court order, and they were free to advertise that they were previously affiliated with *Shuffle Along*, the groundbreaking musical comedy that they had conceived and written.

Runnin' Wild arrived in New York on October 29, 1923, taking up residency at the Colonial Theatre on Sixty-Second, just around the corner from where they had first struck theatrical gold. The 1,293-seat venue was packed, and throughout the performance, patrons stomped their feet in time with the orchestra's percussionists and whistled at the dancing chorus girls. Even the most refined members of the audience found themselves overcome by the sounds of the lively jazz score. However, while the general public was impressed, a critic for the *New York Tribune* wrote a sardonic critique of the show—which had its leading Black actors performing in blackface—for not being performatively Black enough. "There is no particular reason why one should travel all the way to Sixty-Second Street to get his vaudeville, unless he insists that its protagonists be a little second rate and a trifle diluted with African," he wrote. "The best dancer is not as good as [white vaudevillian] Buster West in *The Greenwich Village Follies*, nor the best negro comedian anywhere near as good as [white performer] Eddie Cantor as an imitator of one. Outside of Miller and Lyles…no certainty could be arrived at as to whether the actors were African fish or Caucasian fowl. One small girl in the chorus had limbs of such a pristine whiteness that there was no small doubt regarding whether or not she belonged. Arms and legs were really the only reputable means of judging the color scheme for all the faces (with the exception of the very funny Miller and Lyles) were obtrusively raddled with brick red paint."

Conversely, the Black-owned *New York Amsterdam News* had a far more optimistic take. "The thing uppermost in our mind was the apprehension that they might have fallen from the high standard they set in the previous show, hence it was with a feeling akin to the joy that rises within us at the success of the worthy that we found *Runnin' Wild* adhering to a standard which, if maintained, will keep the Miller and Lyles offerings before the American public for a long time," they wrote. "It is easy to rise and remark that *Runnin' Wild* has been successful in accomplishing that which no other colored show has done, and that is to remain in the class of shows like *Shuffle Along*."

Beyond Miller and Lyles's comedic performances, what commanded the most attention in *Runnin' Wild* was a unique number, "Charleston," which kicked off an inescapable social dance craze that would last throughout the rest of the decade. Instead of having the orchestra play, the accompaniment harkened back to the tradition of what James Weldon Johnson describes as "primitive Negro music… [They] had the major part of the chorus supplement the band by beating out the time with hand-clapping and foot-patting. The effect was electrical. Such a demonstration of beating out complex rhythms had never been seen on a stage in New York."

While *Runnin' Wild* was credited for bringing the dance, which was already popular in the Black community, into the mainstream, several other African American artists argued they were responsible for the dance craze. Black dancer Leonard Harper, from the Lafayette Theatre's 1922 *Plantation Days* revue, said he was the first to do the now-famous steps onstage. Irvin C. Miller, Flournoy's brother, said audiences saw the dance first in *Liza*, which costarred Gertrude Saunders and was staged by Walter Brooks—the director who provided "that Broadway touch" to *Shuffle Along*—in November 1922. Frank Montgomery, who staged the dances for the all-Black revue *How Come?* five months later, said his show was deserving of the distinction. Even Sissle and Blake entered the fray, claiming that the *Shuffle Along* dancers were the first to popularize the dance moves.

Clearly, none of those artists had *created* the dance, and regardless of who brought a version of the Charleston to the stage first, it was Elida Webb's interpretation and the way it was enthusiastically performed by the *Runnin' Wild* chorus that made it a phenomenon. The choreographer said she discovered the dance when she saw some children practicing it on the streets of New York, and when she asked them where they had gotten their moves from, they said they learned from someone who had just moved to the city from Charleston, South Carolina. She was fascinated by their rhythm and built upon the steps she observed to "improve the nucleus" of the dance. After she made her modifications, she taught the cast of *Runnin' Wild* how to fast kick and step, forward and back, and add a little tap, which they perfected with increasing pace and jubilation. Once the dance caught on, Webb was asked to teach it to Josephine Baker as well as white performers Bee Jackson, Nora Bayes, and Elsie de Wolfe.

The Charleston quickly became popular among whites, causing some in the Black community to take umbrage. The *Baltimore Afro-American* addressed the debate in a short editorial beneath the plainly stated headline, Dance Belongs to Negroes: "The Charleston dance, like the folk song, is [of] the race heritage and of his conception. This established, there can be no quarrel with those who refine the basic steps and modernize them. There is a tendency in many quarters to criticize our artists for showing these steps to the white professionals, but the other side is this: if they do not teach, it will be copied and desecrated as have been the Spirituals, and thus a double injury results. The only person toward whom censure should be directed is one who appears in a cabaret or theatre, and 'does his stuff' for a half pint, and the flattery of a lot of 'pirating' 'ofays.'"

Curiously, while Blacks had clearly created the Charleston, several years after the dance craze took off, the *New York Times* credited George White with having created it as well as the Black Bottom dance that first appeared in Irvin C. Miller's *Dinah* in 1923. Will Marion Cook wrote a letter to the paper to set the record straight and give credit to those whom he felt had a hand in the dance sensation, which they ran on December 26, 1926. "I have the greatest respect for Mr. White...but why do an injustice to the black folk of America by taking from them the credit of creating new and characteristic dances? From 'Old Jim Crow' to 'Black Bottom,' the negro dances came from the Cotton Belt, the levee, the Mississippi River, and are African in inspiration," he said. "The American negro, in search of outlet for emotional expression, recreates and broadens these dances. Either in their crude state, or revised form, in St. Louis, Chicago or New York the dance is discovered...by white theatrical producers and sold to the public as an original creation.

"The 'Charleston' has been done in the South, especially in the little island lying off Charleston, S. C., for more than forty years to my knowledge," he continued. "The dance reached New York five years ago. In Harlem any evening a group of negro children could be seen 'Doin' the Charleston' and collecting pennies. This dance was first staged in a real production by Frank Montgomery in *How Come*. Leonard Harper, a colored man, used a few steps of the dance. The first music with this fascinating rhythm was the 'Charleston Strut,' written by Tommy Morris and published by Jack Mills, Inc., about four years ago. Jimmy Johnson, a negro song writer, first conceived the idea of a Charleston songs [*sic*], and in his score of *Runnin' Wild*, for Miller and Lyles, wrote the famous 'Charleston,' which was staged by Elida Webb, and the craze was on. It is doubtful if Mr. White even saw a 'Charleston' until he attended the final rehearsals of *Runnin' Wild*."

Questions of authorship and ownership of creative

materials had become commonplace, and in December 1923, Flournoy Miller and Aubrey Lyles found themselves at the center of yet another lawsuit; however, this time, they were the plaintiffs. One of the comedic highlights of *Runnin' Wild* was a slate adding bit, wherein the two performers had to complete a simple calculation, and after they disagreed on the answer, one would lead the other to a chalkboard and explain how either $7 \times 13 = 28$ or $6 \times 13 = 24$, depending on the situation. Of course, the comedy emanated from the flagrant misuse of the numbers in the "ones" and "tens" columns, much to the confusion and frustration of the other comic onstage, who initially had the right answer and became increasingly irate while trying to follow the math equation gone awry. As with most of Miller and Lyles's routines and many bits born out of the blackface minstrel tradition, the sketch served as a Rorschach test. Depending on their predisposition, an audience member might see the errant arithmetician as either dim-witted or a clever trickster. Although Miller and Lyles hadn't created the routine, white vaudevillian Raymond Hitchcock, who authored it, granted them permission to use it. And when the stars of *Runnin' Wild* learned that John Philbrick and Sadie DeVoe, another comedy duo, had incorporated it into their act, they successfully had them stopped.

These public squabbles point to just how significant the jazz scene was becoming to the American ethos at large and how both Black and white people fought to claim ownership for these defining moments in popular culture. Those who lived in Manhattan saw the metamorphosis up close, as underground nightclubs and speakeasies became even more prevalent uptown in the early years of the Prohibition Era, providing a space not only for both Black and white patrons to listen and dance to jazz as they drank their contraband liquor, but also a venue for African American musicians and dancers to make a living performing. Just like in the early days of Black men performing in minstrel shows, white audiences were increasingly looking for the most "authentic" form of Black entertainment, which made Harlem the natural after-hours hub.

One of the most prominent nightspots, the Cotton Club, opened on 142nd Street and Lenox Avenue during *Runnin' Wild*'s Broadway engagement. Former heavyweight champion Jack Johnson, who was set to star in 1921's *Put and Take*, was the first to run and operate the nightspot, which he called Club Deluxe, but it wasn't until 1923, when he sold it to Owen "Owney" Madden, a noted gangster and bootlegger, that things took off. Madden was primarily interested in selling beer, and running the top nightclub in New York was a means to that end. He kept Johnson on as manager, and after extensive renovations that made the high-end club resemble a swinging Southern plantation like Lew Leslie had done, the spot reopened as the premiere location—for whites only—to enjoy "authentic" Black entertainment. Each night, "tall, tan, and terrific" African American women—all of whom had to be at least five foot six, light-skinned, and under twenty-one years old—wore tiny outfits that left little to the imagination and danced in the nightly floor show. The waitstaff were all Black and provided table service while dressed in red tuxedos, making them resemble butlers. Like the performers, they were strictly prohibited from mingling with the white patrons. In addition to the allure of the talented female chorus, there were also singers, comedians, and male dancers, who all provided a daily program of entertainment that helped put the Cotton Club on the map, even before the likes of Duke Ellington, Lena Horne, and Louis Armstrong became associated with the establishment.

As 1923 drew to an end, J. A. Jackson dedicated his weekly column in *Billboard* to assessing the previous year in Black entertainment. Without a doubt, the preceding 365 days had been an unprecedented period for Black artistry. "As a whole, the showfolks of the race have done well," he wrote. "True, there have been some flops. But the big gain, the acceptance of the Negro in virtually every phase of the show business remains an established fact." Jackson pointed out that *Shuffle Along*, which had been playing throughout the nation continuously since March 1921, had "very definitely established itself in theatrical history as a landmark" and that it was initially "presented to a Broadway public that came to scoff, and remained to admire the colored artist and their production. The sincere flattery bestowed upon its imitators of every race credits the production with having introduced some novelties into musical comedy that will long be remembered.

"The George Wintz road show of the same title has been from Coast to Coast, and from lakes to gulf," he wrote of the *Shuffle Along* Number Three touring company. "This company is in its eighty-third week of uniform success. To it will always be credited a certain distinction for breaking thru [*sic*] the wall of prejudice against Negro attractions in the better houses of the southland. The credit should be equally divided between the writers of the book and songs and the performers who made up the show. The personal deportment and diplomatic manner of the latter were quite as much responsible for the result as was the artistry they disclosed with their work."

It is impossible to overstate just how significant it was for Black individuals throughout the United States to see that a simple show like *Shuffle Along*, which lacked the typical Broadway flourishes even in the zenith of its success, was accepted by audiences across North America and clamored for by producers in Europe. What the show lacked in glitz, it made up for in talent, from Miller and Lyles's witty writing to Sissle and Blake's snappy songs, and a standard of excellence and professionalism that was upheld across three distinct performing companies. For a country still grappling with the stains of slavery, each person who had a hand in the production was an ambassador for racial justice and acceptance, and Black people, by and large, were appreciative of it. It became typical for African American citizens to write their local newspapers of the hopefulness they felt when *Shuffle Along* came to town, just as Howard C. Washington did after he saw the main company perform in Columbus, Ohio, in December 1923. "In haste I'm writing you a few brief lines to inform you that I have many reasons to feel proud of the progress that our people are making in the theatrical world," he wrote to the *Chicago Defender*. "First, they are creating a commercial demand for their productions and services through the ability to please the most critical, thus increasing the box-office receipts wherever they play an engagement—this alone is enough to cause the walls of prejudice to crumble, as the dollar is the real factor in the commercial world.

"The proof of it all is the engagement of our famous Sissle & Blake *Shuffle Along* musical production at the Hartman Theater, this city, the present week," he continued. "This organization has the honor of being the first Race production to play this house and have opened the avenue for our many Race productions to play the same in the future. Why? First reason, because the music-lovers of such productions demanded that this much talked-of production must be brought to this city; second reason, they came, they conquered, and the critics state, 'the best show of the season.' The best reason of all is the third reason—the house was sold out for the week three days before the production came to Columbus, something that has not occurred at this house in years, and this theater played the world's greatest productions... While viewing this wonderful production, I had many reasons to feel proud."

Meanwhile, Sissle and Blake were plotting their next move. Thanks to *Shuffle Along* backer John Scholl, the two contributed a dozen songs to *Elsie*, a show with and all-white cast that he was producing. While lukewarm reviews ultimately plagued its brief Broadway run in the spring of 1923, the songs were largely celebrated. For example, while he was pessimistic that the show would attract an audience, white theater critic Aston Stevens declared Sissle and Blake to be the "black hope" for the musical's success.

As the new year was approaching, they were approached by B. C. Whitney and Abraham Lincoln Erlanger, two powerful

Broadway producers, to write a follow-up to *Shuffle Along*, just as Miller and Lyles had successfully done with *Runnin' Wild*. The musicians weren't book writers, so they enlisted the assistance of Lew Payton, who was playing Steve Jenkins with them on the road, and once a script materialized, they rehearsed the new show during the day while continuing to perform *Shuffle Along* by night. On January 11, 1924, the trades announced that the musicians had opened a new office in Manhattan and were planning on leaving their highly successful show to start a new production, possibly due to discord between them and the company's board of directors, and on February 2, the two played their final performance with *Shuffle Along*—for the second time—in Providence, Rhode Island. The next few days followed a familiar pattern. Upon their exit, Milton Gosdorfer bought them out of their stocks in Shuffle Along Inc., giving the company's president a majority stake in the company as the musicians turned their sights to their new venture, which they planned on calling *Sissle and Blake's Shuffles of 1924*, until that idea was shut down. They toyed around with naming their new show *Bandanna Days* or *Bandanna Land*, both references to their popular song, but they finally decided on *The Chocolate Dandies*. Of course, not to be outdone, Miller and Lyles announced days later that they, too, were considering opening their own office and writing yet another show together.

Just as their comedian counterparts had done with *Runnin' Wild*, Sissle and Blake brought along as many members of the *Shuffle Along* main company for this new venture as they could, including coauthor of the book Lew Payton, Lottie Gee, Edith

Spencer, the Harmony Kings, and Josephine Baker. Charlie Davis, who was one of the star dancers, choreographed the show, but once again, just before they opened and despite Noble Sissle's best efforts, the producers hired white director Julian Mitchell to give the show "that Broadway touch." Mitchell was a giant within the industry and had directed a much-celebrated extravagant musical adaptation of *The Wizard of Oz* in 1902 and several editions of Ziegfeld's *Follies*. However, even more so than Walter Brooks on *Shuffle Along*, the director was little more than a figurehead. The septuagenarian had become so hard of hearing that during music rehearsals, he had to press his ear against the piano to hear even a faint sound. However, even with this unnecessary albatross, Sissle and Blake were glad to have Al Mayer, who had been so instrumental to their previous show's success, serving as manager for this production as well. "Al Mayer worked night and day for us," Eubie Blake recalled. "It's funny, but the only people who ever helped us were Jewish. I owe them a great debt."

In terms of budget and spectacle, *The Chocolate Dandies* was as far from *Shuffle Along* as one could get. The production cost approximately $100,000 to stage and featured a cast of over one hundred people, whose salaries totaled $7,500 weekly, and three live horses. Even with a $2.50 top ticket price, the financial hill was always going to be difficult to climb. Noble Sissle communicated as much to a reporter who asked about the expense, stating that if the show were a hit, they would begin to turn a profit after six months. If it wasn't, they'd end up with a lot of debt and regrets.

In the run-up to its premiere, the cast and crew were a bundle of nerves, as they had all endured marathon days of run-throughs and rewrites. "I had become a veteran of all-night rehearsals, endless cups of coffee, anxiety, doubt, cries of 'It simply doesn't work, take it out!' and 'I like it. Let's try it again,'" Josephine Baker recalled. "Scenes had been taken apart and reconstructed.

"There were moments of self-hatred brought on by exhaustion and spells of self-love," she continued. "The stage is a fragile ship which must be ready to weather rough sailing, but this time, we hoped for sunshine." Hopes aside, the combination of an unprecedented budget for a Black musical comedy, a book that lacked the comedic cleverness Miller and Lyles had perfected over their decades performing together, and a show that deviated significantly from the *Shuffle Along* template conspired to create a perfect storm that seemed poised to capsize *The Chocolate Dandies* as soon as it left the dock.

VALADA SNOW (CENTER) PERFORMING "MANDA" IN *THE CHOCOLATE DANDIES*, 1924. THE INSCRIPTION FROM SNOW TO EUBIE BLAKE'S WIFE, AVIS, READS: "TO A BROAD-MINDED WOMAN WITH A NO GOOD HUSBAND."

Courtesy of the Maryland Center for History and Culture, Item ID #PP301.319

11

BETTER THAN SALARY

1924–1925

Just before the new Sissle and Blake musical comedy's premiere at the Lyceum Theatre in Rochester, New York, on March 10, the producers changed its name to *In Bamville*, an on-the-nose reference to the fictional Mississippi plantation municipality where the show is set. The story begins on the last day of the town fair and centers on a horse race, as the track is the hub of Bamville's economic and social scene. Mose Washington, Lew Payton's character, falls asleep and dreams his horse came in first, and after winning the prize money, Washington becomes the most respected and powerful person in town. Comedy ensues during the extended dream sequence, and when he wakes, Washington finds that his horse wasn't victorious after all. Instead, Dan Jackson, played by Ivan Harold Browning of the Harmony Kings, had the winning animal, and the show ends with Jackson and Lottie Gee's character, Angeline Brown, the daughter of the manager of the Bamville Fair, marrying while surrounded by "a million little cupids."

Despite the best efforts of the company in staging this highly ambitious theatrical extravaganza, early reviews were mixed. *Variety* issued one of the most generous, declaring the show "tuneful" and "pleasing" while countering that "it ran nearly an hour too long, was slow in spots, and much of the comedy misfired." Others weren't as kind. While the production certainly looked the part of a big Broadway show, white theater critic Ashton Stevens felt the writers and performers were trying too hard to prove themselves capable and worthy of playing in the heart of the Manhattan theater district. "This show seems to suffer from too much white man; it is both sophisticated and conventional," he wrote. "You feel the arresting, the civilizing hand of Julian Mitchell in the direction. Nobody seems to go out of his head. Where we used to have splendid barbarians, we now have splendid barbers. It is...the fatal influence of the white man that makes the show seem second rate for all its costly costumes and scenery. There is too much so-called politeness, too much platitudinous refinement, and not enough of the razor-edged. There is, in a word, too much 'art' and not enough Africa. Yes, even in the music of that gifted melodist, Eubie Blake... No stab of originality. No feeling within you that Victor Herbert couldn't have composed [the music] on a bet."

Ashton Stevens's critique—which echoed the sentiments of several white critics—points not only to the misconception some had that "art" and "Africa" were mutually exclusive but also the way Black performers were damned if they attempted to conform to the conventional standards of Broadway and damned if they didn't. *Shuffle Along* was unable to secure a booking at a major house in Midtown, yet audiences came because it was different. But even though it had proven its concept time and again, the show still struggled—and more often than not failed—to break into the major theater chains around the nation, relying instead on independent houses, even as the show raked in money hand over fist. However, when a show was offered with all the Broadway trimmings, it was dismissed out of hand for not being sufficiently Black enough, or worse yet, many critics rhetorically asked why the public should spend top dollar to see Black performers do the same thing whites could. The seemingly unsolvable riddle was reminiscent of the criticism *Darkydom* faced in 1915 and James Reese Europe's long-held belief that Blacks would never prosper when attempting to beat whites at their own game. Although Sissle and Blake weren't necessarily trying to *win* the game, their sin was that they had simply dared to play it.

Sissle and Blake understood that the public might not accept a Black show that wasn't rough around the edges and sufficiently uninhibited—i.e., "primitive"—in its presentation, but at least at first, they believed *In Bamville* would find an audience nevertheless. "Friends had encouraged us, and so Sissle and I thought that after *Shuffle Along* we could write any show we wanted," Eubie Blake said. "We were wrong. People who went to a colored show—most people, not *all* people—expected only fast dancing and Negroid humor, and when they got something else, they put it down." However, even as journalists started to coalesce around the sentiment that *In Bamville* had fallen short of expectations, Noble Sissle defended the choice to stage something that deviated from their prosperous predecessor. "*Shuffle Along* was a corporation," he said. "When it played out, we were all free to start over again. Three years before the public had taught us several lessons. We learned what the white audience wants, and why. We learned that the whites, without question, will accept colored artists and production of merit. They do not demand that we be buffoons and clowns, either.

"Of course, there must be comedy, for an audience comes to a musical comedy primarily to laugh, but the more real art we can work into the different scenes and situations, the better the show takes with the public," he continued. "The singing and dancing are big parts of our success. The jokes are clever, but not vulgar. And we portray Negro characters—not try to give an imitation of whites. Our love scenes are not as romantic as the whites, but they have the same universal touch and are applauded and appreciated."

However, despite their public defense, Eubie Blake realized early in the show's run that they might have been traveling on unstable ground when he observed the audience's reaction to "Dixie Moon," a number that elicited a curious response. The sequence was the opening of the second act, and the stage was set with several rows of long moss hanging from tree branches, creating a beautifully tranquil Southern atmosphere. As the song began, a moon slowly rose above the stage, completing the dusky ambiance. While performer George Jones and the Harmony Kings sang, dressed in expensive pongee suits like fine Southern gentlemen, Blake heard the audience ooh and aah as they attempted to take in the picturesque and musically striking scene. But as the brown-skinned chorus girls emerged in white dresses with multitiered hoop skirts and oversize white headpieces, the young women would literally stun the audience into silence.

After one performance, Eubie Blake finally mustered the nerve to resolve the issue with B. C. Whitney, one of the show's producers. "Mr. Whitney, I didn't come to tell you how to run the show," he began. "I just know how to write music and conduct the orchestra, but everywhere we play, the audience stops dead when they see the girls in the hoop skirts. The scene is too *beautiful* for a colored show. *Our* girls wouldn't wear hoops in their dresses—it's just not the way they would dress." The producer let him finish and then succinctly explained the reality. "Eubie, this is *not* a colored show," he said. "This is Sissle and Blake's show for Broadway."

However, even as *In Bamville* was struggling to impress critics and turn a profit, most of the cast enjoyed being part of the highly polished production. As Eubie Blake's anxiety heightened

backstage—"Unless we can net $16,000, we're through!"—
Josephine Baker felt like a star for the first time. While the show
was being criticized for taking itself too seriously, the teenage
chorine was free to act as wild as she wanted onstage. When
she was approached to be in the show while *Shuffle Along* was
still on the road, she asked if Noble Sissle and Lew Payton could
write a special part just for her. She had always enjoyed making
people laugh while onstage, and her comedic turns in *Shuffle
Along* had won her praise, even though she was just another
girl in the line. Why not give the people what she knew they
wanted? She begged Sissle to write her a blackface number, and
since few African American women blackened up, she thought it
would help her stand out and make headlines. Sissle acquiesced
to the request, although he wasn't particularly fond of "darky
humor," and when the show opened, she appeared onstage in
full minstrel drag, her face covered in burnt cork, with painted
white lips, a checkered dress cut up to her thighs, a sash with
a large bow, black stockings, and oversize floppy black shoes.
"I imitated the sound of a muted saxophone. A grinning girl
making all the silly faces I could think of," she said. "At $125 a
week, I was the best paid girl in the chorus, all because I could
cross my eyes!"

However, while Baker's heart was set on comedy, part of
her didn't want to miss out on the opportunity to wear a beautiful costume as the rest of the cast would be doing. As the show
began to materialize, the enterprising young woman returned to
Sissle and begged him to write a second part for her: "You think
I can only make people laugh? I can be a vamp!" She continued

to wear them down until she had earned an additional role—the Deserted Female—appearing alongside Lew Payton, the show's star, in a gold lamé gown with a thigh-high slit, revealing one of her long legs, that reached the floor and clung to her body. Of the two characters she played in the show, the audience had a harder time buying Josephine Baker as a seductress, but the teenager enjoyed the chance to play dress-up, whether she was appreciated doing so or not.

Another breakout star in the show was Valada Snow, who despite being only nineteen years old had already lived a full life. She was born in 1904 in Chattanooga, Tennessee. Her mother, Etta, was a music teacher and graduate of Howard University who taught her daughter how to play nearly a dozen string and wind instruments—the violin was her specialty—as well as sing, and her father, John, was a minister. As a side venture, the patri-

arch of the family assembled a group of talented kids, including his five-year-old daughter, to perform at Black theaters and vaudeville houses, branding them as the Pickaninny Troubadours. After her father died, she married another performer, Samuel Lewis Lanier, a physically abusive man, when she was fifteen years old. Their union was short-lived, and Snow relocated to New York in

LEW PAYTON (L.) AND AN UNIDENTIFIED ACTOR, LIKELY LLOYD KEYES, WITH JOSEPHINE BAKER AS THE DESERTED FEMALE IN *THE CHOCOLATE DANDIES*, 1924

Courtesy of the archives of Robert Kimball

1921, where she appeared in *Holiday in Dixieland*, a musical revue, and by the following year, she had secured a job singing at Barron Wilkins's Exclusive Club in Harlem, the same open-all-night establishment where Florence Mills performed before she was cast in *Shuffle Along*.

Snow continued to garner attention while at the Exclusive Club until she landed a coveted place in the new Sissle and Blake musical. When Snow appeared onstage in *In Bamville*, smiling brightly in a ruffled one-piece white jumper with matching arm pieces and oversize bow tie, white stockings, white heels, and an oversize white top hat, she became a favorite of the audiences and critics alike. She was a consummate entertainer who also knew how to give a captivating interview and work her way into the papers.

After one performance, Snow invited a reporter backstage— "Sit down if you can find a place. These dressing rooms are stuffy!"—seemingly letting her guard down while consciously turning on the charm. She sat in front of a vanity in a satin negligee, nonchalantly dabbing her fingers into a large jar of cold cream, removing the stage makeup off her smiling face, while singing the praises of the show's writers and the other young women in the cast. "Aren't you pleased with the progress we are making? It is remarkable, and to think, we are just the beginning," she said. "Our biggest hope is to interest the better class in the show business. You say the chorus of *In Bamville* is attractive? It is no wonder! Sissle and Blake are our Ziegfelds. They choose the good-looking talented girl with a careful ear and eye to her breeding and character. The bad girl hasn't any place in the modern first-class show. Some of our girls are from well-known colleges, others are gifted in the arts, and many were society belles in their own hometowns. They work hard, are well paid, and for the most part, take life seriously."

Besides talking about her current role in the chorus, Snow also used the opportunity to express her goal of becoming a musical director: "I am so full of music, maybe I can impart the knowledge to others." This wasn't just wide-eyed dreaming or promotional puffery; her dream was true. Thanks to her mother, Snow was a uniquely proficient player and musical prodigy, capable of giving the show's orchestra leader a run for his money. While in transit to one of their stops, Snow heard Eubie Blake strike the A-440 fork he used to get the orchestra in tune. "Mr. Blake," she said. "Your tuning fork's flat." He looked back at her with skepticism and condemnation—*how could a tuning fork be flat?* The two got into some back and forth. "I say your tuning fork's flat," she affirmed. When they finally reached their next stop, the pianist took Snow by the arm and found the nearest music store. The proprietor of the shop took in the story, asked for Blake's tuning fork, grabbed another one from the shelf, and struck them both. He listened closely as the sound reverberated, with Blake and Snow watching him carefully. He struck one separately, put his ear to it, and then did the same with the other. He carefully examined Blake's tuning fork, which the conductor had kept casually tossed in his luggage while traveling, and gestured to one of its prongs. "She's right," the shop owner said. "It's a tiny bit bent."

After Rochester, the company of *In Bamville* traveled to

Pittsburgh, hoping they would find better luck, but shortly after they arrived, tragedy hit. During rehearsals for the show in upstate New York, Al Mayer had fallen ill and returned to Manhattan. He was operated on at the Van Cortlandt Sanitarium on March 12, but there were complications, and he died eight days later. He was forty-five years old. Upon receiving word, Sissle and Blake took a night train from Pittsburgh to pay their respects to their manager and business partner. "We are deeply moved by Mr. Mayer's death," Noble Sissle said in a statement. "It was due to his sacrifices that *Shuffle Along*, the first show containing an all-Negro cast, was put onstage. We are sorry that Mr. Mayer did not see our current show, patterned after his first success and played by the original characters." Besides the fact that Mayer's death was unanticipated and bewildering, there were practical ramifications that warranted immediate attention. Abraham Lincoln Erlanger, one of *In Bamville*'s producers, struggled to find someone to manage the production on short notice and flippantly hired Jack Yorke, an associate of his with whom Sissle and Blake had no familiarity and who lacked Mayer's unique ability to keep a show running even when the coffers had run dry.

With their new manager on board, *In Bamville* continued its Pittsburgh run at the Nixon Theatre, where it opened to relatively positive reviews and strong audiences. Perhaps reassured by the reaction they had received, Noble Sissle reaffirmed his belief that they had perfectly calibrated the show to succeed with Pennsylvania audiences. "If you saw *Shuffle Along* in New York and noticed what a small place we had for scenery, you can appreciate what it means to us to be in a place like this," he said to a reporter while being interviewed in the theater. "Then we had only a mediocre show, but the novelty of the cast made up for the shortcomings. But when we got on the road, we realized where we must do better the next time. For instance, in the [Sixty-Third Street Theatre], the only place we could get, those who were sophisticated enough not to be captivated by the idea of a 'colored' cast saw at a glance that we didn't have room to spread out and do better. But after our astonishing successes there, the big houses opened up to us and we had the embarrassing experience of taking a play designed for a small house into theaters whose patrons were accustomed to lavish display.

"Even though our novelty helped somewhat, we were at a disadvantage. Take this place," he continued, gesturing to the large venue they were in. "People who are accustomed to attending the Nixon expect to see similar scenery each week, and if we didn't have the show to match, the audience would feel they didn't get their money's worth. The fact that it was 'colored' wouldn't count large. So *Shuffle Along* on the road taught us we must build our next production on a mammoth scale, with the idea of going into the biggest houses from the start."

As *In Bamville* continued its tour of big houses, it was regularly met with contradictory reviews. Even among those who enjoyed it, the issue of race and specifically whether the show was an appropriate show for Black artists to stage remained at the forefront of nearly every write-up. "*In Bamville* is a distinct credit to its architects if they had in mind building something that was racially distinctive," Fred Hollman wrote in his largely positive review for *Billboard* while the show was in Chicago. "Sissle, Blake, Payton, and Mitchell have put together something that oozes Negro entertainment at its best. In the realm of the harmonies, the Negro has something that is all his own that white entertainers have sought to duplicate for fifty years or longer. Some of them have succeeded moderately well. But in *Bamville*, a gorgeous crazy-quilt of color, nimble stepping, and riotous song, the collaborators have written a narrative combining elemental qualities of their race, brought up to the minute in a product of remarkable finish and tone... It may be objected that it follows a little too much the routine of the white companies when a lot of clever racial innovations were open to its use, but the objection must be a potent one to stand up against the fire and surging energy, the joyous abandon, and the flash and spirit of what the writer believes to be about the best—maybe the best—Negro production that has crossed his theatrical path."

While *In Bamville* was only a month and a half into its pre-Broadway tour, some in the Black intelligentsia were beginning to voice their displeasure with the public discord surrounding the show, especially in light of the widespread national hysteria over Pulitzer Prize–winning white playwright Eugene O'Neill's latest drama, *All God's Chillun Got Wings*. The play was highly controversial for dealing with the topic of miscegenation, wherein onstage, a Black man, played by Paul Robeson, kissed his white wife on the hand. Months before the show opened, white journalists were predicting there would be race riots upon the show's premiere. Activists and thought leaders like A. L. Jackson found the outcry surrounding both shows to be indicative of a larger problem with the way whites evaluated Black representation. "We have not yet seen Sissle and Blake's *In Bamville*, but we note the dissatisfaction some of the white critics express with the fact that overalls and buck and wing dancing seem to be conspicuous by their absence," Jackson wrote in the *Chicago Defender*. "They proclaim that the show is too white. A while back, they were complaining because O'Neill was giving them a play that was too black. Whenever you get away from the role assigned to you by the traditions of the white man, you fail to satisfy him. Despite the fact that he sells you clothes and earned culture, he hates to see you wear those same clothes as if they belonged to you, or give expression to that culture as he would give expression to it. By these signs, we are led to believe that Sissle and Blake have a good show."

Noble Sissle and Eubie Blake addressed the issue of race head-on in a no-holds-barred interview with Archie Bell, a notable white drama and music critic, while *In Bamville* was in Cleveland. While the two hoped their show would be evaluated on its own merits, they also wanted to make it clear that they wanted the audience to see them not only as performers but as Black performers who were just as capable—and deserving—of the accolades that were regularly bestowed upon their white counterparts. "We haven't been thinking about the money. We have been so happy in our work, so pleased with our reception by the public, and so anxious to perform what we have seriously considered a 'mission,' that we haven't been thinking so much about the dollars," Eubie Blake said. "It isn't the money that interests us. Partner and I want to be paid for our work. That's natural and laudable, I believe. We want to live well, provide for our families, and such things. But what we want is to do everything we can to convince skeptical white people of the country that the Negro has a legitimate place on the stage as an entertainer, a logical and proper place, as anyone else... Always understand that we are not trying to be white actors, because we know that we have something of our own to develop which we believe—and have reason to believe—is acceptable to white audiences as well as to audiences of our own Race."

"Propagandists—that's what you think of us? That word has been used too much lately—since the war—and yet that's exactly what we want to be, if you use the word correctly," Noble Sissle added. "Take my case. Here I was, the son of a Cleveland Colored preacher of the gospel. Now, [my] father was liberal-minded and no doubt would have been interested in my career, had he lived; but he had not the slightest doubt that I would become a singing evangelist. That was in his mind during the years I was getting an education. Now, I'll give you something to smile about—that's, in reality, what I have become. Or more correctly speaking, that's how I think of myself, and I know that my present work is the development of the evangelical idea.

"I believe that my father would not be disappointed in me," he continued. "I am in the theater and I am not singing in the churches as an evangelist. Still, my partner and I want to be evangelists. We want to do something for the Negro race, to which we belong. And if we compel white audiences to listen to us; if we entertain them and if out of ten thousand persons who see and hear us, one hundred think a little better of the Colored man than in the past, then we have done something that's better than salary. In fact, that's what we want to do. It is our biggest aim. "

As *In Bamville* continued its half-year tour on its journey to Manhattan, Flournoy Miller and Aubrey Lyles were still doing well with *Runnin' Wild* at the Colonial Theatre on Sixty-Second Street. Although the show had found a loyal audience, after 228 performances—a staggering number, especially with a show entirely made up of Black performers—the musical comedy left New York on May 3, 1924. However, despite its closing, the show was far from over. The company moved on to Philadelphia for the first stop on its post-Broadway tour, where it quickly became the biggest box-office hit of the season. The engagement in Pennsylvania was so well received that, following a brief engagement in Newark, New Jersey, the musical comedy triumphantly returned to Broadway on June 23, the week of the Democratic National Convention, which happened to be in New York. The thought was that delegates from throughout the country would take advantage of the opportunity to see the popular theatrical attraction, but even the influx of visitors to the city couldn't keep the show afloat. After an embarrassing $1,100 haul, *Runnin' Wild* vacated the Colonial once again on June 28, truncating its planned three-week-long return, in search of more profitable pastures.

Sissle and Blake's musical finally opened on Broadway at the Colonial Theatre, the same venue *Runnin' Wild* had played, on September 1, 1924; however, just before it opened in Manhattan, the title was changed back to *The Chocolate Dandies*, the name that was first announced to the press back in February. The musicians had finally achieved a significant milestone— matching their former partners by playing Broadway for the second time in a show they had written—and even though they were still out of the way of the proper theater district, at least they were one street closer. It was unusually warm on opening night, but the temperature did little to depress the overflowing premiere audience, which represented a true cross-section of the city. B. C. Whitney, one of the producers, insisted that members of the press sit in the front row so they could observe Eubie Blake's dexterous and unmatched playing of the piano. Behind them sat a row of flappers, most of whom were accompanied by young men, who hooted and hollered, springing out of their seats every time the music moved them and dancing when they weren't stomping their feet in rhythm. In the box seats, there were several members of New York's upper crust, the women dressed in long gowns, the men in tuxedos. Their formal wear proved to be a mere costume, as when the audience below started to buzz with excitement, those in the box seats reacted in kind. And above the white masses sat the Harlemites, the common man and the intellectuals alike, the latter identifiable both by their more conservative dress and pince-nez eyewear.

While the performance was imperfect—some of the jokes failed to get a laugh, there were several miscues, and at one point, two men who were sharing a horse costume were nearly exposed to the audience—the critics seemed more forgiving than many on the road had been. Josephine Baker was well aware of the increased attention that would be on the newly rebranded musical and did her best to steal focus. She had been observing Johnny Hudgins, one of the leads in the show who was regularly praised in the press for his comedic timing—which conjured up Baker's jealousy—and began pilfering his bits, imitating his body movements, and upstaging her colleague, even when they weren't in the same scene. "I used to go up to the balcony and I'd watch her, and it was like seeing myself in a mirror," he recalled. "So the next night, I'd put in something new, and sure enough, she'd be doing the new thing the day after." However, there wouldn't be many more days for Baker to pull her stunt. Five days after they opened at the Colonial, Hudgins gave his notice, believing, like Gertrude Saunders had in the early days of *Shuffle Along*'s New York run, that he had better cash in his chips and move on to the next job while he was earning positive press.

Even more than being on Broadway, Josephine Baker enjoyed being back in Harlem, sharing an apartment with several of the other chorines on the fifth floor above the H. Adolph Howell Funeral Chapel on West 137th Street—she had the smallest of four bedrooms—and, as the city had yet to cool down for the fall, walking down Lenox Avenue with the rest of her castmates, trying on hats and enjoying the warm weather. But their time back in New York was short-lived. After just three months, *The Chocolate Dandies* ended its Broadway run on November 22, 1924, playing a disappointing ninety-four performances. However, despite their premature closing, the show's producers were determined to press on with a post-Broadway tour, crisscrossing Flournoy Miller and Aubrey Lyles, who were still doing the same with *Runnin' Wild*.

Noble Sissle, Eubie Blake, Flournoy Miller, and Aubrey Lyles had all left New York once again, but in late December, *Shuffle Along* returned to Harlem's Lafayette Theatre for a two-week run that extended into the new year. The cast was almost entirely different—save for a few familiar faces among the chorus—but the press welcomed the new company back to the city with open arms nonetheless. "*Shuffle Along*, the title that began the renaissance of the Negro in musical comedy... bears all indications of becoming an institution," J. A. Jackson wrote in *Billboard*. While there were plenty of available seats at the Lafayette and the show's original players had left big shoes to fill, those who attended clearly enjoyed having *Shuffle Along* home for the holidays. The show continued to play in major cities throughout the country until February 18, when the *Shuffle Along* touring company reached the end of the road in Youngstown, Ohio.

It wasn't until the news broke of the show's closure that the public was aware of the financial trouble the touring company was in. About two months earlier, shortly after Christmas, Walter Forbish and John W. Vogel, the show's managers, abandoned the production while it was in New York. They had owed $3,000 in royalties to Shuffle Along Inc., and instead of paying up or dealing with the consequences of poverty, they left town. The musical director and stage manager assumed their roles, getting *Shuffle Along* to its subsequent stops, but while they were in Cleveland, Ohio, they discovered they didn't have enough to pay the company. George Wintz was called in to resolve the issue, and after the producer paid what everyone was owed and brought the show to Youngstown, its next location, he concluded that there was no way to continue on financially. The decision to close the show was disappointing, but his commitment to taking care of the company's salaries was largely appreciated and applauded. "It is unfortunate to see the famed title removed from the active list, but the manner of closing is an eternally favorable reflection upon a man who will long be remembered by colored artists as one of the squarest friends the Negro performer ever had dealings with," a journalist wrote in *Billboard*. "George Wintz's name will long be regarded as a standard by which to measure businessmen. In the two years that he owned, and Clem Shaeffer managed, the *Shuffle Along* show, they made friends and commanded the respect of the whole profession."

While *Runnin' Wild* and *The Chocolate Dandies* continued throughout the winter months, they both struggled to maintain their footing. There were salary cuts—Josephine Baker may have bragged about making $125 weekly, but her checks eventually became $25 lighter—which eroded morale and, in some cases, violated contracts. In March 1925, *Runnin' Wild* actress Mattie Wilkes sued George White for $1,700 plus interest for payment she had been promised but lost due to salary cutbacks. Meanwhile, that same month, Lottie Gee shocked the company of *The Chocolate Dandies*—and Eubie Blake, in particular—by giving her notice. Once her salary was reduced by $50 a week, she began to take stock of her professional, and likely also her personal, situation. *Shuffle Along* had made her a star, and while she had been willing to accept modest pay to be alongside the maritally unavailable love of her life, she finally felt it was time to value her worth. She was returning to Harlem to consider her options. The show's producers were determined to continue without her.

While Sissle and Blake's production was moving forward, the financial issues plaguing Miller and Lyles's show finally came to a head on April 11, 1925. The performance at Brooklyn's Montauk Theatre began normally, but during intermission between the acts, Clifford Gray, the producer who had assumed the road rights to the show from George White, delivered IOU slips to the company in lieu of payment. The cast and crew mistook them for box office orders, believing they could be redeemed at the ticket window, and when they were denied there, all hell broke loose. The actors wouldn't step onstage, and even if they would have, the stagehands said they wouldn't raise the curtain and the orchestra wouldn't play another note. The audience started to suspect something was up after a half hour transpired without the second half of the show starting. Word quickly spread among the company that while the rest of them had been stiffed, Miller and Lyles had received their salaries, just as the sheriff arrived with an order to collect $700 on behalf of Mattie Wilkes. *Runnin' Wild* had finally lived up to its name, and when it was clear the show wasn't going to play its second half—or any other performances—the stagehands took up a collection for carfare to get the actors back to their respective homes.

After twenty months, which included a lengthy stay on Broadway, Miller and Lyles's show had met its unceremonious and unexpected end. While it may have been tempting to view their financially fraught venture as a failure, by nearly every metric, members of the Black press saw it as a success, even though some within the race felt the blackface comedians were doing more damage than good by perpetuating harmful stereotypes. "The colored theatrical profession has much to thank Miller and Lyles for," a journalist for the *New York Amsterdam News* said upon *Runnin' Wild*'s closing. "We expect many to differ with this opinion, but differences of opinion cannot change what we know to be the truth. Both Miller and Lyles have been the butt of some of the most ungrateful digs they have been forced to receive, at the hands of those for whom they made it possible, but we believe after close contact with Flournoy Miller, over a period of many years, he is fully aware that it is simply a part of the price for the success he and his partner attained after many years of sacrifice.

"Aside from the things accomplished before the footlights, there are numerous innovations made by these boys that really had a great deal to do with the hearty manner in which the colored performer was received on Broadway after a decade," they continued. "Clean, upstanding, and a youngster with the courage of his convictions, Flournoy Miller can very well look back and feel proud of what he had accomplished." However, Miller and Lyles weren't ready for a retrospective; they were looking forward, having accepted a slot in George White's upcoming edition of *Scandals*, his revue made up primarily of white artists.

Although *Runnin' Wild* had a long run, the show would

soon be forgotten, possibly due to its reliance on blackface and "darky humor," which some perceived as outdated and harmful to African Americans even during the production's run. However, it is more likely that the show has become forgotten simply because it was never again staged after the 1920s, an unfortunate consequence of Miller and Lyles's creative process. "I'll tell you the reason that there have not been any revivals," cast member Revella Hughes said. "Nothing was ever written down but the music. Miller and Lyles just talked. No one took it down. No one realized what was going on. No one could do it but them. It was improvised—ad-libbed. Of course, we followed the frame; the story did not change. The lines that were funny were kept in from performance to performance. And, of course, the cues were well set. But anything else could change from show to show—the lines, the stage business, all of it. We had a lot of fun."

While *Runnin' Wild*'s raucous final performance made headlines, a month later, it was Sissle and Blake's turn to take part in a scandal. The musicians had been hired to play a private party at the King Edward Hotel while they were on tour with *The Chocolate Dandies* in Toronto, where a white man, Carl Lynn, was murdered. While one might have expected the death to be of utmost importance, when the police arrived on the scene, an officer noticed "a suspicious bulge" in Noble Sissle's pocket, and upon inspection, discovered he had three bottles of whiskey. The duo was arrested for the illegal purchase of alcohol, and at trial, the scene nearly played out like a bit in one of their musical comedies. Eubie Blake admitted to having seen the bottles, but they were sitting on a table unsupervised and, uninvited, he decided to help himself to a taste. When he was asked if he knew how his partner ended up with the bottles, he said he assumed they had been handed to him—not illegally purchased.

When it was Sissle's turn, he testified that a masked man had given him the alcohol, and either way, no crime had been committed because he wasn't a drinking man; he had only had two glasses of ale at the party, and neither had any "kick." Once the judge was through listening to their story, the charges were dismissed against Blake, Sissle was fined $50, and the two were sent on their way. Remarkably, when the story was reported by the *Baltimore Afro-American*, the headline ran in large type—SISSLE AND BLAKE ARRESTED IN TORONTO—with a subheading in a significantly smaller font: PURCHASED WHISKEY ILLEGALLY IT WAS ALLEGED AFTER PARTY WHERE MAN WAS KILLED. Clearly, their interest was with the Black artists as opposed to the dearly departed.

As Sissle and Blake were getting into trouble, Lottie Gee had finally plotted her next move. She accepted an offer to star in *The Chocolate Kiddies*—a revue featuring forty-two other Black performers, including *Shuffle Along* and *Runnin' Wild* alumna Adelaide Hall—which was embarking on a European tour. For the actress, it was a welcome opportunity to not only earn a fair wage but also revisit a continent that she had been longing to return to. "European audiences give me real inspiration," she had said over a year earlier when she was still in Sissle and Blake's show. "They do not hold back for prejudice or horrid injustices of any kind, but give spontaneous applause and pleasing comment to whatever they enjoy."

While the news of Lottie Gee's departure was bittersweet for Eubie Blake, it couldn't have come at a worse time. He had been anxious about *The Chocolate Dandies'* finances since its pre-Broadway run, and conditions hadn't improved. Despite what the critics said, audiences were still enjoying the show, but the overhead was too high and the producers were hemorrhaging money. By May 1925, rumors began circulating that a closing was imminent, and Josephine Baker, who had just been the subject of a feature article in the *New York Amsterdam News* alongside a large picture of her with a beaming smile, prayed for the show's luck to change. She slept with a good-luck penny under her window and wished good thoughts, and one morning, she received a knock on her dressing room door. It was a letter with an offer for her to appear at the Plantation, the nightclub where Florence Mills had appeared after she'd left *Shuffle Along*. Josephine Baker's luck had improved after all.

But she never had the opportunity to give her notice. *The Chocolate Dandies* played its final performance on May 23, 1925, at Werba's Brooklyn Theatre in New York. Similarly to *Runnin' Wild*, the show was in arrears. To break even, the production needed to average $16,000 a week at the box office—and play to full capacity houses every day—which it was only able to do five times throughout its run. By the time they arrived in Brooklyn, the show was over $60,000 in debt and, with the exception of the stage crew, was unable to pay the company their salaries from the box office. The actors and musicians who sought payment from producer B. C. Whitney's offices were denied, leaving them essentially stranded in Manhattan, looking for work. However, despite the show's "disastrous" end, Eubie Blake maintained that, from a musical standpoint, *The Chocolate Dandies* was his best work with Noble Sissle. "That's the score," he said. "I know the world thinks *Shuffle Along* was the best but that is more because it was such a novelty when it came out. It was the first, and it left an indelible mark on people's minds. But I have never written a score to compare with *The Chocolate Dandies*. I know there is nothing in *Shuffle Along* anywhere near the melodies of 'Dixie Moon' and 'Jassamine Lane.' I know what people say, but I still fight the world on it. You know, you have a lot of nerve to tell the whole world off, but that's how I feel."

Just three years earlier, the stars of *Shuffle Along* had more money than they knew what to do with, but by the end of 1925, they were struggling. Noble Sissle and Eubie Blake had returned to vaudeville with their duo act following *The Chocolate Dandies'* closing, but in July, the vocalist filed for bankruptcy. Sissle claimed he was due $6,000 in back pay from the production, owed $3,000 to various debtors, and owned nothing. Even the piano in his home, he said, was a premarital asset of his wife's, as she'd inherited it from her deceased first husband. Five months later, just before Christmas, Aubrey Lyles had also gone broke and sought relief from the courts, as he had only $39.50 to his name and over $19,000 in liabilities—a haberdashery, clothing store, and Shuffle Along Inc. were among his creditors. And although Gertrude Saunders had maintained steady work since leaving *Shuffle Along* in 1921—starring in both Irvin C. Miller's *Liza* and *Dinah* revues, as well as a number of burlesque shows—she too found herself in dire financial straits. She sued Shuffle Along Inc. for $800 in back pay, as her salary was also cut before she left, in violation of her contract.

There were more Black artists working in the entertainment industry throughout the United States than ever before, and yet the creators of *Shuffle Along* were scraping to get by. Miller and Lyles had taken George White up on his offer to appear in *Scandals*, and in August 1925, Sissle and Blake were offered a lifeline of their own. William Morris, of the famous talent agency, offered to book the musicians on an eight-month tour of England, Scotland, and France—no longer as the Dixie Duo but as the American Ambassadors of Syncopation. Just a few weeks later, on the evening of September 18, the two musicians joined their wives aboard the *Olympic*, a luxury liner set to cross the Atlantic. Sissle and Blake took to a piano and played some of their hits from *Shuffle Along* and *The Chocolate Dandies* and a few tunes from their vaudeville act that hadn't made it onto the Broadway stage, and the brief concert was broadcast live on WEAF in New York. At midnight, the ship departed, and the four waved their goodbyes to a throng of family, friends, and fans.

As they set sail, Noble Sissle turned his attention to the seemingly infinite ocean and the possibilities he knew awaited them once they had reached land again, while Eubie Blake couldn't help but look back at the country he was leaving behind. He missed America already.

EUBIE BLAKE SURROUNDED BY CHORINES IN A PUBLICITY STILL FOR *SHUFFLE ALONG OF 1933*

Photo by White Studio, © New York Public Library for the Performing Arts

12

ANOTHER
SECOND CHANCE

1925–1933

Noble Sissle was having the time of his life. In less than a year, he and Eubie Blake had gone from secretly praying there was enough in the *Chocolate Dandies'* box office till to keep the company happy for a little bit longer to headlining a highly successful European tour with a top talent agent behind them. It felt like old times, playing for the rich and refined, who all dropped their pretense once Blake began wobbling the bass, bouncing on his piano stool, and synchronizing with Sissle's melodious vocals. While in England, they played the Coliseum, wowed at the Piccadilly, and were the main entertainment for the Kit Kat Club's floor show, where they played to the Prince of Wales. The London *Daily Telegraph* declared, "Sissle and Blake have the kind of quality that grows on you and makes their work appear at the second visit to be even better than you remembered it. In their own original songs, Noble Sissle and Eubie Blake give us the very essence of syncopation."

While they were scratching out stops on their packed itinerary—and sneaking in a few extra engagements whenever they could—they once again caught the attention of Charles B. Cochran, the producer who had unsuccessfully attempted to bring *Shuffle Along* to England in 1922. The theater impresario had already missed one opportunity to work with the top musicians, and he was eager for another shot at bringing some of that Sissle and Blake magic to his stage. He commissioned them to write a few songs for his upcoming annual revue—he was the Florenz Ziegfeld of England—and two of them, "Tahiti" and "Let's Get Married Right Away," became hits. Pleased with their work, as their eight months overseas were coming toward their natural end, Cochran asked them to remain in London and write his entire 1927 show. And just as the offer was put on the table, Noble Sissle, who'd always managed the business affairs for the pair, had even more good news to share with his partner.

"Hi, kid! Hi, kid! Well, I did it again!" Sissle said, enthusiastically running into Eubie Blake's hotel room, beaming from ear to ear. "I booked a return engagement for the tour! We're going around again!"

Blake sat on the bed, unable to come close to matching his partner's enthusiasm. After eight months, the pianist was ready to go home. "No, Sissle," he said, taking all the air out of the room. "I ain't goin' on that tour again."

For the first time since they'd met in 1915, the two really failed to see eye to eye professionally. The Europeans couldn't get enough of their act, and Sissle couldn't believe Blake would pass up these golden opportunities. The pair and their wives had been treated excellently throughout their stay, and the tour was a boon financially, but Blake had been quietly counting down the days until it was over, and he couldn't imagine pushing their departure back. "I didn't like London. In fact, I don't like Europe at all. I love this country over here, and he wants to stay over there, and I want to come home," he later recalled. The two got into an argument, but despite his best efforts and to his great frustration, Sissle couldn't make Blake stay. They turned down Cochran's deal and prepared to go back home.

But before they departed Europe, Sissle and Blake made arrangements to see an old friend. After *The Chocolate Dandies* folded, Josephine Baker accepted the offer to perform at the Plantation above the Winter Garden, where she earned praise in the press for doing an impression of Johnny Hudgins, clearly having found another way to benefit from her old cast member's comic sensibilities. But just weeks after she began performing at the club, Baker was asked to join an all-Black revue set to open in Paris. She didn't know it at the time, but Florence Mills had been approached first but was unaffordable. Baker thought it was a risky venture, but when she learned she would be given a wardrobe of expensive clothes, pearls, and $200 a week, she signed on the dotted line and prepared to set sail on September 15 alongside two dozen other Black performers.

When she arrived, it was pouring rain. As she made her way off the ship and onto French soil, in her black-and-white-checked gardening overalls and an extravagant hat she was fortunate to be wearing, she said out loud to no one in particular, "So, this is Paris." She wanted to board the ship and return to America already, until she began to take in the locale. "One look at Paris and I was good as new," she recalled. "I was... struck by the women's clothes. In New York I had heard that Parisiennes wore corsets and leg-of-mutton sleeves. Not at all. Their bodies moved freely, their sleeves were closely fitted, their heels were extremely high and the little hats they wore perched on their heads like the dots of an *i*. Everyone seemed to be bursting with life. And most surprisingly of all, I saw couples kissing in the streets. In America you went to jail for that! It was true—this *was* a free country. France was a wonderful place!"

La Revue Nègre opened at the Théâtre des Champs-Élysées on October 2, 1925, and the comedienne from the chorus became a global sensation overnight. Baker danced a frenetic Charleston, and in the show's finale, she appeared in a feathered costume with her slick dark hair plastered to her scalp. She became wild, flittering madly "like a hummingbird," with her body—and not her comedy—attracting the audience's full attention. When the performance was over, the crowd chanted her name, "Jo-se-phine, Jo-se-phine!" Paris correspondent Janet Flanner, who was on her first assignment for the *New Yorker*, reviewed the premiere: "Her magnificent dark body, a new model to the French, proved for the first time that black was beautiful." In France, Baker felt truly uninhibited—and appreciated. "I didn't get my first break on Broadway," she recalled. "I was only in the chorus in *Shuffle Along* and *Chocolate Dandies*. I became famous first in France." Before long, she was performing at the Folies Bergère with the star dressing room, which was filled with a menagerie of exotic animals, in little more than a waistband with sixteen bananas attached to it, a wide smile, and the big bright eyes that had brought her into *Shuffle Along*'s main company in Boston.

Before Noble Sissle and Eubie Blake returned to the States, they had to see Baker for themselves. When they arrived at her apartment, there were boa constrictors, monkeys, and two cheetahs. Blake was invited to get a closer look, but he declined, opting instead to stick with the humans with whom he was better acquainted. There were over forty thousand fan letters strewn about, with several thousand containing marriage proposals. The three enjoyed a nice chat—Sissle, Blake, and the star they had helped discover—and shortly thereafter, the musicians and their wives boarded the *Paris*, another luxury liner, heading back to New York in April 1926.

Upon their return to the States, Blake was eager to reconnect with the familiar. His first trip was to visit his mother in Baltimore—his dad had died in 1917—where he also found time to impart a few wise words to the readers of the Black press. "My advice to all American Negroes is to stay away from Europe," he told the *Baltimore Afro-American*. "Particularly is this so if you are poor. No matter what happens or what the conditions are in America, they can be nothing like the deplorable conditions that exist in London. I have seen thousands sleeping in the streets...and other distresses that I hate to remember."

Eubie Blake may have been frustrated with his time overseas, but Noble Sissle found it difficult to readjust to the United States. After two Broadway shows and a barn-burning European tour, returning to vaudeville felt like a downgrade. Furthermore, while he and his wife had gotten along well enough in Europe, his marriage was causing him more pain than pleasure. Harriett was arrested for larceny in October 1926, and while the charges were subsequently found to be fraudulent and dropped the following February, the ordeal was embarrassing and further strained their already tenuous union. After spending the summer trying his best to paper over his unhappiness, smiling in front of audiences while getting into arguments behind the scenes, Sissle knew it was time to make a move, especially with the changes that were taking place in the world of entertainment. "Tending to the business and looking ahead from that point of view, the American theater had gone practically dead— the musical theater—because the talkies had just started," he explained. While *The Jazz Singer*, the first feature film with lip-synchronous singing and speech, wouldn't have its premiere until October, the developments of the talking picture were covered regularly in the press throughout the early portion of 1927, even prior to Al Jolson being attached to the project. *The*

Jazz Singer was the beginning of the future, and Sissle thought the more prudent career choice was for he and Blake to bide their time in Europe and try to reinstate their business relationship with Charles Cochran in the process. "But, brother, Blake got so cold," Sissle said. With both partners unwilling to budge on their position, Noble and Harriett Sissle ventured to Paris, where he performed in music halls and theaters, while Eubie Blake remained behind. On September 21, 1927, a headline in *Variety* made it official: Sissle-Blake Split.

Part of Noble Sissle's frustration likely emanated from seeing his old partners, Flournoy Miller and Aubrey Lyles, doing well for themselves while he and Blake were making the rounds again in vaudeville. After appearing in George White's *Scandals*, the duo continued performing together and attempted to drum up investors for what they hoped would be their crowning achievement—opening a legitimate Broadway house for Black-centered productions. "We want to establish in New York finally a theater which shall present plays by and of our race, treating us not as mere cartoons of humanity, but in a serious though sometimes a comedy spirit, as human beings created in the image of God," Flournoy Miller told the *Pittsburgh Courier* in May 1926, recalling his early days with Lyles at the world's first Black-owned theater. "The Pekin did not have the serious aim that we have now. We were young then—very young— and we aimed only to amuse... White people when they go to our plays want a certain amount of hokum, and we gave them hokum all right. So we succeeded in getting popular with white people in Chicago. But once you begin to use hokum you begin to go down hill [*sic*], artistically... But we are older...and have done a lot of thinking since then. I find myself becoming more seriously inclined.

"We realize that our fathers were always right," he continued, telling the reporter that both he and Lyles were encouraged to go to Fisk University by their dads. "We really had serious thoughts of working for the betterment of our race until we began to write and put on the college shows... I do not really think we gave up our serious ambitions until one field day in 1904, when we worked out a clown boxing act... And we then and there made up our minds that we would not only go on to the stage, but have a theater of our own."

"And now we feel that we should return to something of the original purposes of our lives. We have merely amused long enough," Lyles added.

"Naturally, whenever the plot called for the presence of occasional white characters, we would use white actors," Miller explained. "Neither the plays presented nor the theater would be in the hands of white men. We ourselves and our associates would handle every detail. But our appeal would be to a cosmopolitan audience. We would aim artistic productions presenting us as we are. It would be a cross-section of a phase of life, and whatever moral there might be in that particular cross-section would adhere to the result. I believe that the needs of our race and a better understanding of us would broadcast through such a theater."

But their dreams of pushing comedy aside and opening their own Broadway theater would have to wait. As Miller and Lyles struggled to secure backers for their venture, in early 1927, they were approached to star in *Rang Tang*, a musical comedy with a book by white actress-turned-playwright Kaj Gynt, who was originally from Scandinavia, music by Ford Dabney, and lyrics by Jo Trent. The show was seemingly written for them, as it was another story set in Jimtown and centered on Steve Jenkins and Sam Peck, who are now local barbers with a mountain of debt. Faced with prosecution for nonpayment to their creditors, the two steal an airplane and set off to find safe harbor anywhere they can. They ultimately find themselves on the coast of Africa, where the locals greet them with song and dance. Jenkins and Peck are soon up to their old shenanigans once again, getting into comedic situations while on African shores, and eventually return to the United States—Harlem, "the black belt" of the country, in particular—with a box of diamonds. They had left the country poor, but they returned "the richest men in the world."

Rang Tang opened on July 12 at the newly opened Royale Theatre, a 1,036-seat venue on West Forty-Fifth Street, right in the center of the Manhattan theater district. Even though Miller and Lyles hadn't written the book—although Flournoy did direct the show—the comedians' return was welcomed, especially with the industry once again in an economic slump. "With the Broadway box-office business still on the wane and over 40 legitimate houses dark, an attempt is being made to revive interest in the theater thru [*sic*] the negro musicals," a journalist wrote in *Billboard*. "A similar move was successfully made several seasons ago when *Shuffle Along* and *Runnin' Wild* prospered thru [*sic*] long runs." *Rang Tang* wasn't the only

Black show in New York—there were at least five presented that season—but it was the production that seemed best poised to succeed. Initial reviews were mixed, led by the *New York Times* bemoaning that "Harlem continued its invasion of the Broadway stage" on the night of its premiere and the *New York Herald Tribune* calling the show "another child-like imitation of dull, white extravaganza."

The *Pittsburgh Courier* said that the show "rivals Ziegfeld production in costumes and scenery," but just as Sissle and Blake had focused too much on music and not enough on comedy in *The Chocolate Dandies*, the paper felt Miller and Lyles's latest project was guilty of the opposite, and both suffered from too much spectacle and not enough substance. "The show is most pretentious," the critic wrote. "It sets out to be a big-time musical comedy, but it starts at the wrong end. It has acquired all the trappings in the line of numbers, clothes, and settings, but has overlooked the fact that first of all, a musical comedy should have music and not just tricky arrangements... One experiences the keen disappointment that comes after biting into a very elaborate and ornate confection and finding it full of air. *Rang Tang* has no filling." *Variety* declared it "more dress than show," and *Billboard* thought it was "dull and uninteresting," with the reviewer also taking issue with Miller and Lyles's continued recycling of their material. "They get over with their old boxing clog and with the arithmetic trick; this year three times seventeen make twenty-four, and occasionally one of their original gags proves to be still reliable. For the most part, however, the show is discouragingly humorless."

However, despite the initial reviews and the heat wave—the longest and most intense of the summer—depressing attendance at venues throughout the city, *Rang Tang* brought in just over $9,000 in its first week. Unforgiving high temperatures continued to be a drag on the industry in the weeks that followed, yet while other shows were forced to fold, *Rang Tang* held its own. The weather finally broke by the first week of August, and Broadway's numbers improved across the board. *Rang Tang* was no exception, grossing over $12,000, with no sign of slowing. In the beginning of September, the production moved around the corner to the Majestic, which had about six hundred more seats than the Royale, where it ultimately reached $16,000 by the end of the month.

While Miller and Lyles were back on Broadway, a face familiar to music lovers around the world was experiencing her own homecoming. Since leaving *Shuffle Along* for Lew Leslie's *Plantation Revue* in 1922, Florence Mills had become one of the most popular Black entertainers in the world. The following year, Charles Cochran had brought the company to England and developed a new show around them, *Dover Street to Dixie*, a two-act revue that featured white performers in the first half and the *Plantation Revue* players in the second. The English adored the show, and upon her return to New York, Mills continued to draw high praise and top dollar, performing in cafés and cabarets and Lew Leslie's 1924 *Dixie to Broadway*, a large-scale all-Black revue that the producer created for her to star in. In his review for *Variety*, African American performer and theater aficionado George Bell praised the production. "Although limited by the producer's obvious economy in the matter of adequate settings, the show is thoroughly well done by a good company," he wrote. "It is a credit to the colored race, rather than a ridicule. The show is not as boisterous as either *Runnin' Wild* or *Shuffle Along*, but suffers nothing in comparison with these two in either the singing or the stepping... Florence Mills, the star, has personality and a splendid voice. She is ably supported by well-known colored artists, whose efforts, and the work of the chorus, succeed in uplifting the Negro in the artistic world."

When the show opened at Philadelphia's Lyric Theatre, the *Pittsburgh Courier* declared that Florence Mills "is the apothesis [*sic*] of pep, she is the nth degree of personality; she can put over any old song, as artfully and artistically as can Nora Bayes or Fanny Brice."

After *Dixie*, Mills contin-ued playing nightclubs and headlining venues like the Palace until she was invited back to the Plantation above the Winter Garden in November 1925 to headline Lew Leslie's *Blackbirds of 1926*, an all-Black revue the producer hoped would become an annual affair in the style of Ziegfeld's *Follies* and George

FLORENCE MILLS IN COSTUME FOR HER "JUNGLE NUMBER" IN A PROMOTIONAL STILL FOR *DIXIE TO BROADWAY*, 1925

Photo by Atelier Rembrand/ullstein bild via Getty Images

White's *Scandals*. Six months later, the show moved to Harlem's Alhambra Theatre, a vaudeville house on the Keith circuit, which was being leased out for the first time to house an all-Black production. The revue was expanded to two acts and seven scenes, with a cast of seventy-five, and patrons were charged a $2 top ticket price for what was shaping up to be a major theatrical event. In the show's opening number, Florence Mills emerged from an oversized birthday cake in a simplistic dress and without any flashy jewelry, a stark contrast to the overdone and underdressed Ziegfeld girls and a reminder of her ability to captivate with her performance skills alone.

The show opened to capacity audiences, and in May 1926, Lew Leslie brought the show to Paris for a brief engagement. "Many changes, startling and significant, have come upon Paris in the days since the war, but among the innovations in the theater, none has been more astonishing than Lew Leslie's presentation of Florence Mills at the Ambassador cabaret," the *Chicago Defender* wrote under the headline PARIS WILD ABOUT FLORENCE. "Night life in this city is being made to conform to the high standard and high prices which Leslie's fast stepping Americans demand. Quite as much interest has been created by the change which Miss Mills has brought to the Ambassador as by the character of her entertainment." *Blackbirds* performer Johnny Dunn confirmed to the *Baltimore Afro-American* that the company was accepted by the Parisians, both onstage and off. "We were treated royally by the French," he said. "There was no evidence of prejudice against us anywhere, except from the American tourists." In

September, Charles Cochran brought the show to London's Pavilion Theatre, where it played 276 performances. The Prince of Wales saw the show at least nineteen times, and the English press found Mills "small but remarkable, not only as a manifestation of great energy in a small compass, but as a burlesque comedienne, singer, and dancer."

Florence Mills quickly became to London what Josephine Baker was to Paris, a Black artist who was able to ascend to heights overseas that probably would have been more challenging had she stayed in America. In January 1927, the singer wrote about her experience with race prejudice both in the United States and abroad in an editorial for London's *Sun-Chronicle*. "'What a pity she isn't white.' This was the remark made by a woman as I left the stage door the other evening," she wrote. "It was not the first time such a comment has been passed. It is the eternal burden of the colored people—the penalization for an accident of birth—to be made to feel out of focus with the rest of humanity. There are some people I have met who appear to find it difficult to credit the Negro with a soul. Perhaps they are prepared to admit that he has a 'soul of sorts,' but that is not on the same plane as that of the white race they refuse to acknowledge.

"A few years ago this attitude towards colored people was very marked. Today it is not so much in evidence, but it still exists," she continued. "But there is not the slightest doubt that the status of the Negro is generally improving. Color barriers are tottering, and he is getting his foot on the ladder of equality. There are still Negroes who are lynched simply because they are Negroes, but there are also colored men who are barristers, doctors, prominent musicians, actors, poets, and writers. And their numbers are steadily increasing. In America, despite the very real prejudice that exists, the Negro race is rearing its head, in all aspects of social life. In England, where the color line is practically nonexistent, Negroes have achieved a virtual equality."

Blackbirds remained a hit throughout 1927, so much so that its producer attempted to stage a knock-off—except with white performers. The results were less than optimal. "It is amusing how Lew Leslie tried to produce a white revue and named it *Whitebirds*, copying everything after his *Blackbirds* revue and, and thus far, *Whitebirds* has been a complete failure," Ivan Harold Browning of the Harmony Kings wrote while on tour in Europe. "In view of this fact, Leslie has started a third edition of his *Blackbirds* revue. He is like all Ofays, using the Negro when he can't do any better."

Florence Mills's English fans wanted her to remain there indefinitely, as the country had taken her in as one of its own, but on September 27, 1927, she and her husband returned to America. Although she had many offers on the table, the performer was in need of a rest. Upon her arrival back, she was greeted by hundreds of fans at the pier—a genuine surprise to Mills—before a caravan escorted her back to her Harlem home on West 133rd Street.

On October 7, Florence Mills was the guest of honor at a star-studded reception at the Footlights Club on West 131st Street. Irvin C. Miller served as chair of the seven-member arrangements committee, which also included Flournoy Miller,

Aubrey Lyles, and Eubie Blake—Noble Sissle was still in Europe. Gertrude Saunders, Mills's *Shuffle Along* predecessor, was also in attendance. A ten-course dinner was served as the guests performed musical selections and delivered speeches, with Aubrey Lyles's address garnering the most attention. After about ten other people spoke, the comedian passionately warned Mills to avoid Carl Van Vechten, the white cultural critic and jazz enthusiast who had been welcomed by many in the Black community, so much so that he saw himself as a genuine Harlemite as opposed to a welcomed guest. Van Vechten financed a studio for *Shuffle Along* and *Chocolate Dandies* alumnus Charlie Davis— who also choreographed specialty numbers for George White's *Scandals*—to teach white dancers how to move like Black performers, and two years earlier, he had published *Nigger Heaven*, a highly controversial, albeit likely well-intentioned, novel that he wrote to shed light on what life was like for the "real Negro" living in Harlem as opposed to the Southern caricatures white audiences were used to seeing.

"Nigger heaven" was an outdated, derogatory phrase from the early days of the Reconstruction Era for the highest seating area of a theater, where Blacks were regulated. Van Vechten knew the title was provocative but thought it would help the book garner attention, in addition to serving as a fitting metaphor for modern race relations. "Nigger Heaven! That's what Harlem is," one of his characters says in the novel. "We sit in our places in the gallery of this New York theatre and watch the white world sitting down below in the good seats in the orchestra. Occasionally they turn their faces up towards us, their hard, cruel faces, to laugh or sneer, but they never beckon." The novel's plot centered on Mary, an uptight librarian who wishes she could "act naturally" as other Negroes do, as opposed to in her hoity-toity college-educated way, and Byron, an aspiring writer with whom she has a brief relationship, whose work and career are thwarted by condescending white editors. The narrative also includes a colorful cast of characters, including pimps, nightclub owners, and gamblers, and plenty of Black folks speaking in stereotypical "darky" dialect. The novel was polarizing, not just for its title but also its content. Some African Americans felt it was capable of humanizing Blacks to whites, while others felt the book was paternalistic in its conception and execution—a Caucasian author speaking with authority on the everyday life of colored people. W. E. B. Du Bois wrote in *The Crisis* that the novel was "an affront to the hospitality of black folk and to the intelligence of white."

Aubrey Lyles shared Du Bois's sentiment. He said that many Black performers had become susceptible to Van Vechten's wiles, but in reality, the cultural critic was interested in maintaining "white supremacy" by perpetuating a narrow and inauthentic view of Black life. Additionally, Van Vechten, who helped make some white folks who felt leery about "slumming it" in Harlem feel comfortable taking the excursion uptown, was a believer that African Americans were innately different—in speech, movement, lifestyle, and ability—from whites. With *Nigger Heaven* a bestseller and Van Vechten beloved and defended by many of the race, Aubrey Lyles urged Mills, "representing our highest and best," to not end up "gobbled up by a flattering Van Vechten."

Six years after *Shuffle Along* arrived in New York, interest in Black life and culture—even if, in most cases, it was often a simplistic and occasionally problematic version of it—had not just remained but had grown stronger. But this sustained attention had its drawbacks, particularly for some in the Black community who took issue with Harlem, once a somewhat exclusive bastion for members of the race, becoming a trendy location for whites to listen to music, buy illicit alcohol, and go on "slumming" excursions. When Rudolph Fisher, an African American writer, orator, and Brown University graduate, returned to his neighborhood after a five-year absence and discovered the landscape had changed, he voiced his surprise in "The Caucasian Storms Harlem," a 1927 essay published in the *American Mercury*. "I was entirely unprepared for what I found when I returned to Harlem recently," he wrote. "I remembered one place especially where my own crowd used to hold forth; and, hoping to find some old-timers there still, I sought it out one midnight. The old, familiar plunkety-plunk welcomed me from below as I entered. I descended the same old narrow stairs, came into the same smoke-misty basement, and found myself a chair at one of the ancient white-porcelain, mirror-smooth tables. I drew a deep breath and looked about, seeking familiar faces. 'What a lot of 'fays!' I thought, as I noticed the number of white guests. Presently I grew puzzled and began to stare, then I gaped—and gasped. I found myself wondering if this was the right place—if, indeed, this was Harlem at all. I suddenly became aware that, except for the waiters and members of the orchestra, I was the only Negro in the place.

"After a while I left it and wandered about in a daze from night-club to night-club," he continued. "I tried the Nest, Small's, Connie's Inn, the Capitol, Happy's, the Cotton Club. There was no mistake; my discovery was real and was repeatedly confirmed. No wonder my old crowd was not to be found in any of them. The best of Harlem's black cabarets have changed their names and turned white... The managers don't hesitate to say that it is upon these predominant white patrons that they depend for success. These places therefore are no longer mine but theirs. Not that I'm barred, any more than they were seven or eight years ago. Once known, I'm even welcome, just as some of them used to be. But the complexion of the place is theirs, not mine. I? Why, I am actually stared at, I frequently feel uncomfortable and out of place, and when I go out on the floor to dance I am lost in a sea of white faces. As another observer put it to me since, time was when white people went to Negro cabarets to see how Negroes acted; now Negroes go to these same cabarets to see how white people act."

Harlem *was* changing, and while thought leaders like Rudolph Fisher were mourning the vicissitudes in their neighborhood, the Black community experienced a significantly damning loss. On October 24, less than a month after her return to New York, Florence Mills was rushed from her home to the Hospital for Joint Diseases on 124th Street, where she was operated on for appendicitis. But the surgery went poorly, and she developed peritonitis. Her husband donated his blood for a transfusion, but she never recovered. On November 1, 1927, Florence Mills died in the early morning hours, at thirty-two years old and the zenith of a career that still confounded many, as she failed to fit into any preconceived notions of what it took to be a successful female performer—Black or otherwise. "Nobody understood Florence Mills," the *Atlanta Constitution* declared the day after she died. "She made weekly profits which would have bought a half dozen farms down south where her parents were born. But she submitted without comment to restrictions of the white race in a care-free manner which won her all the more adoration."

"Her contribution to the stage is greater than that made by any female of the race since the death of the late Aida Overton Walker, and it is well to here point out that whatever she did was without at any time resorting to the smut and suggestiveness which so many fool themselves into believing is necessary to their success," a journalist wrote in the *New York Amsterdam News*. "Her name will be lasting because she built on a firm and clean foundation… Florence Mills did not pander to the so called 'art' of the present day. She did not become a pet of the seekers of notoriety, nor did she crave to bask in the smiles of those perverts of the underworld sent to us by a white society tired of their 'free love' and other tenets to which only the fools among us subscribe. True art needs no embellishment."

The day after her death, over ten thousand Harlemites—including "practically all of the colored actors and actresses in the city" and a delegation of five hundred children—paid their respects at the H. Adolph Howell Funeral Chapel on 137th Street and Seventh Avenue, where Mills's body was dressed in a simple white satin performance dress and laid in a $10,000 hammered bronze casket. New York governor Al Smith and the city's mayor, Jimmy Walker, were among the many who sent telegrams of condolence. Her body continued to lie in state at the parlor until her funeral, and by November 4, over forty thousand people had come to catch a final glimpse of the star. She had been redressed in her final burial outfit, a silver metallic cloth evening dress, trimmed in rhinestones, with matching mesh hose and cloth evening slippers. An ivory rosary was placed in her folded hands, and a string of pearls were clasped around her neck.

Two days later, on November 6, Harlem turned out in spectacular fashion to wish Florence Mills a final farewell. Police were on hand to manage the thousands of well-wishers attempting to push their way inside Zion M. E. Church on West 137th Street, where an estimated five thousand had squeezed into the hall built to hold just twenty-three hundred people. Throughout the funeral services, several women of the choir wailed and fainted before being quickly tended to by white-uniformed African American nurses from the Red Cross. The two-hour-long service also came to a halt when Mills's friend Juanita Stinnette performed an original song, "Florence." Before she concluded, several ushers had to carry her out of the church as she became overcome by grief and emotion, screaming "Florence! Florence!" in agony as her voice reverberated throughout the chapel. During the funeral procession, Robert Brown, one of the musicians playing behind the hearse, collapsed from a heart attack and died before the ambulance arrived. After the services, over 150,000 of the neighborhood's residents lined the streets, along with the countless others who hung out of windows, latched on to fire escapes, and looked down from rooftops as they withstood the wind and cool temperatures to watch and weep as a ten-car motorcade transported large floral bouquets through twenty-six blocks within the epicenter of Black art and culture. She was buried at Woodlawn Cemetery in the Bronx.

Florence Mills's death came at an otherwise promising time for Black entertainers. Although Flournoy Miller and Aubrey Lyles had just concluded their Broadway run of *Rang Tang* after 119 performances—a respectable number, despite falling short of their previous ventures—on October 12, 1927, *Variety* ran a front-page story projecting that the upcoming Broadway season was set to have more African American performers onstage than ever before, and not only in Black shows, as more white producers were "demand[ing] colored atmosphere." The Theatre Guild had just opened *Porgy*, which starred Black actors, with many more in the company of forty. Florenz Ziegfeld was producing an adaptation of Edna Ferber's novel *Show Boat*, which was set to include Blacks. There were thirty Black actors in David Belasco's *Lulu Belle*, which was on tour; ten in both *Sidewalks of New York* and *Black Velvet*; six in Gene Buck's *Take the Air*; and, of course, eighty in *Rang Tang*, which was set to embark on tour.

While Miller and Lyles were on the road and Noble Sissle was performing overseas, Eubie Blake developed a new act with Broadway Jones, the performer he partnered with in 1918 while Sissle was at war. They opened at the Lincoln Theatre in Union City, New Jersey, where they received $162.50, combined, over the course of four days and nearly a dozen performances. They continued to Patchogue and Lynbrook, two villages on Long

Island, as well as New Britain, Connecticut, where their financial prospects weren't much better. The pair averaged about $50 a day at those stops throughout a rough winter season. Were it not for Eubie Blake's royalty checks from the American Society of Composers, Authors, and Publishers (ASCAP), he and Broadway Jones would have had to resort to literally singing for their supper. They ventured to Palm Beach in the winter of 1928, where Broadway Jones usually had success throughout the season playing private events, and by March, they were back home. The press was buzzing with reports that Lew Leslie was looking to unite Josephine Baker, Johnny Hudgins, Adelaide Hall—who was now starring in the latest edition of *Blackbirds*—and several other notable Black stars for a lavish floor show, and he wanted Eubie Blake to provide the music. The producer leaked word to the press, seemingly in an attempt to strong-arm Baker into agreeing to the proposition, but the Parisian star declined.

Broadway Jones had an idea. He and Eubie Blake were just making ends meet playing as a pair, but what if they expanded and rebranded their act? The two quickly pulled together a show they called *Shuffle Along Jr.*, which ran anywhere between a half hour and close to ninety minutes, depending on the length of their booking. Blake and Jones appeared in the show—*Variety* noted that the pianist didn't just play and sing but also danced—alongside eleven others: four principals and a seven-member chorus. Their short revue hit the vaudeville circuit in August 1928, and while they weren't making significantly more money, the revue garnered them moderately more income than they were making before. *Billboard* called the show a "fairly enter-taining vehicle, but not as good as the old Sissle and Blake act," and although the *Baltimore Afro-American* said the revue was "making quite a stir on the big time," *Shuffle Along Jr.* seemed to embody its name—as it made its way across the nation, it wasn't a hit nor a flop but simply ambled across America until it reached its conclusion in 1929.

Meanwhile, Noble Sissle was hitting his stride across the Atlantic, thanks to a chance meeting he had with white composer Cole Porter while walking on the Champs-Élysées in Paris shortly after the singer's arrival in 1927. Porter recognized Sissle straightaway and asked how he was doing.

"I'm starvin' to death," the vocalist responded.

"Why don't you get a band together?" Porter replied. "I think I can find a spot for you."

Sissle didn't know of any Black musicians in Paris, but with Porter's assistance, he found a score of expatriate African American players in Montmartre. With the vocalist serving as bandleader, Noble Sissle's Syncopators prospered at Les Ambassadeurs in Paris. The band would eventually travel to Monte Carlo, Deauville, Ostend, London, and Glasgow, earning enthusiastic applause in every city.

Things were also going well for Miller and Lyles after they'd hit another rough patch. *Rang Tang*'s post-Broadway tour began well, but by January 1928, members of the company were writing home and begging for money—many in the chorus declared they hadn't been paid in weeks—and Charlie Davis, who staged the production, sued for $500 in unpaid wages as the show was struggling to stay above water financially. Nearly as soon as that production closed, their Steve Jenkins and Sam Peck characters were back in a new Jimtown musical comedy—*Keep Shufflin'*—which, following a two-week tryout in Philadelphia, made its Broadway debut on February 27, 1928 at Daly's Sixty-Third Street Theatre, the renamed former home of *Shuffle Along*. This time, Jenkins and Peck appear as benevolent bank robbers who are president and vice president of the Equal Got Club, a comical take on socialism based on the principles that everyone in Jimtown should "git" what everyone else "got." The thin plot sees the two emptying the local bank—because the money has been sitting there too long—so they can enrich everyone in the town. Their pre-Broadway reviews were stellar, and it was clear that the production had pulled out all the stops—a cast of ninety, book by Miller and Lyles, with music by some of the most significant musicians of the Harlem jazz scene: Jimmy Johnson, Thomas "Fats" Waller, and Clarence Todd composed the music, while Henry Creamer and Andy Razaf wrote the score. On the night of its premiere, a large canvas banner hung across Sixty-Third, welcoming them back to the venue that had catapulted the comedians into the stratosphere.

But upon its opening, it was unclear how things would fare in the long term, as the critical assessments were mixed. "Last night's performance gave indications of late revisions and hurried changes. But for all an occasional lack of smoothness, it did maintain a break-neck pace which augured well for the show's continuance," the *New York Times* wrote in its lukewarm review. "The tunes are pleasant, if not rememberable, and the dancing is, of course, fast and furious." Jack Pulaski at *Variety* was even kinder. "Had its sponsors kept the show out for another week or two for smoothing, *Shufflin'* would have wowed Broadway. Hot babe, it's there anyhow—and how!" he wrote. "It is well dressed, has the weight in numbers, and doesn't pretend to be anything else than it is—an excellent colored musical comedy." But the *Baltimore Afro-American* thought the show left a lot to be desired. "With all due regard to Messrs. Miller and Lyles, whose comic antics have won them a cherished place in the heart of the theater-going public, it is evident that two master artists are here working with material that is of an inferior quality," they wrote. "There is a ragged libretto, which itself, jars one forcibly, and the attempts at humor, particularly in the first act, are brutally blunt."

However, despite the inconsistent reviews, the general public and the Black press in particular were generally optimistic about the show's chances for success, even given *Rang Tang*'s recent abrupt ending. The *New York Amsterdam News* praised the arrival of *Keep Shufflin'*, seeing it as another example of Miller and Lyles doing their part to move the nation toward racial harmony. "The contest which the Negro is constantly waging for equality and a rightful share of that much abused something which Nordics term 'democracy' has reached an important stage during the past twelve months. This is particularly true in New York City, where the citizens of Harlem are enjoying more tolerance from the pale brethren...than is meted out to Negroes in other American municipalities. If one stops to analyze the superior state of the colored citizen of New York it will readily be realized that the newborn tolerance has resulted from the fact that the Negro has been particularly active in theatrical circles of late in the Great White Way.

"There is, perhaps, no single instrument of propaganda that is quite so effectual as the theatre," they continued. "Despite the fact that most Nordics are still of the opinion that the Negro is 'easily kidded' and does not 'know the road' like the members of the white race, nevertheless the Negro has what is called in the vernacular 'the low down' on just how valuable theatre actually is in breaking down race prejudice. It does not take a dusky-hued college professor, or even the average colored businessman, to know that the best way of spreading publicity and propaganda is to hand these elements to a person when a person is being entertained... As a propaganda instrument, *Keep Shufflin'* will go far to break down the little prejudice that is left in the narrow minds of narrow-minded Nordics, and is a great omen for the further advance of the great Negro stars in the theatrical world of tomorrow, and that [is] whether it hits or not."

With a first week gross of $13,500, it appeared that *Keep Shufflin'* had hit. On April 14, 1928, Miller and Lyles took advantage of another opportunity to celebrate. Over three thousand people—mostly Black and from the entertainment industry—filed into the Manhattan Casino in Harlem on Eighth Avenue and 155th Street to celebrate the twenty-fifth anniversary of the comedians' professional partnership. Jack Dempsey, the white heavyweight boxer who'd accompanied *Shuffle Along*'s creators to a benefit while the show was in Boston, awarded the two with a large silver cup, and the evening continued well beyond midnight with music, dancing, and laughter. However, despite the festivities, *Keep Shufflin'* was in trouble. In the next week, the show's box office returns, which had been on a steady decline, were a mere $7,500, and the production moved to the Eltinge Forty-Second Street Theatre, where it played for just shy of a month. On May 26, after 101 performances, Miller and Lyles left Broadway once again. The cast told the press that the men spontaneously announced they were calling it quits because they were "tired."

By July, the two were back to vaudeville. Reviews were rough, as it seemed audiences and critics alike were growing "tired" themselves of seeing the boxing and arithmetic bits for the umpteenth time. In a musical comedy, those old gags might be a familiar callback, but in a brief set, they felt particularly trite. The two reassembled the cast and crew of *Keep Shufflin'* in September for a tour, with the money quietly put up by Arnold Rothstein, a white millionaire gambler and racketeer. When their "angel investor" was murdered, the show found itself in a precarious position. The company went unpaid, and on November 19, it disbanded in Chicago.

The comedians were undeterred by the second ending of *Keep Shufflin'*. Talking pictures were becoming all the rage, and Miller and Lyles were able to capitalize on the trend. The duo starred in two Vitaphone "all-talking" short films, *The Mayor of Jimtown* and *Jimtown's Speakeasy*, based on their popular bits, which introduced the comics to an even wider audience across the nation. After another vaudeville attempt stateside, in March 1929, the two decided to press their luck overseas on a month-long tour of London, and upon their return, they joined the cast of *Great Day*, a "black and tan"—with both Black and white races—large-scale musical revue on the road, as well as continuing to headline their own vaudeville act.

When the world was rocked on October 29, 1929, the day of the stock market crash that crippled the global economy and began the Great Depression, otherwise known as Black Tuesday, the theater scene was hit just as hard as everyone else. For too many, expendable income became a thing of the past, as folks were no longer lining the sidewalks to enter theaters—they were standing in breadlines and hitting the pavement in a futile effort to find work. The unemployment rate rose precipitously, and over the next year, over four million people who were actively seeking a job were unable to find one. For Eubie Blake, Flournoy Miller, and Aubrey Lyles, who were all in vaudeville at the time of the crash, their financial situations immediately went from bad to worse, and Miller was dealt another blow when his partner suddenly packed his bags and left the United States shortly before 1929 came to a close.

Flournoy Miller didn't know exactly where his partner was going—just "somewhere in Africa"—or what had caused him to leave. The trades announced that Miller and Lyles had split up, a charge that Miller vehemently denied as he continued to tour with an indefinite stand-in for his partner. However, even with Lyles out of the country, the comedy duo found themselves at the center of a curious controversy when they were billed as the stars of *Shuffle Along of 1930*, a new musical comedy revue named after an old favorite, produced by Flournoy's brother Irvin C. Miller and starring Valada Snow. The production opened at

Webra's Flatbush Theatre in Brooklyn on April 21, 1930, but while many were happy about Miller and Lyles's return to the show, the comedians didn't share that enthusiasm—especially since they weren't involved with the revival at all. The patrons who saw the show weren't happy either, as many wrote angry letters and demanded refunds. Flournoy's lawyer got involved, and his brother claimed it was an honest mistake, but the damage had already been done, with one newspaper writing that the stunt "seems to have been a joke at the public's expense."

However, the dispute over *Shuffle Along of 1930* was nothing compared to the storm that was brewing. Charles Correll and Freeman Gosden, a pair of white comedians, had a highly successful radio show, *Amos 'n' Andy*, wherein the two performed in vocal blackface, with a thick Southern dialect and "darky humor." Although the characters were originally based in Georgia, by 1930, the fictional duo had moved to Harlem, and the show was so popular it was being broadcast from coast to coast by the National Broadcasting Company (NBC) to forty million listeners. Correll and Gosden were paid a combined $100,000 for their services, which they split with their announcer, Bill Hay. But just as things seemed as if they couldn't have been going better for them, in April 1930, Flournoy Miller slapped NBC with a lawsuit for copyright infringement, demanding that Correll and Godsen stop performing bits that he had written unless they made a large payment to use his material. "Many phrases being used by the white men have come to be associated with Miller and Lyles, who first sent them over the footlights to convulse audiences all over the country," the *New York*

Amsterdam News explained. "Friends of the Negro comedians have been expecting this move for some time and, whether they are successful or not in the effort to restrain the white comedians, many will feel that the work of *Amos 'n' Andy* was inspired by that of Miller and Lyles, whose 'I'm regusted,' etc., furnished so much of the fun in everything in which the colored comedians have been associated."

Miller's lawsuit against NBC came at a low point for the comedian. Motion pictures were doing big business—nearly all major studio releases were "talkies" by mid-1929, due to *The Jazz Singer*'s revolution of the industry—and vaudeville and Broadway were on the decline. The performer was rudderless until he received an offer from Lew Leslie, who wanted Miller to write the book for the upcoming edition of his *Blackbirds*, which had somehow been able to withstand the theater industry's dark days, with his annual revue now outgrossing Ziegfeld's *Follies* and George White's *Scandals*. Miller quickly signed on, and concurrently, Lew Leslie hired Andy Razaf to pen the show's lyrics. Razaf had just scored a hit with "Ain't Misbehavin'," which he cowrote with Fats Waller, and Leslie felt he could give *Blackbirds* what it needed to best the competition.

Still, the producer wanted a little extra insurance. He asked Eubie Blake to collaborate with Razaf on twenty-eight songs for *Blackbirds*. With a $3,000 cash advance thrown in for good measure and Blake just as down and out as Miller was professionally, the composer thanked his lucky stars and signed on. "Andy's working method is like no one else's I have ever seen," Eubie Blake later recalled. "He will hear a tune once through, sit right down, and write out the lyric in one sitting. In all the time we worked together—and we wrote four shows together—once he wrote a line it was down there. I never saw him change a line with me." They collaborated on two of the songs: "You're Lucky to Me," which was performed by Ethel Waters, and "Memories of You," which Blake wrote specifically for Minto Cato, a soprano with a large vocal range.

However, when auditions were held at the end of July, Lew Leslie—and Flournoy Miller—were hopeful that the comedian would reunite with his partner for *Blackbirds of 1930*. Aubrey Lyles was back in the country and was heavily courted by the producer but chose to star in *We'se Risin'*, a Black musical comedy, opposite Leigh Whipper instead. Miller joined Lew Leslie's cast alongside Mantan Moreland, a resident comedian at the popular Harlem nightspot Connie's Inn, who was also in the highly successful 1928 edition of *Blackbirds*. For the first time in over a quarter of a century, Miller and Lyles were both performing with separate comedic partners.

In the run-up to *We'se Risin'* opening at the Maryland Theatre in November 1930, Aubrey Lyles spoke with the *Baltimore Afro-American* about his life-changing trip to Monrovia, Liberia, where he was making an investment in his family's future. "While my friends thought I was wasting my money in fast living, I was looking far ahead of them all," he said. "Land is the one thing that the African has plenty of and you can buy it for a song. There is no telling what there is on your land, what there is in your jungle, what there is under your land... There may be gold and diamonds down under my house.

Who can tell?" But besides economic reasons, Lyles stated that he wanted to relocate to Africa because he was "intensely interested in his own race." Ever since he was a boy growing up in Tennessee, where he saw and experienced prejudice and discrimination regularly, one of his life's desires was to live in and contribute to the land of his forefathers. "I may never realize that dream," he said, "but I hope that my son or his son will be a force in Liberia."

But perhaps the greatest lesson the star learned while in Africa was one of humility and the fallacy of believing too strongly in American exceptionalism. "You can't go over there feeling that because you have lived in the greatest civilized country on earth that you are better than they are," he said. "You've got to come right down to earth and realize that in Africa, the youngest African is your superior. He is born with instincts that we have lost by transmigration. A 12-year-old boy can tell you by the looks of the foliage whether an animal has passed through, and whether he is coming back. He knows the use of every twig and plant. He knows Africa."

While Aubrey Lyles was talking up his time out of the country to the *Baltimore Afro-American*, the same month, Eubie Blake sat down with the newspaper to trash Noble Sissle, who was still overseas. The composer revealed that the two had not been friends nor spoken to each other socially for a decade, following an argument they had in 1920 while in New Haven, Connecticut. Blake described Sissle as a "moral fanatic" who tried to regulate his behavior both on- and offstage, and the pianist didn't take kindly to having orders snapped at him by a hifalutin, self-appointed surrogate parent. The paper wrote that, according to Blake, from that point on, "whenever they played a theatre, they had separate dressing rooms on opposite sides of the stage, and ofttimes one did not know that the other was in the theatre until he saw the other enter the wings from the opposite side." Blake's remarks were surprising, especially considering how close the pair seemed to be in the eyes of the public, and may have just been the result of lingering hurt feelings over their breakup. However, even though he was eager to publicly air out their dirty laundry, Eubie Blake made it clear that his complaints with Sissle were strictly personal, not professional. "Blake was loud in his praise of the honesty and integrity of his former partner, declaring him to be one of the smartest men in the theatrical business," the paper wrote. "Although they did not socialize, the pianist always had implicit faith in the fairness of his crooning partner and left all of the business arrangements of the act to him. On many occasions, he has been surprised, he said, when they have entertained at society events and Sissle give [sic] him many times more than what he expected. If ever a check came for the two for a performance, Sissle could have cheated him without knowledge, but never once did his partner resort to any form of chicanery."

Although Noble Sissle wasn't on American soil to clarify the record at the time Blake's interview was published, on Christmas Eve 1930, the bandleader returned to New York with his Ambassadeurs band. As with Josephine Baker before him, Paris had been overwhelmingly receptive to his act, and reports were regularly sent back to the United States of his great success and the strides he was making for the race while overseas. Sissle returned to find that his old colleagues were in a very different place in their careers than when he had last seen them. Despite seemingly having all the right elements, Flournoy Miller and Eubie Blake's tenure with *Blackbirds of 1930* was a "failure" according to *Variety*—lasting only sixty-two performances—while Aubrey Lyles's attempt at forging his own path in *We'se Risin'*, which never played on Broadway, was forgotten almost immediately. Luckily, now that Noble Sissle was back home, he shared his reason for returning to the States, while tears formed in his eyes, with a reporter from the *Baltimore Afro-American*. He wanted to reunite his former collaborators for a revival of *Shuffle Along*, as he had always believed it could have been an institution like Ziegfeld's *Follies* and George White's *Scandals*, producing new editions every year. However, as the newspaper put it, "this dream was shattered by petty jealousy and lack of vision on the part of those whom *Shuffle Along* had made famous." But Sissle was game for another chance and was determined to make it happen. As a testament to his seriousness, before he left Paris, he dropped by to see Josephine Baker and ask if she would be willing to sign on, but she politely declined. She was thankful for the offer— "My exposure to Sissle and Blake helped teach me the technique of using entertainment as a way to open white eyes to the black world," she said—but she felt more comfortable in the "white man's world" of Paris than she had ever been in her own country.

The jury was still out on how receptive Eubie Blake, Flournoy Miller, and Aubrey Lyles would be to the idea. As Noble Sissle returned to vaudeville, headlining at the Palace in New York with the Ambassadeurs, Blake continued playing the circuit with his own orchestra as well. Meanwhile, Miller and Lyles had teamed back up, at least legally, to continue their efforts against *Amos 'n' Andy*. Throughout 1931, the *Pittsburgh Courier*, with the blessing of the NAACP, initiated a petition against the program, charging the show with the "exploitation of Negroes for profit, portrayal of demeaning characters, and making the Negroes' means of support suspect." However, despite widespread participation in the campaign from Blacks across the nation, Romeo L. Dougherty, a reporter for the *New York Amsterdam News*, believed time would reveal that the paper and the African American community were engaged in a futile effort. "We have no quarrel with the *Pittsburgh Courier* in leading the losing fight against *Amos 'n' Andy*," he wrote. "In the days to come the *Courier* will recognize that it will take money to get *Amos 'n' Andy* off the air, and that in the sense of this economic strength which does not come to us via politics because of our inability to make those large contributions to campaign funds and which leaves us always looking for something instead of contributing something."

While the *Courier* was unsuccessful in getting the radio program banned, over 750,000 people signed the petition, and in the summer of 1931, Miller and Lyles won a victory of their own—they were given a contract for their own competing syndicated radio program, which was broadcast twice a week by the Columbia Broadcasting System (CBS). In the days after their July 22 debut, telegrams of support flooded into the network and their affiliates from forty-three states,

Canada, and Central America. The duo was an immediate hit in yet another medium, and even though they maintained that Charles Correll and Freeman Gosden had lifted material from their act, Flournoy Miller was happy to write all new bits lest the public believe the Black comedians were the ones who were cribbing from the white act. "We won't use 'regusted,' 'Let me resplain to you,' or 'sho-sho,'" he said, referring to dialectical bastardizations of the English language that had become popular catchphrases for both pairs of comics. "We do not want to imitate established stars."

Even better yet, in October 1931, the two signed on as the leads in a new Broadway-bound Steve Jenkins and Sam Peck musical comedy, *Sugar Hill*, with a book by Charles Tazewell, a white playwright primarily known for his work in radio; music by Jimmy Johnson; and lyrics by Jo Trent. The show opened on Christmas evening, and by January 2, 1932, it was already playing its final performance. "Even though I am more than sorry to say so, I must admit that [Miller and Lyles] did not return in all their glory," Geraldyn Dismond wrote in the *Baltimore Afro-American*. "For *Sugar Hill*, which brought Miller and Lyles to the Forrest Theatre, isn't exactly what I would call a good show. And even though this *Sugar Hill* is described as 'an epoch of Negro life in Harlem,' I have my doubts that it really is. For, if I know my English grammar, an epoch is one thing, and *Sugar Hill* is another; or to come right out and say so, it is a cross between musical comedy and vaudeville. And what I regret most is the fact that, all things considered, it is neither good musical comedy nor vaudeville."

Miller and Lyles took the loss on the chin—they still had their radio show—and while *Sugar Hill* had failed to resonate with audiences and critics, the comedians were credited with doing the best they could with lackluster material. And they would soon have another chance to prove themselves to the public. On May 20, 1932, the *Chicago Defender* was given an exclusive tip that Noble Sissle, Eubie Blake, Flournoy Miller, and Aubrey Lyles had signed back on for the *Shuffle Along* revival that Sissle had been dreaming of. The news was unexpected, as Sissle and Blake had yet to reunite publicly. Eubie Blake appeared in and provided music for *Harlem Is Heaven*, an independent feature-length film starring Bill "Bojangles" Robinson—with an overture that includes "I'm Just Wild About Harry"—and *Pie, Pie, Blackbird*, a Vitaphone Warner Bros. short starring Nina Mae McKinney and the Nicholas Brothers. Both Blake and Sissle had continued touring with their own orchestras and bands, respectively, but somehow, outside the public's eye, the two had clearly been able to reconcile. "It was not a feud," Blake explained. "Sissle and I saw that promoters didn't want to pay us the kind of money we were accustomed to earning so we decided to form separate orchestras. Then each of us could make as much money as before." Nevertheless, the press and public were ecstatic about the prospects of another *Shuffle Along*, even as details were sparse.

Unfortunately, Noble Sissle's dream would go unrealized, at least in the way he envisioned it. On June 24, while the four men were working together on the new edition of *Shuffle Along* at Eubie Blake's studio, Aubrey Lyles collapsed. He was rushed to the Wiley Wilson Sanitarium on 138th Street and Seventh Avenue, where his stomach was operated on for an undisclosed issue. His wife, Myrtle, remained by his side while he was recovering, and Lyles enjoyed frequent visits from Sissle, Blake, and Miller. The comedian was eager to work on their big Broadway comeback. Every time his partners came to visit, one of them would tell him, "It's coming along fine, but we need you badly," and Lyles would tell Flournoy Miller, "Tell them to play the music louder, kid; I'll be there."

For a while, that seemed likely. On July 16, the *Chicago Defender* reported that the comedian was "much improved." Although he never fully recovered, Lyles remained in relatively high spirits as his unexpected hospital visit turned into a prolonged stay. At the time the *Defender* article was published, Lyles was showing signs of strength. He was able to walk around his room. He was an avid baseball fan, and whenever someone came to visit, he'd ask whether the New York Yankees had won their most recent game. Even if it wasn't true, he was always assured that they had. He had shown such signs of improvement, he was scheduled to be discharged on July 30, until he began to relapse two days beforehand. Within no time, the performer had a full audience at his bedside: his wife, Myrtle; sister, Louella Lyles Cabel of Providence, Kentucky; her three children, Helen, Norma, and DeWitt; the wives of his partners, Harriett Sissle, Avis Blake, and Bessie Miller; and their husbands.

There were no laughs to be had. Myrtle Lyles leaned over, prostrate with grief, while her husband said his final goodbyes. Aubrey Lyles held out his hand, and Noble Sissle took the comedian's in his, with the two never exchanging words. Eubie Blake was too distraught and left to wait in a separate room, while Flournoy Miller came to his friend's side. "Kid," Lyles said, shaking his partner's hand. "It won't be long now." And it wasn't. Miller was the last among the living to speak to Aubrey Lyles before he died on July 28, 1932, from pulmonary tuberculosis, which he had secretly been living with for years, and related intestinal ailments. His two children—Oswald, who lived in Boston, and Audrey Lyles McLerrey, his daughter from his first marriage, coming in from Chicago—arrived shortly after he died. He was forty-eight years old.

An estimated seven thousand people visited his body while it lay in state at Mamie L. Anderson Pratt's undertaking parlor on West 131st Street. "Every walk of life was represented," the *New York Amsterdam News* wrote. "Of the number, some were recognized operatic stars, while others were classed as princes and princesses of the radio world, the motion picture realm, and the legitimate stage, who owe their present prominence to the start they received in *Shuffle Along*." An intimate funeral was held on August 1 at Grace Congregational Church on West 139th Street, and Aubrey Lyles was buried at Cedar Grove Cemetery on Long Island immediately after.

Variety published a 111-word obituary, the *New York Times'* was slightly longer, but the Black press gave Aubrey Lyles the most deserving homegoing eulogies, with Theophilus Lewis's send-off in the *New York Amsterdam News* among the most poignant. "It sometimes happens that when two individuals combine their talents in a definite line of work their joint product is superior to anything either of them could have achieved alone. This is especially true when creative or interpretive minds are associated for a long period of time," he wrote. "As the importance of the work grows it tends to displace its authors in public interest and even to overshadow their existence. People...sing the praises of Gilbert and Sullivan, but cannot distinguish Gilbert from Sullivan. In the end, every jointly achieved success becomes a sort of benevolent Frankenstein that destroys the separate reputations of its creators. Aubrey Lyles, who passed away last week, was a victim of successful collaboration. His merits as a citizen and his personal gifts as an actor were dwarfed and obscured by the vast popularity he won as the team-mate of Flournoy Miller. Only his family and intimates share the bereavement caused by the loss of a relative and friend. The public is saddened by the breakup of a popular team of showmen, the black out of an inimitably hilarious act.

"Many will claim that *Shuffle Along*, in production and performance, was the highest achievement of the Negro stage," he continued. "That may be claiming too much, but few will deny that all their shows, considered from the box-office angle as well as from the point of view of artistic merit, were among the best ever produced in the Aframerican theatre. Miller and Lyles gave Broadway almost half of the successful colored shows that appeared there during the present generation. To do that, they had to be good... The success of their shows depended on their unique style of comedy. It was a style which, in its essence, defied imitation... One can say that each was a perfect foil for the other and no more. For the effects they achieved seemed to consist of something more than the combined total of their separate talents. Something neither Flournoy Miller nor Aubrey Lyles possessed separately appeared as a result of their blended efforts. The public never thought of Miller the comedian or Lyles the comic. It was always Miller and Lyles, the comedy team. And it always will be."

And yet, the show went on. Sissle, Blake, and Miller moved forward with their new *Shuffle Along*, with George Wintz, licensor of the original production's Number Three touring company, attached as producer. They held auditions on September 26 and 27 at the Renaissance Ballroom on 138th Street, attracting a plethora of Black singers, dancers, and actors. Mantan Moreland, Flournoy's old partner from *Blackbirds*, was invited to fill in for Aubrey Lyles. A lot was riding on the success of the production. On November 5, Miller filed for bankruptcy, citing $27,921 in debt and no assets. Among his creditors were forty-four unpaid performers from the various musical comedies he and Lyles had staged. The comedian stated that he and his late partner had invested all their money in a new production they planned on staging at Harlem's Lafayette Theatre—the first time they were making a serious play as producers, a step toward the Broadway venue they hoped to open together—but with Lyles gone, the project fell apart, and the majority of what they had invested couldn't be recouped. A month later, Noble Sissle also sought relief from the courts, as he had gone broke again, this time owing $12,889. "I've not even subway fare," he claimed. "But I'll get a break—I'll get a break."

Shuffle Along of 1932 opened at the Lyric Theatre in Allentown, Pennsylvania, on November 9 to strong attendance and mediocre reviews. This iteration of *Shuffle Along* begins with Tom Sharpe (Noble Sissle) convincing rival grocery store owners Steve Jenkins (Flournoy Miller) and Caesar Jones (Mantan Moreland, ostensibly in the Sam Peck role) to invest in a molasses factory. Jenkins and Jones decide to jump in, becoming copresidents of the project, which ends up becoming a fruitful success for all involved. Once again, there is a subplot with Harry Walton (Clarence Robinson) and his fiancé, Sally Joyce (Fay Conty). While Sissle and Blake enjoyed "a few minutes" together in the original production, this time, Blake took to the stage alone to play the piano and sing through some of the hits from 1921. Later in the evening, Sissle performed with his new orchestra—perhaps an indication of a continuing fissure between the musicians.

Although there were traces of the original in the show, the production didn't connect with critics in the same way. The *Baltimore Afro-American* described Miller's book as "wordy and wearisome" and Sissle and Blake's score as "below the standard set in the original show and…lack[ing] the warmth and sponta- neity we are wont to associate with the music of Eubie Blake," adding that "one of the young composers should be called in to put the necessary virility into the impotent score Blake has written." A tryout at the Majestic Theatre in Brooklyn followed, with the reviews slightly better. "While not as fresh and original as the first edition, this new show…promises also to be a hit," the *Brooklyn Eagle* wrote. "Everything about it is different from the original edition. Everything, that is to say, but the dancing. Here is the same old acrobatic, knockabout dancing that helped to make the first edition famous. And interwoven in the noisy dance numbers are several bits of chorus work, fully the equal of any done by well-trained white women." The show continued to play very brief engagements in major cities along the East Coast, reminiscent of its first graveyard tour, until December 26 when *Shuffle Along of 1933*—the show's title was updated in anticipation of the new year—opened at the Mansfield Theatre on West Forty-Seventh Street, a legitimate Broadway house in the heart of the theater district.

Sissle, Blake, and Miller had finally made it to Midtown Manhattan together, but it was unclear how long they'd remain there. "Just what the family relationship, if any, between *Shuffle Along of 1933*...and the *Shuffle Along* of a decade ago, may be, was not explained in the program, but one suspects it to be pretty remote," the *New York Herald Tribune* wrote. "The latter was an unusually successful Negro revue. Last night's entertainment was a rather ordinary Harlem song-and-dance show, strung on a dull book, with little to explain its appearance on Broadway." But the most telling critique came from Thomas R. Dash writing for *Women's Wear Daily*: "Why will bookmakers fall back on the cliches of negro comedy? Why do they insist on showing the gullibility and ignorance of the simple negro? It is too banal as

NOBLE SISSLE, AT PIANO, WITH MANTAN MORELAND AND FLOURNOY MILLER, IN CHARACTER, IN A PROMOTIONAL STILL FOR *SHUFFLE ALONG OF 1933*

Photo by White Studio, © New York Public Library for the Performing Arts

comedy and it seems to us too slanderous to be in good taste. Producers of colored shows should be too proud to parade off the cultural frailties of their own people. It is too undignified from the viewpoint of the more intelligent colored people or the more intelligent white folk."

The only thing left was for Manhattan's theatergoers to weigh in, and when they did, it was clear that *Shuffle Along of 1933* wouldn't live up to its predecessor. The highly anticipated production earned just under $6,500 in its first week. Performances continued until January 7, and after a scheduled day off on the eighth, the performances on the ninth were canceled, allegedly due to Noble Sissle haven fallen ill. They promised to return on the tenth, but they didn't, and they admitted on the eleventh that, unceremoniously, *Shuffle Along* had played its final performance four days earlier, after only two weeks on Broadway and seventeen performances. "We saw it wasn't going anywhere," Eubie Blake explained. "It wasn't the show, it was the times."

Instead of cutting their losses completely, Flournoy Miller suggested they shorten the show and bring it to movie houses—many of which were former vaudeville theaters—that wanted live entertainment before the motion picture ran. Sissle and Blake would have considered their options, had any serious ones existed. "We didn't have any choice," Blake conceded. "We already had the costumes, scenery, and props, all that stuff." With a stripped-down version of *Shuffle Along of 1933*, Noble Sissle, Eubie Blake, and Flournoy Miller took their company on the road in the hopes that somewhere in America, they would find a wanting audience again.

WHITE CHORUS DANCERS CROSSING A NEW YORK STREET, PASSING THE
MARQUEE FOR *SHUFFLE ALONG OF 1952* AT THE BROADWAY THEATRE

Photo by Leonard Mccombe/The LIFE Images Collection via Getty Images/Getty Images

13

WHITE FOLKS FOLLOW

1933–1952

*S*huffle Along of 1933's tepid reception followed the musical
out of New York and throughout the United States. The
stripped-down version of the show was a welcome addition
to theater owners, as live entertainment almost always caused
a minor uptick in attendance for the feature film being shown
afterward, but it did little to improve upon the bank accounts
of *Shuffle Along*'s creators—or the lasting legacy of the original
1921 show. In fact, the latest iteration of the production was a

reminder of how much had changed since the men first took the stage together.

"The success of *Shuffle Along* and the collapse of the men who produced it gives rise to the question, 'Why?' From many fronts it is argued that the bulk of the money made by *Shuffle Along* went into Nordic hands, and that Miller and Lyles and Sissle and Blake earned a handsome living and that was all," Edward W. Smith wrote in the *Chicago Defender*. "On the other hand, it is said that the principals of *Shuffle Along* were content to rest on their laurels thus won and were of the opinion that *Shuffle Along* would pave their way for all future productions... The actors... sent their production careening to acknowledged heights, turned like a rocket, and swerved to the ground, and when it burst, it found the principals of *Shuffle Along* without a leg to stand on."

Nigger Heaven author Carl Van Vechten had a separate theory as to why *Shuffle Along of 1933* struggled to catch on, chalking the show's lackluster Broadway run up to the fact that a dozen years after they hit it big, Noble Sissle, Eubie Blake, and Flournoy Miller were no longer original and unique but another part of the overpopulated Black theatrical mosaic. He wrote, "When I first began attending the Negro Theatre, it was possible to enjoy the entertainments of Williams and Walker or Sissieretta Jones, the 'Black Patti,' or Cole and Johnson or Ernest Hogan, no mean entertainments to be sure. At the present day, however, the famous Negro stars on the concert, music hall, burlesque, motion picture, and 'legitimate' stages of two continents are so numerous that merely to list them all in small type would require a page or two.

"If you are as old as I am," he continued, "and were accustomed to reading the newspapers and periodicals of thirty years ago, you will recall that the principal items concerning Negroes referred to lynchings and race riots. Nowadays you can scarcely pick up any Sunday supplement without reading about Negro dancing or the blues. It is likewise significant that nearly every third play now produced has one or more Negro characters and that these are now played by Negroes and not by white actors in blackface as was the ludicrous custom three decades ago. Mixed casts like those of *Show Boat*, *Golden Dawn*, *Kongo*, *Deep River*, and *Goin' Home* are no longer uncommon, although it was but a short time back that Paul Robeson's appearance in *All God's Chillun* raised a storm of protest. These are a few of the bald facts."

The *Baltimore Afro-American* summed up Van Vechten's opinion simply, arguing that the original *Shuffle Along* had been a double-edged sword. The fact that the show had led to a significant uptick in African American representation on the stage had inadvertently made it harder for Black artists to compete and succeed in that space—a problem that white performers and producers never faced. "The thing that keeps *Shuffle Along of 1933* from being the sensation that its predecessor was is that in between there have been too many of the calibre of Florence Mills, Ethel Waters, Bill Robinson, Valaida [the former Valada] Snow, Cab Calloway, and an insurmountable list that is growing day by day. There have been in between too many *Blackbirds*, *Hot Chocolates*, *Green Pastures*, *Porgies*. There have been in between too many radio and Vitaphone celebrities.

These advances of Negro artists mark milestones on the road of progress for the theatre, but they all combine to make *Shuffle Along of 1933* just another colored show."

Of course, in some ways, *Shuffle Along of 1933* was just another Black production that failed to live up to its namesake in terms of talent. The original production was advertised as "a musical mélange," and it was. Noble Sissle and Eubie Blake pulled from the best of their songbook and incorporated the best of their material into the production, while the new songs they wrote for the show, like "Love Will Find a Way," were perfectly tailored both for mainstream Manhattan theatergoers and the Jazz Age. There were few better than Eubie Blake at keeping a long index finger on the pulse of the public's developing interest in what was commonly thought of as Black music. "It's the song that makes a fellow want to get right up, no matter where he is, and begin whistling and dancing all over the place, that makes a hit these days," he said in 1921, shortly after *Shuffle Along*'s debut in New York. "A modern song, to make any kind of a hit at all, must have 'pep' to it, and also must have a 'catchy tune' that unconsciously sticks to the mind of the hearer. I have made it a point to study the audiences at every performance of *Shuffle Along* in order to note whether my songs have produced the results which I have first mentioned. I have found that such songs as 'Love Will Find a Way,' 'Bandana Days,' 'Low Down Blues,' [and] 'Baltimore Buzz' invariably set a large part of the audience, particularly the younger members, to beating with their feet and swinging their shoulders rhythmically. Also, I have never failed to hear after the performance and between the acts a number of men whistling snatches of 'Gypsy Blues,' 'Shuffle Along,' 'Full of Jazz,' or any one of the songs from the play.

"The successful song writer of today must be something more than a mere juggler of harmonious sounds. He must be a student of what the public wants—a sort of psychologist," he continued. "The mushy, snobby, sentimental love songs of twenty or more years ago would not be at all popular today. Nor would the semi-martial music of songs popular during the United States' participation in the war make a hit now. What the public wants today are lively, jazzy songs, not too jazzy, with love interest, but without the sickly sentimentality in vogue a generation ago."

In writing the original iteration of the show, Flournoy Miller gave a similar methodological approach to constructing the book. "In *Shuffle Along*, there are not five minutes of straight conversation," he said during the main company's tour in 1923. "As soon as there was the slightest danger of its getting 'talky,' we slipped in a song, dance, or specialty [act, like the Harmony Kings], as a result, one rarely, if ever, has any of that buzzing during our performance, for the audience is too busy trying to see everything and too afraid of missing a dancing step or a bit of comedy, to bother to talk." Essentially, in hoping to create an annual revue in the style of Ziegfeld's *Follies* or George White's *Scandals*, the writers of *Shuffle Along* may have lost track of what made their 1921 production so successful in the first place: they had a gifted cast, several of whom would become international superstars; the music and book were carefully calibrated to resonate with African American and white audiences alike;

the show's creators helped bring Black artistry to the stage for the first time in over a decade in the middle of a tumultuous period for race relations in America; and the four were truly ahead of the curve. Now, as they tried in vain to make *Shuffle Along of 1933* work while embarking on a nationwide tour, Sissle, Blake, and Miller were largely attempting to recapture their old success and trade on nostalgia.

"We went on the road. We really worked," Eubie Blake recalled. "We gave it all we had. But it was no use." While there were still more dates on the itinerary, Noble Sissle left the tour in mid-February 1933, returning to bandleading, while Miller, Blake, and the rest of the cast continued ahead. While there were several times when the company disbanded and reassembled and casting changes were made, *Shuffle Along of 1933* ran intermittently until May 1937, when the show "busted up" in Long Beach, California. The show had been playing along the West Coast for months when the producers unexpectedly realized they didn't have enough money to get the company back home. The performers were forced to disband and left to fend for themselves, leaving one of the young band members— eighteen-year-old Nat Cole—who was unable to afford fare back to Chicago, stranded. He decided to remain in Los Angeles with his wife, Nadine Robinson, who was part of the cast, where he soon found work playing in nightclubs and adopted the nickname "King."

In a sense, Noble Sissle achieved his dream after all. As the shortened *Shuffle Along* roadshow played for years throughout the country, the year at the end of its name was updated annually—*Shuffle Along of 1934*, *Shuffle Along of 1935*, and so on—giving the appearance that the show was just as fresh and of the day, when it really was more of the same. But while Flournoy Miller had remained a constant with the show, the performer was making headlines for becoming increasingly vocal about what he saw as continued injustices in the entertainment industry after a reported case in 1935 of a white theater owner allegedly striking an African American performer who worked for him in the face. The isolated incident, Miller argued, was part of a larger systemic problem where white men felt they had ownership over Black artists. "Men like [Lew] Leslie are enemies of our race," he said. "They talk about him making Florence Mills. He did not make her. Florence Mills made Lew Leslie. When he ran into her, he scarcely had a quarter. She made it possible for him. But he gets the credit for being a great benefactor to the Negro race. We are his benefactor. After such men reach positions of influence, they do all they can to throttle legitimate Negro endeavor in the theatrical world.

"Negro producers, who seek to show their wares, find they are interfered with all along the line," he continued. "They run into brick walls and treacherous shoals, all placed by such men as Leslie. Sometimes these men, who have risen on the backs of Negroes, actually turn their backs on them." However, while Miller continued to muse on ways that Black performers could be independent of white producers, the constant presence of the touring revue gave way to what seemed like a promising opportunity. In June 1935, it was reported that *Shuffle Along* had been optioned by Campbell Productions for a musical feature film based on the original show. The "glamorous production" was to be shot in Virginia—locations were allegedly already scouted, as shooting was expected to commence before the end of the summer—and a $60,000 budget had been secured. Noble Sissle, Eubie Blake, Flournoy Miller, and Mantan Moreland were all slated to star in what was announced as a major motion picture event.

Even though the 1933 Broadway revival was a flop, news of a *Shuffle Along* film was somewhat unsurprising. By 1935, Hollywood was beginning to bet on Blacks, with every major studio boasting at least one motion picture with African American performers in the pipeline. Paramount was developing an adaptation of white playwright Marc Connelly's *The Green Pastures*, a comedy centered on a Southern Black child's interpretation of the Old Testament, and three African American performers were just in *So Red the Rose*, a Civil War–era romance directed by King Vidor. Warner Bros.' last film with Al Jolson under contract, *The Singing Kid*, costarred Cab Calloway. Metro-Goldwyn-Mayer and RKO Radio Pictures had musicals in preproduction with both Black and white actors, while Twentieth Century Fox was developing a film starring Bill "Bojangles" Robinson and Stepin Fetchit set below the Mason-Dixon line. Columbia Pictures was working on *Georgianna*, a musical that stalled in preproduction, and Universal was prepping a heavily anticipated motion picture version of *Show Boat*.

Hollywood's sudden interest in Black performers was due in large part to the international success of *Sanders of the*

River, a British film by director Zoltan Korda that starred Paul Robeson and Nina Mae McKinney. While the movie didn't fare well in the States, studio executives took notice of its reception overseas nonetheless and made the calculation that even if films with Black actors did poorly in the South, production companies should be able to offset the deficit with outsize box office in major cities in the North. Coincidentally, even though the film was an accidental proof of concept for Hollywood, Paul Robeson despised it, leading him to publicly disavow it three years after its release. The film is based in Nigeria—Robeson plays an educated tribal chief named Bosambo—and the actor took the part believing it would be an accurate portrayal of the African people and would help show audiences, Black and white alike, the depth of the country's culture. However, after principal photography wrapped, Robeson was summoned for five days of reshoots where he realized the plot had been rewritten to justify white imperialism. In a complete deviation from the film Robeson thought he had signed on to, the Africans were treated as children when they weren't being deceitful and violent, and the finished movie begins with a dedication to "the handful of white men whose everyday work is an unsung saga of courage and efficiency." Appearing in *Sanders of the River* would forever be one of Robeson's largest regrets.

However, even though plenty of chances were being taken on Black films, a *Shuffle Along* movie never materialized, and instead, the show became the center of another Miller family feud. In the summer of 1935, Flournoy's brother Quintard successfully deceived the owners of the Odeon Theatre in St.

Louis into booking a "mediocre" new show that he was passing off as another iteration of *Shuffle Along*. Not only did its production not include any of the music, lyrics, material, or cast from the 1921 show, it also had not been sanctioned by anyone associated with the original venture, including Quintard's own kin. Flournoy's lawyer successfully secured an injunction against Quintard, who had enraged the public by his antics, making them think they were seeing a show they knew and loved, not a subpar cash grab by a con artist with a last name that gave him an air of legitimacy.

As the *Shuffle Along* brand was becoming marred by false starts, failed comebacks, and fraudulent revivals, Broadway was moving forward. By the end of 1935, there were Black artists in five successful productions: *At Home Abroad* at the Winter Garden, where Ethel Waters starred alongside white actress Beatrice Lillie; the Langston Hughes–penned *Mulatto*, a "starkly real" drama with a cast made up of Blacks and whites; *Three Men on a Horse*, a comedy that featured Black actor Richard Huey; *Connie's Inn Revue*, which starred "a host of Harlem favorites" including Louis Armstrong, the king of trumpeters; and the George and Ira Gershwin's English-language opera *Porgy and Bess*, with over sixty Black actors in the cast of ninety. The *Chicago Defender* argued that the presence—and financial success—of these productions marked a significant turning point, as not only did they demonstrate that African Americans could be accepted in "white shows," but also that audiences would pay to see actors of color in more than just stereotypical comedic roles. "All of which goes to prove that the success of the Negro actors will be found, in the greatest degree, in variety," Floyd J. Calvin wrote for the paper. "The time was, and only a few seasons ago, that it was thought, even by Negro actors themselves, when if they did not stick to the musical comedy type of show, like the old *Shuffle Along* production, they were lost. It was thought that was the only type of vehicle in which colored actors in any appreciable numbers would be received by Broadway.

"The motif was exploitation of the ignorant mouthings of grotesquely blackface comedians, with a supporting 'Chocolate Brown' chorus. Strange as it may seem, not one of the current Broadway productions is built around the blackfaced comedian. On the contract, the Negro as a distinctive American personality is the basis of all the current shows in which Negroes have a part," he continued. "At last the old 'blackface' stereotype has been broken. White people now pay to see Negroes be themselves, and rate them on the faithful interpretation of character, rather than on the faithful portrayal of preconceived prejudiced notions. It is fitting, indeed, and a very good omen, that this is so far the best season for the Negro artist in Broadway history."

In the mid-1930s, Hollywood and Broadway were moving toward the future, and so was Noble Sissle, although those major American entertainment institutions and the Black bandleader had very different visions of what the future looked like. While there was an influx of African American actors on the stage and the screen in "legitimate" projects, many of those ventures underperformed. While many Blacks and whites saw it as a sign of progress that performers of color were being backed by the white establishment, Noble Sissle saw the white benefactors as an impediment. The secret to success was putting Blacks in control of their own storytelling, because when that happened, white folks followed. "Show me a man or a group of men with $50,000 and I can show them how to make a fortune," he said. "The real Negro stage shows have made their creators money... and plenty of money. The big white studios, when they try to depict Negro life, depict it from the white man's angle, casting the Negro in unnatural roles. But Negroes know Negroes as no one else does. What has been done on the stage can be done in the movies.

"Can you imagine an all-colored movie, built up around such stars as 'Bojangles' Bill Robinson, Ethel Waters, Stepin Fetchit, the Mills Brothers, a tantalizing, dancing brownskin chorus, plus all the other innovations Negroes have? Why, the white musical extravaganzas couldn't touch 'em," he continued. "A man would get his money back from houses that cater to Negro patronage, and he'd make a fortune from white theaters...because they buy what the public wants. It would have to be done on a high-class plane, though, with the very latest in photography, technical art, direction, continuity, and so forth. But a real film of the Negro, with these and other stars, would be a natural."

While *Shuffle Along*'s creators had white backers like John and Harry Cort and Al Mayer behind them in their initial venture—and none of their theatrical projects had been funded by African Americans—Noble Sissle felt that his success in show business was due to always being part of projects where

Blacks were in the driver's seat, even if they were simply leasing the car. He had been working quietly behind the scenes with several African American entertainers on a new organization they felt would be an equalizing force within the entertainment industry, and on December 16, 1937, the Negro Actors Guild was formally founded in New York with the crème de la crème of Black artists, with Noble Sissle elected as president. Other officers included Duke Ellington, Ethel Waters, Louis Armstrong, Paul Robeson, and James Weldon Johnson. Additionally, Cab Calloway was elected chairman of the executive board, and Bill "Bojangles" Robinson was voted in as honorary president. One of the organization's primary goals was to eradicate the stereotypical depictions of Blacks on the stage and screen and advocate for more realistic roles for African American artists. However, the Negro Actors Guild was also founded as a mechanism to provide vital resources to performers in need, particularly, but not exclusively, Black ones. "Membership will not be restricted to those of the colored race, but voting power will be confined to the colored complement," the *Pittsburgh Courier* explained. With the new venture, African Americans finally had their own organization for fundraising, modeled similarly to the Jewish, Episcopalian, and Catholic Guilds.

Among the all-star officers and members of the board, Fredi Washington, the ivory skin–toned *Shuffle Along* chorine who befriended Josephine Baker in Boston, was elected as the Negro Actors Guild's executive director. After entering the film business playing a dying Cotton Club performer in RKO's short musical film *Black and Tan* in 1929, which featured

Duke Ellington, Washington followed up with a minor role in the 1933 Paul Robeson vehicle *The Emperor Jones*, the screen adaptation of Eugene O'Neill's 1920 drama, and as the main love interest in *Cab Calloway's Hi-De-Ho*, a 1934 musical short released by Paramount. But Washington rose to prominence when she was cast in 1934's *Imitation of Life* as Peola, a fair-skinned African American teenager who is ashamed of her race and instead chooses to pass as white. The film faced difficulty circumventing the censors at the newly established Production Code Administration, which argued that the film was "extremely dangerous," would "surely...prove troublesome," and would be "universally condemned" for implying that Peola's skin tone was the result of miscegenation that occurred on one of the higher branches of her family tree. However, despite the challenges behind the scenes, the film was nominated for three Academy Awards, including Best Picture.

But while *Imitation of Life* was the pinnacle of Fredi Washington's film career, the movie led to public discourse over her own racial identity. Many within the Black community wondered aloud whether the actress was similarly passing as white and ashamed of her race, charges that Washington vehemently denied. "I don't want to pass because I can't stand insincerities and shams," she told the *Pittsburgh Courier* in 1934. "I am just as much Negro as any of the others identified with the race." A year later, she reaffirmed her position to the *Chicago Defender*: "I have never tried to 'pass for white,' and never had any desire to do so. On the stage in New York I have appeared in such colored revues as *Shuffle Along* and *Singing the Blues*, and opposite Paul Robeson in *Black Boy*. On the screen I have been in *Emperor Jones* and other pictures—but always as a colored girl. Perhaps I might have been able to show in [*Imitation of Life*] how a girl might feel under the circumstances, but I was not showing how I feel myself." Despite receiving critical acclaim for her role, Washington found it difficult to continue getting work within an industry where Blacks were still relegated to typical roles. Her skin tone and European features prevented her from being cast as a domestic in white films or as an African American woman in Black ones, resulting in her being eligible for only a narrow sliver of roles where the visual contradiction of her race and color were plot points.

Washington's cofounding of the Negro Actors Guild was significant, as she was firmly reaffirming her place in both a race and industry where many felt she did not fit. Her priorities soon shifted from performing to activism, with Washington using her platform and privilege as a light-skinned Black woman to speak out against race discrimination. "You see I'm a mighty proud gal and I can't for the life of me find any valid reason why anyone should lie about their origin or anything else for that matter," she told the *Chicago Defender* in 1945. "Frankly, I do not ascribe to the stupid theory of white supremacy and to try to hide the fact that I am a Negro for economic or any other reasons, says in effect that to be a Negro makes me inferior, [and] that I have swallowed whole hog all of the propaganda dished out by our fascist-minded white citizens.

"I am an American citizen and by God, we all have inalienable rights and whenever and wherever those rights are tampered with, there is nothing left to do but fight," she continued. "We someday are going to put into practice all of the beautiful ideals which many of us up to now have been giving little more than lip service to. If we on the home front think the issues can be side-tracked for long, I have a hunch that the boys who have been doing the fighting and dying will set us straight and quick. They vow their buddies shall not have died in vain. We have much to look forward to, but it will only come about if we are willing each to do our share in bringing the good life to realization."

Under Noble Sissle's leadership, the Negro Actors Guild hit the ground running with both action and advocacy. "For many actors, the Guild has been a salvation for them in dire times," Black playwright Abram Hill wrote in 1939. "Probably the greatest benefit the Guild has rendered the public besides its welfare work to the actor has been the immense public interest awakened among the Negro people as well as the general public... The American Negro thanks the Negro Actors Guild of America for reminding him that the Negro actor has a soul."

However, while the organization was making inroads within the industry, by the end of the 1930s, it was clear there was still much work to do. Even though both Blacks and whites increasingly considered blackface to be offensive and outdated, the practice was still regularly seen in major Hollywood films. In 1934's *Wonder Bar*, Al Jolson, who was generally seen as an ally to Blacks even though he built his career on wearing burnt cork and co-opting and mimicking aspects of African American culture, goes to Heaven—a Black version of Heaven, as envisioned by white filmmakers. In an extended musical sequence, Jolson appears with dozens of other actors who all have artificially blackened skin in a version of the afterlife in which pork chops grow on trees, live chickens are thrown through a machine where they are immediately defeathered and fried, and the deceased tap-dance joyfully against a backdrop of overgrown watermelon slices. Two years later, Fred Astaire paid tribute to Bill "Bojangles" Robinson, one of his heroes, in *Swing Time*, appearing in blackface and a flamboyant suit alongside two dozen chorines dressed in sequined antebellum-inspired showgirl costumes.

Concurrently, *Shuffle Along* was experiencing renewed interest within the film industry, as Sissle and Blake's "I'm Just Wild About Harry" was sung by white actresses Alice Faye and Priscilla Lane in *Rose of Washington Square* and *The Roaring Twenties*, respectively, which were both released in 1939. The same year, teen stars Mickey Rooney and Judy Garland both performed the song in blackface—the latter's more subtly applied, while the former's skin is the color of tar, with oversize white lips—as part of a minstrel show sequence in *Babes in Arms*, alongside a cavalcade of supporting dancers in equally flashy costumes and dark skin. While the movie industry had made some overtures to Black actors—a year before Fred Astaire paid him homage, Bill "Bojangles" Robinson was holding hands, singing, and tap-dancing on a staircase with Shirley Temple in *The Little Colonel*—it was clear that African American culture and artistry were still best appreciated when funneled through white storytellers and narratives that maintained the racial status quo.

In addition to his work with the Negro Actors Guild, Noble Sissle continued as a bandleader, with a steady engagement at theater mogul Billy Rose's Diamond Horseshoe nightclub in the basement of the Paramount Hotel in Times Square, a job he picked up in 1938. His old partner Eubie Blake was making a living as best he could, sustaining himself primarily from relatively meager ASCAP royalty checks. In 1937, he teamed up with lyricist Milton Reddie to write the score for *Swing It*, a Broadway musical "made up chiefly of actors of the old school" with a book by Cecil Mack. The show played thirty-six performances at the Adelphi Theatre on West Fifty-Fourth Street. The show was produced with funding from the Works Progress Administration (WPA), a program developed by President Franklin D. Roosevelt to help lift the still-economically anemic country out of the Great Depression. Upon the show's closing, the *Baltimore Afro-American* noted that the show was a source of salvation for the struggling artists who took part in the venture. "Actors with long records of European and American successes associated with their names cluster all over the stage in this show," they noted. "Broadway agents and movie managers could not give these performers work. Vaudeville had been knocked out long ago by the movies, leaving hundreds of colored actors idle until Uncle Sam came along with that WPA idea."

However, while *Swing It* had been a brief glimmer of hope, Blake experienced the most devastating blow of his life when Avis, his wife of twenty-nine years, died in 1939 of tuberculosis. "In my life I never knew what it was to be alone," he said in 1979. "At first when Avis got sick, I thought she just had a cold, but when time passed and she didn't get better, I made her go to a doctor and we found out she had TB. Now they know how to cure that, but forty years ago they really didn't know nothin' about it, see... Doctors, they try and tell you she might get better—wait a while and see how she does. But no matter how much you hope, see, if they don't know how to fix it, it ain't gonna fix itself. I suppose I knew from when we found out she had the TB, I understood that it was just a matter of time."

Avis's death was doubly painful. Although it was likely a biological impossibility at the time she passed, both she and Eubie had always wanted children but never prioritized having them. When she died, the pianist not only mourned her life but lives the two wished they had brought into the world. "If anybody asked me in 1935 or 1937 did I love Avis, I'd have told them, 'Sure I love my wife.' But I wouldn't be knowin' what I was talking about," he said. "When I really knew it is when I saw I was gonna lose her. God! People who got kids don't know how lucky they are... I didn't know what to do [when she died]. I didn't have any reason to do anything. Who was I gonna do it for? No kids, see? Nobody."

While Flournoy Miller had engagements playing stand-up comedy sets at Harlem haunts like the Cotton Club, he also appeared in a number of pioneering Black western films throughout the latter half of the 1930s. His first, 1937's *Harlem on the Prairie*, became the highest-grossing film with an all–African American cast, a record that held at least into the next decade. Miller appeared in the movie with Mantan Moreland, and when the two weren't on set Moreland had an active film career of his own—they went back on the road in a seemingly endless string of *Shuffle Along* revues that yielded ever-diminishing returns. The *Hollywood Reporter* called their 1939 edition "unhappy," writing that the musical "disappointed its audience by proving a very disappointing and dull show, which at times fell below the standard amateur tryouts. The presentation of fourteen scenes was very sloppily done, with microphones not working, lights going on and off during the sketches, and the pointless dialogue dragging throughout." *Billboard* gave an equally harrowing report, calling the show "too amateurish" and citing that it "smacks of high school theatricals." They noted that on the night of its first performance in Los Angeles, the production "was far from ready to open. It started slow and kept the same pace thruout [*sic*] the evening, with a good portion of [the] crowd walking out during intermission. The cast was given very poor material, the few effective songs were dragged out too long, and the scenes lacked punch."

By the end of the 1930s, *Shuffle Along*'s three surviving creators were struggling financially. Even though Noble Sissle was at the Diamond Horseshoe, on May 26, 1939, he once again filed for bankruptcy, listing $9,689 in liabilities and claiming only $965 in assets. Against a landscape of hard times—not only for themselves but for Black performers generally—Noble Sissle, Eubie Blake, and Flournoy Miller thought the timing was right to stage a proper *Shuffle Along* revival, which they hoped would once again bring African American artists back to the stage in spectacular fashion, just as the 1921 production had done. "Their coming opus will feature more singing and hot dancing than has been seen on Broadway since *Shuffle Along* and *Blackbirds* bowed out of the picture," Major Robinson wrote in the *Chicago Defender* in February 1940. "This idea, it's said, is the answer to the critic's cry that the days of the hot jazz band musical comedies were a thing of the past. During the last year the Race musicals that were fortunate to open—ending in an unfortunate closing—lacked what the playgoers expected of any colored musical that went past 110th Street. Keen observers of the theatre believe that Sissle, Blake, and Miller have had the practical experience necessary to make such a show, as they now plan, a hit. Many of the modern producers they say haven't knowledge when it comes to casting Race members in shows that will show them off their best advantage."

Initial reports stated that Sissle and Blake had already written three new songs and that the new *Shuffle Along* was scheduled to play on Broadway in the spring of 1940. Eubie Blake explained that the biggest challenge would be finding a cast, as Black performers were no longer centralized in New York but were spread throughout the country. He stated that they had discovered a woman who was of "the Florence Mills type" in Detroit but had yet to offer her a role. By April, Sissle, Blake, and Miller announced that the show had been cast and would be starting rehearsals within three or four weeks, and after a brief out-of-town tryout, it would be on Broadway by the end of the summer. By the next month, when vaudevillian Apus Brooks was declared the successor to Aubrey Lyles's Sam Peck part and Nina Mae McKinney had been cast as Ruth Little, the role originated by Gertrude Saunders and reinvented by Florence

Mills, the press was skeptical, which gave way to downright distrust when the show's opening was pushed back yet again to "perhaps along about the Christmas holiday."

However, just as the production seemed poised for perpetual purgatory, Diamond Horseshoe owner and theater producer Billy Rose declared that he was ready to back a *Shuffle Along* revival "in modernized form" and that he would "keep the original script and give it a 1940 touch." The update was a sign of seriousness that the show was moving forward, even though industry insiders thought Rose's investment was either a heavy or careless gamble. It was clear from the beginning that the show's creators and their new financier had different visions for the revival. While the producer thought songs from the original production were "tops then," he thought they lacked what was needed to win over a modern Broadway audience. Sissle and Blake were encouraged to write an entirely new score, with a few of the hits of 1921, like "I'm Just Wild About Harry" and "Love Will Find a Way," included but relegated only to "a few minutes" at the end of the production.

But spring came and went. By the end of the summer of 1940, talk of another *Shuffle Along* had tapered off, and from its ashes, Flournoy and Irvin C. Miller wrote the book for *Tan Manhattan*, a musical revue that was described by some as "the new *Shuffle Along*." The production included music by Eubie Blake and Andy Razaf as well as a sizable company reminiscent of the Black musical comedies of the early 1920s. The show had its premiere at the Howard Theatre in Washington, DC, on January 19, 1941, to a packed house and middling reviews.

However, Eubie Blake remained unfazed, telling the press that he and Andy Razaf were carefully monitoring the opening week reception to see what needed tweaking before the show moved to New York. "After being in the show business thirty-five years, a man ought to learn something," Blake said. "And in opening in a colored house, we felt we could accomplish more than we could if we had opened down town." *Tan Manhattan* ultimately landed in New York as the inaugural show at the Ubangi Club on Broadway between Fifty-Second and Fifty-Third Streets.

While *Tan Manhattan* was getting underway, the press revealed that Noble Sissle had quietly remarried—his union with Harriett had ended in divorce just months earlier—and his new bride was Ethel Watkins, one of the Cotton Club's "tall, tan, and terrific" chorines who originally hailed from Miami, Florida. Two children, Cynthia and Noble Jr., would soon follow. While of a completely different order, Flournoy Miller entered into a new marriage of sorts as well when in November 1941, he joined the *Amos 'n' Andy* radio show as a writer, seemingly adopting the mantra of "if you can't beat 'em once they've beaten you, join 'em." In addition to his work in radio, when Twentieth Century Fox announced in 1942 that they were going to take a shot at bringing *Shuffle Along* to the big screen, it was also revealed that Flournoy Miller was hired by the studio to advise on the project. The performer had remained active in the film industry, appearing alongside Mantan Moreland in a host of comedies, including 1941's *Mr. Washington Goes to Town*, and *Lucky Ghost* and *Professor Creeps*, both released in 1942, and Fox wanted him to help them develop musical adaptations of

Shuffle Along, *Runnin' Wild*, *The Chocolate Dandies*, and *Keep Shufflin'*. Noble Sissle and Eubie Blake were "expected" to lend their services and expertise once again. However, once again, none of these projects materialized.

While not on screen, *Shuffle Along* did receive another lease on life in 1942. The United States was embroiled in World War II, and the three remaining creators thought *Shuffle Along* would be the right blend of comedy, music, and nostalgia to entertain the troops. They quickly trimmed their original script—Johnny Lee filled the vacancy left by Aubrey Lyles, with both Lee and Flournoy Miller continuing to perform in blackface—and retained several beloved songs from the 1921 show, including "Love Will Find a Way," "I'm Just Wild About Harry," and "Bandana Days." With the necessary assistance of the United Service Organizations (USO), Eubie Blake and Flournoy Miller began bringing their "Camp Shows" edition of *Shuffle Along* to military theaters and bases in the United States—where it was regularly resoundingly received—and by 1945, Noble Sissle had joined the outfit for a European tour while Blake stayed behind. For Sissle, having the opportunity to entertain the U.S. troops in Europe during a second war was a distinct honor and, he felt, the best service an American entertainer could do for his country. "I feel that if we can get to entertain them and let them know we are proud of them, and love them for the great job their commanders have said they have done, then they may come home with happier hearts and their gallant fight," he said while embarking overseas with the thirty-eight member company.

According to Captain Douglass Hall, who saw the show

while stationed in Caserta, Italy, Sissle and his colleagues succeeded in their mission. "I have just seen the 'best' USO show that has been presented in this section," he wrote in a special column for the *Baltimore Afro-American.* "Don't blame me for the evaluation. It is not mine. It is just what hundreds of men and women who are stationed in this theatre are saying. I have just seen Noble Sissle's GI edition of *Shuffle Along.* For one hour before the show was scheduled to jump-off, long lines of GIs sat on the anxious seat in the vicinity of the theatre. That was a definite compliment to the show because GIs have shown little interest in many of the shows that have come over with the explanation: 'Oh well, if you have seen one USO show you have seen them all, because they are all alike.'... It's safe to say that *Shuffle Along* offers more laughs per minute than any other show that these GIs have seen. It has good music, moves fast, and the costumes are tops. It is different from other shows that have been booked over here in that it is a full stage production."

After Italy, the show went to Germany where, in March 1946, Noble Sissle, Flournoy Miller, and Ivan Harold Browning of the Harmony Kings, who was part of the cast, reunited with Josephine Baker backstage at the Alhambra Theatre in Brussels after the opening of her new show, *Revue du Rythme.* The gathering was commemorated with a photograph—the three men in servicemen's jackets, Baker in a long formal gown with embroidery around the collar, and all four with hands and arms connecting them to the person they were nearest. It was a reminder of how far each of them had come, exactly 3,657 miles from the heart of New York City. Throughout the tour, it was rumored and reported that *Shuffle Along Revue*, the name that emerged to distinguish the ninety-minute USO version from its various predecessors, was headed back to Broadway after completing its overseas engagement. However, when Sissle and Miller returned to the States after playing over 150 performances throughout Italy, France, Germany, and Australia

FLOURNOY MILLER, JOSEPHINE BAKER, NOBLE SISSLE, AND IVAN HAROLD BROWNING IN BRUSSELS, MARCH 1946

Courtesy of Photographs and Prints Division, Schomburg Center for Research in Black Culture, The New York Public Library / used with permission of the United Services Organization

to over 1.25 million soldiers, they put *Shuffle Along* away on the shelf. Both they and the show needed a break.

That was until—to the complete surprise of Sissle, Blake, and Miller—President Harry S. Truman adopted "I'm Just Wild About Harry" as the song for his reelection campaign against New York governor Thomas E. Dewey. When Truman won in a surprising upset, Sissle and Blake were invited to Washington, DC, to sing the song at the inaugural celebration, but at the last minute, the event organizers requested that Alice Faye, who sang the number in 1939's *Rose of Washington Square*, perform the number instead. Blake, who was already in the nation's capital, was asked to work alongside Fletcher Henderson on a special arrangement of the song for the festivities. Even though they had been slighted, for the composers, the resurrection of the number in the election of 1948 was a fitting completion of a circle where art imitated life, which then imitated art yet again.

"The interesting thing about 'Harry' was that it actually was written as an election song in a show whose plot was almost a parallel to the 1948 Presidential Campaign," Sissle and Blake wrote in a letter to the president. "Our hero, Harry Walton, was the underdog in his race just as you were in the Election of 1948. Although we did not have a *Chicago Tribune* telling the people that his rival had been elected, it first appeared that one of the candidates opposing Harry in our race had won.

"Oh, yes, our Harry had more than one opponent just as you did in 1948," they continued. "Well, a friend asked the ingenue how she felt about Harry when he'd apparently lost. She replied, 'I'm just wild about Harry,' and went into the song. Harry won our election and, of course, won the Election of 1948."

With the presidential race bringing "I'm Just Wild About Harry" to radio airwaves and countless campaign events throughout the United States—and Truman emerging victorious—it once again seemed appropriate to strike while the iron was hot and revamp *Shuffle Along* for Broadway. While there were several African American performers like Harry Belafonte, Sammy Davis Jr., Lena Horne, and Eartha Kitt raking in money playing Las Vegas nightclubs, the state of Black musical theater in Manhattan had changed significantly. There had been a few recent hits with all-Black casts, such as *Carmen Jones*, which was penned by white composers Oscar Hammerstein II and Georges Bizet and ran over 500 performances. *Bloomer Girl* and *Finian's Rainbow*—both also with all-white creative teams—had integrated casts and grappled with complex social issues such as racial justice and women's rights in a bold and progressive way. They were undeniable successes, running 657 and 725 performances on Broadway, respectively. However, the days of multiple all-Black shows written and produced by all-Black creators were long gone. In many ways, it already seemed unfathomable that it had even occurred at all.

Nevertheless, Noble Sissle, Eubie Blake, and Flournoy Miller had faced this challenge before. If they could bring about a renaissance in 1921 with little more than ambition and talent, they felt they could do it again. On March 25, 1949, the *New York Times* reported that *Shuffle Along*, "the Negro musical of yesteryear," was being "brought up to date" for a new production, backed by Irving Gaumont and directed by John Murray Anderson, a multihyphenate and multitalented creative who had worked in vaudeville, theater, and film. Anderson cut his teeth on both the Ziegfeld and Greenwich Village *Follies*, making him the perfect person to give the new production "that Broadway touch." Pearl Bailey, a veteran of the nightclub circuit who had performed with Cab Calloway and Duke Ellington and had recently made the transition to Broadway, was publicly floated as a contender for the show's leading lady, and the production would once again reunite Sissle, Blake, and Miller, as well as Miller's daughter, Olivette, who was now a famous harpist.Eubie Blake, who was completing a course in musical composition at New York University and was looking forward to spending the rest of his career composing instrumental and "semi-classical" music, anticipated the new iteration of *Shuffle Along* being his final time writing for the stage.

"I'm tired of fighting Broadway," he said, "but I will continue to write music as long as I can hold a pen."

While the show seemed off to a legitimate start, the budding revival was badly in need of financing. Industry insiders projected it would take about $150,000 for the show to hit Broadway—a marked increase from being $21,000 in the hole on the 1921 production's opening night at the Sixty-Third Street Theatre—and investors would have to put in at least $3,000 for a one-percent share. It took until June 1951, over two years after the show was announced, for Gaumont to raise $115,000 to bring *Shuffle Along* back to the stage. The production was back on track, but some in the press were beginning to question whether the show would meet the same fate as the revival of 1930's *The Green Pastures*, which was unsuccessfully resurrected before dying a second time in front of a piddling audience. "Critics went overboard to praise the show and a competent cast labored to keep it alive," Frank Morton wrote for the Associated Negro Press. "But the show had outlived its usefulness—or so theatergoers felt. A big house was necessary for the big production and critics said this took lots away from the intimacy of the production. Now another group is sponsoring a [*Shuffle Along*] revival, it is hoped, next spring of the show that won acclaim everywhere in the United States and enjoyed a long and prosperous run. Doubting Thomases are standing by with tongues in cheek. They defend their position by saying that *Shuffle Along*, no matter how it is brought up to date, will suffer the same fate because it is not in keeping with the tempo of today's stage hits. There have been several tabloid revivals of the show done by USO groups...but a Broadway presentation, where competition is better, is another question."

But *Shuffle Along* had a greater chance of success by every objective standard, especially since the show had a star. By the summer of 1951, Pearl Bailey had become formally attached to the project, with a $2,000 guarantee against a 7.5 percent gross of the profits. With Bailey and several other members of the cast on board, Irving Gaumont refocused his efforts to raising the remaining $35,000 needed to bring the show to Broadway. Promotional booklets were soon sent to New York's top theatrical investors. A photograph of Bailey appeared prominently on its cover, alongside several other women of the cast, above a large illustration of three physically nondescript Black men in tuxedos, one shy of the quartet that made the original production a success. Its backside featured newspaper clippings highlighting "what the critics said about *Shuffle Along*," but they were nearly all close to thirty years old and about the 1921 run. The lone exception was an excerpt from *Variety* in 1951, wherein Ivan Harold Browning was reminding the outlet that Josephine Baker had gotten her start with the show's original company. Even that, it seemed, had become forgotten. Inside there were two brief notes from Pearl

THE COVER OF IRVING GAUMONT'S PROMOTIONAL BOOKLET FOR *SHUFFLE ALONG* OF 1952

Photo courtesy of the author's personal collection.

Bailey; one to Noble Sissle "for the wonderful things you taught me in show business" and the other to Gaumont. "Here's hoping life will give you the best," she said. "And give me *Shuffle Along.*"

In November, the *New York Times* reported that the show was premiering on New Year's Eve in Boston, where it would enjoy a three-week run before opening in New York on January 21. Sissle and Blake had written an almost entirely new score, with a few "old favorites" from the original production, including "Love Will Find a Way" and "I'm Just Wild About Harry," making the cut. Flournoy Miller's original book hadn't "undergone much alteration," and everything was moving forward as planned. But nearly as soon as their article was written, there were reports that Pearl Bailey had finally laid eyes on the script—and she wasn't pleased. Concurrently, the public doubts about the show's prospects for success continued to grow louder. "*Shuffle Along* is dated," the Associated Negro Press declared as a matter of fact in a syndicated article that was likely to be seen by over four million African Americans. "It represents a phase of theater Negroes prefer not to be reminded of." In an attempt to keep Pearl Bailey—and perhaps also the potential paying customers— happy, the producers pushed back the start date of the show and ordered immediate changes.

The theater industry had changed significantly in the thirty years since 1921. While there were obviously challenges to getting a show to Broadway—financial and racial especially—in the 1920s, it was easier for creatives to remain in control when it came to the finished product that appeared onstage. The four who'd conceived *Shuffle Along* had had a hand in the casting, and each had a vote and a stake in the show's production company. When bits didn't work, they changed them; when a leading lady left, they quickly found a replacement; when the company didn't have a place to sleep, they helped beg, borrow, and steal; and when the show made good, they became rich too. But that artist-driven system no longer existed. The entertainment industry had become so competitive across various media that producers were less inclined to gamble with the house money. *Shuffle Along* had name recognition, but it was far from a certainty that a revival would turn a profit. The producers were lucky to have a star like Pearl Bailey, and they were going to do whatever was needed to keep her.

By the beginning of 1952, John Murray Anderson was replaced with George Hale, a noted choreographer who was beginning to make a name for himself as a director. Additionally, producer Irving Gaumont hired playwright John McGowan, whose credits included 1928's *Hold Everything*, 1930's *Girl Crazy*, and 1931's *Singin' the Blues*, to doctor the script. He was tasked with expanding Pearl Bailey's role and writing new songs that catered to her comedic singing style. By the end of January, the moneymen told reporters that *Shuffle Along of 1952*, as the show as now being called, would have a completely new story, which Flournoy Miller would consult on with McGowan, and that three new songs had been specifically written for Bailey. Miller was summoned to Charleston, South Carolina, where McGowan lived and had already hammered out a revision of the show's first act, to work on rewrites alongside Paul Gerard Smith, who had written several Buster Keaton films and the books for the 1924, 1925, and 1926 editions of Ziegfeld's *Follies*. The press was invited to watch them work, putting Flournoy Miller in the awkward position of having to explain why his original book was unsuitable for the current times. "The show is planned as entertainment and nothing else... Nobody uses burnt cork anymore," he said, although he had just blackened up for the USO version of the show six years earlier.

However, journalist Thomas R. Waring quickly picked up on the issues being altered from *Shuffle Along*'s original book, which Flournoy Miller had failed to address in his retooling of the script before reinforcements were brought in. "Like almost everything else, humor about colored people has changed since the Roaring Twenties. What was funny then is stale or unintelligible today," Warning wrote. "One of the big guffaws in the original *Shuffle Along* was about a Negro who was elected mayor of a mythical town and couldn't spell 'C-A-T.' Nowadays, when most colored people can read even in the deep country, the joke would fall flat. Another gag, illustrating the laziness of the characters, was laid in a grocery. The clerks were so dull they told the customers to wait on themselves. In this age of the supermarket, everybody serves himself and an audience would be left cold by a dated wisecrack." Eliminating the show's racial stereotypes may have been a tall order, but John McGowan was certain the three men could do it. "With Miller's knowledge of Negro humor and the theater experience of all three of us, we expect to turn out a new book in short order," he said.

Once the book was completed and back in New York, Irving Gaumont rescheduled its opening at the Colonial Theatre in Boston for March 31, 1952. However, that day came and went, with the production being delayed yet again when the revival's star, Pearl Bailey, quit

FLOURNOY MILLER, DELORES MARTIN, AND MANTAN MORELAND IN REHEARSALS FOR *SHUFFLE ALONG OF 1952*

Courtesy of Photofest

just as rehearsals were scheduled to begin. While it wasn't reported publicly at the time, the actress thought that the show, even in its restructured state, was antiquated, tone-deaf, and inappropriate for the current—or any—moment. Instead, Delores Martin, a singer and actress who was recently in *Finian's Rainbow*, was quickly cast as her replacement. Furthermore, George Hale was out as director—he would stay on to "oversee" the production—and script doctor Jack McGowan was in. Rehearsals finally commenced in earnest in mid-March, with the premiere set for the end of April at the Shubert Theatre in New Haven, Connecticut, followed by a brief tryout in Philadelphia before arriving on Broadway at the end of May.

The constant changes regarding *Shuffle Along of 1952* were frustrating for the show's creators, especially as every development was covered by the press. Years later, Noble Sissle recounted the behind-the-scenes chaos for the *Baltimore Afro-American*, from the moment the show was announced to when their star left for another sky. "We both have a good right reason to be put out with her," he said, referring to both himself and Eubie Blake. "We had to get $50,000 subscribed before we could even go into rehearsals. Well, we got the money after a year's struggle, and approached Pearl Bailey to play the lead. She was to have the part Florence Mills played in the original production. Pearl said o.k., to go on with the plans and she'd be back in town when rehearsals were set. We hired designers, a theatre, set decorators, lighting engineers, costumes, orchestra—the works. Then came the time for Pearl to sign the contract. 'Well, I don't know,' she said, 'that show is kinda Uncle Tom, and I don't want to get mixed up with anything like that.' After a bit of haggling, we rewrote the show entirely, hired a show doctor, rewrote the lyrics to all the songs—in fact, made it a tailor-made production for her. To make a long story short—she never did sing."

Shuffle Along of 1952 began with promise, but it soon revealed itself to be ill-planned, or perhaps just ill-fated. Days into rehearsals, the set pieces designed by Albert Johnson, a twenty-year Broadway veteran with over thirty credits to his name, were destroyed in a fire that ravaged a scenic design studio in Fort Lee, New Jersey. To make matters worse, just prior to the incident, a representative from the production office had brought Johnson's original design sketches to the studio to inspect his work, and they went up in flames as well. With Irving Gaumont set against pushing the show back any further, the designer had no choice but to recreate everything as best he could from memory, in just a matter of weeks. Then, just days before the show was scheduled to premiere, Noble Sissle stepped backward while rehearsing onstage, lost his balance, and fell into the orchestra pit. The singer was rushed to the hospital and treated for a back injury—which would give him problems for the rest of his life—but promised to be onstage with the rest of the company on opening night. And throughout it all, the press—particularly the Black press—continued their assault on the revival, sight unseen. "This column has said it before and will say it again and again. Broadway can get along without such shows as *Shuffle Along*," James Hicks wrote in the *Baltimore Afro-American*. "We hope when the play hits the Big Town it will be shunned like poison ivy. Especially so when the man who once helped write the *Amos and Andy* [*sic*] script is helping to write *Shuffle Along*. Isn't it silly that it's so hard for some folks to realize that colored people these days are walking on their feet instead of 'shuffling along' on their knees?"

The hits kept coming. Noble Sissle's injury was worse than originally thought, causing him to miss the first few shows, and just before April 23, when *Shuffle Along of 1952* played its first of five performances in New Haven, John McGowan fell ill and was replaced as director by his colleague Paul Gerard Smith. But despite the repeated changes in who was in charge, or perhaps because of it, the revival left critics with much to be desired. "If they ever decide what they want to do with this all-Negro musical, maybe they can whip it into hit proportions before it's too late. Otherwise the whole thing will just be a case of shuffle off to Buffalo," *Variety* wrote of its first preview performance. "A series of preparatory headaches that involved star replacement, a shift in directors, an injury to one of the principals, and similar obstacles, brought the production up to its preem curtain in a floundering condition. Opening performance was merely a series of songs and dances scotch-taped together by a pretty weak semblance of a book, the net result being nothing more than a blueprint of what might be expected if potentialities are exploited along more entertainment-conscious lines." The show's inaugural week was a disappointment, grossing just $7,000 with a $4.80 top ticket price. To add insult to injury, there was yet another shake-up. On the final night of its run in Connecticut, for reasons left unexplained, Eubie Blake was replaced as the orchestra's conductor in the middle of the show, with William "Billy" Butler, who had led the pit for Lew Leslie's *Blackbirds*, taking his place after intermission.

The show began what was intended to be a two-week run at the Shubert Theatre in Philadelphia on April 28, but Irving Gaumont made the confounding decision to stop its run on May 3, a week early. Instead, the producer canceled the show's previously scheduled Boston engagement and moved the New York opening at the aptly named Broadway Theatre up by three weeks, stating that it was "based on his belief that the new version of the fabulous hit of the Nineteen Twenties is ready for local examination." However, *Variety* told a different story. The show grossed under $10,000 while in Philadelphia, making it necessary for Gaumont to save money by pulling all local newspaper advertisements and fast-tracking the show to New York to avoid future losses.

Gaumont's spin around the show's premature Manhattan transfer was sullied by Pearl Bailey making news of her own on the same day. The actress attended the opening of *Shuffle Along of 1952* in Philadelphia and took the opportunity to share for the first time, in her own words, why she'd abandoned the revival. "In the first place, the part had no laughs, and I need laughs," she said, but her real objection? "The script was written in dialect! I know I have a natural drawl, but I don't want somebody to write 'dem' for me when I'm supposed to say 'them,' and who wants to hear things like 'who dat?' We don't need to go back that far!" Nevertheless, on the eve of the New York opening, Gaumont and his team were still projecting confidence that *Shuffle Along of 1952* had the potential of recreating the success of the original and all the show's problems were just par for the course. "Believers in omens, it was said yesterday by a spokesman for the attraction, can take comfort in the knowledge that practically similar troubles dogged the pre-New York footsteps of the first of the musical series," Louis Calta wrote in the *New York Times*. "Overcoming its difficulties, the original *Shuffle Along* went on to enjoy long runs on Broadway and on the road with two companies touring simultaneously for three years."

On May 8, 1952, the third Broadway iteration of *Shuffle Along* had its Manhattan premiere. Sixty-two-year-old Noble Sissle rejoined the cast, still reeling from his back injury, ready to relive his glory days with Eubie Blake, three years his senior, who joined him onstage at the end of the show for "a few minutes" to perform a medley of the hits from moons ago. While it had been kept relatively quiet, almost all of the show's score had been revamped by lyricist Floyd Huddleston and composer Joseph Meyer, white musicians who had written for Frank Sinatra, Judy Garland, and Al Jolson. "They threw my music out of *Shuffle*

Along," Blake recalled decades later, still annoyed with what had happened right under his nose.

The show's book was tinkered with until the last minute, but when the curtain rose, time had finally run out. The narrative, which was once again universally criticized as being "thin" despite the six weeks that were spent modernizing the 1921 story, began in Italy just after World War II ended. A unit of Black American men and women serving overseas vow to remain together when they return to New York so they can open a salon with the latest in women's fashion. Along the way, several of the characters fall in love, and there are the necessary shenanigans for comedic effect, all of which are ancillary to the main plot. While there were a few generous reviews, overall, the critics were unsurprisingly ruthless. "The only similarity between *Shuffle Along* of 1921 and the *Shuffle Along* of 1952 is the title," John Chapman wrote in the *New York Daily News*. "The old show was fast, hard-dancing, and light-hearted; the new one...is slow and muddled."

John Chapman's assessment was shared across the board. "Noble Sissle and Eubie Blake had two big tunes, 'I'm Just Wild About Harry' and 'Love Will Find a Way'... The two songs [are] as tuneful as ever, with nostalgia thrown in this time. The rest of the score is commonplace, the dancing really nothing to write to the coast about, and this is the big disappointment what with an all-Negro cast," Sid Garfield wrote in the *Hollywood Reporter*. "There are so many happy and eager people in *Shuffle Along*, I feel like a heel saying this. But I found it, generally, a tedious, mediocre presentation." Walter E. Kerr wrote in the *New York Herald Tribune*, "The new edition of *Shuffle Along* has endured so many vicissitudes...that one wishes all the agony might have ended in triumph. But the show...is no more than a minor vaudeville masquerading as a full-fledged comedy... With the book dragging itself about the stage, and the dancing numbers blending lazily into one another, *Shuffle* is a rather extravagant word for the pace of the show at the Broadway [Theatre]. I'm afraid that this latest version of a once beloved song-and-dance frolic is distinguished only by its ancestry."

On May 10, after just four performances on Broadway, *Shuffle Along of 1952* became history. The show was abruptly canceled, with a reopening to be scheduled "after revisions suggested by the critics have been made," which never happened. Although John Chapman had given the production a lackluster review in the *New York Daily News*, he still lamented the loss for the theatergoers and performers of all races. "The closing... of *Shuffle Along* was inevitable—but regrettable, for it meant at least temporary defeat for great talent," he wrote. "Tragically little use is being made of the Negro on the stage, and the tragedy is the white man's as much as it is his. It seems to me that the Negro was born for the stage, and when he isn't being used it is the theatre's loss. He is, of course, the best dancer alive—agile, precise, graceful, and tireless. There was a great lift to *Shuffle Along* whenever the chorus got to dancing, and there should have been more dancing. Somewhere in our theatre there should be more serious dancing, too; a Negro ballet company could be the new sensation of the ballet world... Great talent and great ambition are being wasted. I'd like to see Negro productions of the classics—any classics; and not in Harlem, but on Broadway, where they belong. My bet is that we'd see some astonishing acting. Meanwhile, good luck to *Shuffle Along*."

For Noble Sissle, Eubie Blake, and Flournoy Miller, the failure of the revival was more than just an embarrassment—it was a signal to each of them that they were living legends, men who had shaped the course of history while also being left behind by it. "A man gets to feelin' that enough is enough," Blake said. "I was disappointed. I knew it wasn't my fault or Sissle's fault that it was no good. My God, we had some of the most talented people in the world. But I wasn't broken up like some kid seeing his first show go down the drain. Now I was almost seventy years old. Most men seventy years old—I felt it myself—they think there's not much future left… I'm long past the time when a flop can be a disaster, and I already was then. Of course, while it's happenin' it's no fun at all. You look at what they done to your show and you know they don't know what the—what they're doin'. And if you've been in show business all your life, it hurts more than anything to see an audience that's not getting what they paid to see."

What was more discouraging than anything was that after the great strides that had been made to increase Black representation in all forms of entertainment, parts for African American performers were incredibly limited in theaters and cinemas, and they were virtually nonexistent on television. "It wasn't only the talent that changed, it was the business itself," Blake explained. "In those times if you looked at the TV, you'd think there were no Negroes in the whole world. Well, *Amos 'n' Andy*. They had to go to Negroes for that show on TV. On radio those parts were played by white actors. Sometimes a Jones [a colloquialism for "Black person"] could get a part as a maid or porter. In fact, one lady got her own series playin' a maid," he said, referring to Louise Beavers in *Beulah*. "But they shoulda been more advanced by that time. But they weren't. People don't realize, but Martin Luther King done all that. He started everything for Negroes."

While it may have been difficult for Eubie Blake and his partners to see at the time, they, too, had played an integral part in "starting everything." While there were other attempts to bring back *Shuffle Along*—a Las Vegas revue, another Broadway revival, and the elusive feature film were all ideas bandied about— the show's creators would never reunite to stage another version of their sensationally simple show that brought a new sound to Manhattan theatergoers and changed the face of the Great White Way. It had introduced the world to the likes of Josephine Baker, Paul Robeson, Florence Mills, and dozens of other artists who would go on to make lasting contributions to American culture. "I will always believe that if Miller and Lyles and Sissle and Blake had stuck together, the colored stage would have been entirely different," Lottie Gee, the star of the original *Shuffle Along*, said.

Following the closing of *Shuffle Along of 1952*, the show's main creators remained adjacent to the entertainment business but were essentially retired and absent from high-profile projects. "After the white writers learned how to write syncopation, they didn't need us," Eubie Blake explained. "There was no more room for us." Flournoy Miller remained in California, close to Hollywood, while Eubie Blake and his wife, Marion—he remarried in 1945 while Sissle and Miller were overseas with the USO edition of the show—remained comfortable in Brooklyn. Noble Sissle relocated to Florida to be near his children after he and his wife divorced in 1947 and she moved back to the Sunshine State. Of his many accomplishments, one of the things Sissle felt proudest of was the role he'd played in elevating Black women, who were routinely marginalized—when they weren't completely absent—onstage until *Shuffle Along* made the chorines a focal point of the production and the leading actresses future international stars. "If there's anything we leave behind for posterity, I think it's an effort that we did bring to the American theater, the Negro shows, to glorify the colored woman," he said.

"We always felt that theatre was designed for art," Flournoy Miller said. "In those days, the Negro was not typed. Anything he could do, comedy or otherwise, if he could do it well, he was given a chance." And when given that opportunity, Noble Sissle felt, they would show America that despite all the obstacles in their way—or perhaps even because of them—Black performers were capable of exceeding the expectations that whites had for them and overcoming all limitations imposed upon them. "Negro artists and composers were placed by Fate at the bottom rung of the ladder of opportunity in this great country of ours," he said. "But having had to wait on the bottom rung for our chance to move up, we thus had the opportunity to take stock of those above us—and really know what makes America 'tick.'"

Margaret Truman, daughter of President Harry S. Truman, and Noble Sissle look on as Eubie Blake plays "I'm Just Wild About Harry" after presenting a manuscript of the song to the Truman Memorial Library on September 26, 1967

Courtesy of Jacob Harris/AP/Shutterstock

EPILOGUE

ENCORES

B lack comedian Flip Wilson stood in front of a chalkboard with fourteen-year-old Michael Jackson in front of a studio audience and television cameras on October 26, 1972, faced with two different answers to a simple math problem. The host of NBC's highly rated *The Flip Wilson Show* was attempting to contribute his share toward a $28 lunch tab, which Jackson had paid, and since seven of them had agreed to split the bill, Wilson calculated that he owed $4. The teenager contested, claiming the actual amount owed was $13. The comedian was incredulous, but after the singer demonstrated several different ways that twenty-eight, when divided by seven, equaled thirteen, the audience was in stitches—and Flip Wilson was out $13.

On November 14, Olivette Miller Darby, Flournoy Miller's daughter, sued both the network and television show host in federal court for copyright infringement and misappropriation of her father's work, to the tune of $500,000. The accused maintained their innocence. After all, it was difficult to establish exactly who had originated the bit. Bud Abbott and Lou Costello had similar trouble with numbers in their 1941 film *In the Navy*, as did Ma and Pa Kettle ten years later in *Ma and Pa Kettle Back on the Farm*. Miller Darby claimed that the sketch had been written for *Shuffle Along* in 1921, which she couldn't prove, likely because it wasn't true. Miller and Lyles had popularized the routine, and it had been frequently ripped off, usually by white comedians, but they hadn't created it—although they had used it with permission—and they first worked the routine into 1923's *Runnin' Wild*. In the end, Olivette Miller Darby agreed to drop the charges in exchange for $1,000, even though the facts didn't fully add up.

Flournoy Miller died at eighty-four years old on June 6, 1971, at a convalescent home in Hollywood, survived by his wife and daughter, who was left to tend to all his business affairs. In 1974, Broadway and film producer Cyma Rubin attempted to bring *The Laughmaker*, a feature film biopic of Miller's life, based on an unpublished memoir written by his daughter, to the big screen. Bill Cosby was set to star, and Eubie Blake was involved in the preproduction process. However, issues with his estate led to the project being canceled, even though a screenplay was written and financing was secured.

At the time of Miller's death, *Shuffle Along* was experiencing renewed attention, thanks in large part to the 1969 release of *The Eighty-Six Years of Eubie Blake*, a double LP album celebrating the long life and career of the famed ragtime pianist, who had largely receded from the public eye. The album's title was derived from the composer's declared age, although like Miller and Lyles, he began playing with the numbers by the mid-1960s, claiming to have been born in 1883, four years earlier than he truly was.

The recording sessions took place in front of live audiences on three days between December 1968 and March 1969, and on one of those occasions, Noble Sissle joined his old partner for several numbers, including on their first hit, "It's All Your Fault," and a rollicking, nearly seven-minute-long *Shuffle Along* medley. Anyone listening to the two vocally ad-libbing and harmonizing on numbers like "Gypsy Blues" and "If You've Never Been Vamped By a Brown Skin" would be forgiven for not realizing that the two hadn't performed together in over fifteen years. Toward the end of the dynamite performance, Eubie Blake exploded into a short piano solo during "I'm Just Wild About Harry," with the octogenarian's fingers ricocheting off the piano keys with incredible speed, deftness, energy, and jubilation. His old partner excitedly egged him on, reminding the composer that even though the number had been covered by Al Jolson, Carmen Miranda, and even Daffy Duck, it belonged to him: "Go 'head, now! You wrote it, play it!"

The album was a surprise hit for Columbia Records, and almost immediately, Eubie Blake, finally a Grammy Award nominee, was in high demand. His datebook was filled with appointments to give lectures and play on college campuses, chat with newspaper journalists writing nostalgic think pieces, and have a laugh with late-night television hosts eager to speak with one of the surviving giants of a long-lost era. With Noble Sissle, he contributed extensively to *Reminiscing with Sissle and Blake*, a retrospective illustrated book by Robert Kimball and William Bolcom commemorating the musicians' decades of professional partnership, which was published to critical success in 1973. Its release was accompanied by an extensive promotional campaign, from which Noble Sissle was largely absent.

The following January, Eubie Blake and his wife, Marion, traveled to Tampa, Florida, to see Sissle, who was experiencing concerning bouts of extreme memory loss. It would be the last time the two men would see each other. "That was terrible," Blake said afterward. "I never should have gone. Poor Sissle. He kept asking me if I had any trouble finding the subway. There's no subway in Tampa. He don't even know he ain't in New York. I felt so bad seeing him like that." However, the trip was more than a social visit. The singer's son, Noble Sissle Jr., worked in television and wanted to sit down with both Eubie Blake and his father in front of an audience for a short biographical video, knowing there would be few opportunities left to capture the two men together on film.

"He said Sissle would be all right, but I didn't believe it," Blake recalled. As the cameras rolled, the pianist sat in a black swivel chair at a small organ, prepared to play while expecting the worst. His partner sat to his right in an identical chair. The two senior citizens sat across from Noble Jr., who looked every bit as modern as they looked of the past: decked out in a sand-colored suit with a mile-high afro, appearing about seven feet tall sitting in a chair with mustard cushions. Blake began playing "Gee! I'm Glad That I'm from Dixie," which was always the first number in their old vaudeville act, but his partner never came in, leaning back with his left leg crossed over the right, with an index finger never leaving his cheek.

The pianist continued carrying the conversation and performance until his long fingers tickled the introductory notes to "I'm Just Wild About Harry," and to his surprise, Noble Sissle perked up. He uncrossed his legs, leaned forward, and with a voice just as strong and smooth as it ever was, began singing right on time. Blake winced in surprise and began playing softer, not fully believing what he had just heard, but his partner kept the tempo and rhythm going, forcing the pianist to match his energy. With a smile and a head nod to Noble Jr., Blake liberated his fingers to do what they did best, and Noble Sissle called his digits to attention as well, punctuating his singing with expressive hand movements. The cameraperson zoomed in on the vocalist, and when the two reached the chorus, the audience applauded, causing the singer's eyes to twinkle and his mouth to curl upward into a smile.

Even if it was just for a day, for one final song, Sissle and Blake were back. "Right after we got done, he started talkin' nonsense," the pianist said regretfully. "I couldn't *stand* that." Noble Sissle died a year later, on December 17, 1975, at eighty-six years old.

In the years after *Shuffle Along of 1952*, Blacks continued to make strides on Broadway, in both comedies and dramas. In 1959, Black playwright Lorraine Hansberry's *A Raisin in the Sun*, starring Sidney Poitier and Ruby Dee, ran for 530 performances. The production featured a predominantly Black cast and was nominated for four Tony Awards, which led to an engagement on London's West End and a 1961 Golden Globe–nominated feature film. In 1967, Pearl Bailey and Cab Calloway costarred in a well-received revival of *Hello, Dolly!* with an all–African American cast, earning Bailey a special Tony Award. Two years later, James Earl Jones became the first Black performer to win a Tony for Best Actor in a Play.

In 1975, *The Wiz*, a "super soul musical" reimagining of L. Frank Baum's *The Wonderful Wizard of Oz*, opened on Broadway. While the book was penned by white playwright William F. Brown, Black artists such as composer and lyricist Charlie Smalls, orchestrator Harold Wheeler, and singer-songwriter Luther Vandross made up the majority of the creative team. The production won seven of the eight Tony Awards it was nominated for and became the first show with an all-Black cast to win the evening's top honor of Best Musical. Geoffrey Holder also made history that night, becoming the first African American to win Best Director of a Musical and Best Costume Design in a Musical. The show ultimately ran for four years and 1,672 performances.

The following year, "Love Will Find a Way" and "In Honeysuckle Time" from *Shuffle Along* were featured in *Bubbling Brown Sugar*, a Tony-nominated revue inspired by the music of the Harlem Renaissance. And as encouraging as it was to hear two of his songs on a Manhattan stage again, in 1978, another failed attempt to revive *Shuffle Along* on Broadway led to *Eubie!*, a celebrated revue made up of twenty-four of the composer's hits, including numbers from *Shuffle Along*, *The Chocolate Dandies*, *Blackbirds of 1930*, and *Tan Manhattan*. The produc-

EUBIE BLAKE STANDS UNDER THE MARQUEE FOR *EUBIE!* AT NEW YORK'S AMBASSADOR THEATER ON SEPTEMBER 13, 1978

Courtesy of R Howard/AP/Shutterstock

tion starred Gregory Hines, who was Tony-nominated for his performance. Not to be left out, Noble Sissle, Flournoy Miller, Andy Razaf, and James Reese Europe were all posthumously nominated for Best Original Score, alongside musician Johnny Brandon and, of course, Eubie Blake himself.

The pianist had always bristled at discussing race discrimination he had faced over the course of his career, but as he reached his nineties—his *actual* nineties—his attitude began to change. He freely agreed that too many white Americans suffered from the disease of racism—"A lot of people are still fighting the Civil War. And they don't know it yet, but they lost"—and publicly reflected on his role in the fight for equal treatment for Blacks.

"You can't fight with your hands tied behind your back," he said to a white journalist in 1980. "I had money in my pocket, but there were places that wouldn't serve me because I was a Negro. People wonder how we stood all of this. Well, we said something about it, but we didn't fight it. You people had all the pistols, all the food, all the clothes, all the houses, and the money to build our schools. You didn't have to shoot us; you could starve us. When Martin Luther King came along and told us, 'Don't hit back,' I didn't agree. I thought he was crazy. But he was talking about the same things we practiced. My mother and father were slaves. When slavery was over, where did they go? Back to the white man. Ain't no other place to go. Well, things have changed in some ways, but our hands are still tied sometimes.

"If I was white and had the influence, I would never come out to say nothin' in the Negroes' favor," he said in summation. "Because just about every one who did, from John Brown on—see if they don't kill him. Every last one of them except for Truman. For the others, it was suicide. But remember this. There are a lot of people who got on their minds, 'We must keep the Negro down.' That's where they lose, you see. Because in order to keep me down in the gutter, you gotta stay down in the gutter with me. If you get up, I do too."

However, Blake's criticism wasn't reserved exclusively for white folks. He often expressed frustration that many within the Black community, whom he felt he had helped make great advances for, had forgotten the doors he broke down with Noble Sissle, Flournoy Miller, and Aubrey Lyles. While being forgotten by many stung, the more painful wound was that, to some, Blake was seen as a blemish on African American history. "I'm not going to name the lady—she's a great star now, she's a great artist—but she called Sissle and Blake 'Uncle Toms' because we wrote 'Bandana Days.' Now, she didn't know that when there's a book to a show, you write according to the book. Sissle changed some of the lyrics—it wasn't a 'Tom' lyric, 'cause Sissle wasn't that kind of a fella. Nobody in the world was as good as Sissle *to Sissle*, you understand? He loved Noble Sissle, so he couldn't have been that way. I was born in the ghetto; I had more inhibitions than he had, but that's what hurt us. Hurt my feelings. Hurt Sissle's feelings.

"When Miller and Lyles and Sissle and Blake put that show on, *Shuffle Along*, and it swept this country—not just New York, swept the whole country—then they should look at that, what we did," he added, his voice filled with equal parts pride and defiance. "But we put Negroes *back* on this great Broadway. *We* put 'em back there."

On October 9, 1981, President Ronald Reagan awarded Eubie Blake with the Presidential Medal of Freedom, the highest honor that can be bestowed upon a civilian. In December of that year, he lived to see *Dreamgirls*, a musical with an all-Black cast and primarily-white production team, act as a shot in the arm to the African American theater scene and an overall struggling Broadway season. At capacity, the show made $83,000 a week— and it was frequently at capacity. It ultimately ran for 1,521 performances at the Imperial Theatre and won six of the thirteen Tony Awards it was nominated for as well as two Grammys for its highly successful soundtrack. Although he was in his golden years, Blake never lost his wits—when a reporter asked him at what age one starts to lose their sex drive, Blake quickly replied, "You'll have to ask somebody older than me"—and the composer continued to play piano until his death on February 12, 1983, just five days after his purported hundredth birthday.

For the century following its premiere, *Shuffle Along* was never revived on Broadway in its original iteration. Some argue that that would be impossible to do in the next hundred years as well, given the show's use of racialized humor that was offensive to some in 1921 and would be considered far more objectionable to twenty-first-century audiences. These concerns are valid, but they raise equally fair questions: How can we avoid erasing significant shows like *Shuffle Along* from our shared cultural memory, even if aspects of them may be distasteful?

Is there a double standard that permits "classic" shows by white playwrights and composers with sexist, homophobic, culturally insensitive, and yes, even racist content to continue to be revived on Broadway, performed in local high schools and community theaters, and considered part of the theatrical canon, but equally important ones like *Shuffle Along* are forced into early retirement?

In 2002, Jack Viertel, senior vice president of Jujamcyn Theaters and artistic director for Encores!, a nonprofit that produces concert versions of lesser-known American musicals at New York City Center, seriously considered staging a book-in-hand version of the 1921 *Shuffle Along*, complete with full orchestrations. His organization had never staged a production written by an all-Black creative team before, and as the show was of extreme cultural importance and a bit clandestine— Viertel found its book at the Library of Congress and the original orchestrations at the Maryland Historical Society's archives in Eubie Blake's hometown of Baltimore—he thought the show would be of interest to the theatergoing public.

Of course, he had concerns about how the show would be perceived in a modern world, and as a white man, he thought it would be prudent to ask a person of color for their opinion. Viertel reached out to his friend, Pulitzer Prize–winning playwright August Wilson, and explained his dilemma. Wilson was a distinct voice in the theater and Black communities who had a unique ability to evaluate and untangle complex issues of race, culture, and history, making him among the best to weigh in. "There is, I believe, a historical imperative that suggests we have a responsibility to recognize the contributions of African American writers for the theater of the '20s and '30s," he wrote in a letter to Wilson. "And on its own terms, the work has a lot of merit—terrific songs, a good deal of wit, and a satirical perspective on politics of that time.

"However, not surprisingly, a reading of the script reveals it to be a long (if very well turned out) *Amos 'n' Andy* episode, created in part for Miller and Lyles to demonstrate their skills as comedians," he continued. "There is even a character reminiscent of Stepin Fetchit. This mitigates against the work in obvious ways and suggests that it might meet with enormous political resistance, especially from the very population we'd be trying to honor... It's not a problem I would ask for you to solve, but I'd be very curious as to your wisdom on the subject. One of my own ideas was to gather together a small committee of artists of color to discuss it, maybe even read part of the piece, and try to gain some consensus about the larger subject—how to honor the Millers and the Lyles, and the Bert Williams of the world without insulting or outraging the very audiences they would have been proudest to perform for."

"*Shuffle Along*, the musical, has value as an historical

document," August Wilson wrote in response. "It illustrates the ideas and attitudes of American society at a certain point in time, as well as the development of American popular music. So does *Oklahoma!*... My first reaction was to think of *Amos 'n' Andy* and the protest that led to its removal from the [television] airwaves. I rather liked *Amos 'n' Andy*. I thought it was an example of two comedians working at the top of their craft and sometimes working brilliantly. I did not understand at the time why *Amos 'n' Andy* should have been looked at any differently than say, *The Three Stooges* or *The Honeymooners*. Certainly no one thought that all whites were like *The Three Stooges*. But those Blacks who were moving into the main stream [*sic*] and were beginning to make inroads into places and positions in the society that had previously been closed to them were, understandably, anxious that whites not think all Blacks were, like the character clowns and buffoons, of suspect intelligence. They had, after all, to encounter their white colleagues at the office water cooler the next day.

"Later I came to understand that there were many other presentations of white America on the television, in the movies, the opera houses, and in business and commerce and science and medicine and government," he continued. "*Amos 'n' Andy* was virtually the only portrayal of blacks on television and in many instances the only one that white America saw. That is certainly not the situation today in 2002. Blacks have moved into such high-profile positions in government and business, as well as other areas of American social and cultural life, as to make that point moot... Since I am aware of expressions of Black culture that reveal Blacks to be men and women of high purpose, and since I know and am aware that whites have often thought less of us than we think of ourselves, I have no objection in witnessing an historical document and accepting its portrayal of blacks as historical evidence. In fact, it is important to remember, and it might be interesting to explore these ideas and attitudes from the 1920s to see how they are reflected in the ideas and attitudes the larger society has about blacks in 2002.

"Finally, I think it is a good idea to assemble the committee and see what thoughts and feelings are out there," he concluded. "I think if you ultimately decide to produce *Shuffle Along* you will probably be praised. And you will probably be condemned. For me, the Black contribution to musical theater, musical forms and idioms has a long and illustrious history. *Shuffle Along* is one. Its presentation would be a historical reminder of that contribution, and its images and portrayal of blacks, though less than sterling, would not be a perpetuation of these images, but a historical reminder of a time when such portrayals were part of the popular culture. I think that is important."

However, despite August Wilson's conclusion that it was necessary for America to sit with the discomfort of revisiting *Shuffle Along* in its original form, as a reminder not only of the artistry and achievements of its creators but the limitations they had to work within, Jack Viertel ultimately decided against reviving the show on the New York City Center stage.

The musical and the four men who created it had largely disappeared from the national consciousness until 2015, when Black writer-director George C. Wolfe assembled a company of fellow Tony Award winners and fresh-faced, fast-stepping newcomers for *Shuffle Along, or, the Making of the Musical Sensation of 1921 and All That Followed*. As its title suggests, the show was less a revival and more a behind-the-scenes look at the original production and its aftermath. However, even though some of the most accomplished Black Broadway performers of the day were part of the cast, the original *Shuffle Along* had escaped most of them until they heard about Wolfe's project. "This is a part of my history, and I didn't know it," Audra McDonald, who played Lottie Gee and holds six Tony Awards, more than any other actor, said in the run-up to its opening. Her comments were echoed by several other principal cast members, which included the Tony-nominated Joshua Henry as Noble Sissle and Brandon Victor Dixon as Eubie Blake, as well as Tony winners Brian Stokes Mitchell as Flournoy Miller and Billy Porter as Aubrey Lyles.

When Wolfe's *Shuffle Along* opened in the spring of 2016, the show was uniformly celebrated for its strong performances, bold and vibrant costumes, and Tony Award–winner Savion Glover's choreography. Perhaps out of concerns shared by Jack Viertel, most of Miller and Lyles's material was jettisoned, and similarly, the show brushed by the issue of blackface fairly quickly.

Conversely, Sissle and Blake's songbook was well-represented, with all the best-remembered numbers from the original show helping to comprise the score, supplemented by several songs from the duo's days in vaudeville and other theatrical ventures. To help advance the plot, the writer-director added a handful of expository original tunes for good measure.

While there would have been no way to predict this at the time of the show's conception, Wolfe's production was notable for not only shining a light on a hidden gem of musical theater—and American—history but also for being part of Broadway's brownest season in recent memory. At that year's Tony Awards, where *Shuffle Along* was nominated in ten categories, including Best Musical, host James Corden greeted the audience by saying, "Think of tonight as the Oscars but with diversity," as *The Color Purple, Allegiance, Eclipsed, On Your Feet!,* and a little-known musical that would end up sweeping the night, each with casts made up entirely—or almost entirely—with people of color, were all vying for honors.

Shuffle Along was a strong contender to pull some upset victories, yet coincidentally, the show about the Broadway sensation of last century was overshadowed by the Broadway sensation of the current one, as Lin-Manuel Miranda's historic *Hamilton: An American Musical* prevented it from winning a single award.

In many ways, the inability of the 2016 *Shuffle Along* to snag a Tony speaks less to the failures of that production and more to the success of its 1921 predecessor. Thanks in large part to the efforts of Noble Sissle, Eubie Blake, Flournoy Miller, Aubrey Lyles, and every member of the company who agreed to go on the ride alongside them, even though success was unlikely and failure was a near certainty, it is no longer unusual to see people of color onstage. More Black and brown folks were telling stories than ever before, even though many of the challenges the creators of the original *Shuffle Along* faced still existed in too many facets of the theater industry and American society as a whole.

Perhaps it's fitting that Wolfe's *Shuffle Along* was bested by another show that brought music genres borne out of Black culture—rap, hip-hop, and R&B—and packaged it in a way that white audiences would pay top dollar to enjoy. Like *Shuffle Along*, with its predominantly Black and brown cast, *Hamilton* held a mirror to its audiences, asking them to reexamine the way they saw America and the people of color who inhabit it, who also had stories to tell and deserved space to do so. The fight for representation, inclusion, and an entertainment industry that more closely reflects the population of the United States wouldn't end with *Hamilton*, just as it didn't end with *Shuffle Along* in 1921, but both shows changed perceptions and helped pave the way for artists of color to grab the baton and make even more drastic strides in the right direction.

Unfortunately, like each of its revival predecessors, the 2016 version of *Shuffle Along* eventually found itself steeped in controversy. Despite impressive ticket sales, critical acclaim, and strong word-of-mouth praise, Scott Rudin, the show's white lead producer who had a problematic history when it came to race and privilege, sent shockwaves throughout the theater industry when he announced on June 23, just two weeks after the Tony Awards, that the show would be closing the following month. Audra McDonald had recently announced to the press that she was pregnant, and in his statement, Rudin explained that "the need for Audra to take a prolonged and unexpected hiatus from the show has determined the unfortunate inevitability of our running at a loss for significantly longer than the show can responsibly absorb."

On July 24, after thirty-eight previews, a hundred regular performances, and box office receipts totaling over $11 million, *Shuffle Along* vacated the Music Box Theatre on West Forty-Fifth Street. That November, Rudin and his production team sued their insurer, Lloyd's of London, for close to $13 million in damages, which they claimed were entirely caused by Audra McDonald. Their insurance policy covered the show in the event that the actress "was unable to perform because of an accident or illness," but Lloyd's refused to pay out, arguing that just because McDonald's pregnancy was a surprise, it was not an "accident" nor an "illness." They added that "by virtue of the all-star cast, Ms. McDonald's temporary absence does not appear fatal to the show's continued success."

For close to four years, in an unsettling—yet patently predictable—prolonged legal battle, scores of white men unwillingly put a Black woman and her body in their crosshairs as they fought over money that she would never see a dollar of. The parties settled out of court in October 2020, but in the interim, the premature closure, and the circumstances surrounding it, led to widespread criticism. In a piece entitled "Don't Blame Pregnancy for *Shuffle Along* Closing," Catherine M. Young hypothesized that there likely were a number of factors that led to the show's closure—like the show's inability to find its way out of *Hamilton*'s shadow—but Scott Rudin took the easy, sexist, and fiscally convenient way out by claiming that McDonald singularly forced his hand: "Imagine a world where a host of complex capitalist decisions didn't come down on one woman's body."

Beyond the reasons Young spelled out, cast member Phillip Attmore, who played William Grant Still in the production, has another theory as to why the show met its early end. "With *Shuffle Along*, I think it's a show that was beautiful and also a hard pill to swallow for some in terms of the indictment that it brings to all of the Broadway community, so for that reason it didn't run long enough, as long as it should have," he said. "It wasn't a show to see a company of talented Black performers perform; it was a show where through these elements of performance we were hitting home a deeper truth."

Broadway Black, an organization that fosters and inspires artistic diversity and excellence in theater, also expressed criticism for Rudin and compassion for McDonald before its final performance. "She is putting other working mothers to shame out on that stage six times a week and this is how you throw her under the bus?!," web content editor Alicia Samuel wrote on their online platform. She concluded her scathing editorial with a promise that was as hopeful as it would prove to be somber. "The original *Shuffle Along* that made history and changed an entire culture in 1921 was eventually forgotten, but the same will not be said for the *Shuffle Along* of 2016," she said. "We will remember every single soul that gave this piece life and we will honor the legacy this show leaves behind."

In his final moments on stage before he's struck dead by Aaron Burr's bullet, Alexander Hamilton, as imagined by Lin-Manuel Miranda, considers his life after death. "What is legacy," he asks, before answering his own question. "It's planting seeds in a garden you never get to see." In her piece, Alicia Samuel acknowledged the importance of remembering to cultivate those seeds that had been planted, lest they never grow into that garden. But the cliché is often true—when something is out of sight, it's easy for it to go out of mind, and *Shuffle Along*, once again, was being pushed to the margins. With the sounds of tapping feet no longer emanating from the theater walls onto West Forty-Fifth Street, how would "we," the countless people Samuel evokes in her piece, make sure that this time we remembered to never forget *Shuffle Along*?

In an interview prior to the show's opening, George C. Wolfe discussed the delicate nature of theater and historical memory. "You know, I still have people come up to me and say, 'I saw [your 1996 four-time Tony Award-winning Broadway musical *Bring in 'da Noise, Bring in 'da Funk*] ten times. It was the most extraordinary thing I've ever seen.' And then you walk up to other people and they say, 'What's that show?' It's gone," Wolfe said. "Theatre is fragile that way. Theatre is incredibly fragile. Unless the right people write about it, it becomes somebody's distant memory."

The centennial of the original *Shuffle Along* arrived in May 2021, providing the perfect opportunity to evaluate how we have collectively remembered the groundbreaking all-Black musical, its creators, and as George C. Wolfe put it, "all that followed." It's understandable that people still might not have known much about the century-old show that had been largely buried underground, but what remained in the public consciousness of the relatively recent, critically acclaimed, financially successful attempt on Broadway to solidify the show's legacy? How well had we tended to that garden?

Perhaps it's still too early to tell. In the modern era, it is relatively easy for theatrical works to gain immortality. Shows that have been procured by a licensing company can be performed by theater companies and schools around the world, but Wolfe's *Shuffle Along* hasn't been acquired. Because Wolfe continued to tinker with the book throughout its entire run—on opening night, Brian Stokes Mitchell asked if the show was "frozen," as in, if there would be no further changes, and the writer-director forebodingly responded that "there's ice"—it's unlikely that a bound copy of the libretto will find its way to bookshops. A professional video recording, or "pro-shot," can preserve a show's record and, in an abstract sense, ensure that it never really closes, but unless you're a researcher with access to the New York Public Library's archives at Lincoln Center, there is no publicly available way to see Wolfe's production.

Arguably the most popular way a musical extends its reach, and lifespan, is through an Original Broadway Cast recording, but almost unbelievably, the 2016 cast of *Shuffle Along* never ventured into the recording studio to preserve their work. For many involved with the production, these omissions, and how they will impact the historical memory of their show, continue to sting. "Can we go back and do a *Shuffle Along* cast album," Adrienne Warren, who was Tony Award-nominated for her performance of both Gertrude Saunders and Florence Mills in the show, tweeted in 2021. "Cause I'm still tight about that…"

"[The show's closing] felt like a death in the family. Close. Not the second cousin twice removed. It felt like something you love, that was close to you, was taken," cast member Amber Iman said that same year. "If you talk to any of us about *Shuffle* five years later, we also have this exact same energy. And that's how you know how hurtful it was.…We are still hot. I think in twenty years if you asked me about *Shuffle Along*, I will still be this level of pissed because it hurts in so many different ways. I think half of it is because the reason to revive the show, and bring it back to life and tell it in a new way, was to honor the show from 1921. To honor those names, to tell their stories, to keep their names in the space, and to sing the songs that they wrote and speak the words that they wrote. The least we could have done was preserve it in some way. Let's say we got a cast album but no film, or a film but no cast album. To work that hard to bring this story back to life… and not even preserve it? It's insulting. You know what I'm saying?"

"Working on [*Shuffle Along*] was an extraordinary experience, and the loss of it was extraordinary. And the memory of it," George C. Wolfe said in 2017, seemingly still trying to work his way through the stages of grief in real time. "I felt so deeply connected to that show in an astonishing way. I created a show about a show that didn't last, and then the show didn't last. And it should have."

Much like its distant relative from 1921, one might argue that Wolfe's *Shuffle Along* failed to leave a lasting impression on our collective consciousness. However, there are other ways to appraise a legacy. On July 6, 2016, Philando Castile, a Black man, was shot and killed by police Jeronimo Yanez during a traffic stop. His girlfriend, Diamond Reynolds, and her four-year-old daughter were in the car with him. The incident sent reverberations throughout the nation, in large part because Reynolds's Facebook livestream of the fatal encounter went viral. It was the latest in a string of nationwide events where law enforcement killed Black men first, then developed answers to tough questions later.

In the final weeks of *Shuffle Along*'s 2016 Broadway run, several members of the cast started to wonder if they were doing enough to speak to the issues that were plaguing the Black community. "I was onstage performing in front of a sea of white people that had no idea this entire cast was hurting so deeply," Adrienne Warren said. "I remember looking out onto our stage and our ensemble was performing some incredible number, and they had tears in their eyes and smiles on their faces."

On August 1, just a week after the 2016 *Shuffle Along* closed, several cast members organized an event called Broadway for Black Lives Matter, a forum where artists, activists, and members of the New York Police Department could discuss issues of racial justice and collectively think through ways to better build community. Cast members Audra McDonald, Brian Stokes Mitchell, and Joshua Henry performed for more than one thousand people who attended. The successful event led several cast members to cofound the Broadway Advocacy Coalition. "We're often asked to hold the red bucket [for Broadway Cares/Equity Fights AIDS] or get dressed and raise money at a gala, but when it comes to police brutality and racism and mass incarceration, there's something beyond raising money that needs to happen," Britton Smith, one of the show's swings, said. "We decided it was important for the arts to finally meet law and policies, so we built this relationship with the folks at Columbia Law School and since 2016 we've really deepened our practices of how art and law and policy work for the people." On September 26, 2021, less than two weeks after Broadway reopened from its year-and-a-half long shutdown, the organization was awarded a Special Tony Award for its work to ensure the arts industry takes a more impactful role in combating racism.

Once Broadway reopened in September 2021, the lasting impact of America's "racial reckoning" after George Floyd and Breonna Taylor were both killed by police officers, and the efforts of organizations like Broadway Advocacy Coalition and Black Theatre United, a coalition cofounded by *Shuffle Along* alum Audra McDonald, Brian Stokes Mitchell, and Billy Porter, could already be felt. The latter advocacy group developed "A New Deal for Broadway," a pledge that would increase representation for Black artists. For example, directors and writers who signed vowed to "never assemble an all-white creative team on a production again, regardless of the subject matter of the show." Theater owners agreed to name at least one of their theaters after a Black artist. In March 2022, The Shubert Organization announced that they were renaming the Cort Theatre, where auditions were held for the 1921 *Shuffle Along*, after James Earl Jones. Ultimately, "A New Deal for Broadway" garnered widespread support and was signed by owners and operators for nearly every Broadway theater, as well as the Broadway League, a trade organization representing producers, and the Actors' Equity Association labor union, which represents performers and stage managers.

It wasn't enough that professional theater was back—artists of color wanted to ensure that upon its return, Broadway also was Black.

Of course, it would be unfair to the disproportionally credit Wolfe's *Shuffle Along* and its alumni for what seems to be the beginning of a potentially seismic shift; this was the result of several different coordinated industry-wide efforts to make Manhattan a more welcoming space for Black artists and patrons. For example, in 2020, over twenty past and present cast members from *The Book of Mormon* pushed for the show's satirical elements to be sharpened so audiences were clear that Africans weren't simply the butt of the joke, and for tweaks to be made to narrative elements that, now that that lens was more finetuned in a post-George Floyd world, played as overtly-racist. The show's writers, Matt Stone, Trey Stone, and Robert Lopez, made a number of edits over a two-week period with one clear goal: "Make sure everything works and everybody feels good." The end result was a show that not only centered on paternalistic Mormon missionaries from America, but also the Ugandan people they attempted to "civilize," who had their own culture before the white men arrived to "save them."

A hundred years after *Shuffle Along* first challenged social norms on Broadway, it seemed the future of the great white way had become brighter—and darker—than ever before. This is cause for celebration, but perhaps only cautiously. After all, New

York had seen a Black renaissance on Broadway a century ago, and many of those productions, including the one that started it all, have become a distant memory, even if its impact was long-lasting.

"Theatre is fragile that way. Theatre is incredibly fragile. Unless the right people write about it, it becomes somebody's distant memory."

But as Lin-Manuel Miranda memorably states in *Hamilton*, "you have no control who lives, who dies, who tells your story." What, then, of the original *Shuffle Along*? Will the time ever be right to tell that story again onstage, even if, as August Wilson suggests, those who do so may be derided for it? Perhaps not. However, it's worth considering why that is and what the repercussions are for Black folks who grew up never knowing that, in 1921, one of the biggest sensations of the year was a show where everyone in the cast looked like someone in their family and that the foundational theatrical texts extend beyond the works of George and Ira Gershwin, Rodgers and Hammerstein, Cole Porter, and Irving Berlin.

Noble Sissle, Eubie Blake, Flournoy Miller, and Aubrey Lyles were there too, each with several Broadway productions under their belts, and their works, contributions, and lives matter even though, as Laurence Maslon put it in the *Washington Post* in 2021, it seems the fate of the show's creators "to be marginalized even when celebrated." Though lingering concerns about reintroducing *Shuffle Along* to a modern audience are well intentioned, American history is a tapestry of imperfect icons and flawed works. While some are permitted to repeatedly press their feet into the wet cement of time, others are papered over, shuffled off to the sidelines, and relegated to little more than historical footnotes.

In the meantime, those who know the impact of this groundbreaking musical share responsibility in telling its story, and celebrating its creators, again and again and again.

READING GROUP GUIDE

1. In the opening of the book, Sissle, Miller, and Lyles brace for the worst during *Shuffle Along*'s most sincere love song. Why were they so afraid of the fallout from that particular scene?

2. In describing Miller's childhood, Gaines draws attention to the relationship between economic class and racism. How would you describe that relationship? What are some ways in which race and class intersect throughout the narrative?

3. Diverse racial representation has a marked impact on audiences, but what effect does it have on future productions? How did *Shuffle Along* build on the accomplishments of earlier all-Black shows like *A Trip to Coontown*, *In Dahomey*, and *Bandanna Land*?

4. What did you think of Black performers including blackface in their own productions? What advantages and disadvantages did they court by perpetuating minstrelsy tropes and broader Black stereotypes?

5. Blake's parents disagreed about whether to talk about their pasts. Blake's mother would never even admit that she had been enslaved, while his father thought discussing slavery was crucial. Who did you agree with and why?

6. When the James Reese Europe's Society Orchestra is served dishwater instead of the meal they were promised, Blake observes that "Jim Europe didn't get where he is with the white folks by complainin'." How does this capture the tenuous balance the performers were trying to strike between large-scale success and respect?

7. Describe Jim Europe's impact on Noble Sissle. How did Europe's example guide Sissle in advancing his career and highlighting the artistry of other Black performers?

8. During their vaudeville days, Blake and Sissle had contrasting views on their never-ending travel, a lifestyle that could be dangerous for Black performers. Would you travel most of the year if it meant you could follow your dream, or would you rather have a consistent place to call home?

9. *Shuffle Along* was celebrated for introducing Black women to the stage but earned a reputation for rejecting or sidelining chorus girls for being "too dark."

Were the show's creators wrong for casting based on skin color? How does colorism compare to racism more generally?

10. Miller and Lyles thought that it was unfair that Blake and Sissle were making more money from the show and its music. Did you think Miller and Lyles were entitled to any portion of the royalties from *Shuffle Along*'s sheet music?

11. In their later ventures, Sissle and Blake were challenged by (white) critics who thought their shows had "too much 'art' and not enough Africa." How did they handle this criticism? What would you have done in their position?

12. In your opinion, what is *Shuffle Along*'s most lasting impact? Do you think it should be revived? How can we preserve the contributions it made to the theatrical canon?

SELECTED BIBLIOGRAPHY

Armstead-Johnson, Helen. "*Shuffle Along*: Keynote of the Harlem Renaissance." In *The Theatre of Black Americans*, edited by Errol Hill. New York: Applause, 1987.

Badger, Reid. *A Life in Ragtime: A Biography of James Reese Europe*. New York: Oxford University Press, 1995.

Baker, Jean-Claude, and Chris Chase. *Josephine: The Hungry Heart*. New York: Cooper Square, 2001.

Baker, Josephine, and Jo Bouillon. *Josephine*. New York: Marlowe, 1994.

Bloom, Ken, and Richard Carlin. *Eubie Blake: Rags, Rhythm, and Race*. New York: Oxford University Press, 2020.

Bricktop, and James Haskins. *Bricktop*. New York: Atheneum, 1983.

Brook, Tim, and Richard K. Spottswood. *Lost Sounds: Blacks and the Birth of the Recording Industry, 1890–1919*. Urbana: University of Illinois Press, 2005.

Duberman, Martin. *Paul Robeson*. New York: New Press, 2005.

Egan, Bill. *Florence Mills: Harlem Jazz Queen*. Lanham, MD: Scarecrow, 2004.

Forbes, Camille F. *Introducing Bert Williams: Burnt Cork, Broadway, and the Story of America's First Black Star*. New York: Basic Civitas, 2008.

Furia, Philip, and Michael L. Lasser. *America's Songs: The Stories behind the Songs of Broadway, Hollywood, and Tin Pan Alley*. New York: Routledge, 2008.

Glasser, Ruth. *My Music Is My Flag: Puerto Rican Musicians and Their New York Communities, 1917–1940*. Berkeley: University of California Press, 2000.

Graziano, John. "The Early Life and Career of the 'Black Patti': The Odyssey of an African American Singer in the Late Nineteenth Century." *Journal of the American Musicological Society* 53, no. 3 (2000): 543–96. https://doi.org/https://www.jstor.org/stable/831938.

Jasen, David A., and Gene Jones. *Black Bottom Stomp: Eight Masters of Ragtime and Early Jazz*. New York: Routledge, 2002.

——. *Spreadin' Rhythm Around: Black Popular Songwriters, 1880–1930*. New York: Schirmer, 1998.

Johnson, James Weldon. *Black Manhattan*. New York: Da Capo, 1991.

Kimball, Robert, and William Bolcom. *Reminiscing with Noble Sissle and Eubie Blake*. New York: Cooper Square, 2000.

Little, Arthur West. *From Harlem to the Rhine: The Story of New York's Colored Volunteers*. New York: Haskell House, 1974.

Perlis, Vivian, and Libby Van Cleve. *Composers' Voices*

from Ives to Ellington: An Oral History of American Music. New Haven, NJ: Yale University Press, 2005.

Rose, Al. *Eubie Blake*. New York: Schirmer, 1983.

———. *I Remember Jazz: Six Decades among the Great Jazzmen*. Baton Rouge: Louisiana State University Press, 1987.

Seaton, Sandra. "*Shuffle Along* and Ethnic Humor: 'The Proper Push.'" *Dramatist* 18, no. 5 (May/June 2016): 45–50.

Staggs, Sam. *Born to Be Hurt: The Untold Story of Imitation of Life*. New York: St. Martin's Griffin, 2010.

Stearns, Marshall, and Jean Stearns. *Jazz Dance: The Story of American Vernacular Dance*. New York: Da Capo, 1994.

Strausbaugh, John. *Black like You: Blackface, Whiteface, Insult & Imitation in American Popular Culture*. New York: Jeremy P. Tarcher/Penguin, 2007.

Taylor, Yuval, and Jake Austen. *Darkest America: Black Minstrelsy from Slavery to Hip-Hop*. New York: W. W. Norton, 2012.

Thompson, David S. "Shuffling Roles: Alterations and Audiences in *Shuffle Along*." *Theatre Symposium* 20, no. 1 (2012): 97–108. https://doi.org/10.1353/tsy.2012.0002.

U.S. Department of Veterans Affairs. *Noble Sissle's Syncopated Ragtime*. February 6, 2020. https://youtu.be/5VaOfBpfykE.

Wood, Ean. *The Josephine Baker Story*. London: Sanctuary, 2002.

NOTES

INTRODUCTION

"**The proudest day**" Michael Kantor and Laurence Maslon, *Broadway: The American Musical* (Guilford, Connecticut: Applause Theatre & Cinema Books, 2019), 81.

PROLOGUE: THE CROWD-PLEASER

Opening night was going Robert Kimball and William Bolcom, *Reminiscing with Noble Sissle and Eubie Blake* (New York: Cooper Square, 2000), 93.

"**Harry, you can't lose**" Flournoy E. Miller et al., *Shuffle Along: The 1921 Broadway Musical: Complete Libretto* (Theatre Arts, 2015), 11.

"**Love will find a way**" Miller et al., *Shuffle Along*, 12.

he had longed to compose a song Al Rose, *Eubie Blake* (New York: Schirmer Books, 1979), 18.

who were shoehorned Ibee, "On Broadway: Shuffle Along," *Variety*, May 27, 1921.

comfortable with mammies David Pilgrim, "The Mammy Caricature," Jim Crow Museum of Racist Memorabilia, Ferris State University, last modified 2012, https://www.ferris.edu/HTMLS/news/jimcrow/mammies/.

laugh at sapphires David Pilgrim, "The Sapphire Caricature," Jim Crow Museum of Racist Memorabilia, Ferris State University, last modified 2012, https://www.ferris.edu/HTMLS/news/jimcrow/antiblack/sapphire.htm.

familiar with jezebels David Pilgrim, "The Jezebel Stereotype," Jim Crow Museum of Racist Memorabilia, Ferris State University, last modified 2012, https://www.ferris.edu/jimcrow/jezebel/.

hearts bled for tragic mulattas David Pilgrim, "The Tragic Mulatto Myth," Jim Crow Museum of Racist Memorabilia, Ferris State University, last modified 2012, https://www.ferris.edu/htmls/news/jimcrow/mulatto/.

Encore! Encore! Kimball and Bolcom, *Reminiscing*, 93.

when the act was over Kimball and Bolcom, *Reminiscing*, 93.

$21,000 shy of being flat broke "Dramatic Story of Success of 'Shuffle Along' Told by Noble Sissle, Eubie Blake: Present Stars of Phenomenal All-Color Show Tell of Trials Before Play 'Went Over' From Detroit Time Piece," *Pittsburgh Courier*, September 22, 1923.

in a venue that Marshall Stearns and Jean Stearns, *Jazz Dance: The Story of American Vernacular Dance* (New York: Da Capo, 1994), 136.

PART ONE: THE WAY THERE

CHAPTER 1: THE BLACKER THE BAIT

born and raised Flournoy Miller, unpublished autobiography, Flournoy Miller Collection, Sc MG 599, Schomburg Center for Research in Black Culture, Manuscripts, Archives, and Rare Books Division, New York Public Library.

"the KKK must have" Miller, unpublished autobiography.

"The Cotton Factory folks" Miller, unpublished autobiography.

Jones was a classically trained John Graziano, "The Early Life and Career of the 'Black Patti': The Odyssey of an African American Singer in the Late Nineteenth Century," *Journal of the American Musicological Society* 53, no. 3 (2000): 579, https://doi.org/10.2307/831938.

In 1892, she performed Graziano, "'Black Patti,'" 568–69.

The following year Graziano, "'Black Patti,'" 574–75.

By 1894 Graziano, "'Black Patti,'" 580–81.

The Millers snagged tickets Miller, unpublished autobiography.

he served as the Miller, unpublished autobiography.

"right side of the desk" Miller, unpublished autobiography.

"As I look back" Miller, unpublished autobiography.

involved Louis Wright "Riot in Theater Leads to Lynching of Negro Minstrel," *St. Louis Republic*, February 18, 1902.

Lyles was also from Tennessee David S. Thompson, "Shuffling Roles: Alterations and Audiences in *Shuffle Along*," *Theatre Symposium* 20, no. 1 (2012): 99, https://doi.org/10.1353/tsy.2012.0002.

be an Episcopal minister "Miller and Lyles Hope for Theatre Devoted to Negro," *Pittsburgh Courier*, May 22, 1926.

developed a comedy routine Miller, unpublished autobiography.

centerpiece of their act Miller, unpublished autobiography.

John Robinson's famous touring circus "Aubrey Lyle's Stage Debut Was Made in Gymnasium," *Baltimore Sun*, November 2, 1930.

prosperous Black neighborhood Alex Bean, "The Incredible History and Cultural Legacy of the Bronzeville Neighborhood," Chicago Detours, February 22, 2016, https://www.chicagodetours.com/bronzeville-neighborhood/.

arrived in the Windy City Bernard L. Peterson Jr., *The African American Theatre Directory, 1816–1960: A Comprehensive Guide to Early Black Theatre Organizations, Companies, Theatres, and Performing Groups* (Westport, CT: Greenwood, 1997), 164–65.

quickly wrote the book Miller, unpublished autobiography.

premiere production at the Pekin "Only Colored Play-House," *Billboard*, October 20, 1906.

Lyles met and married Miller, unpublished autobiography.

"This little playhouse" Frank Wiesberg, "Correspondence: Chicago, Ill.," *Variety*, September 1, 1906.

"We felt that we had" Miller, unpublished autobiography.

One of their most successful Lester A. Walton, "Death of Ernest Hogan," *New York Age*, May 27, 1909.

which began in 1896 Krystyn R. Moon, David Krasner, and Thomas L. Riis, "Forgotten Manuscripts: A Trip to Coontown," *African American Review* 44, no. 1–2 (2011): 7–24, https://doi.org/10.1353 /afa.2011.0012.

who marketed themselves Camille F. Forbes, *Introducing Bert Williams: Burnt Cork, Broadway, and the Story of America's First Black Star* (New York: Basic Civitas, 2008), 58–59.

in 1898, they starred "Clorindy: The Origin of the Cakewalk (1898)," Black Work Broadway, accessed November 9, 2020, https:// blackworkbroadway.com/Clorindy-The-Origin-of-the-Cakewalk-1898.

"Negroes were at last on Broadway" Will Marion Cook, "Clorindy: The Origin of the Cakewalk," *Theatre Arts* (September 1947), 61–65, reprinted in *Readings in Black American Music*, ed. Eileen Southern (New York: W. W. Norton, 1971), 223.

there were concerns "Dahomey on Broadway," *New York Times*, February 19, 1903.

In Dahomey ran "In Dahomey: A Negro Musical Comedy (1903)," Black Work Broadway, accessed November 9, 2020, https://blackwork broadway.com/In-Dahomey-A-Negro-Musical-Comedy-1903.

1906's Abyssinia "Abyssinia," Internet Broadway Database (hereafter cited as IBDB), accessed November 9, 2020, https://www.ibdb.com /broadway-production/abyssinia-6176.

1908's *Bandanna Land* "Bandanna Land," IBDB, accessed November 9, 2020, https://www.ibdb.com/broadway-production/bandanna-land-6508.

George Walker became ill Forbes, *Introducing Bert Williams*, 162.

starring in the musical Forbes, *Introducing Bert Williams*, 191.

suffered the loss Walton, "Death of Ernest Hogan."

ever-whitening state Lester A. Walton, "About the Colored Shows," *New York Age*, July 21, 1910.

a new nickname "The Great White Way," Spotlight on Broadway, accessed October 23, 2020, https://www.spotlightonbroadway.com/the-great-white-way-0.

their best approach Miller, unpublished autobiography.

laughed in their faces Miller, unpublished autobiography.

They turned on their heels Miller, unpublished autobiography.

a "syncopated argument" Miller, unpublished autobiography.

practice of European performers John Strausbaugh, *Black Like You: Blackface, Whiteface, Insult & Imitation in American Popular Culture* (New York: Jeremy P. Tarcher/Penguin, 2007), 35–36.

popularized in 1828 Yuval Taylor and Jake Austen, *Darkest America: Black Minstrelsy from Slavery to Hip-Hop* (New York: W. W. Norton, 2012), 37.

getting into the act too Taylor and Austen, *Darkest America*, 47.

claimed to be recently freed Robert C. Toll, *Blacking Up: The Minstrel Show in Nineteenth-Century America* (London: Oxford University Press, 1977), 198, 236–37.

when he conceded that Frederick Douglass, "Gavitt's Original Ethiopian Serenaders," *North Star* (Rochester), June 29, 1849, reproduced in Stephen Railton, "Douglass on Minstrelsy," Uncle Tom's Cabin and American Culture, http://utc.iath.virginia.edu/minstrel/miar03at.html.

After an eight-week tour Miller, unpublished autobiography.

"We were the first 'talking act'" Stephen Breszka, "Flournoy Miller Is in Fighting Mood," *Pittsburgh Courier*, February 9, 1935.

The Charity Girl Wynn, "The Charity Girl," *Variety*, August 9, 1912.

one of the chorines "Studebaker Theatre, Charity Girl (September 2, 1912)," Chicago Public Library Digital Collections, accessed November 9, 2020, http://digital.chipublib.org/digital/collection /CPB01/id/4920/.

They married in New York Charles Rosenberg, "Miller, Flournoy Eakin," Oxford African American Studies Center, May 31, 2016, https://doi .org/10.1093/acref/9780195301731.013.72948.

declared would usher in "Way Down South," *New York Age*, September 16, 1915.

CHAPTER 2: KNOW YOUR AUDIENCE

Joe Porter's Famous Dixie Serenaders Rose, *Eubie Blake*, 55.

He'd been playing with the group "A Tribute to Eubie Blake," Tony Brown's Journal, 1983, https://www.tonybrownsjournal .com/a-tribute-to-eubie-blake.

carrying a patent leather valise "Interview with Eubie Blake," National Great Blacks in Wax Museum, 1973, http://www.greatblacksinwax .org/Exhibits/Eubie_blake/Eubie_Blake2.htm.

hastily introduced the newcomer "Tribute to Eubie Blake."

written the lyrics for *Catalog of Copyright Entries*, vol. 9 (Washington: Government Printing Office, 1914), entry 389.

an obscure number Bernard L. Peterson, *Profiles of African American Stage Performers and Theatre People, 1816–1960* (Westport, CT: Greenwood Press, 2001), 267.

The pianist fired back "Tribute to Eubie Blake."

Noble's father, George U.S. Dept. of Veterans Affairs, *Veterans Legacy Program: Noble Sissle's Syncopated Ragtime*, February 6, 2020, https://youtu.be/5VaOfBpfykE.

Martha was given "Sissle, George A. and Martha A.," Notable Kentucky African Americans Database, accessed November 4, 2020, https://nkaa.uky.edu/nkaa/items/show/1683.

vocal in church "Entertainment at Allen Chapel Last Night," *Indianapolis News*, April 27, 1892.

and current state "Preachers of Two Sects," *Indianapolis News*, October 14, 1889.

Noble Sissle also grew into himself *Noble Sissle's Syncopated Ragtime*.

"I used to get a great thrill" Kimberley L. Phillips, *AlabamaNorth: African-American Migrants, Community, and Working-Class Activism in Cleveland, 1915–45* (Urbana: University of Illinois Press, 1999), 176.

Sissle's parents enrolled him Kimball and Bolcom, *Reminiscing*, 30.

which John D. Rockefeller attended "Central High School," Encyclopedia of Cleveland History, accessed November 4, 2020, https://case.edu/ech/articles/c/central-high-school.

Of the fifteen hundred students Kimball and Bolcom, *Reminiscing*, 30.

Sissle was warmly welcomed Tim Brook and Richard K. Spottswood, *Lost Sounds: Blacks and the Birth of the Recording Industry, 1890–1919* (Urbana: University of Illinois Press, 2005), 365.

His first professional engagement David A. Jasen and Gene Jones, *Spreadin' Rhythm Around: Black Popular Songwriters, 1880–1930* (New York: Schirmer, 1998), 340.

he wrote the school's fight song Kimball and Bolcom, *Reminiscing*, 33.

Sissle arrived in Baltimore on May 16 Rose, *Eubie Blake*, 55.

Blake quickly picked up Jasen and Jones, *Spreadin' Rhythm Around*, 340.

a teacher falsely accused him "Baltimore Bordellos to Broadway," undated newspaper clipping, MS 2800, Eubie Blake Manuscript and Ephemera Collection, H. Furlong Baldwin Library, Maryland Center for History and Culture (hereafter cited as Eubie Blake Collection).

at the local market Rose, *Eubie Blake*, 11.

"This child is a *genius*!" Rose, *Eubie Blake*, 11.

she carried Jesus around Amy Lee, "Eubie Blake at Home and on 86-Year Discs," *Christian Science Monitor*, August 7, 1970.

She wasn't exactly fanatical Glenn Giffen, "Man on the Eighty-Eight Is Just That," *Denver Post*, May 6, 1971.

managed to bypass Rose, *Eubie Blake*, 11.

able to plunk out John S. Wilson, "Eubie Blake," *International Musician* (July 1972): 6.

next-door neighbor David A. Jasen and Gene Jones, *Black Bottom Stomp: Eight Masters of Ragtime and Early Jazz* (New York: Routledge, 2002), 35.

"Mister Blake" Max Morath, "The 93 Years of Eubie Blake," *American Heritage* 27, no. 6 (October 1976), https://www.americanheritage.com /93-years-eubie-blake.

He had never heard the word Rose, *Eubie Blake*, 12–13.

a local piano player Morath, "93 Years of Eubie Blake."

"All the girls'd" Katie M. Hemphill, *Bawdy City: Commercial Sex and Regulation in Baltimore, 1790–1915* (New York: Cambridge University Press, 2020), 254.

Even though Aggie Hemphill, *Bawdy City*, 254.

Blake could still bring Morath, "93 Years of Eubie Blake."

father and son John S. Wilson, "Eubie Blake, Ragtime Composer, Dies 5 Days After 100th Birthday," *New York Times*, February 13, 1983.

"We kept it from Mama" Sara Carroll, "Performer Young at Heart," *Columbus Dispatch*, April 7, 1974.

families were broken up Morath, "93 Years of Eubie Blake."

for about three days Helen Armstead-Johnson, "*Shuffle Along*: Keynote of the Harlem Renaissance," in *The Theatre of Black Americans*, ed. Errol Hill (New York: Applause, 1987), 130.

twenty-seven children Rose, *Eubie Blake*, 6.

sit with his shirt off Rose, *Eubie Blake*, 8.

The patriarch spoke Rose, *Eubie Blake*, 8–9.

get beaten up Alice Otto, "Eubie Blake: He Never Learned How to Hate," *Ann Arbor News*, January 19, 1974.

"peculiar institution" Rose, *Eubie Blake*, 8.

a more practical reason Rose, *Eubie Blake*, 8.

moved on to play Morath, "93 Years of Eubie Blake."

found his way into a stint Eubie Blake, interview by John Hunt, *Options* on NPR, audio, 1978.

Fourth of July Sara Carroll, "Performer Young at Heart," *Columbus Dispatch*, April 7, 1974.

jumped ship Jasen and Jones, *Black Bottom Stomp*, 36.

perform as a buck dancer Kimball and Bolcom, *Reminiscing*, 43–44.

his mother paid Robert W. Matthews, "The Afro Visits with Sissle and Blake," *Afro Magazine*, September 13, 1958.

spending his summers Rose, *Eubie Blake*, 49–50.

It wasn't until 1914 Richard Carlin and Ken Bloom, *Eubie Blake: Rags, Rhythm, and Race* (New York: Oxford University Press, 2020), 43–44.

A year earlier Carlin and Bloom, *Eubie Blake*, 43–44.

"I began to walk" Lori Harrison-Kahan, *The White Negress: Literature,*

Minstrelsy, and the Black-Jewish Imaginary (New Brunswick, NJ: Rutgers University Press, 2011), 32.

her biggest hit Sophie Tucker, *Some of These Days*, cited in "Sophie Tucker and 'Some of These Days,'" Museum of the City of San Francisco, accessed November 4, 2020, http://www.sfmuseum.net/hist2/days.html.

The two quickly wrote Rose, *Eubie Blake*, 55.

"all brass" Rose, *Eubie Blake*, 55.

"Sissle was more aggressive" "Interview with Eubie Blake."

"It was an instant hit" Rose, *Eubie Blake*, 56.

Although the number was only known "Interview with Eubie Blake."

quickly followed up Rose, *Eubie Blake*, 57.

The Serenaders disbanded Brook and Spottswood. *Lost Sounds*, 365.

enough of a springboard "Washington (D.C.) Stage Notes," *Indianapolis Freeman*, October 9, 1915.

CHAPTER 3: HIGH SOCIETY

a more proper engagement Reid Badger, *A Life in Ragtime: A Biography of James Reese Europe* (New York: Oxford University Press, 1995), 128–29.

"If the management consults" R. W. Thompson, "Darkydom," *Indianapolis Freeman*, October 30, 1915.

"Miller and Lyles, as per their work" Sime, "Darkydom," *Variety*, November 5, 1915.

It was also reported that Uno, "Miller & Lyles Score a Big Hit," *New York Age*, October 28, 1915.

then bringing it to Broadway "'Darkydom' for London?" *Variety*, December 24, 1915.

a "historical" portrayal *The Birth of a Nation*, directed by David W. Griffith, 1915.

a nationwide smash Richard Brody, "The Black Activist Who Fought Against D. W. Griffith's 'The Birth of a Nation,'" *New Yorker*, February 6, 2017, https://www.newyorker.com/culture/richard-brody/the-black-activist-who-fought-against-d-w-griffiths-the-birth-of-a-nation.

In March 1916 *Variety*, March 17, 1916.

a scenic view "Royal Poinciana Hotel History. Interesting Tourism for Students," Darwin Essay, August 28, 2017, https://darwinessay.net/royal-poinciana-hotel-history-interesting-tourism-students/.

the Poinciana's owners invited Noble Seisle [*sic*], "Palm Beach Notes," *Indianapolis Freeman*, February 12, 1916.

Palm Beach suits by day Kimball and Bolcom, *Reminiscing*, 52.

he couldn't do much more Rose, *Eubie Blake*, 57.

and one socialite Kimball and Bolcom, *Reminiscing*, 52.

Vaudeville star Nora Bayes "Will Sing for 'Sweet Charity' in Royal Poinciana Ball Room," *Palm Beach Post*, February 28, 1916.

and E. F. Albee Badger, *Life in Ragtime*, 133.

Europe revolutionized Negro musicianship Reid Badger, "James Reese Europe," Encyclopedia of Alabama, August 17, 2017, http://www.encyclopediaofalabama.org/article/h-2470.

"Our symphony orchestra never tries" "The Negro's Place in Music," *New York Evening Post*, March 13, 1914.

his working relationship Reid Badger, "James Reese Europe and the Prehistory of Jazz," *American Music* 7, no. 1 (Spring 1989): 48–67, https://doi.org/10.2307/3052049.

frequently hired-out vocalist Badger, *Life in Ragtime*, 133–34.

Europe arranged for Blake Rose, *Eubie Blake*, 57.

he was less impressed Rose, *Eubie Blake*, 58–59.

It would strike Rose, *Eubie Blake*, 58–59.

"The colored bands jazz a tune" Daniel B. Moskowitz, "Jazzman James Reese Europe Taught White America How to Swing," HistoryNet, accessed November 4, 2020, https://www.historynet.com/jazzman -james-reese-europe-taught-white-america-how-to-swing.htm.

revenues of over $100,000 Jonathan Gill, *Harlem: The Four Hundred Year History from Dutch Village to Capital of Black America* (New York: Grove Press, 2012), 196.

the bandleader responded frankly "The Negro Musician," *Lancaster News Journal*, November 6, 1915.

"I myself have written" "Negro Composer on Race's Music," *New York Tribune*, November 22, 1914.

The United States had so far Badger, *Life in Ragtime*, 140–41.

on September 18 Badger, *Life in Ragtime*, 141.

The singer was reluctant Noble Lee Sissle, *Memoirs of "Jim" Europe*, unpublished manuscript, 1942, 36–37, African American Odyssey, Library of Congress Music Division, https://memory.loc.gov/ammem /aaohtml/exhibit/aopart7.html#0717.

A month earlier Kimball and Bolcom, *Reminiscing*, 52.

A week after they spoke Sissle, *Memoirs of "Jim" Europe*, 37.

overall enrollment in the 15th Arthur West Little, *From Harlem to the Rhine: The Story of New York's Colored Volunteers* (New York: Haskell House, 1974), 119.

Europe knew there was a shortage Little, *From Harlem*, 120.

With only three days Badger, *Life in Ragtime*, 147–48.

the rank of sergeant *Memoirs of "Jim" Europe*, 45.

When they'd run Rose, *Eubie Blake*, 60.

Black soldiers from the 24th "Houston Race Riot," *New York Age*, August 30, 1917.

with Spartanburg Mayor J. F. Floyd "Fear Negro Troops in Spartanburg," *New York Times*, August 31, 1917.

A group of Southern troops "Men of the 15th Resent Insult," *Philadelphia Tribune*, October 6, 1917.

W. E. B. Du Bois advocated W. E. B. Du Bois, "Close Ranks," *The Crisis*, July 1918.

On October 10 Badger, *Life in Ragtime*, 155–56.

soldiers from the 7th Regiment Little, *From Harlem*, 59–62.

On the evening of October 20 Sissle, *Memoirs of "Jim" Europe*, 78–83.

While they had planned Badger, *Life in Ragtime*, 158.

"I'm sure sorry" Sissle, *Memoirs of "Jim" Europe*, 85.

CHAPTER 4: NO MAN'S LAND

Just slightly more Badger, *Life in Ragtime*, 166–67.

disastrous from the start Badger, *Life in Ragtime*, 161–62.

"I believe that" Little, *From Harlem*, 92.

The 15th New York Infantry made history Sissle, *Memoirs of "Jim" Europe*, 106–107.

The regiment was ordered Badger, *Life in Ragtime*, 161–62.

but on February 10 "Ragtime by U.S. Army Band Gets Everyone 'Over There,'" *St. Louis Post-Dispatch*, June 10, 1918.

a swoop that came down Sissle, *Memoirs of "Jim" Europe*, 119–121.

Lieut. Europe was no longer Sissle, *Memoirs of "Jim" Europe*, 119–121.

"eagle rocking fit" Sissle, *Memoirs of "Jim" Europe*, 119–121.

when the band had Sissle, *Memoirs of "Jim" Europe*, 119–121.

On one memorable occasion Little, *From Harlem*, 137.

While on the way Little, *From Harlem*, 130.

the irony wasn't lost Little, *From Harlem*, 145–46.

The troops in search Badger, *Life in Ragtime*, 172.

they received word "Famous Dancer Killed," *Statesman*, February 15, 1918.

but a true ally Nahum Daniel Brascher, "'Jim' Europe Lives," *Chicago Defender*, May 17, 1919.

he received a letter James Reese Europe to Eubie Blake, April 9, 1918, Eubie Blake Collection.

He recorded several songs Bill Edwards, "James Hubert 'Eubie' Blake," RagPiano.com, accessed November 9, 2020, http://ragpiano.com /comps/hblake.shtml.

They'd retained their uniforms *Noble Sissle's Syncopated Ragtime*.

Europe was soon out Badger, *Life in Ragtime*, 183.

no performance caused more anxiety Sissle, *Memoirs of "Jim" Europe*, 145–51.

We were both of the same Sissle, *Memoirs of "Jim" Europe*, 145–51.

until his report Irvin S. Cobb, "Young Black Joe," *Saturday Evening Post*, August 24, 1918.

Early that morning Badger, *Life in Ragtime*, 185–86.

"if ever proof were needed" Cobb, "Young Black Joe."

Louis A. Mitchell Louis A. Mitchell to Eubie Blake, August 21, 1918, Eubie Blake Collection.

until he received word Sissle, *Memoirs of "Jim" Europe*, 167–70.

By September Badger, *Life in Ragtime*, 191–93.

the regimental band kick-started Badger, *Life in Ragtime*, 195.

"When our country" Sissle, *Memoirs of "Jim" Europe*, 118.

most memorable performance Badger, *Life in Ragtime*, 193–94.

"We have our own racial feeling" Grenville Vernon, "That Mysterious 'Jazz,'" *New York Tribune*, March 30, 1919.

who ultimately achieved Badger, *Life in Ragtime*, 147.

On October 14 Noble Sissle to Eubie Blake, October 14, 1918, reprinted in Kimball and Bolcom, *Reminiscing*, 69–72.

"Soon" came Badger, *Life in Ragtime*, 196.

prepared to leave Little, *From Harlem*, 352–55.

The officers in charge Badger, *Life in Ragtime*, 200–201.

"They did not give" Martha Gruening, "The Fifteenth Regiment," *New York Herald Tribune*, September 27, 1936.

CHAPTER 5: THE RED SUMMER

The United States had fallen Dave Roos, "When WWI, Pandemic and Slump Ended, Americans Sprung into the Roaring Twenties," History .com, accessed April 24, 2020, https://www.history.com/news /pandemic-world-war-i-roaring-twenties.

Southern Blacks continued "The Great Migration," History.com, updated January 16, 2020, https://www.history.com/topics/black-history/great-migration.

ongoing health crisis Michael Wilson, "What New York Looked Like During the 1918 Flu Pandemic," *New York Times*, April 2, 2020, https://www .nytimes.com/2020/04/02/nyregion/spanish-flu-nyc-virus.html.

While classrooms were closed Alexandra Minna Stern, Mary Beth Reilly, Martin S. Cetron, and Howard Markel, "'Better Off in School': School Medical Inspection as a Public Health Strategy during the 1918–1919 Influenza Pandemic in the United States," *Public Health Reports* 125, suppl. 3 (April 2010): 63–70, https://doi .org/10.1177/00333549101250S309.

In October 1918 Richard Berglund, "Social Distancing Halted Baltimore's 1918 Flu Epidemic, but Not Soon Enough," Dying to Tell Their Stories, March 28, 2020, https://www.dyingtotelltheirstories.com

/home/2020/3/28/social-distancing-eventually-halted-baltimores
-1918-flu-epidemic-but-not-soon-enough.

a group of Negro soldiers Christopher Klein, "How America Struggled to Bury Its Dead During the 1918 Flu Pandemic," History.com, February 12, 2020, https://www.history.com/news/spanish-flu-pandemic-dead.

On December 16, 1918 "Negro Soldier Lynched for Resisting Arrest," *Statesman*, December 16, 1918.

The next day "Remembering Black Veterans Targeted for Racial Terror Lynchings," Equal Justice Initiative, November 15, 2019, https:// eji.org/news/remembering-black-veterans-and-racial-terror-lynchings/.

The NAACP demanded "Negro Protest at Mob Murder," *Brooklyn Citizen*, December 19, 1918.

The Boston branch "Notified President of Soldier Lynching," *Kansas City Advocate*, January 24, 1919.

In March 1919 "All Negroes Want Is Chance to Make Good, Says Writer," *Chattanooga Daily Times*, March 5, 1919.

Even if only "Square Deal Urged for Negro," *Springfield Republican*, March 20, 1919.

The Hellfighters recorded Badger, *Life in Ragtime*, 209.

alongside booking agent Pat Casey Sissle, *Memoirs of "Jim" Europe*, 1.

The tour kicked off Sissle, *Memoirs of "Jim" Europe*, 197–200.

save for a snag "Theater Boycotted, Band Embarrassed," *Chicago Defender*, May 3, 1919.

a white mob "April 13, 1919: Jenkins County Riot," Zinn Education Project, accessed November 5, 2020, https://www.zinnedproject.org/news/tdih /jenkins-county-riot/.

In the aftermath W. E. B. Du Bois, "Returning Soldiers," *The Crisis*, May 1919.

the tour moved on Sissle, *Memoirs of "Jim" Europe*, 220–22.

a few of the players Sissle, *Memoirs of "Jim" Europe*, 224.

a term Europe coined Badger, *Life in Ragtime*, 135.

But despite the weather Sissle, *Memoirs of "Jim" Europe*, 224.

performing at a benefit "Successful Benefit for Actors' Fund," *Boston Daily Globe*, May 17, 1919.

surprised his old friend Sissle, *Memoirs of "Jim" Europe*, 223–26.

The show began as usual Sissle, *Memoirs of "Jim" Europe*, 227–28.

Wright returned Sissle, *Memoirs of "Jim" Europe*, 229–30.

Just as Europe was set Sissle, *Memoirs of "Jim" Europe*, 229–33.

Sissle didn't realize Sissle, *Memoirs of "Jim" Europe*, 233–34.

Boston City Hospital Sissle, *Memoirs of "Jim" Europe*, 234–35.

The next morning Sissle, *Memoirs of "Jim" Europe*, 235.

Eubie Blake was the manager Advertisement in *New York Age*, May 10, 1919.

on May 13 "Funeral of Famous Bandmaster Held on Tuesday," *New York Age*, May 17, 1919.

"You see, Siss" Sissle, *Memoirs of "Jim" Europe*, 27–30.

I vowed that if Sissle, *Memoirs of "Jim" Europe*, 27–30.

"There was only one" Kimball and Bolcom, *Reminiscing*, 78.

As he brainstormed Kimball and Bolcom, *Reminiscing*, 80.

earning him the moniker Kimball and Bolcom, *Reminiscing*, 74–75.

Gossler Brothers' Campus Restaurant Kimball and Bolcom, *Reminiscing*, 77.

"He come on stage" Rose, *Eubie Blake*, 60–61.

before stepping out Rose, *Eubie Blake*, 65.

CHAPTER 6: PARTNERED

"Hey you!" "Tribute to Eubie Blake."

Even though the song Rose, *Eubie Blake*, 60.

"Don't start to bombing" Noble Sissle, Eubie Blake, and James Reese Europe, "On Patrol in No Man's Land," M. Witmark & Sons, 1919.

made their debut Kimball and Bolcom, *Reminiscing*, 80.

The venue's manager loved Vivian Perlis and Libby Van Cleve, *Composers' Voices from Ives to Ellington: An Oral History of American Music* (New Haven, NJ: Yale University Press, 2005), 58–59.

"They're not going" Perlis and Van Cleve, *Composers' Voices*, 58–59.

with lobby cards "Charles B. Falls 1918 New York City Show Bert Williams," poster, https://www.worpoint.com/worthopedia/charles-falls-1918-york -city-show-1790932773.

Casey offered an ultimatum Perlis and Van Cleve, *Composers' Voices*, 58–59.

but when Sissle and Blake debuted Advertisement in *New York Tribune*, June 29, 1919.

given the second performance spot Kimball and Bolcom, *Reminiscing*, 81.

a lukewarm start Ibee, "Palace," *Variety*, July 4, 1919.

"You play the Palace" "'Piano-Plunker' Blake Going Strong at 91," *University of Massachusetts*, March 6, 1974.

did a week Advertisement in *Baltimore American*, July 6, 1919.

before proceeding Advertisement in *Boston Herald*, July 20, 1919.

they were given higher Len Libbey, "Show Reviews: Keiths, Boston," *Variety*, July 25, 1919.

the two signed "Vaudeville: With the Music Men," *Variety*, July 25, 1919.

They were paid Rose, *Eubie Blake*, 63.

"Sissle and Blake stop" "The Song World: Sissle and Blake Stop Show," *Billboard*, September 13, 1919.

at the Royal Theatre "Vaudeville," *New York Tribune*, August 31, 1919.

Keith's on Chestnut Street Advertisement in *Philadelphia Inquirer*, September 14, 1919.

the Empress in Grand Rapids "The Theaters Attractions of the Week," *Grand Rapids Press*, September 27, 1919.

and the E. F. Albee Theatre Advertisement in *Evening Times* (Pawtucket), October 25, 1919.

climb further up the bill Kimball and Bolcom, *Reminiscing*, 81.

$300 a week Morath, "93 Years of Eubie Blake."

Their dressing rooms Kimball and Bolcom, *Reminiscing*, 81.

Finding adequate hotels Rose, *Eubie Blake*, 64.

written up positively "Jim Europe's Band Major at Palace," *Hartford Courant*, December 2, 1919.

a negative experience Eubie Blake, interview by John Hunt.

"They found ways" Rose, *Eubie Blake*, 64.

Blake was bothered Eubie Blake, interview by John Hunt.

playing the Shuberts' theater Advertisement in *Hartford Courant*, November 23, 1919.

"We were two" Ted Gioia, "A Megastar Long Buried Under a Layer of Blackface," *New York Times*, October 22, 2000, https://www.nytimes.com/2000/10/22/arts/music-a-megastar-long-buried-under-a-layer-of-blackface.html.

"They put you out" Eubie Blake, interview by John Hunt.

"I've never been homesick" Rose, *Eubie Blake*, 64.

had grown tired Rose, *Eubie Blake*, 64.

with a stop in Rhode Island Advertisement in *Evening Times* (Pawtucket), December 17, 1919.

Sissle slipped away "Marriages," *Billboard*, January 10, 1920.

bootleg alcohol Rose, *Eubie Blake*, 63.

"If you didn't know Sissle" Rose, *Eubie Blake*, 65.

"I missed my wife" Rose, *Eubie Blake*, 65.

followed by an encore Rose, *Eubie Blake*, 71.

were expected to remain "Cables: Variety Hits Abroad," *Variety*, December 15, 1916.

filled out their draft cards World War I Draft Registration Cards, 1917–1918, for Aubrey Lee Lyles, accessed via Ancestry.com.

Lyles remarried Donna L. Harper, "Lyles, Aubrey Lee," Oxford African American Studies Center, accessed November 5, 2020, https://doi .org/10.1093/acref/9780195301731.013.78471.

"You guys are so good" Rose, *Eubie Blake*, 71.

"Broadway was the goal" Miller, unpublished autobiography.

As luck would have it Rose, *Eubie Blake*, 71.

couldn't help but think Kimball and Bolcom, *Reminiscing*, 86.

PART TWO: MAKING IT

CHAPTER 7: BLACK BOHEMIANS

sought out E. C. Brown Lyn Schenbeck and Lawrence Schenbeck, *Noble Sissle and Eubie Blake: Shuffle Along* (Middleton, WI: A-R Editions, 2018), xx.

The pitch Noble Lee Sissle, *Autobiography of Noble Sissle*, unpublished manuscript, 7–8, Helen Armstead-Johnson Miscellaneous Theater Collections, Sc MG 599, Schomburg Center for Research in Black Culture.

banker didn't bite Schenbeck and Schenbeck, *Noble Sissle and Eubie Blake*, xxi.

"I had always believed" "Dramatic Story of Success."

"There has never been" "Dramatic Story of Success."

at his beautiful "Cort Theatre," Shubert Organization, accessed November 5, 2020, https://shubert.nyc/theatres/cort/.

Al Mayer invited Kimball and Bolcom, *Reminiscing*, 88.

Miller also offered Ean Wood, *The Josephine Baker Story* (London: Omnibus, 2000), 62.

In the end Kimball and Bolcom, *Reminiscing*, 88.

The economy remained Michael Lerner, "Prohibition: Unintended Consequences," PBS, accessed November 5, 2020, http://www.pbs.org/kenburns/prohibition/unintended-consequences/.

The divorce rate Alexander A. Plateris, "100 Years of Marriage and Divorce Statistics, United States, 1867–1967," *Vital and Health Statistics* 21, no. 24 (December 1973), https://www.cdc.gov/nchs/data/series/sr_21/sr21_024.pdf.

with the ratification Sharon Harley, "African American Women and the Nineteenth Amendment," National Park Service, updated April 10, 2019, https://www.nps.gov/articles/african-american-women-and-the-nineteenth-amendment.htm.

"With us as colored women" Mary B. Talbert, "Women and Colored Women," *The Crisis*, August 1915.

middle-class Black families "Ragtime: The Music That Grew Up With the Race in Gotham," *Baltimore Afro-American*, October 20, 1934.

found a new home J. A. Jackson, "Jackson Tells Where Jazz in Cabarets Was Born," *Baltimore Afro-American*, October 12, 1929.

Eastern European Jews Bruce Perry, *Malcolm* (Hamburg: Junius, 1993), 154–55.

Italian immigrants Gill, *Harlem*, 169.

Payton was a former Doni Glover, "Editorial: Do You Know about Philip A. Payton, Jr., the Father of Harlem?," *Harlem Business Journal*, accessed April 25, 2020, https://www.harlembusinessjournal.com /editorial-do-you-know-about-philip-a-payton-jr-the-father-of-harlem/.

The company was founded Adeel Hassan, "Philip Payton, the Real Estate Mogul Who Made Harlem a Black Mecca," *New York Times*, February 1, 2019, https://www.nytimes.com/interactive/2019/obituaries/philip -a-payton-jr-overlooked.html.

Payton's earliest successes came Clement Richardson, *The National Cyclopedia of the Colored Race* (Montgomery, AL: National Publishing, 1919), 1:258.

Two landlords "Local Realty Men Doing Big Business," *New York Age*, December 5, 1912.

He solicited Advertisement in *New York Age*, February 23, 1905.

"Race prejudice is a luxury" "A Race Prejudice Mint for Profits in Reality," *New York Times*, October 27, 1906.

there was a whitelash "Real Estate Race War Is Started in Harlem," *New York Times*, December 17, 1905.

financial and legal trouble Edward T. O'Donnell, "A Neighborhood of Their Own," *New York Times*, June 6, 2004, https://www.nytimes .com/2004/06/06/nyregion/city-lore-a-neighborhood-of-their-own.html.

he was sued "Race Prejudice Mint."

He was charged "Mr. Payton Arrested," *New York Age*, January 31, 1907.

and in 1908 "Philip A. Payton Jr., Harlem Real Estate Visionary," *Harlem World*, February 26, 2018, https://www.harlemworldmagazine.com /philip-a-payton-jr-harlem-real-estate-visionary/.

and Marcus Garvey Tony Martin, *Marcus Garvey, Hero: A First Biography* (Dover, MA: Majority Press, 1983), 27–28.

In exchange for his help Kimball and Bolcom, *Reminiscing*, 88.

News leaked J. A. Jackson, "Miller and Lyles; Sissle and Blake," *Billboard*, January 29, 1921.

"I maght be" Miller et al., *Shuffle Along*, 17.

"That's the way" Helen McNamara, "Presenting the World's Oldest Ragtime Pianist (and Black Philosopher)," newspaper clipping, Eubie Blake Collection.

"Oh, I said dat" Miller et al., *Shuffle Along*, 41–42.

They settle the score Stearns and Stearns, *Jazz Dance*, 133.

John Cort offered Sissle, *Autobiography of Noble Sissle*, 10.

"There were a lot" "Dramatic Story of Success."

Twenty-six-year-old Frank C. Taylor and Gerald Cook, *Alberta Hunter: A Celebration in Blues* (New York: McGraw-Hill, 1988), 51–52.

Ethel Waters Taylor and Cook, *Alberta Hunter*, 51–52.

Of the eighty Schenbeck and Schenbeck, *Noble Sissle and Eubie Blake*, lxiii.

She had separated "Gee, Charlotte 'Lottie,'" Notable Kentucky African Americans Database, accessed November 5, 2020, https://nkaa.uky.edu/nkaa/items/show/300003652.

concluded a tour Howard Rye, "Southern Syncopated Orchestra: The Roster," *Black Music Research Journal* 30, no. 1 (2010): 33–34, https://doi.org/10.5406/blacmusiresej.30.1.0019.

For a country "Rankin, Jeannette," History, Art & Archives, U.S. House of Representatives, accessed November 5, 2020, https://history.house.gov/People/Listing/R/RANKIN,-Jeannette-(R000055)/.

who had spent years Bernard L. Peterson, *A Century of Musicals in Black and White: An Encyclopedia of Musical Stage Works by, about, or Involving African Americans* (Westport, CT: Greenwood, 1993), 52.

"none of that wedding stuff" Miller et al., *Shuffle Along*, 10.

frenzied number Schenbeck and Schenbeck, *Noble Sissle and Eubie Blake*, lxvii.

a versatile performer Allen C. White, "Lawrence Deas," *Chicago Defender*, January 5, 1924.

With money tight Miller, unpublished autobiography.

"I'll show you how" Carlin and Bloom, *Eubie Blake*, 121.

Cort also found Rose, *Eubie Blake*, 73.

when Harry discovered Rose, *Eubie Blake*, 73–74.

Sissle and Blake wrote Kimball and Bolcom, *Reminiscing*, 88.

"In those dear old" Noble Sissle and Eubie Blake, "Bandana Days," M. Witmark & Sons, 1921.

a reference to Robert J. Gangewere, "Stephen Foster and Uncle Ned," *Pittsburgh Post-Gazette*, August 22, 2017, https://www.post-gazette. com/opinion/Op-Ed/2017/08/27/Stephen-Foster-and-Uncle-Ned /stories/201708230295.

Cort found some kimonos Kimball and Bolcom, *Reminiscing*, 88.

"Now, first, you take" Noble Sissle and Eubie Blake, "Baltimore Buzz," M. Witmark & Sons, 1921.

"I'm just wild about Baby" Noble Sissle and Eubie Blake, "My Loving Baby," H. Federoff Maryland Music, 1916.

a Viennese waltz Kimball and Bolcom, *Reminiscing*, 106.

"That cut me" Philip Furia and Michael L. Lasser, *America's Songs: The Stories behind the Songs of Broadway, Hollywood, and Tin Pan Alley* (New York: Routledge, 2008), 31.

The goal was to test "Dramatic Story of Success."

fast-moving tap dancer Stearns and Stearns, *Jazz Dance*, 134.

"Everyone in town" Noble Sissle and Eubie Blake, "Shuffle Along," M. Witmark & Sons, 1921.

With their bags packed Kimball and Bolcom, *Reminiscing*, 88–89.

"Lawrence Deas, whose experience" J. A. Jackson, "'Shuffle Along' Opens," *Billboard*, April 9, 1921.

Perhaps as a result Jackson, "'Shuffle Along' Opens."

Mayer recalled "Dramatic Story of Success."

In his memory Kimball and Bolcom, *Reminiscing*, 90.

"Noble Sissle and Eubie Blake" Daniel Chase, "News of the Week around Washington," *Norfolk Journal and Guide*, April 9, 1921.

One of the theater's employees Kimball and Bolcom, *Reminiscing*, 90.

It was pouring Jean-Claude Baker and Chris Chase, *Josephine: The Hungry Heart* (New York: Cooper Square, 2001), 49.

What if she hadn't run Josephine Baker and Jo Bouillon, *Josephine* (New York: Marlowe, 1994), 26.

She walked into the theater Baker and Bouillon, *Josephine*, 26–27.

Tears filled her eyes Wood, *Josephine Baker Story*, 62.

When she met back up Baker and Bouillon, *Josephine*, 27–28.

It was announced "'Shuffle Along' Stand Set," *Billboard*, April 9, 1921.

a modestly sized "The Greenwich Village Theatre: A Brief but Fruitful History," Researching Greenwich Village History, November 5, 2013, https://greenwichvillagehistory.wordpress.com/2013/11/05/the-greenwich-village-theatre-a-brief-but-fruitful-history/.

The musical had been playing "Cort Colored Show 'A Riot' in Philly," *Variety*, April 22, 1921.

"A splendid performance" J. A. Jackson, "Reports on 'Shuffle Along,'" *Billboard*, April 23, 1921.

"laughed themselves sick" Stearns and Stearns, *Jazz Dance*, 135.

"No one knew us" Kimball and Bolcom, *Reminiscing*, 89.

One evening Kimball and Bolcom, *Reminiscing*, 89.

"Blake and Lyles were always" Stearns and Stearns, *Jazz Dance*, 136.

"We didn't have money" Rose, *Eubie Blake*, 74.

"At the next town" "'Shuffle Along,' Started on $1.50, Yields Million," *Chicago Herald and Examiner*, December 3, 1922.

"You learn a lot" Stearns and Stearns, *Jazz Dance*, 136.

In another city Kimball and Bolcom, *Reminiscing*, 89–90.

an old lecture hall Kimball and Bolcom, *Reminiscing*, 88.

the May 9 engagement "Cort's Colored Show Soon," *Variety*, May 9, 1921.

On May 9, 1921 "Theatrical Notes," *New York Times*, May 9, 1921.

Someone who worked Miller, unpublished autobiography.

"It was only a thread" Eubie Blake, interview by John Hunt.

"If anything approaching" James Weldon Johnson, *Black Manhattan* (New York: Da Capo, 1991), 171.

One of the male chorus Kimball and Bolcom, *Reminiscing*, 106.

she recorded two J. A. Jackson, "Gertrude Saunders," *Billboard*, May 7, 1921.

$21,000 in debt "Dramatic Story of Success."

M. Witmark & Sons "Vaudeville: News of the Music Men," *Variety*, May 20, 1921.

several unofficial business agreements "Legitimate: 'Shuffle Along' Make Up," *Variety*, May 20, 1921.

A few days before Eubie Blake, interview by John Hunt.

CHAPTER 8: NEVERTHELESS, THEY SUCCEEDED

one of its bleakest "Legitimate: Start of Summer Shows Put Back; New Capital Cagey," *Variety*, May 20, 1921.

designed to be Stearns and Stearns, *Jazz Dance*, 136.

was its capacity "Daly's 63rd Street Theatre," IBDB, accessed November 9, 2020, https://www.ibdb.com/theatre/dalys-63rd-street-theatre-1025.

The show's preview Ibee, "On Broadway: Shuffle Along."

the full company Kimball and Bolcom, *Reminiscing*, 95.

"People cheered" Kimball and Bolcom, *Reminiscing*, 93.

their ticket pricing Rose, *Eubie Blake*, 83.

most stringent criticism James Whittaker, "Carbon Carusos Bright Stars of 'Shuffle Along,'" *New York Daily News*, May 26, 1921.

credited positive reviews Kimball and Bolcom, *Reminiscing*, 94.

The composer was Mark Tucker, "In Search of Will Vodery," *Black Music Research Journal* 16, no. 1 (Spring 1996): 123–82, https://doi .org/10.2307/779380.

but also Puerto Ricans Ruth Glasser, *My Music Is My Flag: Puerto Rican Musicians and Their New York Communities, 1917–1940* (Berkeley: University of California Press, 2000), 67–68.

While there were Glasser, *My Music*, 69–70.

"They brought in" Stearns and Stearns, *Jazz Dance*, 137.

brought in receipts "Legitimate: Shows in N.Y. and Comment," *Variety*, June 3, 1921.

Variety noted "Legitimate: Shrewd Showmen Predict Autumn Boom for Theatres," *Variety*, May 27, 1921.

when the show "Legitimate: Shows in N.Y. and Comment," *Variety*, June 10, 1921.

break-even point Kimball and Bolcom, *Reminiscing*, 123.

Just days after "Tulsa Race Massacre," History.com, March 8, 2018, https://www.history.com/topics/roaring-twenties/tulsa-race-massacre.

According to local "Citizens of Tulsa Tell of Conditions There Preceding the Race Riot," *St. Louis Post-Dispatch*, June 5, 1922.

chalked up Sissle, *Autobiography of Noble Sissle*, unpublished manuscript, 4–5.

producers canceling Advertisement in *New York Times*, May 30, 1921.

"White show people" Stearns and Stearns, *Jazz Dance*, 136.

"Then Negroes came" Stearns and Stearns, *Jazz Dance*, 137.

"**Irving Berlin used to**" Giffen, "Man on the Eighty-Eight."

The politician was Stearns and Stearns, *Jazz Dance*, 133.

"**La Guardia came**" Stearns and Stearns, *Jazz Dance*, 137.

While Broadway continued "Legitimate: Shuffle On [*sic*] to Determine How Many Shows for B'way," *Variety*, June 3, 1921.

one white producer "'Shuffle Along,' Race Musical Comedy, Is Real Broadway 'Wow,'" *Chicago Defender*, August 27, 1921.

On June 5, 1921 Burns Mantle, "Vacationists Will Find Much in the New York Theaters," *Louisville Courier Journal*, June 5, 1921.

$3 top Advertisement in *New York Times*, June 6, 1921.

the city designated Advertisement in *New York Tribune*, July 24, 1921.

Just a month "'Shuffle Along': What It Means to the Colored Artist," *Baltimore Afro-American*, June 24, 1921.

In August 1921 "Legitimate: Jack Johnson, Star with New Show," *Variety*, August 12, 1921.

$2,000 weekly "Jack Johnson, Star with New Show."

expressed optimism "Put and Take Opens in N.Y.," *Baltimore Afro-American*, September 2, 1921.

Variety's **Jack Lait** "Jack Lait's Reviews: Put and Take," *Variety*, August 26, 1921.

"**bent on outgyrating each other**" "'Put and Take' Has Many Catchy Numbers," *Music Trades*, October 1, 1921.

closing abruptly "'Put and Take' Blows," *Variety*, September 23, 1921.

$8,000 weekly "Legitimate: Shows in N.Y. and Comment," *Variety*, September 2, 1921.

"**awful flop**" "Legitimate: Shows in N.Y. and Comment," *Variety*, September 9, 1921.

increasing its weekly "Legitimate: Shows in N.Y. and Comment," *Variety*, August 26, 1921.

The musical was in "Cables: Cochran's Offer," *Variety*, September 9, 1921.

spending a few weeks J. A. Jackson, "J. A. Jackson's Page: Here and There Among the Folks," *Billboard*, September 10, 1921.

onstage for Hurtig Con, "Burlesque: Burlesque Reviews—Big Wonder Show," *Variety*, September 16, 1921.

and a headache Kimball and Bolcom, *Reminiscing*, 118.

"She threw it" Barbara Lewis, "The Shuffles of Yesteryear Remembered," *New York Amsterdam News*, February 11, 1978.

"never missed a thing" Lynn Abbott and Doug Seroff, *The Original Blues: The Emergence of the Blues in African American Vaudeville* (Jackson: University Press of Mississippi, 2017), 251.

"looked like someone" Lewis, "Shuffles of Yesteryear Remembered."

she proved instrumental Bricktop and James Haskins, *Bricktop* (New York: Atheneum, 1983), 79.

"Flo was a star" Lewis, "Shuffles of Yesteryear Remembered."

Harriett agreed to bring Kimball and Bolcom, *Reminiscing*, 118.

Mills was offered Kimball and Bolcom, *Reminiscing*, 126.

as a condition Stearns and Stearns, *Jazz Dance*, 135.

The cast was excited Bill Egan, *Florence Mills: Harlem Jazz Queen* (Lanham, MD: Scarecrow, 2004), 61.

"She had these" Lewis, "Shuffles of Yesteryear Remembered."

Mills's interpretation Kimball and Bolcom, *Reminiscing*, 118.

"She sang a song" Abbott and Seroff, *Original Blues*, 252.

"She had a little" Carlin and Bloom, *Eubie Blake*, 141–42.

"If Lottie mentioned" Lewis, "Shuffles of Yesteryear Remembered."

as far as Ohio Langston Hughes, *The Big Sea: An Autobiography* (New York: Farrar, Straus and Giroux, 2015), 63, 85.

until early September J. A. Jackson, "J. A. Jackson's Page: Here and There Among the Folks," *Billboard*, September 24, 1921.

Of the numbers Doris Evans McGinty, "Conversation with Revella Hughes: From the Classics to Broadway to Swing," *Black Perspective in Music* 16, no. 1 (Spring 1988): 81–104, https://doi .org/10.2307/1215128.

"of phenomenal sweetness" "'Ledger' Writer Discusses 'Shuffle Along,'" *Billboard*, March 11, 1922.

"It sho' is!" McGinty, "Conversation with Revella Hughes."

"had he been born" "'Ledger' Writer Discusses 'Shuffle Along.'"

its best week "Legitimate: Shows in N.Y. and Comment," *Variety*, October 7, 1921.

make the show accessible "Shuffle Along," *The Crisis*, January 1922, 114–115.

several notable members Egan, *Florence Mills*, 63.

by November 1921 "Legitimate: Shows in N.Y. and Comment," *Variety*, November 11, 1921.

"all occasions" Kimball and Bolcom, *Reminiscing*, 114.

became a staple Arnold Shaw, *The Jazz Age: Popular Music in the 1920s* (New York: Oxford University Press, 2000), 81.

hit up three or four Eubie Blake, interview by John Hunt.

its share of critics William H. Ferris, "The Negro in Dramatic Art," 1922, reprinted in Tony Martin, *African Fundamentalism: A Literary and Cultural Anthology of Garvey's Harlem Renaissance* (Dover, MA: Majority, 1991).

A bold black headline "Plan Negro Grand Opera," *Variety*, December 9, 1921.

about $15,000 "Legitimate: Shows in N.Y. and Comment," *Variety*, November 18, 1921.

They organized a pair "Theatre Notes," *New York Daily News*, December 14, 1921.

Just before the New Year "N.A.A.C.P. Commends Shuffle Along Company," *Black Dispatch* (Oklahoma City), December 29, 1921.

a second group "Legitimate: No. 2 'SHUFFLE ALONG,'" *Variety*, January 27, 1922.

"We were afraid" Kimball and Bolcom, *Reminiscing*, 95.

"The 1920s were" Hughes, *Big Sea*, 223–24.

all but guaranteed Egan, *Florence Mills*, 64.

Leslie successfully lobbied "Vaudeville: 'Aunt Jemima' in Show," *Variety*, April 22, 1921.

"We really went" Egan, *Florence Mills*, 64.

truly unique and novel "Burlesque: Cabaret," *Variety*, March 17, 1922.

and a cotton field "All-Colored Show at Folies Bergère," *Billboard*, February 11, 1922.

Its opening was Egan, *Florence Mills*, 65.

Mills's five weeks Egan, *Florence Mills*, 68.

In March 1922 Egan, *Florence Mills*, 68.

name glistened in bright lights J. A. Jackson, "J. A. Jackson's Page: Florence Mills in Lights," *Billboard*, May 20, 1922.

spawned several imitators "Vaudeville: Cabaret," *Variety*, May 19, 1922.

The show opened Advertisement in *New York Daily News*, April 26, 1922.

With the exception "Vaudeville: Cabarets," *Variety*, May 5, 1922.

On April 14 "Legitimate: Inside Stuff," *Variety*, April 14, 1922.

evaluated their banner J. A. Jackson, "J. A. Jackson's Page: 'Shuffle Along,'" *Billboard*, May 13, 1922.

prominent loss "Pneumonia Kills Bert Williams, Noted Comedian," *Chicago Daily Tribune*, March 5, 1922.

"That's a nice way" Brook and Spottswood, *Lost Sounds*, 141.

brought back "Pneumonia Kills Bert Williams."

his final correspondence "Bert's Last Letter a Forecast," *Chicago Defender*, April 2, 1955.

well acquainted Rose, *Eubie Blake*, 34.

leading more producers J. A. Jackson, "J. A. Jackson's Page: New Revue at Reisenweber's," *Billboard*, June 24, 1922.

"Many of our" Elmer J. Walters, "Lost, Strayed or Stolen!," *Billboard*, October 8, 1921.

Alan Dale also Alan Dale, "'Shuffle Along' Full of Pep and Real Melody," *New York American*, reprinted in Kimball and Bolcom, *Reminiscing*, 99.

"Such girls are" "Chorus Girls of 'Shuffle Along' Delight in Hard Work," *Boston Daily Globe*, August 6, 1922.

most ambitious attempts Ibee, "Legitimate: Strut Miss Lizzie," *Variety*, June 23, 1922.

"glorified minstrelsy" Barry Singer, *Black and Blue: The Life and Lyrics of Andy Razaf* (New York: Schirmer, 1995), 56.

white lace costume Burns Mantle, "New York Stage: Ziegfeld Stages Sixteenth 'Follies'—and Broadway Gets into Its Old Stride Once More," *Louisville Courier Journal*, June 11, 1922.

who all performed "Ziegfeld Follies of 1922 'It's Getting Dark on Old Broadway,'" American Memory: Remaining Collections, December 16, 2015, http://memory.loc.gov/diglib/ihas/loc.music.tda.4702 /default.html.

"It's getting very dark" Gene Buck, Victor Herbert, Louis A. Hirsch, and Dave Stamper, "It's Getting Dark on Old Broadway," HARMS Inc., 1922.

original concept "Musical Comedy: Dancer Out of 'Follies,'" *Billboard*, June 17, 1922.

"The Negro has" Ashton Stevens, "In the Spotlight with Ashton Stevens," *Chicago Herald-Examiner*, December 18, 1922.

revolutionary development Rose, *Eubie Blake*, 87–89.

the weekly box office "Legitimate: Shows in N.Y. and Comment," *Variety*, June 16, 1922.

The main cast "Legitimate: Heat Drives out Shows, but 'Follies' Gets Record," *Variety*, June 16, 1922.

had to resort "Legitimate: Shows in N.Y. and Comment," *Variety*, June 16, 1922.

change their focus Brook and Spottswood, *Lost Sounds*, 457.

earned him a write-up "Men of the Month," *The Crisis*, March 1918.

By the end Paul Robeson, "The New Idealism," *The Targum*, June 10, 1919.

Robeson's first moments Martin Duberman, *Paul Robeson* (New York: New Press, 2005), 44–45.

worst on record "Worst B'Way Season Over," *Variety*, July 28, 1922.

CHAPTER 9: VAMPED BY A BROWN SKIN

"New York is a freak" Stearns and Stearns, *Jazz Dance*, 137.

went to the theater Stearns and Stearns, *Jazz Dance*, 137.

"The power of syncopation" "'Shuffle Along' Opens at Selwyn," *Boston Daily Globe*, July 30, 1922.

The opening brought "Legitimate: Colored Show at $1 Is Under Canvas," *Variety*, August 4, 1922.

On one day J. A. Jackson, "Boston Succumbs to 'Shuffle Along' Co.," *Baltimore Afro-American*, August 4, 1922.

The proprietor devised Kimball and Bolcom, *Reminiscing*, 135.

notable white figure Kimball and Bolcom, *Reminiscing* , 134.

At one performance Archie Bell, "Jazz Most Popular Music of the Day," *Chicago Defender*, May 31, 1924.

in need of a tune-up McGinty, "Conversation with Revella Hughes."

ran dance rehearsals "Chorus Girls of 'Shuffle Along.'"

Boston press raved "'Shuffle Along' Breezy Comedy," *Chicago Defender*, August 12, 1922.

she wasn't mentioned by name Baker and Bouillon, *Josephine*, 28–29.

she wasn't Josephine Baker and Bouillon, *Josephine*, 29.

"Word got back" Kimball and Bolcom, *Reminiscing*, 128.

She packed her bag Baker and Bouillon, *Josephine*, 29–30.

He remembered her Baker and Bouillon, *Josephine*, 30.

"She had such a wonderful" Kimball and Bolcom, *Reminiscing*, 128.

She was working Sam Staggs, *Born to Be Hurt: The Untold Story of Imitation of Life* (New York: St. Martin's Griffin, 2010), 364–65.

With her moxie Burritt Wheeler's Broadcast, K.F.I., Los Angeles, California, July 20, 1951, Eubie Blake Collection.

On one occasion Baker and Chase, *Josephine: The Hungry Heart*, 62.

"Talk about discrimination" Baker and Chase, *Josephine: The Hungry Heart*, 64.

Black author Claude McKay, "A Negro Extravaganza," *Liberator*, December 1, 1921.

In the second act Miller et al., *Shuffle Along*, 52.

"If you've never" Noble Sissle and Eubie Blake, "If You've Never Been Vamped by a Brown Skin," M. Witmark & Sons, 1921.

"We girls would share" Baker and Chase, *Josephine: The Hungry Heart*, 63.

freely admitted Rose, *Eubie Blake*, 84–85.

Blake wasn't particularly shy Baker and Chase, *Josephine: The Hungry Heart*, 62–63.

Blake put her up Al Rose, *Eubie Blake*, unpublished draft, 99, Eubie Blake Collection.

"I never bought" Rose, *Eubie Blake*, unpublished draft, 99.

a friend of hers Al Rose, *I Remember Jazz: Six Decades among the Great Jazzmen* (Baton Rouge: Louisiana State University Press, 1987), 104.

"Honey, you see" Rose, *Eubie Blake*, unpublished draft, 100.

"That niggah gave me" Rose, *I Remember Jazz*, 104.

"Kitten, what are you" Rose, *Eubie Blake*, unpublished draft, 100.

Lottie Gee freely admitted Rose, *Eubie Blake*, unpublished draft, 98.

She often received Rose, *Eubie Blake*, unpublished draft, 99.

$14,500 a week "Legitimate: Soft Money in Boston," *Variety*, September 1, 1922.

"We had to jump" Stearns and Stearns, *Jazz Dance*, 138.

straightforward and scathing editorial W. E. B. Du Bois, "We Shuffle Along," *The Crisis*, September 1922.

He was a staunch believer *The Theatre of Black Americans*, ed. Errol Hill (New York: Applause, 1980, 1987), 9.

"*Shuffle Along* is Negro 'Lightin'!" Kimball and Bolcom, *Reminiscing*, 141.

"Any Caucasian producer" "Shuffle Along," *Chicago Journal of Commerce*, November 15, 1922.

recalled their trek Baker and Bouillon, *Josephine*, 34.

"I don't lie" Carole Marks and Diana Edkins, *The Power of Pride: Stylemakers and Rulebreakers of the Harlem Renaissance* (New York: Random House International, 2000), 22.

Instead, Adelaide Hall Iain Cameron Williams, *Underneath a Harlem Moon: The Harlem to Paris Years of Adelaide Hall* (New York: Continuum, 2003), 42–43.

critics remained surprised Richard L. Stokes, "'Shuffle Along' Has Some Nimble Dances," *St. Louis Post-Dispatch*, March 19, 1923.

battling in court "Legitimate: Colored Show Clash," *Variety*, November 17, 1922.

played its final "Miller & Lyle [*sic*] to Leave Shuffle Along Co, but Will Remain Part Owners," *New York Age*, June 23, 1923.

PART THREE: HOLDING ON

CHAPTER 10: PARTIAL OWNERSHIP

It was predetermined "Original 'Shuffle Along' Co. Closes in Atlantic City," *Pittsburgh Courier*, July 7, 1923.

After having grossed "Shuffle Along to Dissolve After Close," *Billboard*, June 16, 1923.

saw it differently "Music Men," *Variety*, June 21, 1923.

staged their own revue "Original 'Shuffle Along' Co. Closes."

audience demanding "Original 'Shuffle Along' Co. Closes."

they were planning "Legitimate: White Philanthropic," *Variety*, August 2, 1923.

On August 3 "Shuffle Along Barred White," *Elmira Star-Gazette*, August 4, 1923.

"Flournoy Miller warrants" "Black Americans Respond to the 'Marsellaise': Asked to Sing Star," *New York Amsterdam News*, July 25, 1923.

was in rehearsals "Geo. White Cannot Use 'Shuffle Along' Title," *Billboard*, August 11, 1923.

Not to be outdone J. A. Jackson, "J. A. Jackson's Page: 'Shuffle Along' in Rehearsal," *Billboard*, August 18, 1923.

Although they collectively "Election Protested by Shuffle Along, Inc.," *Billboard*, August 23, 1924.

over $52,000 "Legitimate: 'Shuffle Along' Wins in Matter of Title," *Variety*, August 9, 1923.

After considering "'Shuffle Along' Wins."

the triumvirate settled "Legitimate: New Colored Shows," *Variety*, August 23, 1923.

over $800 "New Colored Shows."

A theater critic "Legitimate: New Plays Produced Outside New York City—Running Wild," *Variety*, August 30, 1923.

sold out its first "Legitimate: New Colored Show Did $8,000 Weekly," *Variety*, August 30, 1923.

"When Joe Simms sang" Robert P. Edwards, "J. A. Jackson's Page: How 'Shuffle Along' Hit in Canada," *Billboard*, September 29, 1923.

He petitioned the "Legitimate: Colored Show Mystery," *Variety*, August 30, 1923.

"Talk all you may" J. A. Jackson, "Yes, We Have Made Progress," *Billboard*, September 1, 1923.

grossing just shy "Legitimate: 'Runnin' Wild' For N.Y.," *Variety*, September 20, 1923.

a sardonic critique "Negro Musical Comedy Opens White's Colonial," *New York Tribune*, October 30, 1923.

the Black-owned "Season's Offering of Miller and Lyle Should Be Another B'dway Hit," *New York Amsterdam News*, November 7, 1923.

accompaniment harkened James Weldon Johnson, *Black Manhattan* (New York: Da Capo, 1991), 190.

other African American artists argued "Vaudeville: 'Charleston' Dispute," *Variety*, March 11, 1925.

was staged by Walter Brooks "'Liza' at Savoy," *Asbury Park Evening Press*, November 8, 1922.

Frank Montgomery "Vaudeville: 'Charleston' Dispute."

to take umbrage Kennard Williams, "Stage Music: The Spotlight Photo-Plays Broadway Pilot Here," *Baltimore Afro-American*, December 19, 1925.

several years after Will Marion Cook, "'Spirituals' and 'Jazz,'" *New York Times*, December 26, 1926.

comedic highlights Thompson, "Shuffling Roles," 101.

hadn't created the routine "Vaudeville: 'Slate Adding' Bit," *Variety*, December 20, 1923.

most prominent nightspots "A Night at the Cotton Club: Music of Duke Ellington, Harold Arlen & Cab Calloway," Jim Cullum Riverwalk Jazz Collection, accessed November 7, 2020, https:// riverwalkjazz.stanford.edu/program/night-cotton-club-music-duke -ellington-harold-arlen-cab-calloway.

drew to an end J. A. Jackson, "J. A. Jackson's Page: The Gifts of the Year in Colored Amusements," *Billboard*, December 15, 1923.

hopefulness they felt Howard C. Washington, "Howard Writes," *Chicago Defender*, December 15, 1923.

Thanks to *Shuffle Along* backer Kimball and Bolcom, *Reminiscing*, 144.

While lukewarm reviews Ashton Stevens, "Sissle and Blake Are Black Hope of White Man's 'Elsie,' Says Ashton Stevens," *Chicago Herald and Examiner*, January 24, 1923.

the trades announced J. A. Jackson, "In Old New York," *Baltimore Afro-American*, January 11, 1924.

possibly due to discord Jackson, "In Old New York."

on February 2 J. A. Jackson "J. A. Jackson's Page: Picked up by the Page," *Billboard*, January 19, 1924.

Upon their exit "Inside Stuff Legit," *Variety*, January 31, 1924.

they finally decided Kennard Williams, "In the Spotlight," *Baltimore Afro-American*, February 22, 1924.

not to be outdone J. A. Jackson, "J. A. Jackson's Page: Picked up by the Page," *Billboard*, February 9, 1924.

brought along Kimball and Bolcom, *Reminiscing*, 164.

the director was Kimball and Bolcom, *Reminiscing*, 164.

"Al Mayer worked" Stearns and Stearns, *Jazz Dance*, 135.

budget and spectacle "On the Theaters and Concert Halls: Ethel Barrymore Coming," *Rochester Democrat and Chronicle*, February 24, 1924.

a cast of over Kimball and Bolcom, *Reminiscing*, 181.

Noble Sissle communicated Floyd J. Calvin, "'In Bamville' Cost $75,000 at Start; 6 Gowns $300 Each: Noble Sissle, Eubie Blake Talk of What They Learned from 'Shuffle Along' Run," *Pittsburgh Courier*, March 29, 1924.

"I had become" Baker and Bouillon, *Josephine*, 33.

CHAPTER 11: BETTER THAN SALARY

"a million little cupids" Kimball and Bolcom, *Reminiscing*, 166.

declaring the show "Legitimate: New Plays Presented Outside New York City—In Bamville," *Variety*, March 19, 1924.

This show seems to suffer Ashton Stevens, "White Art Rather Than Black Magic, Says Stevens," *Chicago Herald and Examiner*, March 31, 1924.

"Friends had encouraged" Kimball and Bolcom, *Reminiscing*, 166.

Sissle defended the choice Calvin, "'In Bamville' Cost $75,000."

on unstable ground Kimball and Bolcom, *Reminiscing*, 178.

"Unless we can" Baker and Bouillon, *Josephine*, 34.

Josephine Baker felt Baker and Chase, *Josephine: The Hungry Heart*, 74.

"At $125 a week" Baker and Bouillon, *Josephine*, 34.

heart was set Baker and Chase, *Josephine: The Hungry Heart*, 75.

an additional role Baker and Bouillon, *Josephine*, 34.

Another breakout star Giovanni Russonello, "Overlooked No More: Valaida Snow, Charismatic 'Queen of the Trumpet,'" *New York Times*,

February 22, 2020, https://www.nytimes.com/2020/02/22/obituaries /valaida-snow-overlooked-black-history-month.html.

a reporter backstage Rose Atwood, "Bride of a Month, Pretty 'In Bamville' Star, Tells of Hopes and Ambition," *Pittsburgh Courier*, March 29, 1924.

While in transit Kimball and Bolcom, *Reminiscing*, 176.

During rehearsals "Obituary," *Variety*, March 26, 1924.

took a night train Baker and Bouillon, *Josephine*, 34.

"We are deeply moved" "Promoter of 'Shuffle Along' Albert Mayer, Dies in New York," *Gazette Times*, March 21, 1924.

struggled to find Kimball and Bolcom, *Reminiscing*, 166.

reaffirmed his belief Calvin, "'In Bamville' Cost $75,000."

at the forefront Fred Hollman, "The New Plays on Broadway: Chicago: Sissle and Blake," *Billboard*, April 12, 1924.

Activists and thought leaders A. L. Jackson, "The Onlooker: Coolidge Lashes Senate," *Chicago Defender*, April 26, 1924.

"We haven't been" Bell, "Jazz Most Popular Music."

biggest box-office hit J. A. Jackson, "J. A. Jackson's Page: 'Runnin' Wild,'" *Billboard*, June 7, 1924.

triumphantly returned "Donkey Wants 'Runnin 'Wild,'" *Baltimore Afro-American*, June 27, 1924.

$1,100 haul "Legitimate: Shows in N.Y. and Comment," *Variety*, July 2, 1924.

unusually warm M. V. O'C., "'Chocolate Dandies' and the Audience at the Premier," *New York Herald*, September 14, 1924.

several miscues O'C., "'Chocolate Dandies.'"

was well aware Baker and Chase, *Josephine: The Hungry Heart*, 75.

Five days after Baker and Chase, *Josephine: The Hungry Heart*, 75.

sharing an apartment Baker and Chase, *Josephine: The Hungry Heart*, 76.

in late December J. A. Jackson, "J. A. Jackson's Page: 'Shuffle Along,'" *Billboard*, January 3, 1925.

two months earlier "Legitimate: 'Shuffle Along' Closes," *Variety*, March 4, 1925.

largely appreciated "Wins Salary Suit: Mattie Wilkes Gets Judgment Against Miller and Lyle [*sic*] Show," *Chicago Defender*, March 7, 1925.

Mattie Wilkes sued "Mattie Wilkes Gets Judgment."

Lottie Gee shocked "Here and There Among the Folks," *Billboard*, April 4, 1925.

due to the $50 "To Quit 'In Bamville,'" *Baltimore Afro-American*, March 28, 1925.

financial issues "Legitimate: Colored Show Strands in Brooklyn," *Variety*, April 15, 1925.

tempting to view "Miller and Lyles to Be Starred in George White's Scandals Next Season," *New York Amsterdam News*, April 15, 1925.

an unfortunate consequence McGinty, "Conversation with Revella Hughes."

in a scandal "Sissle and Blake Arrested in Toronto," *Baltimore Afro-American*, May 2, 1925.

finally plotted "Stage's Best Dressed Girl Tells of Hard Struggle in Rise to Stardom," *Pittsburgh Courier*, March 15, 1924.

large feature article "A Chorus Girl Who Really Stood Out and Won Acclaim," *New York Amsterdam News*, May 13, 1925.

good-luck penny Baker and Bouillon, *Josephine*, 35.

By the time Kimball and Bolcom, *Reminiscing*, 181.

sought payment "Legitimate: Colored Show Winds Up Owing Salary," *Variety*, May 27, 1925.

"disastrous" end "Colored Show."

"That's the score" Kimball and Bolcom, *Reminiscing*, 181.

filed for bankruptcy "Vaudeville: Sissle Owes $3,000 to Debtors; Has Nothing," *Variety*, July 8, 1925.

just before Christmas "Aubrey Lyle [*sic*] Bankrupt," *Billboard*, December 12, 1925.

dire financial straits "Former 'Shuffle Along' Actress Sues Owners," *New York Amsterdam News*, July 15, 1925.

on the evening of September 18 "Noble Sissle and Eubie Blake to Broadcast Radio Farewell to United States," *Pittsburgh Courier*, September 19, 1925.

CHAPTER 12: ANOTHER SECOND CHANCE

The London *Daily Telegraph* "Sissle and Blake," *Variety*, April 21, 1926.

He commissioned them Kimball and Bolcom, *Reminiscing*, 190.

more good news Rose, *Eubie Blake*, 96.

"I didn't like London" Eubie Blake and Noble Sissle, interview by Valena Minor Williams, *Coffee Break* on WABQ (Cleveland), audio, May 14 and October 29, 1962.

They turned down Kimball and Bolcom, *Reminiscing*, 194.

Baker accepted the offer "Tan Town Topics Great Floor Show," *Baltimore Afro-American*, August 29, 1925.

When she arrived Baker and Bouillon, *Josephine*, 48.

a frenetic Charleston Marks and Edkins, *Power of Pride*, 26–27.

chanted her name Baker and Bouillon, *Josephine*, 52.

Paris correspondent Marks and Edkins, *Power of Pride*, 26–27.

a menagerie Kimball and Bolcom, *Reminiscing*, 198.

sixteen bananas Baker and Bouillon, *Josephine*, 63.

When they arrived Kimball and Bolcom, *Reminiscing*, 198.

boarded the *Paris* Rose, *Eubie Blake*, 96.

eager to reconnect "Eubie Blake Back from Foreign Tour: Sissle and Blake Score Hit in London and Ireland with Act," *Baltimore Afro-American*, April 17, 1926.

Harriett was arrested "Vaudeville: Mrs. Sissle Acquitted," *Variety*, February 9, 1927.

"Tending to the business" Blake and Sissle, interview by Valena Minor Williams.

"But, brother" Blake and Sissle, interview by Valena Minor Williams.

unwilling to budge Kimball and Bolcom, *Reminiscing*, 203.

a headline "Vaudeville: Sissle-Blake Split," *Variety*, September 21, 1927.

drum up investors "Miller and Lyles Hope for Theatre."

written for them "'Rang-Tang' Speedy Show at Tremont," *Boston Daily Globe*, November 22, 1927.

"With the Broadway" "Musical Comedy: Negro Musicals Making Play for Broadway's Summer Favor," *Billboard*, July 9, 1927.

reviews were mixed "'Rang Tang' Opens at Royale Theatre," *New York Times*, July 13, 1927.

calling the show Percy Hammond, "The Theaters: The Colored Folks in Another Child-Like Imitation of Dull, White Extravaganza," *New York Herald Tribune*, July 13, 1927.

The *Pittsburgh Courier* "Geraldyn Dismond Reviews Broadway Shows," *Pittsburgh Courier*, July 23, 1927.

***Variety* declared it** "Legitimate: Plays On Broadway—Rang Tang," *Variety*, August 17, 1927.

***Billboard* thought it was** Gordon M. Leland, "The New Plays on Broadway: Rang Tang," *Billboard*, July 23, 1927.

the heat wave "Heat Takes Toll Along Broadway," *Billboard*, July 23, 1927.

brought in "Legitimate: New Low Grosses From Heat; Last Week Fell Below 4th Term," *Variety*, July 20, 1927.

weather finally broke "Legitimate: Shows in N.Y. and Comment," *Variety*, August 10, 1927.

around the corner "Legitimate: Shows in N.Y. and Comment," *Variety*, September 7, 1927.

ultimately reached "'Rang Tang' Hits $16,000," *Pittsburgh Courier*, October 1, 1927.

The following year George Bell, "Legitimate: Dixie to Broadway," *Variety*, September 17, 1924.

When the show "'Flo' Mills Personification Of Rhythm, Critics Declare," *Pittsburgh Courier*, January 31, 1925.

Six months later "Vaudeville: Once Big Timer Alhambra for Colored Show," *Variety*, March 31, 1926.

opening number "Florence Mills' 'Blackbirds' Fly: New Show at Alhambra, New York, Boasts Topline Company Of 75," *Baltimore Afro-American*, April 10, 1926.

Lew Leslie brought "Foreign: Sailings," *Variety*, May 19, 1926.

"Many changes" "Paris Wild about Florence," *Chicago Defender*, July 24, 1926.

***Blackbirds* performer** "Florence Mills Best London Ever Had," *Baltimore Afro-American*, October 2, 1926.

In September Sam Love, "Famous Negro Singer Rests in Casket Costing $10,000," *Atlanta Constitution*, November 7, 1927.

The Prince of Wales "Nominating Harlem's Little Blackbird," West Harlem Art Fund, June 24, 2018, https://westharlem.art/2018/06/24/nominating-harlems-little-blackbird/.

the English press H. H., "'Blackbirds': Last Night's Revue at Pavilion," *Observer* [London], September 12, 1926.

the singer wrote Florence Mills, "Florence Mills Tells Londoners about 'The Soul of the Negro,'" *Pittsburgh Courier*, January 8, 1927.

attempted to stage "Browning of 'Harmony Kings' Fame Writes from Paris," *Pittsburgh Courier*, July 2, 1927.

but on September 27 "Florence Mills Back from Europe," *New York Times*, September 28, 1927.

Upon her arrival "Florence Mills Receives Warm Welcome at Home," *Chicago Defender*, October 8, 1927.

On October 7 "Lyle [*sic*] Warns 'Flo' Mills against Carl Van Vechten: Caution Amazes Guests W-A-R-N-E-D!," *Pittsburgh Courier*, October 8, 1927.

guests performed "Miss Mills Honored by Her Many Friends," *Chicago Defender*, October 8, 1927.

After about ten "Lyle [*sic*] Warns 'Flo' Mills."

Van Vechten financed Stearns and Stearns, *Jazz Dance*, 134.

highly controversial Kelefa Sanneh, "White Mischief," *New Yorker*, February 10, 2014, https://www.newyorker.com/magazine/2014 /02/17/white-mischief-2.

Du Bois wrote Sanneh, "White Mischief."

"representing our highest" "Lyle [*sic*] Warns 'Flo' Mills."

had its drawbacks Rudolph Fisher, "The Caucasian Storms Harlem," *American Mercury*, August 1927, 393–98.

After a while Fisher, "The Caucasian Storms Harlem."

Mills was rushed "Vaudeville: Florence Mills' Operation," *Variety*, October 26, 1927.

On November 1 "White Light Death Riddle: Jazz Queen Dies Merry as She Lived," *Daily News*, November 2, 1927.

"**Nobody understood**" "Florence Mills, Dusky Mystery Dies at Stage Career's Peak," *Atlanta Constitution*, November 2, 1927.

"**Her contribution to**" "Bye, Bye, Beloved 'Blackbird,'" *New York Amsterdam News*, November 2, 1927.

over ten thousand Harlemites "10,000 Pay Tribute to Florence Mills," *New York Times*, November 3, 1927.

laid in a Love, "Famous Negro Singer Rests."

New York governor "10,000 Pay Tribute."

lie in state "Visitors to Mills Bier Reach 40,000 Third Day," *New York Herald Tribune*, November 5, 1927.

two-hour-long service "Harlem Buries Girl Idol," *Los Angeles Times*, November 7, 1927.

over 150,000 "150,000 Turn Out for Funeral of Florence Mills," *Hartford Courant*, November 7, 1927.

as they withstood "Scores Collapse at Mills Funeral," *New York Times*, November 7, 1927.

ten-car motorcade "150,000 Turn Out."

She was buried "Harlem Buries Girl Idol."

front-page story "Colored Show Folks' Best Season for White Stage Jobs," Variety, October 12, 1927.

ventured to Palm Beach Sam Kopp, "Times Square: Palm Beach," *Variety*, February 29, 1928.

press was buzzing "Eubie Blake and Jo Baker May Head New York Show," *Chicago Defender*, April 21, 1928.

The two quickly Mark, "New Acts: Eubie Blake and CO," *Variety*, September 5, 1928.

ninety minutes Rose, *Eubie Blake*, 99.

play and sing Mark, "New Acts: Eubie Blake."

eleven others Rose, *Eubie Blake*, 99.

short revue "F. F. Proctor's New York Theatres: Eubie Blake and Company of 15 in 'Shuffle Along Jr.,'" *Daily News*, August 16, 1928.

"fairly entertaining" Nat S. Green, "Coast to Coast Vaudeville Reviews: New Palace, Chicago," *Billboard*, February 9, 1929.

"quite a stir" "Race Performers See Busy Season," *Baltimore Afro-American*, September 29, 1928.

chance meeting Rose, *Eubie Blake*, 96–97.

found a score Kimball and Bolcom, *Reminiscing*, 293.

Les Ambassadeurs Billy Jones, "Stars That Shine," *Chicago Defender*, August 25, 1928.

writing home "Legitimate: 'Rang Tang' Trouble?," *Variety*, December 28, 1927.

Charlie Davis "Legitimate: 'Rang Tang' Stager Sues," *Variety*, November 9, 1927.

a new Jimtown "Miller-Lyles in New Show Coming Here: 'Keep Shufflin'" New Musical Comedy," *Philadelphia Tribune*, February 2, 1928.

This time "'Keep Shufflin'" Given at Break-Neck Pace," *New York Times*, February 28, 1928.

The thin plot "'The Wrecker' Crude Play; 'Keep Shufflin'' Is Breezy," *Daily News*, February 28, 1928.

"Last night's" "'Keep Shufflin'" Given."

even kinder Ibee, "Legitimate: Plays on Broadway—Keep Shufflin'," *Variety*, March 7, 1928.

to be desired W. I. Gibson, "'Keep Shufflin'" Saved by Music: Miller Lyles in New Show Work under Handicap of Inferior Material," *Baltimore Afro-American*, February 25, 1928.

generally optimistic "Fight for Broadway Recognition Has Reached a Very Important Point," *New York Amsterdam News*, February 29, 1928.

first week gross "Legitimate: Salary Slicing Too Early in B'Way's Healthy Attractions," *Variety*, March 7, 1928.

Over three thousand "3,000 Shuffle at Miller-Lyles Harlem Jubilee," *New York Herald Tribune*, April 16, 1928.

filed into "Miller and Lyles to Celebrate," *New York Times*, April 9, 1928.

Jack Dempsey "Miller-Lyles Harlem Jubilee."

steady decline "Legitimate: Shows in N.Y. and Comment," *Variety*, April 25, 1928.

they were "tired" "'Keep Shufflin' Gives Up Ghost," *Baltimore Afro-American*, June 2, 1928.

Reviews were rough E. E. S., "New Turns and Returns: Miller and Lyles," *Billboard*, July 14, 1928.

The two reassembled "'Keep Shufflin" at the Windsor: Miller and Lyles Heading Company at Uptown House at the Windsor Theatre," *New York Amsterdam News*, September 5, 1928.

quietly put up "'Keep Shufflin" Folds in Chicago," *Billboard*, November 24, 1928.

two Vitaphone "The Aldine," *Pittsburgh Press*, January 2, 1929.

press their luck "Foreign Show News: Vaude in London," *Variety*, March 6, 1929.

joined the cast "'Great Day' Still in Jamaica: Miller and Lyle, Cora Green, Lois Deppe and Others Score Big," *New York Amsterdam News*, July 10, 1929.

headline their own "Miller and Lyle Are Vaudeville Headliners," *Chicago Defender*, July 27, 1929.

world was rocked "Great Depression History," History.com, October 29, 2009, https://www.history.com/topics/great-depression/great-depression-history.

"somewhere in Africa" "No Miller, No Lyles, in New 'Shuffle' Show," *Daily News*, April 26, 1930.

curious controversy "Theater News," *New York Herald Tribune*, April 11, 1930.

"seems to have been" "Editorial: Inside Stuff-Legit," *Variety*, April 30, 1930.

white comedians "Charles Correll, 82, Andy of Radio, Dies," *New York Times*, September 27, 1972.

slapped NBC "Amos and Andy Sued by Miller and Lyles," *Baltimore Afro-American*, May 10, 1930.

"Many phrases" "Attempts to Restrain 'Amos 'n' Andy,'" *New York Amsterdam News*, April 30, 1930.

extra insurance Rose, *Eubie Blake*, 100.

heavily courted "Thespians Crowd for Places in 'New Blackbirds,'" *Philadelphia Tribune*, July 31, 1930.

chose to star "The Stage and Players: Aubrey Lyle and Leigh Whipper to Star in New Play," *Philadelphia Tribune*, September 25, 1930.

Miller joined "Thespians Crowd for Places."

November 1930 "Deserts Glamour of Broadway to Pioneer in Liberia," *Baltimore Afro-American*, November 15, 1930.

Blake sat down "Did Noble Sissle Go to Europe to Escape Snobs?," *Baltimore Afro-American*, November 8, 1930.

a "failure" "Legitimate: Failures of '30-'31," *Variety*, June 2, 1931.

sixty-two performances Kimball and Bolcom, *Reminiscing*, 214.

shared his reason "Dreams of Sissle May Come True," *Baltimore Afro-American*, February 28, 1931.

before he left Paris Baker and Bouillon, *Josephine*, 88.

"My exposure" Baker and Bouillon, *Josephine*, 30.

"white man's world" Baker and Bouillon, *Josephine*, 88.

returned to vaudeville "Noble Sissle," *Variety*, February 18, 1931.

Throughout 1931 "Pittsburgh Courier, 1931," Amos and Andy, accessed November 7, 2020, https://www.amosandandy.org/2012/09/pittburgh -courier.html.

futile effort Romeo L. Dougherty, "Just a Glance Here and Also There," *New York Amsterdam News*, July 15, 1931.

over 750,000 people Joshua K. Wright, "Reflections on Black Image in Amos 'n' Andy," *Abernathy*, March 1, 2017, https://abernathy magazine.com/reflections-on-black-image-in-amos-n-andy/.

In the days "Miller and Lyles Booked by Columbia to Counter 'Amos 'n' Andy' on National Chain," *Chicago Defender*, July 18, 1931.

telegrams of support "Radio Fans Acclaim Miller and Lyles," *New Journal and Guide*, August 22, 1931.

"We won't use" "Radio Fans."

"Even though I am" Geraldyn Dismond, "'Sugar Hill' is Farce on Life in Harlem," *Baltimore Afro-American*, January 2, 1932.

an exclusive tip "Shuffle Along to Be Revived," *Chicago Defender*, May 21, 1932.

"It was not a feud" "Eubie Blake Brooklyn," newspaper clipping, 1949, Eubie Blake Collection.

On June 24 Edgar T. Rouzeau, "Theatre Stars Mourn at Aubrey Lyles' Bier," *New York Amsterdam News*, August 3, 1932.

that seemed likely "Aubrey Lyles Is Much Improved," *Chicago Defender*, July 16, 1932.

avid baseball fan Rouzeau, "Theatre Stars Mourn."

"Every walk of life" Rouzeau, "Theatre Stars Mourn."

Variety **published** "Outdoors: Obituary," *Variety*, August 2, 1932.

slightly longer "Aubrey Lyles Dies, Negro Comedian," *New York Times*, July 29, 1932.

homegoing eulogies Theophilus Lewis, "The Harlem Sketch Book: Black Out," *New York Amsterdam News*, August 3, 1932.

held auditions "'Shuffle Along' Revival May Be Asset to Stage," *Pittsburgh Courier*, October 1, 1932.

Miller filed "Flournoy Miller Goes Bankrupt 'With Splurge,'" *New York Herald Tribune*, November 6, 1932.

sought relief "Music: Noble Sissle Declares Self Bankrupt; Owes $12,889," *Variety*, September 27, 1932.

"I've not even" "Sissle, 'Broke' Again, Offers 'Creditor Blues,'" *New York Herald Tribune*, September 20, 1932.

opened at the "'Shuffle Along' Is Revived in the East: New York Sees 1932 Edition and Then Raves Second Time," *Chicago Defender*, November 26, 1932.

didn't connect "'Shuffle Along, of 1932,' Has Both Good and Bad Points Critics Say," *Baltimore Afro-American*, November 19, 1932.

"While not as fresh" "'Shuffle Along' Is Revived."

"Just what the family" Arthur Ruhl, "Shuffle Along of 1933," *New York Herald Tribune*, December 27, 1932.

most telling critique Thomas R. Dash, "More Frenzy Than Whit in Ebony Frolic," *Women's Wear Daily*, December 27, 1932.

earned just under "Legitimate: Not One Capacity Broadway Show, Unique Occurrence in Show Memory," *Variety*, January 10, 1933.

allegedly due "Theatrical Notes," *New York Times*, January 10, 1933.

they admitted "Theatrical Notes," *New York Times*, January 11, 1933.

"We saw it wasn't" Rose, *Eubie Blake*, 110.

CHAPTER 13: WHITE FOLKS FOLLOW

"The success of" Edward W. Smith, "Tough Luck on Trail of Old 'Shuffle,'" *Chicago Defender*, November 19, 1932.

separate theory "They Are Concerned with Shuffle Along of 1933,"
Baltimore Afro-American, February 25, 1933.

"The thing that keeps" "They Are Concerned."

"It's the song" "Essentials of the Modern Hit," *New York Evening
Telegram*, undated newspaper clipping, Eubie Blake Collection.

methodological approach "All-Negro Revue 'Shuffle Along' to Come to
American," *St. Louis Star and Times*, March 16, 1923.

"We went on" Rose, *Eubie Blake*, 110.

"busted up" "Shuffle Along Reported 'Busted Up,'" *Chicago Defender*, May 29,
1937.

enough money Rose, *Eubie Blake*, 110.

making headlines Stephen Breszka, "Flournoy Miller Is in Fighting Mood,"
Pittsburgh Courier, February 9, 1935.

been optioned "Campbell Productions Get Option to Buy Shuffle Along
for Film," *Pittsburgh Courier*, July 27, 1935.

bet on Blacks "Hollywood Showing Interest in Negro," *New York
Amsterdam News*, November 16, 1935.

accidental proof Mark Duguid, "Sanders of the River (1935)," BFI
Screenonline, accessed November 8, 2020, http://www.screenonline
.org.uk/film/id/438878/index.html.

Flournoy's brother Quintard "Miller Brothers in Battle over Shuffle
Along," *Baltimore Afro-American*, July 27, 1935.

successful productions Floyd J. Calvin, "Race Actors Capture a Great
Broadway," *Chicago Defender*, December 7, 1935.

"Show me a man" William G. Gunn, "Race Must Finance Own Broadcasts,
Sissle," *Pittsburgh Courier*, January 9, 1937.

working quietly "Sissle Named President of Actors Guild," *Pittsburgh
Courier*, December 18, 1937.

faced difficulty "Imitation of Life: Notes," Turner Classic Movies, accessed October 16, 2020, https://www.tcm.com/tcmdb/title/79028/imitation-of-life#notes.

"I don't want to pass" "Uptown Fredi Washington Gives the Lowdown on Hollywood; No Great Hope for the Sepia Stars," *Pittsburgh Courier*, April 14, 1934.

she reaffirmed her position "'Part in 'Imitation' Is Not Real Me,' Says Fredi," *Chicago Defender*, January 19, 1935.

"You see I'm a mighty" Earl Conrad, "To Pass or Not to Pass?," *Chicago Defender*, June 16, 1945.

"For many actors" "The Negro Actors Guild of America," NYPL Digital Collections, accessed November 8, 2020, https://digitalcollections.nypl.org/items/c0957fe0–8be2–0133-ce21–00505686d14e.

offensive and outdated *Blackface and Hollywood* (Turner Classic Movies, 2020), documentary, https://www.youtube.com/watch?reload=9&v=tf4OKW_fqYU.

steady engagement Kimball and Bolcom, *Reminiscing*, 225 and 228.

"made up chiefly" "Oldtimers Get Break in WPAs Swing It," *Baltimore Afro-American*, September 11, 1937.

produced with funding "Works Progress Administration (WPA)," History.com, July 13, 2017, https://www.history.com/topics/great-depression/works-progress-administration.

"Actors with long" "Oldtimers Get Break."

devastating blow Rose, *Eubie Blake*, 112.

stand-up comedy "Flournoy Miller at Cotton Club," *Pittsburgh Courier*, July 20, 1935.

highest-grossing film "New Motion Picture Company Enters Negro Field in the South," *New York Age*, March 9, 1940.

1939 edition "unhappy" "Shuffle Along Is an Unhappy Revue," *Hollywood Reporter*, November 11, 1938.

harrowing report Dean Owen, "Night Clubs-Vaudeville: 'Shuffle Along' Flops in L.A.; Too Amateurish," *Billboard*, November 26, 1938.

filed for bankruptcy "Sissle Bankrupt," *Chicago Defender*, June 10, 1939.

"Their coming opus" "Miller, Sissle, and Blake to Revive Show," *Chicago Defender*, February 17, 1940.

Initial reports stated "Miller, Sissle, and Blake."

"the Florence Mills type" "Miller, Sissle, and Blake."

show had been cast "News of the Theater," *New York Herald Tribune*, April 12, 1940.

"perhaps along about" "'Shuffle Along' of Past to Be Revived," *Chicago Defender*, May 11, 1940.

Billy Rose declared "'I'll Back Shuffle Along' Billy Rose Tells Critics," *Chicago Defender*, May 18, 1940.

the producer thought "Rose Likes 'Shuffle's' Songs, But Not for '40," newspaper clipping, May 25, 1940, Eubie Blake Collection.

from its ashes "Manhattan Ready for Big Premiere," *New York Amsterdam News*, January 18, 1941.

"After being in" A. White, "Andy Razaf, Eubie Certain Their New Will Please New York," *Philadelphia Tribune*, January 30, 1941.

ultimately landed Maurice Dancer, "Tan Manhattan," *Chicago Defender*, August 30, 1941.

the press revealed "Year Old Marriage of Sissle Revealed," *Baltimore Afro-American*, November 9, 1940.

his union with "Author: Sissle Writes 'Diamond Horseshoe,'" *Baltimore Afro-American*, April 20, 1940.

Two children Kimball and Bolcom, *Reminiscing*, 228.

completely different order "Ex-Star of Miller-Lyle [sic] Team Joins Amos 'n' Andy," *Chicago Defender*, November 22, 1941.

work in radio "Flourney [sic] Miller to Advise on Negro Films for 20th Century-Fox," *New Journal and Guide* (Norfolk, Virginia), October 24, 1942.

necessary assistance Loop, "House Review: Shuffle Along," *Variety*, December 16, 1942.

distinct honor "Noble Sissle Plays to GIs in Two Years," *New Journal and Guide*, November 17, 1945.

"I feel that if" "Sissle Leaves for Overseas," *Chicago Defender*, July 28, 1945.

According to Captain Captain Hall, "The Week: Color in the Army 'Shuffle Along,'" *Baltimore Afro-American*, October 13, 1945.

went to Germany "'Shuffle Along' Reunion in Belgium," *Chicago Defender*, March 30, 1946.

rumored and reported "Europe's 'Shuffle' to Broadway," *Chicago Defender*, November 24, 1945.

1.25 million soldiers "Stars Reunited in Belgium," *Baltimore Afro-American*, June 15, 1946.

away on the shelf "Noble Sissle Back with 'Shuffle Along,'" *Philadelphia Tribune*, May 4, 1946.

inaugural celebration Lillian Scott, "'I'm Just Wild About Harry' Was Original Election Tune," undated newspaper clipping, Eubie Blake Collection.

asked to work John Jasper, "He Disobeyed His Mother," *Baltimore Afro-American*, September 29, 1956.

"The interesting thing" "Truman Library Receives Sissle and Blake Hit Tune," *Baltimore Afro-American*, October 7, 1967.

such as *Carmen Jones* "Carmen Jones - Broadway Musical - Original," IBDB, accessed June 1, 2022, https://www.ibdb.com/broadway-production /carmen-jones-1365

Bloomer's Girl and Finian's "Bloomer Girl - Broadway Musical - Original," IBDB, accessed June 1, 2022, https://www.ibdb.com/broadway-production /bloomer-girl-1583. "Finian's Rainbow - Broadway Musical - Original," IBDB, accessed June 1, 2022, https://www.ibdb.com/broadway-production /finians-rainbow-1507.

March 25, 1949 Sam Zolotow, "Musical of 1921 Will be Revived," *New York Times*, March 25, 1949.

completing a course "Eubie Blake, at 66, Is Learning Music," *New York Times*, August 22, 1949.

insiders projected Robert Sylvester, "Theatre Goes Bigtime with Own Tip Sheet," *Daily News*, September 17, 1949.

Gaumont to raise Danton Walker, "Broadway," *Daily News*, June 16, 1951.

some in the press Frank Morton, "Can 'Shuffle Along' Survive... 'Pastures'?," *Atlanta Daily World*, June 20, 1951.

In November Sam Zolotow, "'Paint Your Wagon' Will Open Tonight," *New York Times*, November 12, 1951.

public doubts "Will 'Shuffle Along' Succeed as Revival?," *Atlanta Daily World*, December 12, 1951.

In an attempt Earl Wilson, "It Happened Last Night," *Delta Democrat-Times* (Greenville, Mississippi), December 7, 1951.

By the beginning "Famed Broadway Singer Never Took a Lesson," *Morning Herald* (Uniontown, Pennsylvania), February 2, 1952.

hired playwright "'Script Doctor' Struggling with 'Shuffle Along,'" *New York Amsterdam News*, January 5, 1952.

the moneymen "Sissle in City Seeking 'Shuffle Along' Talent," *Philadelphia Tribune*, January 29, 1952.

The press was invited Thomas R. Waring, "3 Writers Busy Tailoring '21 'Shuffle Along' to '52," *New York Herald Tribune*, February 10, 1952.

"Like almost everything" "3 Writers Busy Tailoring."

Gaumont rescheduled "Legitimate: Boston Legit Prospects Brighten Season Balance," *Variety*, February 27, 1952.

Delores Martin "'Shuffle Along,' Casting Completed, Eyes Broadway," *Chicago Defender*, April 5, 1952.

Years later "The Afro Visits with Sissle & Blake," *Baltimore Afro-American*, September 13, 1958.

soon revealed itself "New Version of Old Comedy in Rehearsal," *New York Amsterdam News*, March 29, 1952.

set against pushing Robert Sylvester, "'Shuffle Along' Fights Fire," *Daily News*, March 25, 1952.

scheduled to premiere "Noble Sissle Recovering," *New York Amsterdam News*, April 19, 1952.

"This column has said" "Big Towns by James Hicks," *Baltimore Afro-American*, March 1, 1952.

originally thought "Legitimate: 'Shuffle' 7G for Four in New Haven Tryout," *Variety*, April 30, 1952.

"If they ever" Bone, "Legitimate: Plays Out of Town—Shuffle Along," *Variety*, April 30, 1952.

a disappointment "'Shuffle' 7G for Four."

the final night "Philadelphia Portrait," *Philadelphia Tribune*, May 6, 1952.

taking his place "Legitimate: Inside Stuff-Legit," *Variety*, April 30, 1952.

confounding decision "'Shuffle Along' to Open Next Week," *New York Daily News*, May 3, 1952.

"based on his belief" Louis Calta, "'Shuffle Along' Quickening Pace," *New York Times*, May 3, 1952.

a different story "Legitimate: B'way Hits the Late-Spring Skids," *Variety*, May 7, 1952.

"In the first place" Francis Cauthorn, "The Night Shift," *Philadelphia Tribune*, May 3, 1952.

"Believers in omens" Louis Calta, "'Shuffle Along' to Open Tonight," *New York Times*, May 8, 1952.

"They threw my music" Kimball and Bolcom, *Reminiscing*, 232.

"The only similarity" John Chapman, "New Version of 'Shuffle Along' Has Some Nice People but Little Else," *Daily News*, May 9, 1952.

across the board Sid Garfield, "36 Paramount Properties Approved for Production: Irving Gaumont Presents 'Shuffle Along,'" *Hollywood Reporter*, May 9, 1952.

"The new edition of" Walter E. Kerr, "'Shuffle Along,'" *New York Herald Tribune*, May 9, 1952.

On May 10 "Two Plays and Musical Stay; Plans for Summer Playhouses," *Christian Science Monitor*, May 10, 1952.

"after revisions suggested" Louis Calta, "Musical Suspends to Make Revisions," *New York Times*, May 13, 1952.

"The closing...of" John Chapman, "Our Best Singers and Dancers Have Small Stage Opportunities," *Daily News*, May 14, 1952.

"A man gets to feelin'" Rose, *Eubie Blake*, 125.

"It wasn't only" Rose, *Eubie Blake*, 123.

"I will always believe" Lottie Gee, "Broadway Success Did Not Bring Happiness," *Baltimore Afro-American*, October 11, 1930.

"After the white writers" McCandlish Phillips, "Eubie Blake Rides Crest of Ragtime Revival at 89," *New York Times*, December 1, 1972.

"If there's anything" Eubie Blake and Noble Sissle, interview by Valena Minor Williams.

"We always felt" Miller, unpublished autobiography.

"Negro artists and composers" Noble Sissle, "Highlights of the Negro's Contribution in the Development of Music and the Theatre in the American Scene," 6, Flournoy Miller Collection, Sc MG 599, Schomburg Center for Research in Black Culture.

EPILOGUE: ENCORES

On November 14 "Radio-Television: Sue Flip Wilson Show for Lifting a Sketch," *Variety*, November 15, 1972.

who had originated Burkard Polster and Marty Ross, "Movies, Mathematics and Mulsification," Maths Masters, October 8, 2012, https://www.qedcat.com/archive_cleaned/139.html.

agreed to drop Thompson, "Shuffling Roles," 99.

Flournoy Miller died "Obituaries," *Variety*, June 9, 1971.

attempted to bring A. H. Weiler, "News of the Screen: 'Laughmaker' Tells of Miller and Lyles," *New York Times*, June 30, 1974.

issues with his estate Cyma Rubin, in discussion with the author, April 24, 2020.

by the mid-1960s P. L. Prattis, "Horizon: Down Memory Lane," *New Pittsburgh Courier*, June 6, 1964.

recording sessions Jasen and Jones. *Black Bottom Stomp*, 35.

Noble Sissle joined Eubie Blake, *The Eighty-Six Years of Eubie Blake*, Columbia, 1969, LP.

The following January Rose, *Eubie Blake*, 137.

As the cameras *Noble Sissle's Syncopated Ragtime*.

"Right after we got done" Rose, *Eubie Blake*, 137.

Noble Sissle died "Thousands at Funeral of Noble Sissle, Dead at 86," *New York Amsterdam News*, December 27, 1975.

"A lot of people" Harriet Choice, "Theater: Eubie a 97-Year-Old Success Story," *Chicago Tribune*, February 10, 1980.

Blake's criticism "Tribute to Eubie Blake."

$83,000 a week "'Dreamgirls' a Broadway Smash; Can Make 83G a Wk. at Capacity," *Variety*, December 30, 1981.

seriously considered staging Jack Viertel to August Wilson, reprinted in Sandra Seaton, "*Shuffle Along* and Ethnic Humor: 'The Proper Push,'" *Dramatist* 18, no. 5 (May/June 2016): 45–50.

"*Shuffle Along*, the musical" August Wilson to Jack Viertel, reprinted in Seaton, "*Shuffle Along* and Ethnic Humor."

"This is a part" "'Shuffle Along': Re-Imagining Broadway History," CBS News, December 20, 2015, https://www.cbsnews.com/news /shuffle-along-re-imagining-broadway-history/.

"Think of tonight" Diep Tran, "'Hamilton' Swept the Tonys, but Has Diversity Swept Broadway?," *American Theatre*, June 28, 2016, https://www.americantheatre.org/2016/06/28hamilton-swept-the-tonys-but -has-diversity-swept-broadway/.

Despite impressive ticket "'Shuffle Along' Announces Abrupt Closing Date on Broadway," *Hollywood Reporter*, June 27, 2016, https://www.holly woodreporter.com/newsshuffle-along-announces-abrupt-closing-906008.

Rudin and his production Louie Bacani, "Broadway producers sue Lloyd's of London," *Insurance Business*, November 15, 2016, https://www .insurancebusinessmag.com/us/news/breaking-news/broadway -producers-sue-lloyds-of-london-40591.aspx.

The parties settled Michael Paulson, "'Shuffle Along' and Insurer Drop Pregnancy-Prompted Lawsuit", *New York Times*, October 21, 2020,

https://www.nytimes.com/2020/10/21/theater/shuffle-along-audra
-mcdonald-insurer-pregnancy-lawsuit.html.

In a piece Catherine M. Young, "Don't Blame Pregnancy for *Shuffle Along Closing*," Howlround Theatre Commons, July 18, 2016, https://howlround.com/dont-blame-pregnancy-shuffle-along-closing.

"With *Shuffle Along*" "The Forgotten Legacy of Shuffle Along (Phillip Attmore Interview)," YouTube, https://youtu.be/fUlCLYbB5mE.

"She is putting" Alicia Samuel, "Audra McDonald's Pregnancy Is Not 'Unexpected,'" Broadway Black, June 24, 2016, https://web.archive.org/web/20160627054304/http://broadwayblack.com/audra-mcdonalds-pregnancy-not-unexpected/.

"What is legacy" Lin-Manuel Miranda, "The World Was Wide Enough," *Hamilton: An American Musical*, Hal Leonard Corporation, 2016.

"You know, I still" Rob Weinert-Kendt, "What Ever Happened to 'Shuffle Along'? Ask George C. Wolfe," American Theatre, May/June 2016, https://www.americantheatre.org/2016/03/31/what-ever-happened-to-shuffle-along-ask-george-c-wolfe/.

Because Wolfe continued "The Forgotten Legacy of Shuffle Along (Phillip Attmore Interview)," YouTube, https://youtu.be/fUlCLYbB5mE.

"Can we go" Adrienne Warren [@adriennelwarren], "Can we go back and do a Shuffle Along cast album cause I'm still tight about that..." Twitter, November 24, 2021.

"[The show's closing]" Dexter Thomas, "If Everybody Knew, Episode 1: '...about the black musical that disappeared forever, twice," Princeton University Humanities Council, December 1, 2021, https://humaities.princeton.edu/2021/12/01/if-everybody-knew-episode-one/.

"Working on [*Shuffle Along*]" Ashley Lee, "'Immortal Life of Henrietta Lacks' Director on Working with Oprah and the 'Draining' Emotional

Scenes," *Hollywood Reporter*, August 8, 2017, https://www .hollywoodreporter.com/news/general-news/immortal-life-henrietta -lacks-director-working-oprah-draining-emotional-scenes-1026493/.

On July 6 Mitch Smith, "Video of Police Killings of Philando Castile Is Publicly Released," *New York Times*, June 20, 2017, https:// www.nytimes.com/2017/06/20/us/police-shooting-castile-trial -video.html.

"I was onstage" Casey Mink, "The Long-Overdue Conversation About Racism on Broadway," *Backstage*, June 10, 2020, https://www .backstage.com/magazine/article/black-lives-matter-broadway-70891.

On August 1 Diep Tran, "'Instead of call-out culture, we're calling them in," *The Brooklyn Rail*, October 2020, https://brooklynrail .org/2020/10/theater/Instead-of-call-out-culture-were-calling-them -in-Broadway-Advocacy-Coalition-fights-for-change-on-a-grassroots -and-now-industry-wide-level.

"We're often asked" Casey Mink, "The Long-Overdue Conversation About Racism on Broadway," *Backstage*, June 10, 2020, https://www .backstage.com/magazine/article/black-lives-matter-broadway-70891/.

On September 26 Ryan McPhee, "Special Tony Award Honors Will Go to Broadway Advocacy Coalition, *American Utopia, Freestyle Love Supreme*," Playbill, June 22, 2021, https://playbill.com/article /special-tony-award-honors-will-go-to-broadway-advocacy-coalition -american-utopia-freestyle-love-supreme.

The latter advocacy group Ryan McPhee, "Special Tony Award Honors Will Go to Broadway Advocacy Coalition, *American Utopia, Freestyle Love Supreme*," Playbill, June 22, 2021, https://playbill.com/article /special-tony-award-honors-will-go-to-broadway-advocacy-coalition -american-utopia-freestyle-love-supreme.

In March 2022 Logan Culwell-Block, "Broadway's Cort Theatre to Be Re-Named for James Earl Jones," Playbill, March 2, 2022, https:// playbill.com/article/broadways-cort-theatre-to-be-re-named-for-james -earl-jones.

For example, in 2020 Michael Paulson, "As Broadway Returns, Shows Rethink and Restage Depictions of Race," *New York Times*, October 23, 2021, https://www.nytimes.com/2021/10/23/theater /broadway-race-depictions.html.

"you have no control" Lin-Manuel Miranda, "Who Lives, Who Dies, Who Tells Your Story," *Hamilton: An American Musical*, Hal Leonard Corporation, 2016.

Noble Sissle, Eubie Blake Laurence Maslon, "An all-Black musical was a Broadway smash—and then was mostly forgotten," *Washington Post*, July 30, 2021, https://www.washingtonpost.com/outlook/an-all-black-musical -was-a-smash-broadway-hit—and-then-was-mostly-forgotten/2021/07 /28/f26ecc2a-e421–11eb-a41e-c8442c213fa8_story.html.

INDEX

K

L

M

Y

ACKNOWLEDGMENTS

Completing this project required me to flex researching and writing muscles I didn't know I possessed, and it feels like it took forever and no time at all. I am so blessed to have had thoughtful, patient, brilliant, and excited folks who have helped me along the way. I truly could not have told this story without you.

Footnotes began as several different projects, with its most immediate predecessor being one about Broadway's 2016 season overall, of which George C. Wolfe's *Shuffle Along* was a part. However, the universe continued steering me toward this one. Peter Steinberg, my fantastic literary agent, was by my side through it all. It's a cliché, but he believed in this project even when I had my doubts, and for that I am forever indebted. Thank you for recognizing the value and worth of these phenomenal artists. Similar thanks are owed to Grace Menary-Winefield, who acquired this for Sourcebooks and whose enthusiasm was present in my mind throughout the writing process. Thank you for being champions of this project!

Additionally, to Anna Michels, my wonderful editor, thank you for your patience, support, keen eye, and shepherding to help me tell the account of these artists that I wanted to tell. This book would not exist were it not for your advocacy and belief in the importance of telling this story. To Liz Kelsch, BrocheAroe Fabian, Shana Drehs, the amazing teams who worked on the beautiful cover and interior design, the folks in sales and marketing, and everyone else at Sourcebooks who had a hand in crafting and promoting this work, thank you for helping to put this story in front of as many eyes as possible.

I have to take a moment to thank Jen Hale, my friend in Canada, where people haven't completely lost their minds as of the time of publication, for being an amazing reader for this book—and for taking a chance on me in 2009. It was an absolute pleasure to get to work with you again, especially on a project that means so much to me. I cannot thank you enough for your characteristically astute observations, great catches, and tracked changes that kept me laughing even when I was dead exhausted. While on the topic, can I thank the makers of Café Bustelo and the Keurig? But seriously, thank you a million times over for being there this time and all times. Additionally, I am a firm believer that everything I write has benefited from everything I've written, so to the editors of the other books I've written, Kate Napolitano and Chris Prince, thank you as well.

The research process on this book was different from what I was used to, which was initially intimidating, but I soon discovered how exciting it can be paging through old newspapers and photographs, feverishly transcribing audio and video recordings in a public library, and screaming—silently, like a proper person sifting through archives when I'd found the perfect primary source and a piece of it had cracked, broken off, and been forever lost to time. Ashes to ashes, dust to dust, right? I'd like to thank the archivists and librarians who have been helpful to me in this endeavor, particularly but not limited to: Micah Connor, Mallory

Herberger, and Leslie Eames at the Maryland Center for History and Culture in Baltimore, Maryland; Kathleen Shoemaker at the Stuart A. Rose Manuscript, Archives, and Rare Book Library at Emory University in Atlanta, Georgia; Anne Rhodes at Yale University's Oral History of American Music in New Haven, Connecticut; George Feltenstein at Warner Archive Collection; and Alexsandra M. Mitchell and Tiana M. Taliep at the Schomburg Center for Research in Black Culture's Manuscripts, Archives, and Rare Books Division at the New York Public Library in Harlem. Special thanks also go to John Duke Kisch at Separate Cinema, Todd Ifft and Derek at Photofest, and Kira Jones and Julienne Grey for their research help.

I had the pleasure of interviewing several folks for this project to help fill in background information or put events in their proper context. First and foremost, thank you to Noble Sissle Jr. for repeatedly taking time out to chat with me about your dad. It was an honor getting to know you and hearing your stories. Your generosity and participation mean so much to me; I hope you feel this does your dad justice. Additionally, thanks to Daniel Bernardi, William Bolcom, Thomas F. DeFrantz, Robert Kimball, and Cyma Rubin for making time for me as well.

To Laurie Gwen Shapiro and Brian Jay Jones, thank you for helping me at moments when I was particularly up against a wall. Your practical suggestions and author therapy were much needed and helped to get me out of my head and across the finish line. Extra special thanks to Christopher Ryan, my friend, colleague, and former teacher, for giving me a great writing tip that, truthfully, I don't know how this book would have been written in time without. I am so thankful to have fellow writers I can reach out to for support, guidance, a sounding board, a gripe session, or some combination of the aforementioned, like Mathew Klickstein, J. M. Lee, Toney Jackson, Jeff Ryan, Ryan Britt, Blake J. Harris, Alex Simmons, and Omar Holmon. Thank you all for your wisdom and for telling your stories.

When I wrote the original version of these acknowledgments for *Footnotes: The Black Artists Who Rewrote the Rules of the Great White Way*, the hardcover edition of this book, Broadway was dark due to the global COVID-19 pandemic. It was incredibly frustrating and harrowing to live fourteen miles away from Times Square and be unable to comfortably grab a bite, have a drink, and meander down the streets. There were many times when I wanted to venture to where the Sixty-Third Street Theatre once stood, walk through Harlem, and most frequently and regularly—go see a show.

I missed live theater more than I could express, and working on this project caused me to reflect on all the amazing Black actors whose representation on the Broadway stage left a lasting impression on me. I hope I always remember how I felt when I unexpectedly saw Michael Luwoye step onstage as Alexander Hamilton. I looked around as if to make sure everyone else was seeing what I was, and by the end of the opening song, tears had pooled in the bottom lids of my eyes. I was watching the most groundbreaking Broadway show in at least a generation, and a Black man was at the center of it, playing one of the nation's Founding Fathers. Representation matters, so to the following performers of color, all of whom I have had the opportunity to see onstage and be moved by, this book is also for you: Danielle Brooks, Jasmine Cephas Jones, Ariana DeBose, André De Shields, Daveed Diggs, Brandon Victor Dixon, Cynthia Erivo, Renée Elise Goldsberry, Joshua Henry, Jennifer Hudson, Christopher Jackson, LaChanze, Kimberly Marable, Audra McDonald, Lin-Manuel Miranda, Brian Stokes Mitchell, Leslie Odom Jr., Billy Porter, Anthony Ramos, Lance Roberts, Adrienne Warren, Christian Dante White, Elisabeth Withers, and Rachel Zegler, just to name a few.

A world of thanks, gratitude, appreciation, and love goes out to my wife, Johanna Calle, who was the backbone of this book. She has seen me at my peaks and valleys with this project, and more than anyone, she knows how pleased I am that this now exists in the world. Thank you for being understanding of why I have been locked in my office for more time than I can keep track of. Talking through issues I was having or plot points I was excited about always made the book better. You know it's true—this book would not have happened without you.

Several of my friends have also been part of my amazing support system. First off, special thanks to Wendy Salkin for brainstorming the original name for the book over pancakes and conversation—I think you were the one who came up with it!—and the rest of the Wednesday night music crew for helping to keep me sane throughout the quarantine and unknowingly forcing me to take a break from finishing the book: Gaby Alvarez, Josh Bellocchio, Gary Eggers, Angela Glassman, and Katie O'Connell. The following friends are also sincerely appreciated for checking in about how writing was going, expressing their enthusiasm about the project, and/or being understanding as to why I completely had fallen off the grid: Leila Amirhamzeh, Felicia Benson-Kraft, Phil Brophy, Daniel Carola, John and Rose Frontignano, Tim and Casey Hoffman, Rasha Jay, Gregory Liosi, Laura Martin, Jensyn Modero, Maddie Orton, Vanessa "Curly Fries" Perez, Fiona Sarne, Stephanie Shaw, Michele Stein, Tom Terzano, Jared Wexler, and Anthony Zisa. Additionally, thanks to Rosemary Flowers-Jackson and the late Reverend Toney E. Jackson Sr., who provided some encouragement when I needed it.

Last but certainly not least, much love goes out to my family—especially my parents, Bernadette and Curtis; my brother, Curtis Gaines III; and my grandma, Rosetta Gaines—for always being there. I am so blessed to have you in my life. Thank you for encouraging me to use my voice and speak the truth as I see it and for embracing me for who I am.

Much of the "brass tacks" work on this book was done while the world was at a standstill. Throughout that period, the violent and immoral deaths of George Floyd and Breonna Taylor, as well as the depraved shooting of Jacob Blake, led to a racial awakening and reckoning in the United States, this country I love, that I wished kept its promises. Watching and participating in demonstrations has been simultaneously draining and inspiring, but seeing the young people at the forefront of many of these movements has made me incredibly hopeful about the future. The kids are all right. Let's let them lead.

So my last acknowledgment is to my students, past, present, and future, who inspire me every day. You all have the potential to change the world. I can't wait to see it.

ABOUT THE AUTHOR

Credit © Johanna Calle

Author and journalist Caseen Gaines has appeared in *Rolling Stone* and *Vanity Fair*. He holds an MA from Rutgers University in American Studies, focusing on racial representations in popular culture.

He is the award-winning author of several books that explore the lasting impact of significant moments in art and entertainment. His work has been praised by media outlets around the world, including NPR, *The Hollywood Reporter*, and *Esquire*.

Caseen directs theater and teaches literature and writing, drama, journalism, and a course on race and representation at a high school in New Jersey, where he lives. Find Caseen online at caseengaines.com, via email at caseen@caseengaines.com, or on social media @caseengaines and facebook.com/caseengaines.